iOS App Development for Non-Programmers

Book 4: Learn to Code in Swift

Kevin J McNeish

iOS App Development for Non-Programmers
Book 4: Learn to Code in Swift

Author

Kevin J McNeish

Technical Editor

Greg Lee

Photography

Sharlene M McNeish

Copy Editor

Yolande McLean

© 2014 Oak Leaf Enterprises, Inc.

1716 Union Mills Rd.

Troy, VA 22974

434-979-2417

http://iOSAppsForNonProgrammers.com

ISBN 978-0-9882327-7-8

Contents

Dedicated to Steve Jobs

The night Steve Jobs passed away, by coincidence my wife and I already had tickets to San Francisco for early next morning, because I was scheduled to speak at a Silicon Valley Code Camp.

After arriving in San Francisco, we drove to Cupertino to make some sense of the loss of a great visionary. The flags at Apple were flying at half-mast and many people had gathered to honor him with candles, flowers, posters, and apples.

We drove to the home where Steve created the first Apple computer, then on to the last place he called home in Palo Alto where many others were gathering to pay respects and where his silver Mercedes (famously without license plates) still sat in front of his house.

It was there I decided to write this book series and do for iOS app development what Steve had done for users of iOS devices—make app development accessible to the masses of non-programmers, teaching them to create apps that surprise and amaze their users.

Foreword

This book is the fourth in a series designed to teach non-programmers to create iOS apps. Many books for beginning iOS App developers assume *way* too much. This book series intends to rectify that by assuming you know *nothing* about programming.

Learning Swift is the most difficult step for non-programmers in the iOS App-development learning curve. It gets easier after this.

Each chapter, each exercise, and each code sample has been reviewed by people just like you—with little or no experience (mostly "no experience") in writing code, or creating apps. I rewrote many sections of the book multiple times, added diagrams, and improved code samples until all our "beta readers" completely understood each key concept.

Once you master the concepts in this book, you will be able to move forward and learn how to use other technologies such as Xcode, create a great user experience, and make use of the many tools available in Apple's Software Developer Kit. All these topics are covered in other books in our iOS App Development for Non-Programmers series, with you, the non-programmer, in mind.

So, buckle up, and let's get started.

Introduction

At the WWDC 2014 keynote, Apple surprised the developer community by announcing a brand new language called *Swift* that replaces Objective-C as the primary development language for iOS developers. This new language is great news; it includes many of the more modern programming conventions that give you more power and make it easier to write code.

Mastering Swift is one of your biggest learning curves—especially if you have never written code. While you can create prototype applications without writing code, you need to write code to do anything meaningful.

Why You Should Use Swift

You can still create iOS Apps using the Objective-C programming language, but I highly recommend using Swift instead.

Why?

Swift is the future of software development at Apple. You can expect little or no advancements in Objective-C, whereas Apple is putting all their efforts behind Swift. Another reason is that for many computational-intensive tasks, Swift is much faster than Objective-C.

So Swift it is.

Before you start writing code, you need to understand the fundamentals of Swift, something this book covers thoroughly.

Chapter 1: Getting Started

Welcome! This chapter is where you learn how to get yourself and your computer set for app development, get your hands on the code samples that come with this book, and learn some of the basics of iOS App development.

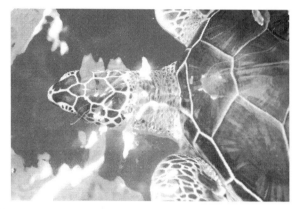

Sections in This Chapter

1. *Getting Set Up*

2. *Downloading the Sample Code*

3. *iOS—The Operating System*

4. *Source Code, Compilers & Machine Code*

5. *The Cocoa Touch Framework*

6. *Designing With Humans in Mind*

Getting Set Up

Before going further in this book, you need to accomplish three primary tasks:

1. Get an Intel-based Mac computer you can build iOS Apps on.

2. Register as an Apple developer (free).

3. Download and install Xcode.

Our first book in this series, iOS App Development For Non-Programmers Book 1: Diving Into iOS contains details of these tasks, so I won't repeat them here.

Downloading the Sample Code

We have spent a lot of time putting together relevant samples for you. Follow these steps to download and install this book's sample code on your Mac:

1. In the browser on your Mac, go to this link:

    http://iOSAppsForNonProgrammers.com/SamplesSwift.html

2. On the download page, click the **Download Sample Code** link (Figure 1.1).

Figure 1.1 Click the Download Sample Code link.

3. If Safari is your default web browser, when you click the link, you will see a blue progress indicator in the upper-right corner of the browser (Figure 1.2).

Figure 1.2 The download progress indicator

4. When the blue progress bar completely fills, and then disappears, the download is complete. To view the downloaded file, click the Show downloads button in the upper-right corner of Safari (Figure 1.3).

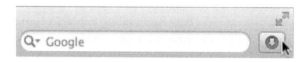

Figure 1.3 Click the Show downloads button.

5. This displays the Downloads popup. Click the small magnifying glass on the right (Figure 1.4).

Figure 1.4 Click the magnifying glass to see the samples.

This displays the downloaded **SamplesSwift** folder in the Finder (Figure 1.5).

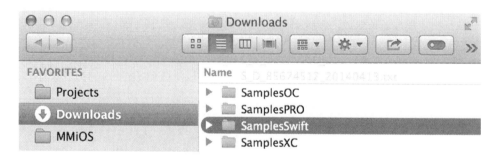

Figure 1.5 The newly downloaded samples

6. Let's make a copy of this folder and save it the **Documents** folder (you can choose a different destination folder if you prefer).

With the **SamplesSwift** folder still selected, press the **Command** key (the key to the left of the spacebar), and while holding the key down, press the **C** key (in other words, press **Command+C**). This makes a copy of the folder in memory.

7. Next, on the left side of the Finder window, click the **Documents** folder (Figure 1.6), and then press **Command+V** to add a copy of the **SamplesSwift** folder into the **Documents** folder.

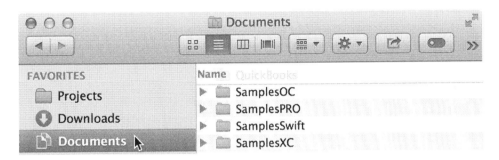

*Figure 1.6 Select the **Documents** folder.*

8. Double-click the **SamplesSwift** folder in the right-hand panel of the Finder window and you will see a list of sample project folders.

Throughout this book are exercises where you change the code in the sample projects. Anytime you need to get a "fresh start" you can always copy projects from the **Downloads** folder to the **Documents/SamplesSwift** folder.

iOS—the Operating System

Apps are not the only software running on an iPhone, iPod Touch, or iPad. They also run the ***iOS operating system***, which manages the device hardware and provides core functionality for all apps running on the device.

When you first turn on an iPhone, the Apple icon displayed on a black screen greets you. During this startup phase, the operating system gets the iPhone ready for use, and displays the user's wallpaper and app icons. It also seeks a carrier signal for the cell phone and a wireless signal for Wi-Fi access.

As Apple releases new versions of the iOS operating system, it continues to improve the core functionality of the device by adding new features, fixing bugs, and even releasing new built-in apps. With each iOS release, you can add new functionality to apps you create by taking advantage of the new features it provides.

The only limit to the apps you can create is your imagination. The hardware and software features of iOS devices can be used for widely different purposes. For example, use the microphone to record voice memos or as an input for a musical wind instrument (check out the *Ocarina* app for an example of this). Use the camera not only to take pictures, but also to view details of the world around you as in augmented reality apps such as the *Yelp* app. Use Internet access to get the latest weather forecast or to retrieve a list of current political candidates. Use the GPS to show your current location on a map or as an altimeter to show current elevation.

Each time you install an app on your smart phone, it gets smarter. The newly installed app empowers your phone with new functionality. And now with the advent of *Siri*, the voice-activated assistant introduced in the iPhone 4s, your phone seems even smarter with a personality to go along with its intelligence (unfortunately, there is currently no way to access Siri's functionality from the apps you create).

Source Code, Compilers & Machine Code

This book helps you learn to use the Swift programming language to write code for your app. Swift is a **_high-level language_**, meaning it is closer to human language than the actual code an iOS device executes when it is running your app. A high-level language makes it easier for you, the app developer, to understand and write code for your app.

Ultimately, an iOS device doesn't understand the Swift programming language. Rather, an iOS device understands a **_machine code_** instruction set consisting of bits of data (ones and zeroes) specific to its **_processor_**. For example, the iPhone 4 and iPad use the Apple A4 processor, the iPhone 4s and iPad 2 use the newer Apple A5 processor, the new iPad uses the A5x processor, and the iPhone 5 uses the A6 processor.

So something needs to interpret or convert the Swift code you write into machine code so your iOS device can actually execute the code. The tool that performs this magic is called a **_compiler_**. As you work through the book's samples you will add code to an Xcode project, and then *build* the project.

This build process is what takes the Swift code you have written and converts it into machine code as shown in Figure 1.7.

Figure 1.7 The compiler converts Swift source code to machine code.

So, whenever you read about compiling or building a project, now you have a high-level picture of what's going on behind the scenes.

The Cocoa Touch Framework
—Oh, the Things You Can Do!

You need more than just Swift to create an app. Everything you do in your app—designing the **user interface (UI)**, writing the **core logic**, and saving and retrieving **data**—gets its functionality from Apple's **Cocoa Touch Framework**. The Cocoa Touch Framework gives you access to important services that allow your app to do great things. Cocoa Touch is actually a set of many smaller frameworks (reusable sets of tools), each focusing on a set of core functionality.

The following table lists some of the most commonly used frameworks and services included in Cocoa Touch as well as describes the functionality that each service provides for your app.

Scanning through this table should give you an idea of the features you can add to your app to provide a compelling experience for your users.

We will only use a few Cocoa Touch frameworks in this book, but for extensive coverage of the other key Cocoa Touch frameworks, check other books in this series.

Cocoa Touch Frameworks

Framework	Description
Foundation	Contains the low-level core classes such as collections, strings, and date and time management.

UIKit	Contains all the standard iOS user-interface controls that you need to design a great user experience including buttons, text fields, sliders, activity indicators, and table views for displaying lists of data.
Address Book	Lets you access the contacts stored on a device from your app.
Cut, Copy and Paste	Allows you to share images, rich text, and HTML between apps.
Core Location	Allows you to determine the location (latitude and longitude) of the device. You can use this information to display points of interest near the user or even show his or her current altitude.
Gyroscope and Accelerometer	Your app can use the device's gyroscope and accelerometer (iPhone 4 and newer) to sense motion, 3D attitude, and rate of rotation. This is great for games or other apps that use motion to improve the user experience.
Compass	Another feature that allows you to improve location and map services by providing the user's heading (the direction they are facing) from the device's magnetometer.
Map Kit	Allows you to add maps to your App that the user can zoom and pan. You can also add overlays with your own custom information.
Event Kit	Allows a user to access his or her existing calendar of events and to add new calendar events and alarms.
Core Data	Provides a high-level graphical interface for designing the structure of your App's data. Core Data is designed to manage potentially large amounts of data.
Multitasking	Allows your app to perform background tasks for better performance and battery life.
iCloud	Lets you store a user's documents and data in a central location on the Internet that can be accessed from any of the user's devices.
System Configuration	Allows you to determine if a Wi-Fi or cell connection is in use and whether a particular host service can be accessed through a connection.
Camera and Photo Library	Allows you to import images from the photo library, take new photos, and create augmented reality Apps using the live camera feed. In iPhone 4 and newer, you can access both front & main cameras.
iPod Media Library	Allows you to play music in the background while your app runs and provides access to the full media library on the device.
Text and Email Messaging	Provides a user interface and underlying components to compose and send text messages and emails from within your app.
Quick Look	Provides your app with an interface for previewing content

	files your app does not directly support such as iWork or Microsoft Office.
Accessories	Lets you control hardware devices attached to the 30-pin connector at the bottom of iOS devices.
Multi-Touch Gestures	Allows you to add standard iOS gesture recognition to your app for gestures such as tap, double-tap, swipe, pinch, rotate, and pan.
Store Kit	Allows you to set up the purchase of content and services from within your app such as unlocking additional app features or new levels in a game.
iAd	Lets you embed ads into your app that users can click to learn more about a particular product. By implementing iAd, you're basically putting an empty billboard into your app onto which Apple fills ad space. iAd allows you to generate more revenue from your app!
Sprite Kit	The Sprite Kit framework (introduced in iOS 7) makes it much easier for beginner developers to create 2D and 2.5D games. It provides the basic infrastructure most games need including a graphic rendering and animation system, sound playback support, and a physics simulation engine.

Designing With Humans in Mind

I know you're itching to put fingers to keyboard and get on with the fun of creating apps, but first, you should absolutely read Apple's *iOS Human Interface Guidelines* document first. One of software development's biggest problems is forgetting about end users. Losing sight of the people who will be using your app, you risk creating an app that is difficult to comprehend and use.

There is a reason Apple has taken over the world with iOS devices in contrast with products like Microsoft's Zune that are now serving as expensive paperweights. Apple has designed its devices and apps with humans in mind. And not just any humans—Apple products are designed for what Apple likes to call "the 80 percent," or the majority of your users.

Sometimes it's hard to ignore the very vocal 20 percent of users, but if you add complex features only to please a smaller percentage of users, the other 80 percent will not be able to easily use your app.

I highly recommend you read this document thoroughly and keep it in mind through the entire adventure of building your apps.

Chapter 2: Understanding Classes & Objects

Swift is an object-oriented programming language, meaning that when you write Swift code, you are mostly interacting with objects. Other object-oriented languages such as Java and C# are similar. Understanding the foundational information in this chapter is key to your success as an iOS app developer.

Sections in This Chapter

User-Interface Objects

When you create iOS Apps, most objects that you work with are user-interface objects. Looking at the iOS clock app in Figure 2.1, you'll see there are many different user-interface objects.

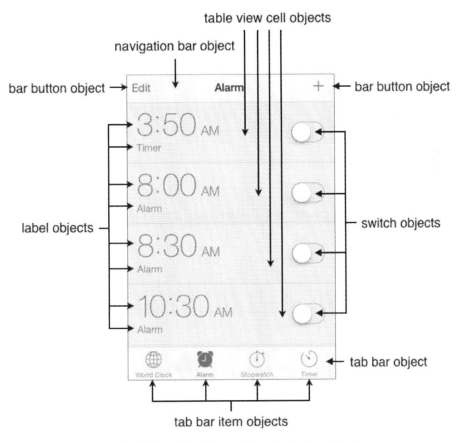

Figure 2.1 User-interface objects in the Clock app

You can interact with some objects by touching, tapping, pinching, and sliding them. Other objects, such as labels, are not interactive; they only display information.

Fortunately, Apple allows you to use, in your own custom apps, the very same user-interface objects that they use in the built-in iOS Apps. When you install Xcode on your computer, you also install a library full of user-interface controls (Figure 2.2).

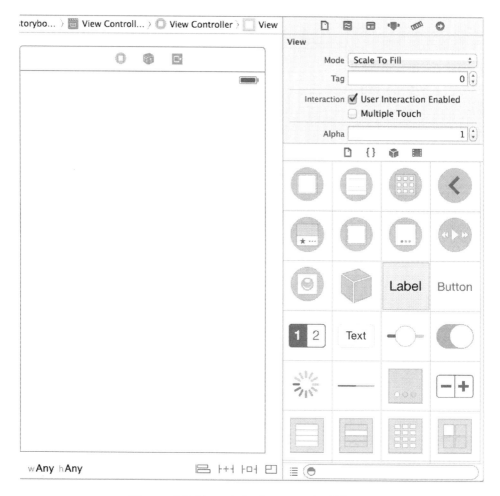

Figure 2.2 User-interface control library

Each user-interface icon on the right represents a class. A ***class*** is like a blueprint for an ***object***. You create objects from a class. For example, by dragging a Label icon from the list on the right and dropping it on the design surface on the left (Figure 2.3), you create a label object from the **UILabel** class.

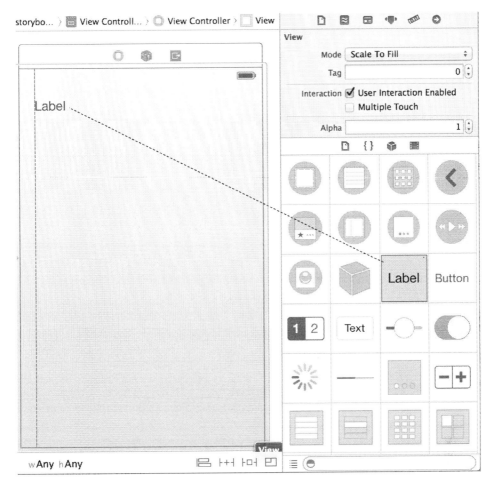

*Figure 2.3 Creating a label object from the **UILabel** class*

You can create many objects from a single class. As shown in Figure 2.4, four text fields have been created from the **UITextField** class by dragging the **Text** field icon and dropping it onto the design surface.

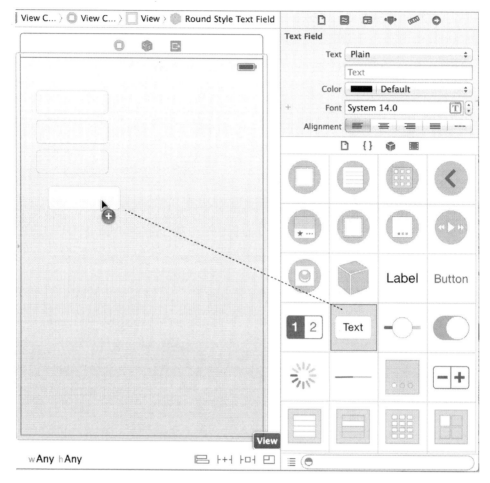

Figure 2.4 Creating multiple objects from a single class

To see which class a particular user-interface icon represents, click the class in the library (Figure 2.5).

Figure 2.5 Click on a user-interface icon to see which class it represents.

Clicking on a user-interface icon pops up a help dialog, telling you what class that it represents (**UITextField** in this example), as well as describing the physical ***attributes*** and behavior of objects created from that class. In object-oriented programming, an object created from a class is called an ***instance*** of the class.

Examining Object Attributes

To see attributes of a user-interface object, use Xcode's Attribute Inspector (Figure 2.6). First, click on a user-interface object in the design surface to select it. Then bring up the Attributes Inspector by selecting **View > Utilities > Show Attributes Inspector** from the menu. You can see the Attributes Inspector in the upper-right corner of Figure 2.6. Whenever you select an object in the design surface, you can see its attributes in the Attribute Inspector. Every object has its own attributes, so you can change an attribute on one object without affecting other objects.

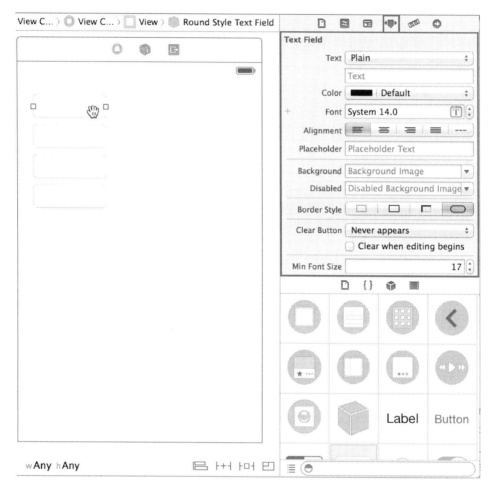

Figure 2.6 Viewing an object's attributes with the Attributes Inspector

As you can see, you can choose from quite a few attributes. Here are descriptions of some:

- **Text** – Specifies the text contained in the text field.

- **Color** – Specifies the color of the text within the text field.

- **Alignment** – Specifies if the text is left-, center-, or right-aligned.

- **Background** – Specifies the background color of the text field.

An object's attributes are defined in the class blueprint the object was created from. Each attribute has a default value, also specified in the class. After an object has been created, you can change the value of its attributes. For example, Figure 2.7 shows the selected text field's **Text** changed to

www.apple.com, its **Alignment** changed to **Centered**, and its text **Color** changed to red.

Figure 2.7 Changing the values of an object's attributes

Understanding Class Properties

Up to now, we have been talking about an object's *attributes*. Ultimately, for every attribute you see in the Attribute Inspector, there is a corresponding ***property*** in the class definition. In fact, Apple could have called it the *Property* Inspector. If you look at Apple's documentation for the **UITextField** class, you see a list of properties such as:

- background

- borderStyle

- clearButtonMode

- clearsOnBeginEditing

- font

- placeholder

- text

- textAlignment

- textColor

In this context, attributes and properties are similar. In Xcode, an object has attributes; in Swift, the class an object is based has properties.

Understanding Class Methods

User-interface objects not only have attributes, but also behavior. For example, when you touch a text field in an iOS app, a keyboard pops up and each letter you type automatically appears in the text field.

An object's behavior or actions it can perform are defined in the class blueprint as **methods**. A method comprises one or more (usually more) lines of code grouped together to perform a task.

Figure 2.8 shows a formal representation of the **UITextField** class known as a **class diagram**. It lists the properties of **UITextField** as well as a few of its commonly used methods.

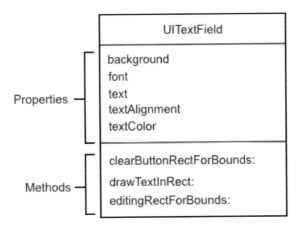

Figure 2.8 **UITextField** *properties and methods*

Each method can be performed individually and has a different effect on the text field. For example, the **drawTextInRect:** method displays the text inside the text field.

All objects created from a single class have the same behavior, because the same method code runs for every object created from that class.

Non-Visual Objects

You can't see or interact with all objects the way you can user-interface objects. A good example of a non-visual object is the *View Controller* object shown on the left in Figure 2.9. On the right side is a *view*. A view contains one screen of information on an iOS device.

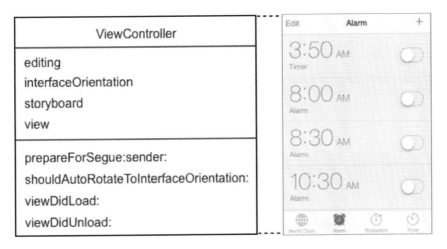

Figure 2.9 The view controller is a non-visual object.

Every view in an iOS app has a view controller that works behind the scenes together with the view. It has properties that (among other things):

• Indicate if the user can edit items in the view.

• Report the user-interface (portrait or landscape).

• Allow you to access user-interface elements.

It has methods that:

• Allow you to navigate to other views.

• Specify the interface orientations the view supports.

• Indicate when the associated view is loaded and unloaded from the screen.

View controller objects are based on the Cocoa Touch Framework's **UIViewController** class, or one of its subclasses.

Another category of non-visual objects that work behind the scenes is ***business objects***. Business objects contain the core business logic of your app. They often represent real-world entities such as a customer, an invoice, a product, or a payment. Figure 2.10 shows a **Calculator** business object that contains the core logic behind the **Calculator** user interface. The **Calculator** business object is created from a custom **Calculator** class (Apple doesn't provide a **Calculator** class in the Cocoa Touch Framework).

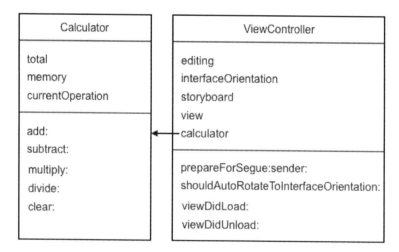

Figure 2.10 The Calculator business object contains core business logic.

Typically, Apple's user-interface classes such as labels, text fields, and buttons do everything you need them to—with no extra programming on your part.

In contrast, you have to add properties and methods to view controller classes that do things specific to the app you are building. For example, you need to add code that responds to the touch of a button or slide of a switch, or that collects information from text fields. When it comes to business objects—such as the Calculator, Invoice, or Customer—you have to do even more coding, because you have to create these from scratch, since no class in the Cocoa Touch Framework has the properties and methods you need.

Check out the **ViewController** code in Figure 2.11.

```
class DetailViewController: UIViewController {

    @IBOutlet var detailDescriptionLabel: UILabel

    var detailItem: AnyObject? {
        didSet {
            // Update the view.
            self.configureView()
        }
    }

    func configureView() {
        // Update the user interface for the detail item.
        if let detail: AnyObject = self.detailItem {
            if let label = self.detailDescriptionLabel {
                label.text = detail.description
            }
        }
    }

    override func viewDidLoad() {
        super.viewDidLoad()
        // Do any additional setup after loading the view,
        self.configureView()
    }

    override func didReceiveMemoryWarning() {
        super.didReceiveMemoryWarning()
        // Dispose of any resources that can be recreated.
    }
}
```

Figure 2.11 View controller code written in Swift

What does this code do? How does it work? How do you change existing methods and add new properties and methods to accomplish tasks you need to perform in your app?

By the time you finish this book, you will know the answers to all these questions and more. You will have learned Swift.

Object-Orientation and Discoverability

Working with an object-oriented language has great advantages. One is **discoverability**—a measure of how easy is it to discover, or find the code you need to perform a particular task.

Apple provides thousands of classes for you to build your apps. When you need to perform a task, your first job is discovering which class will help you get the job done. However, once you discover the class you need, it opens up a world of functionality for you, because each class contains many related methods.

For example, let's say that you are creating an app with one text field for the user's first name and another for their last name (Figure 2.12). When the user clicks the **Done** button, you want to display a welcome message that combines the first and last names (for example, "Welcome Steve Jobs"). So, how do you do this?

Figure 2.12 How do you combine first and last names?

A bit of research reveals that Swift has a **String** class that allows you to manipulate a set of characters. As it turns out, you can use the addition operator (+) to combine strings. Just what you were looking for!

Once you learn that the **String** class exists, the whole world of string manipulation is open to you. In fact, **String** has dozens of methods that you can use to manipulate strings.

In **Table 2.1**, the column on the left lists a few tasks you can perform with **String** and the column on the right lists the associated **String** methods you can use to perform each task.

You don't need to know how all these methods work right now. I just want to give you a sense of the methods available to you.

Object-orientation is "the gift that keeps on giving." Each new Swift or Cocoa Touch Framework class you discover opens a world of functionality for you.

Inheritance

Inheritance is a foundational principle of object-oriented programming, and is important for you to understand. "Inheritance" refers to the concept that a class can be based on or inherit its attributes (properties) and behavior (methods) from another class.

For example, as illustrated in Figure 2.13, illustrates how the **ScientificCalculator** class inherits from the **Calculator** class.

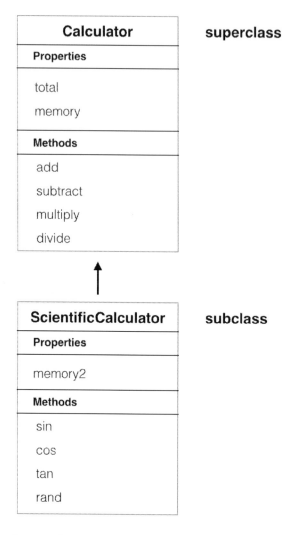

*Figure 2.13 The **ScientificCalculator** class is a subclass of and inherits from the **Calculator** superclass.*

Because of this relationship, **ScientificCalculator** inherits the **Calculator** class's **total** and **memory** properties as well as its methods. In this relationship, **Calculator** is referred to as a ***superclass*** of **ScientificCalculator**. In turn, **ScientificCalculator** is referred to as a ***subclass*** of **Calculator**.

Class inheritance can go further than just one level. For example, tracing the heritage of the **Goalie** class in Figure 2.14 to the top level, you'll find **Goalie** inherits from **FootballPlayer**, which inherits from **Athlete**.

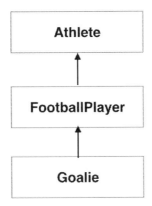

Figure 2.14 The full inheritance chain

Walking the inheritance chain the other way, from top to bottom, you'll see each class becomes more specialized and adds new properties and methods, inherited in turn by the class below it.

In Swift, a class can have only one superclass but can have zero, one, or many subclasses (known as zero-to-many). For example, in Figure 2.15, **Shape** has three subclasses: **Triangle**, **Circle**, and **Rectangle**.

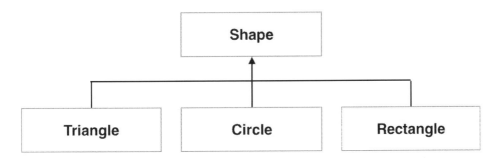

Figure 2.15 Classes can have zero-to-many subclasses.

Where will you come across subclasses in your daily app development? For starters, when you create a new iOS project, Xcode automatically adds view controller subclasses to your project. For example, if you create a Master-Detail app, Xcode adds **MasterViewController** and **DetailViewController** classes to your project, as shown in Figure 2.16 (you will learn all about these classes a little later).

Figure 2.16 **MasterViewController** *and* **DetailViewController** *classes*

In Figure 2.17, you can see **MasterViewController** is a subclass of **UITableViewController**, in turn a subclass of **UIViewController**. The **DetailViewController** class is a direct subclass of **UIViewController**. What makes this interesting is that **MasterViewController** and **DetailViewController** are Swift classes, and **UITableViewController** and **UIViewController** are Objective-C classes, because they are part of the Cocoa Touch Framework still written in Objective-C.

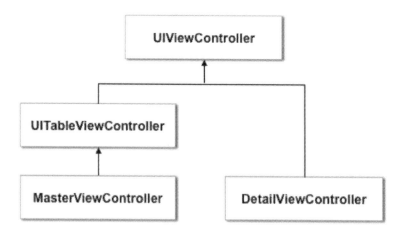

Figure 2.17 View controller class hierarchy

Part of your job as an iOS developer is to modify the **MasterViewController** and **DetailViewController** classes to suit your app's needs. So, it's important for you to understand how the properties and methods of the view controller superclasses work.

Chapter 15: Inheritance and Polymorphism teaches you more about this subject.

AnyObject and Any

In Swift, there is no universal base class. Classes you define without a superclass can become base classes from which you create subclasses.

Since you can declare your own base classes, there has to be another way to refer to any object. That's where **AnyObject** and **Any** Swift keywords come into play.

AnyObject can represent an instance of any class type. It is similar to **id** in Objective-C. **Any** is a little broader in scope and can represent an instance of not just classes, but any type at all, including function types.

Summary

In this chapter, you learned these facts about classes, objects, and inheritance:

- A class is a blueprint objects are created from.

- A class defines the attributes and behavior of objects created from it.

- Class properties define the attributes of objects, and methods define their behavior.

- Inheritance is a key feature of object-oriented programming. It allows a subclass to inherit attributes and behavior from a superclass.

- A class can have zero or more subclasses.

- There is no universal base class in Swift.

- The **AnyObject** keyword can represent an instance of any class type.

- The **Any** keyword can represent an instance of not just classes, but any type at all.

Chapter 3: Variables and Constants

Most books aim to teach you Swift by having you build your own custom classes. For non-programmers, this is like trying to learn to drive by building a car—it can be a bit overwhelming.

So, first I'll teach you to drive; then I'll show you how to build your own custom car. Let's start out with a few easy classes to help you get a feel for Swift.

Sections in This Chapter

1. *Opening the SwiftDemo Sample Project*

2. *Running the Sample App*

3. *Viewing Code Files*

4. *Declaring Variables*

5. *Declaring Constants*

6. *Variable and Constant Names*

7. *Setting Property Values*

8. *Summary*

9. *Step-By-Step Movie 3.1*

Opening the SwiftDemo Sample Project

If you haven't already done so, it's time to download the sample code for this book. Instructions for downloading the sample code appear in *Chapter 1: Getting Started* under the topic Downloading the Sample Code.

To open the **SwiftDemo** sample project:

1. Launch the Xcode application on your computer. If you have never launched Xcode before, it's normally found in the Dock on your Mac. All you have to do is click the Xcode icon to launch it as in Figure 3.1.

Figure 3.1 Launching Xcode from the Mac OS X Dock

2. If you don't see Xcode in your Dock, click the **Applications** icon in your Dock, and then select Xcode from the pop-up list of applications (you may have to scroll down to see it).

3. After Xcode launches, you should see the **Welcome to Xcode** window (as long as you haven't unchecked **Show this window when Xcode launches** located at the bottom of the window) as in Figure 3.2. If you *don't* see the **Welcome to Xcode** window, in Xcode's **Window** menu, select **Welcome to Xcode**.

Figure 3.2 The Welcome to Xcode window lets you create new project or open existing projects.

4. In the bottom-left corner, click the **Open Other...** button to open the sample project.

5. In the Open window, navigate to the location where you have copied the sample code for this book. If you have used the suggested folder, select the **Documents** folder in the **Favorites** panel, and then double-click the **Samples** folder on the right. Expand the **SwiftDemo** folder (Figure 3.3), select the **SwiftDemo.xcodeproj** file, and click **Open**.

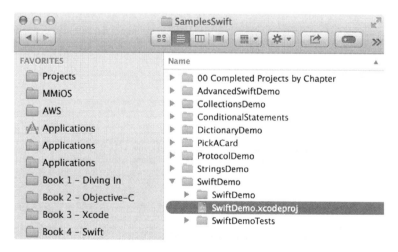

*Figure 3.3 Opening the **SwiftDemo** project*

When you first open the project, it should look like the screen shot in Figure 3.4. On the left side of the Xcode window is the Project Navigator. If you don't see the Project Navigator, press **Command+1** to display it.

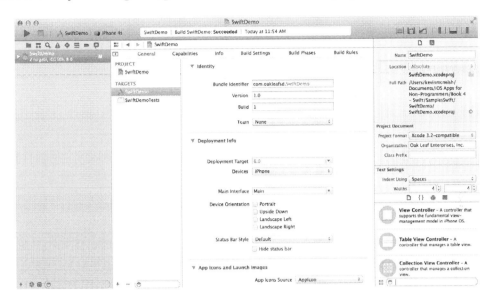

*Figure 3.4 The newly opened **SwiftDemo** project*

Note: Throughout this book, when I mention pressing the **Command** key plus any other key, you should simultaneously hold the **Command** key down and press the other key mentioned (in this case, the number **1**).

The Project Navigator contains the highlighted **SwiftDemo** project item. Click the small gray triangle on the left to expand the project item, and then click the gray arrow to the left of the **SwiftDemo** subfolder to expand it. This folder contains the main code files (Figure 3.5).

Figure 3.5 The Project Navigator contains a list of files.

Click on the **Main.storyboard** file in the Project Navigator to display the app's user interface in Xcode's designer as shown in Figure 3.6. You can see it looks like a blank iPhone screen (except for the label) and even includes a status bar with a battery icon.

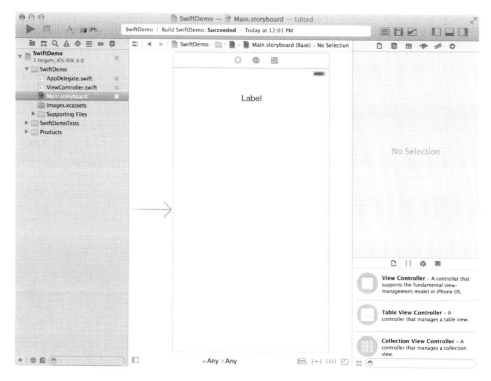

*Figure 3.6 The **SwiftDemo** project's main storyboard*

For now, you just need to know a few things about laying out the user interface. First, the white rectangular area in the middle of the screen that contains the label is a *scene*. Again, a scene displays one screen of information on an iOS device.

Each scene usually has a related view controller class that contains code associated with that scene. In this case, the view controller class is stored in the file named **ViewController.swift**, which you can see in the Project Navigator on the left side of the screen in Figure 3.6. You will learn more about this file in just a bit.

Running the Sample App

To establish a starting point, let's run the project to see what it looks like in the iOS Simulator. First, make sure the **Scheme** control at the top left of the Xcode window is set to **iPhone 5s** (Figure 3.7).

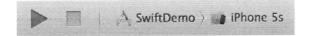

*Figure 3.7 Set the Scheme control to **iPhone 5s**.*

Next, click the **Run** button in the upper-left corner of the Xcode window (Figure 3.8).

*Figure 3.8 Click **Run** to run the app in the Simulator.*

After several seconds, the iOS Simulator appears and displays the app as in Figure 3.9.

*Figure 3.9 The **SwiftDemo** app running in the Simulator*

No surprises here. The screen looks the same as it does in Xcode's design surface.

Viewing Code Files

As a first step to learning Swift, you are going to write a few lines of code that will change the text of the label when the app runs in the Simulator. This is a valuable exercise, because you often need to make such changes in an iOS app. Let's begin by taking a look at one of the project's code files.

1. Go back to Xcode (if you can't see the Xcode window to click on it, press **Command+Tab**) and click the **Stop** button in the upper-left corner of Xcode to stop the app from running in the Simulator.

2. Next, you are going to look at one of the project's code files. When viewing code, it's a good idea to turn off Xcode's Assistant Editor to provide a larger code-editing area in the center of the window. If the Assistant Editor is on, it displays two code windows (either on top of or next to each other) in the center panel of Xcode. Turn it off by clicking the **Show the Standard editor** button, which is the first on the left in the three-button group above the **Editor** label in the top-right corner of the Xcode window (Figure 3.10). If this button is already selected (as it is in the figure), then the Assistant Editor is off.

Figure 3.10 Hiding the Assistant Editor

3. In the Project Navigator on the left, select the **ViewController.swift** file to display it in the Code Editor. Near the top of this file is the following declaration:

```
class ViewController: UIViewController {
```

This declaration tells you this is the **ViewController** class file and that **ViewController** is a subclass of the **UIViewController** class.

Notice the following lines of code a little farther down in the code file:

```
override func viewDidLoad() {
    super.viewDidLoad()
    // Do any additional setup after loading
}
```

This section of code is called a *method*. Remember, a method groups one or more lines of code that are executed as a unit. A Swift class usually has dozens of methods. The left curly brace at the end of the line indicates the beginning of the code block and the ending curly brace indicates the end of the code block. All method code in your app *must* appear within the curly braces of a method. Entering code outside these curly braces is one of the most common mistakes for new iOS developers, so definitely watch out for this!

The name of this method is **viewDidLoad**, and it is inherited from the **UIViewController** class, which you can tell by the **override** keyword (more on this later). This method is automatically executed at run time when the view is first loaded for display. The green, called a **comment**, is used to explain the code that follows. Comments are not code and are therefore not executed.

4. You are now going to add code that changes the label's text at ***run time*** (run time is when the app is running in the Simulator or on an iOS device). To do this, click your mouse pointer to the immediate right of the comment, and then press **return**. This adds a new empty line directly below the existing code.

Note: Throughout this book, when I ask you to create a new empty line, this is how you do it!

Declaring Variables

Now type the following highlighted line of code (each line of code is known as a ***statement***). Make sure you type all characters in upper or lower case as shown in this code sample, because Swift is ***case sensitive***. This means you must type the uppercase and lowercase letters exactly as shown:

```
override func viewDidLoad() {
        super.viewDidLoad()
      // Do any additional setup after loading
      var myString: String = "Swift"
```

```
    }
```

Note: You can break up a single line of code into multiple physical lines in the code file as follows:

```
var myString: String =
      "Swift"
```

The line of code that you added creates a *variable* named **myString**, which contains a *String* object.

A variable is a place in memory where you can store and retrieve information. It's called a variable because you can vary the information that you store in it. You can store one piece of information in a variable then store another piece of information in the same variable. Variables declared within a method are called *local variables*, because they can only be accessed locally, from within the method in which they are declared.

Figure 3.11 provides a breakdown of this variable declaration for us.

Figure 3.11 Declaring a variable

You begin a variable declaration with the **var** keyword followed by the name of the variable. Next, you add a colon, followed by the variable type (known as a *type annotation*.) Afterward, you can assign a value to the variable using the (=) assignment operator. The rest of the line stores the ***string literal*** "Swift" into the new variable. In Swift, a literal is a notation representing a fixed value. You declare a string literal by typing the string between open and closed double quotes.

In review:

*   **myString** is the variable name.

*   **String** is the type of the variable.

*   The equal (=) sign is the assignment operator. It takes the value on its

right and stores it into the variable on its left.

- "Swift" is a string literal.

- Storing the string value in the **myString** variable creates a string object.

Variable Types

In Swift, if you assign an initial value to a variable, you don't need to specify the variable type (Figure 3.12). This is because Swift has something called *type inference* that means it can figure out, or *infer*, the type of the variable based on the value you assign to it.

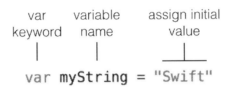

Figure 3.12 If you assign an initial value to a variable, you don't have to specify its type.

Although you can change the information stored in a variable, there is a limit on the type of information you can store. In the line of code that you just added, you declared **myString** as a **String** variable. This means the variable can only store information of the type **String**.

The **String** class is part of Swift and represents a set of characters. So, you can store any set of characters in the **myString** variable, but you can't store other types of information such as integers, true or false values, etc.

Declaring Constants

In contrast with variables, **_constants_** are just that—constant. Their values don't change. Declaring constants in Swift is very similar to declaring a variable. You simply use the **let** keyword rather than the **var** keyword. For example:

```
let margin: Integer = 10
```

This line of code declares a constant named **margin** of type **Integer** and sets the value of the constant to **10**. Once you set the value of a constant, it can't be changed. (That's what makes it constant!)

As with variables, you can also leave out the type annotation when declaring a constant since the compiler can infer the type from what you specify as its value.

Variable and Constant Names

You can name variables and constants anything you want, although something meaningful is best. Here are some rules governing variable and constant names:

- Names must be unique within the same scope. This means you can't have two variables in a method with the same name. However, you can have variables with the same name if they are in different methods.

- You can use almost any character in a variable or constant name, including Unicode characters.

- They can't contain mathematical symbols, arrows, line- or box-drawing characters.

- They can't start with a number, although you can use numbers elsewhere in the name.

- If you need to give a variable or constant the same name as a reserved Swift keyword (avoid this if you can), you can surround the name with back ticks when you declare it and when you reference it. For example:

```
var `extension` = "abc"
`extension` = "123"
```

Setting Property Values

Now type the following highlighted line of code directly below the line of code you previously added:

```
override func viewDidLoad() {
   super.viewDidLoad()
   // Do any additional setup after loading
   var myString: String = "Swift"
   self.lblDemo.text = myString
}
```

of the code that follows. Comments are not code and therefore not executed.

- *Run time* is when the app is running in the Simulator or on an iOS device.

- Swift is *case sensitive*!

Variables

- A variable is a place in an app's memory where you can store and retrieve information.

- It's called a *variable* because you can change the information you store in it.

- Variables declared within a method are called *local variables*, because they can only be accessed locally, from within the method in which they are declared.

- In Swift, a *literal* is a notation representing a fixed value. You declare a string literal by typing the string between open and closed double quotes.

- Here is an example of declaring a variable:

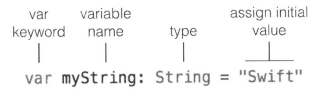

- If you assign an initial value to a variable, you don't need to specify the variable type, because Swift's **type inference** allows it to figure out, or *infer,* the type of the variable based on the value assigned to it.

- Although you can change the information stored in a variable, you can only store one type of information such as strings in a String variable.

- **self** refers to an instance of the class in which you are typing code.

- You type a period (.) after **self** to access an object's properties.

- To store a value into a property or variable, you use the **assignment** *operator*, which is an equal (=) sign. It takes the value on its right and stores it into the property or variable on its left.

Constants

- Declaring a constant in Swift is very similar to declaring a variable. You simply use the **let** keyword rather than the **var** keyword. For example:

```
let margin: Integer = 10
```

- Once you set the value of a constant, it can't be changed.

- Variable and constant names must be unique in the scope in which they are declared.

Step-By-Step Movie 3.1

In case you missed any of the steps along the way, you can enter the link below in your Web browser to see each step performed for you.

Movie 3.1

http://www.iOSAppsForNonProgrammers.com/B4M31.html

Chapter 4: Working with Optionals

Optionals are a new feature in the Swift programming language, unavailable previously in Objective-C. They are similar to optional types in Java and nullable types in the C# programming language. Optionals make your code safer and are part of Swift's type safety!

Sections in This Chapter

1. *Xcode Playgrounds*

2. *Creating a New Playground*

3. *Why Use Optionals?*

4. *nil in Swift*

5. *Accessing Optional Values*

6. *Using Forced Unwrapping*

7. *Using Optional Binding to Unwrap Optionals*

8. *Implicitly Unwrapped Optionals*

9. *Optional Chaining*

10. *Summary*

11. *Step-By-Step Movie 4.1*

Xcode Playgrounds

Before diving into Swift's optionals, let's look at the tool you'll use in this chapter to test-drive your code—playgrounds.

A playground (Figure 4.1) is a new type of document introduced in Xcode 6 that allows you to enter code in the left panel and immediately see the result of each expression in the right panel.

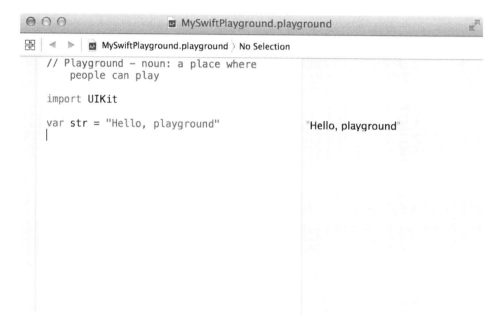

Figure 4.1 A new playground

Every time you add new code or change existing code in the left panel, Xcode runs all your code from top to bottom.

Creating a New Playground

Let's create a playground we can use to experiment with Swift's optionals.

1. Select **File** > **New** > **Playground** in the Xcode menu.

2. In the Create Playground dialog, set the **Name** to **Optionals**, and the **Platform** to **iOS** as in Figure 4.2.

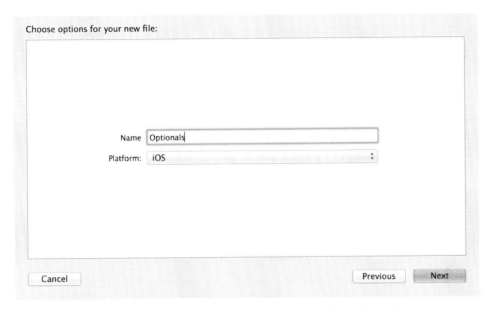

*Figure 4.2 Create a playground named **Optionals**.*

3. In the **Name** box, enter **Optionals**, and in the **Platform** box, enter **iOS**. Then, click **Next**.

4. In the Save dialog, select the folder where you want to save the playground (I like to use the **Documents** folder), and then click **Create**.

   Now, you should now see a new playground as in Figure 4.1. You can see that when you enter code on the left side of the playground window, the results are automatically displayed in the Results sidebar on the right side of the window.

5. Delete the following line of code from the left side of the playground:

   ```
   var str = "Hello, playground"
   ```

   This is sample code automatically included in the playground when you first created it. When you delete this code, the value disappears from the Results sidebar on the right.

6. If a toolbar isn't visible, at the top of the playground, select **View > Show Toolbar** from the Xcode menu.

Now you're ready to learn about Swift's optionals!

Why Use Optionals?

Optionals are a key feature of the Swift programming language. They let you specify that a variable or constant may potentially contain a **nil** (nothing).

Maybe you're thinking, *I can ignore optionals—it's a feature I'll never use,* but I recommend that you read further. You will find you *must* use optionals in Swift if you ever need a value to be **nil** (nothing)!

Optional values in Swift allow you to be more precise in your code by letting you specify when it's OK for a particular value to be empty (and when it's not.) This helps you avoid common programming errors that occur when your app encounters an unexpected **nil** value.

Swift's optionals also help your app's code more closely mirror the ability you have in Core Data to indicate that a particular entity attribute is optional (see Book 3: Navigating Xcode for details on using Core Data). As Figure 4.3 shows, you can specify the type of an attribute (**String**, in this case) as well as indicate if the value is optional.

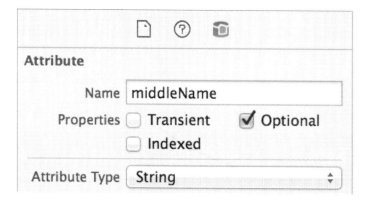

Figure 4.3 You can specify that Core Data entity attributes are optional.

Swift allows you to do the same with your properties and variables. Let's get some hands-on experience with optionals.

1. Open the **Optionals** playground if it's not already open.

2. Add the following line of code to the left side of the playground:

```
var middleName: String
```

This declares a non-optional **String** variable called **middleName**.

3. Now add a question mark at the end of the declaration.

```
var middleName: String?
```

This changes the type of the **middleName** variable to an optional String. This statement is equivalent to marking the **middleName** attribute **Optional** for a Core Data attribute (Figure 4.3).

The question mark (?) after the **String** variable type indicates that the **middleName** variable can contain a value that is either a **String** or **nil**. Anyone looking at this code immediately knows that **middleName** can be **nil**. It's self-documenting!

Notice in the Results sidebar on the right side of the playground, a **nil** appears (Figure 4.4), indicating the value of the **middleName** variable is **nil**.

```
var middleName:String?    nil
```

*Figure 4.4 The **middleName** variable contains **nil**.*

This demonstrates that if you don't specify an initial value for an optional constant or variable, the value is automatically set to **nil**. If you prefer, you can explicitly set the initial value to **nil**:

```
var middleName: String? = nil
```

Now let's take a closer look at how **nil** is used in Swift.

nil in Swift

At first glance this may not be obvious, but *only optionals can be nil*. As stated in Apple's *The Swift Programming Language* book (available for free in the iBooks Store):

***nil** cannot be used with non-optional constants and variables. If a constant or variable in your code needs to be able to cope with the absence of a value under certain conditions, always declare it as an optional value of the appropriate type.*

This means you can't set a non-optional to **nil**. Let's try.

1. Remove the question mark at the end of the **middleName** variable declaration in the playground:

```
var middleName:String
```

This makes the variable non-optional and causes the **nil** to disappear in the Results sidebar.

2. Add the following code to the end of the variable declaration and press **return**:

```
var middleName: String = nil
```

This code attempts to store a **nil** into the non-optional **middleName** variable.

3. This generates a compile-time error as indicated by the red exclamation mark icon to the left of the code. Click on this error icon and it displays the error in Figure 4.5.

```
var middleName:String = nil
   Type 'String' does not conform to protocol 'NilLiteralConvertible'
```

*Figure 4.5 Compiler error when trying to store **nil** into a non-optional variable*

Note that **nil** in Swift is different from **nil** in Objective-C. In Objective-C, **nil** is a pointer to a non-existent object. In Swift, **nil** simply indicates the absence of a value—it is not a pointer. This means you can specify optionals of *any* type, not just object types.

Accessing Optional Values

Unlike other programming languages, in Swift, *you can't access an optional value directly*. You must *unwrap* the optional first to access its underlying value. Let's get some hands-on experience with this.

1. Remove the **middleName** declaration from the playground you created in the previous section.

2. Add the following variable declarations to the playground:

```
var firstName: String = "Ryan"
var middleName: String? = "Michael"
```

```
var firstAndMiddleNames: String
```

This code declares a **firstName** String variable, a **middleName** *optional* String variable, and a **firstAndMiddleNames** String variable.

3. Now add the following code below the variable declarations:

```
firstAndMiddleNames = firstName + " "   +
    middleName
```

This code concatenates (joins) the **firstName** and **middleName** variable values together with a space between them and stores the resulting string in the **firstAndMiddleNames** variable. You may be surprised to find this line of code creates a compile-time error. To see the error, click on the red error icon to the left of the **firstAndMiddleNames** variable (Figure 4.6).

```
var firstName: String = "Ryan"
var middleName: String? = "Michael"
var firstAndMiddleNames: String
    ⊙ Value of optional type 'String?' not unwrapped; did you mean to use '!' or '??'
firstAndMiddleNames = firstName + " "   +
middleName
```

Figure 4.6 "Value not unwrapped" error

Here is the full text of the compiler error:

Value of option type 'String?' not unwrapped; did you mean to use '!' or '?'?

This is one of Swift's protection mechanisms. It forces you to acknowledge that the optional **middleName** variable may be **nil**. So how do you unwrap an optional? The following sections describe two main ways.

Using Forced Unwrapping

As the compiler error in the previous section suggests, one way to unwrap an optional value is to use *forced unwrapping*—add an exclamation mark (!) after the optional to explicitly unwrap it. Let's give this a try.

1. Add an exclamation mark after the reference to the **middleName** variable:

```
firstAndMiddleNames = firstName + " " +
    middleName!
```

2. This manually forces the value of the **middleName** optional to be unwrapped. Notice in the Results sidebar, the value of the **middleName** variable is **Ryan Michael** (Figure 4.7).

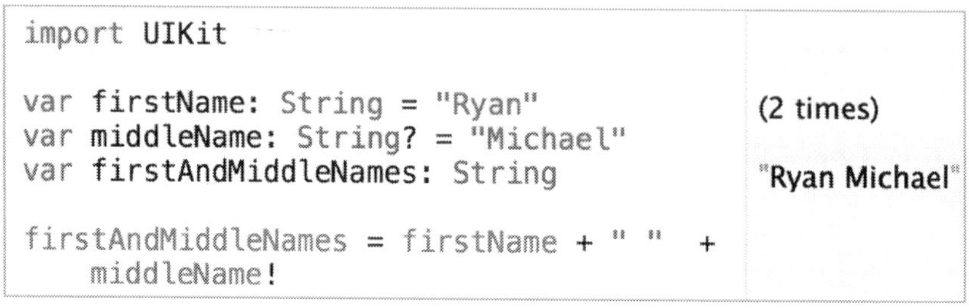

```
import UIKit

var firstName: String = "Ryan"              (2 times)
var middleName: String? = "Michael"
var firstAndMiddleNames: String             "Ryan Michael"

firstAndMiddleNames = firstName + " " +
    middleName!
```

*Figure 4.7 Explicitly unwrapping the **firstName** variable*

Although this works fine for this example, if **middleName** contains a **nil** at run time, this produces a run-time error. Let's see which error is generated.

3. Change the **middleName** variable initialization to the following:

```
var middleName: String? = nil
```

4. Click on the error icon to the left of the code to see the compiler error in Figure 4.8.

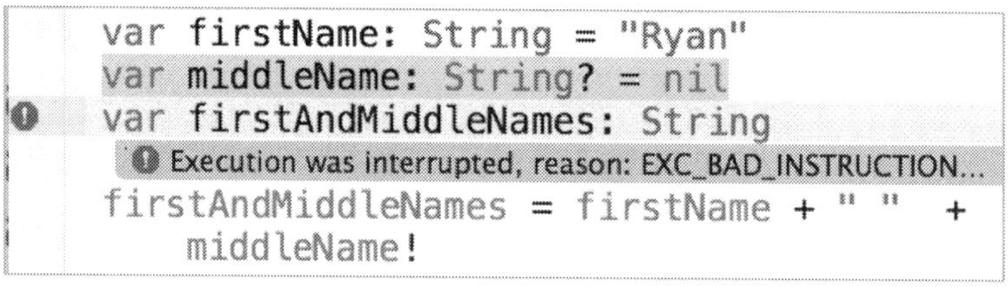

```
var firstName: String = "Ryan"
var middleName: String? = nil
var firstAndMiddleNames: String
  ● Execution was interrupted, reason: EXC_BAD_INSTRUCTION...
firstAndMiddleNames = firstName + " " +
    middleName!
```

*Figure 4.8 Explicitly unwrapping a variable that contains **nil** produces a compiler error!*

The moral of the story is: don't use forced unwrapping unless you are *absolutely sure* the optional value is not **nil**!

Using Optional Binding to Unwrap Optionals

You can use a technique known as **optional binding** to test if an optional contains a value, and, if so, store that value in a temporary variable or constant. Let's see how this works.

1. Change the **middleName** variable initialization to the following:

```
var middleName: String? = "Michael"
```

2. Remove the following code from the playground:

```
firstAndMiddleNames = firstName + " "  +
        middleName!
```

3. Add the following code below the variable declarations:

```
if let middle = middleName
{
    firstAndMiddleNames = firstName + " "  +
        middle
    println("Middle name not nil")
}
else
{
    firstAndMiddleNames = firstName
    println("Middle name is nil")
}
```

When the **if** condition is checked, if the **middleName** variable contains a **String** value:

1) The condition evaluates to **true**

2) The **middleName** variable's value is unwrapped.

3) The value is stored in the **middle** constant.

4) The code within the curly braces is executed.

Since the variable currently contains a value, you will see the results in Figure 4.9.

```
var firstName: String = "Ryan"              (2 times)
var middleName: String? = "Michael"
var firstAndMiddleNames: String             "Ryan Michael"
                                            "Middle name not nil"
if let middle = middleName
{
    firstAndMiddleNames = firstName + "
        " + middle
    println("Middle name not nil")
}
    else
{
    firstAndMiddleNames = firstName
    println("Middle name is nil")
}
```

*Figure 4.9 The **middleName** variable is not **nil**.*

If the **middleName** variable contains **nil**:

1) The condition evaluates to **false**.

2) The optional value is *not* unwrapped.

3) The code in the curly braces of the **else** statement is executed.

4. To test this, store a **nil** in the **middleName** property:

```
var middleName: String? = nil
```

5. Since the variable contains a **nil**, you will see the results in Figure 4.10.

```
var firstName: String = "Ryan"              (2 times)
var middleName: String? = nil
var firstAndMiddleNames: String
                                            "Ryan"
if let middle = middleName                  "Middle name is nil"
{
    firstAndMiddleNames = firstName + "
        " + middle
    println("Middle name not nil")
}
    else
{
    firstAndMiddleNames = firstName
    println("Middle name is nil")
}
```

*Figure 4.10 The **middleName** variable is **nil**.*

Implicitly Unwrapped Optionals

Swift has something called *__implicitly unwrapped optionals__*. These are optionals that do not need to be unwrapped using either forced unwrapping (!) or optional binding, because they are unwrapped implicitly (automatically) when they are declared. They are declared using an exclamation mark (!) rather than a question mark (?). For example:

```
var middleName: String!
```

You often see implicitly unwrapped optionals when working with Cocoa Touch Framework classes. That's because objects in Objective-C can potentially be **nil**, so some APIs that contain a reference to an object must reference it as an optional. However, where you know an object will never be **nil**, it's convenient to use implicitly unwrapped optionals so you don't have to continually unwrap the values manually.

You often see implicitly unwrapped optionals when working with Interface builder outlets (**@IBOutlet** properties.) For example:

```
@IBOutlet weak var lblLabel: UILabel!
```

In this code, an exclamation mark following the **lblLabel** outlet property indicates it is implicitly unwrapped. This allows you to access the property without unwrapping it.

In this example, the outlet property isn't *guaranteed* to contain a reference to a label, but it absolutely *should*. If it doesn't contain a reference to a label, it means the connection between the outlet and the label is broken. In this case, it's OK to have a run-time error, because you want to be alerted that the connection is broken so you can fix it!

Obviously, if you're not 100 percent sure a constant or variable contains a **nil**, you should use a regular optional instead.

Optional Chaining

Where you are accessing a nested optional property or method, you can use optional chaining, which fails gracefully rather than generating a run-time error.

What do I mean by "nested" property or method? Typically, you access a property on an object like this:

```
myObject.myProperty
```

However, at times, an object has a property containing a reference to a second object and you need to access the property on that second object:

```
myFirstObject.mySecondObject.myProperty
```

In this case, **myProperty** is nested. So how do you handle the situation where **mySecondObject** is optional? This is where optional chaining comes to the rescue.

Let's get a hands-on example of how optional chaining works.

1. In the folder where you downloaded this book's sample code, expand the **OptionalChainingDemo** folder and then double click the **.xcodeproj** file to open the project in Xcode.

2. Expand the **OptionalChainingDemo** group folder in the Project Navigator, and look at the code in the **MemberEntity.swift** and **LocationEntity.swift** code files. Here's what you will see in the two files (I have left out the initializer in **MemberEntity** to make the code easier to read):

```
class MemberEntity {

    var location : LocationEntity? = nil
    var firstName : String = ""
    var lastName: String = ""
}

class LocationEntity {

    var locationName = "Cupertino"
    var locationDescription = "Apple's home"
    var locationId: Int32 = 1
}
```

The **MemberEntity** class represents someone who is a member of your app's user base. The **LocationEntity** represents their physical location.

The **MemberEntity** class has a **location** property that can hold a reference to a **LocationEntity** object (Figure 4.11). This property is optional, because not every member wants us to know where they live! So let's try to access the **location** property and its sub-properties in code.

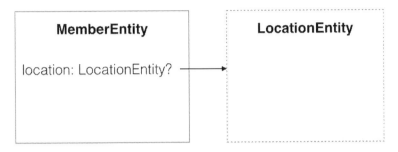

*Figure 4.11 The **MemberEntity** and **LocationEntity** objects*

3. Expand the **OptionalChainingDemoTests** group and select the **OptionalChainingDemoTests.swift** code file. Add the following test method before the closing curly brace of the class:

```
func testOptionalChaining() {

    var memberEntity = MemberEntity()
    var nameOfLocation : String? =
        memberEntity.location?.locationName

    XCTAssertNil(nameOfLocation)
}
}
```

The first line of code creates an instance of the **MemberEntity** class and stores it in the **memberEntity** variable. The next code statement is physically broken up into two lines to save space. This code references the **MemberEntity** object's **location** property and then the location object's **locationName** property. The last line of code is a test to check if the **nameOfLocation** variable is **nil**.

Important to note:

- You need the question mark after **location**, because **location** is an optional property.

- The **nameOfLocation** variable where the return value is stored is declared as an optional string, even though **locationName** is not optional! That's because if the **location** property is nil, then the operation's result is **nil**.

- The act of accessing a value from an optional member is called *optional chaining*.

Let's run the test and see how this code works at run time.

4. Press **Command+B** to build the project and verify that you have no compiler errors.

5. Click in the gutter to the left of the first line of code in the test method to set a breakpoint (Figure 4.12).

```
func testOptionalChaining() {

    var memberEntity = MemberEntity()
    var nameOfLocation : String? =
        memberEntity.location?.locationName
    XCTAssertNil(nameOfLocation)
}
}
```

Figure 4.12 Set a breakpoint on the first line of code.

6. In the Navigator toolbar on the left side of the Xcode window, click the fifth button from the left to select the Test Navigator.

7. Expand the **OptionalChainingDemoTests** node, and then click the Run button to the right of the **testOptionalChaining()** method (Figure 4.13).

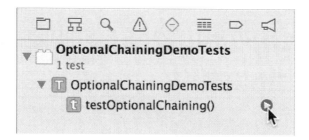

*Figure 4.13 Run the **testOptionalChaining()** test.*

After a few seconds you will hit the breakpoint as Figure 4.14 shows. The method is getting ready to execute the code that creates an instance of the **MemberEntity** class.

```
func testOptionalChaining() {

    var memberEntity = MemberEntity()
    var nameOfLocation : String? =
        memberEntity.location?.locationName
    XCTAssertNil(nameOfLocation)
}
}
```

Figure 4.14 The breakpoint is hit!

8. Next, in the Debug area toolbar, click the **Step into** button to begin stepping into the creation and initialization of the **MemberEntity** object (Figure 4.15).

```
class MemberEntity {

    var location : LocationEntity?
    var firstName : String = ""
    var lastName: String = ""

    init () {

    }
}
```

*Figure 4.15 Stepping into the **MemberEntity** init*

9. Click **Step over** three times to step over the code that initializes the **MemberEntity** object's properties. In the Variables View, expand the self node to see these values (Figure 4.16).

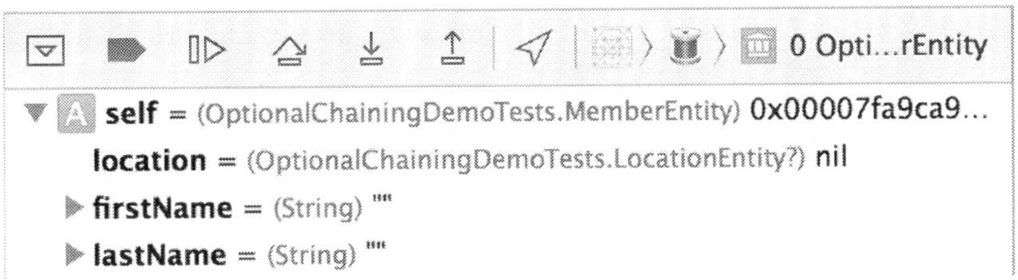

▼ A **self** = (OptionalChainingDemoTests.MemberEntity) 0x00007fa9ca9...
   location = (OptionalChainingDemoTests.LocationEntity?) nil
  ▶ **firstName** = (String) ""
  ▶ **lastName** = (String) ""

*Figure 4.16 The **MemberEntity** initialized properties*

No surprises here. The **location** property is **nil** and the **firstName** and **lastName** properties contain empty strings.

10. Click the **Step out** button to step back to the unit test code and then click **Step over** to execute the code that stores the **MemberEntity** object into the **memberEntity** variable.

11. Now the unit test is ready to execute the line of code that retrieves the value of the nested **locationName** property. Press **Step over** again to execute this line of code, and then check out the value of the **nameOfLocation** variable in the Variables View. As Figure 4.17 shows, it's **nil**. This is because there is no **LocationEntity** object in the **location** property. If there is no **LocationEntity** object, then there is no **locationName** property.

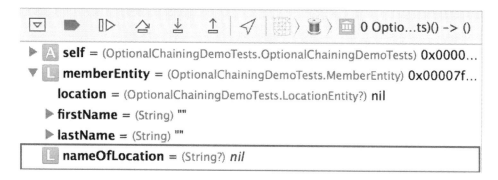

*Figure 4.17 The **nameOfLocation** variable is **nil**.*

When Swift sees the **MemberEntity** object's **location** property is **nil**, it looks no further and simply stores a **nil** in the **nameOfLocation** variable.

12. In the Debug toolbar, click Continue and you should see the test for **nil** pass with flying colors (green, to be specific).

Let's see how the optional property works when it's not **nil**.

1. Select the **OptionalChainingDemoTests.swift** file in the Project Navigator and add the following new method before the closing curly brace of the class:

```swift
func testOptionalChaining2() {
    var memberEntity = MemberEntity()
    memberEntity.location = LocationEntity()
    var nameOfLocation : String? =
        memberEntity.location?.locationName
```

```
            XCTAssertNotNil(nameOfLocation)
        }
    }
```

2. This test method is similar to the other method you created, but has an extra line of code (the second line) that creates a **LocationEntity** object and stores it in the **MemberEntity** object's **location** property. The last line of code checks for *not* **nil** instead of **nil**.

3. Click in the gutter to the left of the first line of code in this method to set a breakpoint.

4. Press **Command+B** to build the project and ensure you have no compiler errors.

5. Next, in the Navigators toolbar, click the fifth button from the left to select the Test Navigator. Click the Run button to the right of the **testOptionalChaining2** method and you should hit the breakpoint.

6. Click **Step over** to execute the line of code that creates the **MemberEntity** object. Now, the unit test is ready to run the line of code that creates a **LocationEntity** object and stores it in the **location** property of the **MemberEntity** object (Figure 4.18).

```
    func testOptionalChaining2() {

        var memberEntity = MemberEntity()
        memberEntity.location = LocationEntity()
        var nameOfLocation : String? =
        memberEntity.location?.locationName
        XCTAssertNotNil(nameOfLocation)
    }
```

Figure 4.18 The breakpoint is hit!

7. Press the **Step into** button twice to begin to step into the initialization of the **LocationEntity** object (Figure 4.19).

```
class LocationEntity {

    var locationName : String = "Cupertino"
    var locationDescription : String = "The home of Apple"
    var locationId: Int32 = 1
}
```

*Figure 4.19 Stepping into the **LocationEntity** init*

8. Click **Step over** three times and then in the Variables View, expand the **self** node and you can see the **LocationEntity** object's properties have been initialized (Figure 4.20). Note the **locationName** property is set to **Cupertino**.

```
▽    ■    ▷    △    ↓    ↑  |  ⊲  |  ▦  ⟩  👕  ⟩  🏛  0 Opti...Entity

▼  A  self = (OptionalChainingDemoTests.LocationEntity) 0x00007ffdb86...
   ▶ locationName = (String) "Cupertino"
   ▶ locationDescription = (String) "The home of Apple"
   ▶ locationId = (Int32) 1
```

*Figure 4.20 The **LocationEntity** object's properties*

9. Click the **Step out** button to be taken back to the next line of code in the unit test that assigns the newly created **LocationEntity** object to the **location** property (Figure 4.21).

```swift
func testOptionalChaining2() {

    var memberEntity = MemberEntity()
    memberEntity.location = LocationEntity()
    var nameOfLocation : String? =
    memberEntity.location?.locationName
    XCTAssertNotNil(nameOfLocation)
}
```

*Figure 4.21 Getting ready to set the **location** property*

10. Press the **Step over** button to execute this line of code and then go to the Variables View, expand the **memberEntity** variable and check out its property values as Figure 4.22 shows. Notice the **location** property contains a reference to the **LocationEntity** object that was just created.

```
▽    ■    ▷    △    ↓    ↑  |  ⊲  |  ▦  ⟩  👕  ⟩  🏛  0 OptionalChai...oTests)() -> ()

▶  A  self = (OptionalChainingDemoTests.OptionalChainingDemoTests) 0x00007ffdb87cb4a0
▼  L  memberEntity = (OptionalChainingDemoTests.MemberEntity) 0x00007ffdb866a390
   ▶ location = (OptionalChainingDemoTests.LocationEntity?) (locationName = "Cupertino"...
   ▶ firstName = (String) ""
   ▶ lastName = (String) ""
▶  L  nameOfLocation = (String?) Some
```

*Figure 4.22 The **location** property contains a reference to the **LocationEntity** object.*

As Figure 4.23 shows, the unit test is ready to execute the line of code that performs the optional chaining. At this point, the location property isn't **nil**. It contains a reference to the **LocationEntity** object, so this line of code should be able to retrieve the **locationName** property value and store it in the **nameOfLocation** variable. Let's see this for ourselves.

```
func testOptionalChaining2() {

    var memberEntity = MemberEntity()
    memberEntity.location = LocationEntity()
    var nameOfLocation : String? =
    memberEntity.location?.locationName
    XCTAssertNotNil(nameOfLocation)
}
```

Figure 4.23 Ready to execute the optional chaining code

11. Click **Step over**, and the Variables View shows the **nameOfLocation** variable set to **Cupertino** (Figure 4.24)!

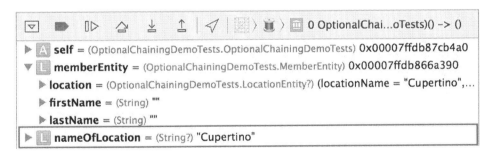

*Figure 4.24 **nameOfLocation** is set to **Cupertino**.*

Now click **Continue** and you should see this test passes, because **nameOfLocation** is not **nil**.

Important points about using optional chaining in other situations:

- Although you can *retrieve* a property value through optional chaining, you can't *set* its value this way.

- You can call methods through optional chaining. For example, if the **LocationEntity** class had a **getFormattedAddress** method, you could access the method like this:

```
var address : String? =
    memberEntity.location?.getFormattedAddress()
```

Again, note the return value is an optional **String**, because any value returned from optional chaining is always an optional.

- If you call a method that doesn't return anything, the return value will be **Void?**, because (again) any value returned from optional chaining is always optional.

- If you use optional chaining to access a value from a subscript, put the question mark before the subscript's braces. For example, if the **MemberEntity** class had an optional **nickNames** collection, you could access the first nickname value like this:

```
var nickName = memberEntity.nickNames?[0].name
```

- Although you can access a value from a subscript using optional chaining, you cannot set a subscript value this way.

The nil Coalescing Operator

The nil coalescing operator (a ?? b) unwraps an optional if it contains a value. If not, it returns a default value. Let's try it.

1. Open **Optionals.playground**.

2. Add the following code to the playground:

```
var textColor: UIColor?
var color = textColor ?? UIColor.blackColor()
```

Since the **textColor** optional contains **nil**, the nil coalescing operator returns the default **blackColor** (Figure 4.25).

```
var textColor: UIColor?                              nil
var color = textColor ?? UIColor.blackColor()        ███ w 0.0 a 1.0
```

*Figure 4.25 The nil coalescing operator sets **color** to black.*

3. Now store a value in the textColor variable:

```
var textColor: UIColor? = UIColor.blueColor()
var color = textColor ?? UIColor.blackColor()
```

Now that **textColor** contains a value, the nil coalescing operator returns **blueColor** (Figure 4.26).

```
var textColor: UIColor? = UIColor.blueColor()     {Some r 0.0 g 0.0 b 1.0 a 1.0}
var color = textColor ?? UIColor.blackColor()      ■ r 0.0 g 0.0 b 1.0 a 1.0
```

*Figure 4.26 The nil coalescing operator set **color** to **blue**.*

Summary

The main points from this chapter:

Playgrounds

- A playground is a new type of document introduced in Xcode 6 that allows you to enter code in the left panel and immediately see the result of each expression in the right panel.

Optionals

- Optionals allow you to specify that a variable or constant may contain a **nil** (nothing).

- To indicate the value is optional, add a question mark after the type of the value:

```
var middleName: String?
```

- If you don't specify an initial value for an optional constant or variable (as shown above) the value is automatically set to **nil** for you.

- Only optionals can be **nil**.

- In Swift, **nil** indicates the absence of a value—it is not a pointer.

- You can't access an optional value directly. You must unwrap the optional first to access its underlying value.

Forced Unwrapping

- One way to unwrap an optional value is to use forced unwrapping—add an exclamation mark (!) after the optional to explicitly unwrap it:

```
firstAndMiddleNames = firstName + " "   +
    middleName!
```

Optional Binding

- Use a technique called *optional binding* to test if an optional contains a value, and if so, store that value in a temporary variable or constant. For example:

```
var firstName: String = "Ryan"
var middleName: String? = "Michael"
var firstAndMiddleNames: String

if let middle = middleName
{
    firstAndMiddleNames = firstName + " " + middle
}
else
{
    firstAndMiddleNames = firstName
}
```

Implicitly Unwrapped Optionals

- Implicitly unwrapped optionals do not need to be unwrapped, because they are unwrapped implicitly (automatically). They are declared using an exclamation mark (!) rather than a question mark (?). For example:

```
@IBOutlet weak var lblDescription: UILabel!
```

Optional Chaining

- Where you are accessing a nested optional property or method, you can use optional chaining, which fails gracefully rather than generating a run time error. For example:

```
var nameOfLocation : String? =
        memberEntity.location?.locationName
```

- You need a question mark after **location**, because **location** is an optional property.

- The result of optional chaining is always an optional value.

- Although you can *retrieve* a property value through optional chaining, you can't *set* its value this way.

- You can call methods through optional chaining.

- If you call a method that doesn't return anything, the return value will be **Void?**, because any value returned from optional chaining is always optional.

- If you use optional chaining to access a value from a subscript, put the question mark before the subscript's braces. For example:

```
var nickName = memberEntity.nickNames?[0].name
```

- Although you can access a value from a subscript using optional chaining, you cannot set a subscript value this way.

- The nil coalescing operator (a **??** b) unwraps an optional if it contains a value. If not, it returns a default value:

```
var textColor: UIColor?
var color = textColor ?? UIColor.blackColor()
```

Step-By-Step Movie 4.1

In case you missed any of the steps along the way, you can enter the link below in your Web browser to see each step performed for you.

Movie 4.1

http://www.iOSAppsForNonProgrammers.com/B4M41.html

Chapter 5: Calling Methods

In creating iOS Apps, you're going to be working with many kinds of objects with a wide variety of methods. In this chapter you will learn the basic skills that will allow you to call any type of method on any class or object.

Sections in This Chapter

1. *The Anatomy of a Method Call*

2. *Calling a Method Step by Step*

3. *Arguments and Parameters*

4. *Figuring Out How to Pass a Message*

5. *Calling Instance Methods*

6. *Calling Type Methods*

7. *Summary*

8. *Exercise 5.1*

9. *Solution Movie 5.1*

method and press **return**.

4. This adds the full method name followed by open and closed parentheses that contain text highlighted in blue (Figure 5.4).

```
self.lblDemo.text =
    myString.stringByAppendingString(aString: String)
```

Figure 5.4 Code completion adds code automatically.

This highlighted text provides a clue to what Xcode expects you to type next. When you call a method on an object, you first pass the name of the method that you want to call (which you just did) and then any additional information the method requires—additional pieces of data we call *arguments*.

In this case, the **stringByAppendingString:** method expects you to pass a single **String** argument. The string you enter here is passed as an argument to the **stringByAppendingString:** method, which appends it to the string stored in the **myString** variable.

5. Now finish the statement by typing the following highlighted text, including the double quotes. There is a space after the first double quote (the code is broken into two lines for space reasons):

```
self.lblDemo.text = myString.stringByAppendingString(" is
for me")
```

When the **stringByAppendingString:** method is executed at run time, the **" is for me"** string argument is appended to the value stored in the **myString** variable and the resulting string is stored in the **text** property of the **lblDemo** label.

6. Let's run the app in the Simulator to see the effect of this new code. To do this, click the **Run** button in the upper-left corner of Xcode. Now the top of your app should look like Figure 5.5.

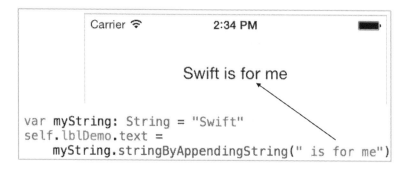

Figure 5.5 The appended string at run time

7. Go back to Xcode and click the **Stop** button.

Congratulations on completing your first method call!

Arguments and Parameters

You often see the words *argument* and *parameter* used interchangeably. However there is a subtle difference. In the previous section you learned an argument is a piece of data you pass to a method. A *parameter* is a part of the method declaration that dictates the argument(s) to be passed to the method. In short, arguments appear in method calls, parameters appear in method declarations.

Figuring Out How to Pass a Message

In writing code for your app, you are going to call many methods on many Cocoa Touch Framework objects. You will use a wide variety of classes and objects, and need them to perform specific tasks for you. Maybe you need to send a text message, find the user's current location, or get the current user's high score in a game. It's one thing to figure out *which* class and method to call; it's another hurdle to figure out *how* to call that method. Many students in my iOS classes have expressed difficulty in figuring out how to call a method, so I'd like to demystify this process for you.

First, you need to know that Swift has two main types of methods—***instance methods*** and ***type methods***. Instance methods are called on instances of an object—meaning you create an object from a class, and then call a method on the object. In contrast, type methods belong to the class or type itself, meaning you call the method on the class directly, without creating an instance of the class.

Calling Instance Methods

Let's start by looking at some instance methods in the **String** class. Afterward, we will look at how to call type methods.

1. Go back to Xcode and at the bottom of the **viewDidLoad** method (right before the ending curly brace), add a new empty line. Next, type the following directly below the code you previously added (the last character is the lowercase letter "s"):

    ```
    myString.s}
    ```

    As soon as you type this, Xcode displays all the methods of the **String** class that begin with the letter "s" as in Figure 5.6. This popup is a great place to learn how to pass a message.

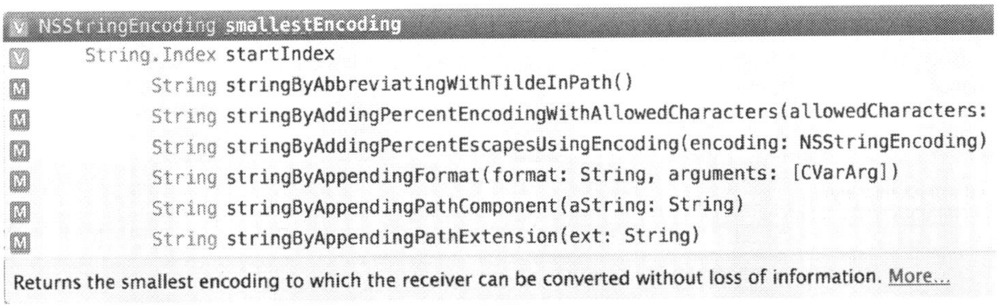

V	NSStringEncoding smallestEncoding
V	String.Index startIndex
M	String stringByAbbreviatingWithTildeInPath()
M	String stringByAddingPercentEncodingWithAllowedCharacters(allowedCharacters:
M	String stringByAddingPercentEscapesUsingEncoding(encoding: NSStringEncoding)
M	String stringByAppendingFormat(format: String, arguments: [CVarArg])
M	String stringByAppendingPathComponent(aString: String)
M	String stringByAppendingPathExtension(ext: String)

Returns the smallest encoding to which the receiver can be converted without loss of information. More...

Figure 5.6 String methods that begin with "s"

Remember, the variable **myString** contains an object that is an instance of the **String** class. You created the object earlier by storing a string into the variable. So, all the methods in the pop-up list are *instance* methods.

The pop-up list contents provide clues on how to call each method:

*   On the far left is an "M" indicating each item that is a method ("V" indicates a property).

*   The next column to the right specifies the type of value returned from each method. For example, the **stringByAbbreviatingWithTildeInPath** method returns a **String** value.

*   The last column specifies the method name and any arguments that you need to pass. For example, **stringByAbbreviatingWithTildeInPath**

accepts no arguments.

2. Highlighting a particular method in the popup, you'll see a mthod description at the bottom as for **stringByAppendingPathExtension** in Figure 5.7.

```
Ⓜ String stringByAppendingFormat(format: String, arguments: [CVarArg])
Ⓜ String stringByAppendingPathComponent(aString: String)
Ⓜ String stringByAppendingPathExtension(ext: String)
Ⓜ String stringByAppendingString(aString: String)
```
Returns a new string made by appending to the `String` an extension separator followed by a given extension.

Figure 5.7 The method description in the Code Completion popup

So, in this example, the pop-up help says:

"Returns a new string made by appending to the 'String' an extension separator followed by a given extension."

Based on the method name and the description provided, you can infer that this means you can call the **stringByAppendingPathExtension:** method on a string object containing a file name without an extension, the method appends a separator character (.) and the specified file extension to the file name.

3. Before we try this, delete the partial line of code you just typed:

```
var myString: String = "Swift"
self.lblDemo.text =
myString.stringByAppendingString(" is for me")
myString.s
```

Table 5.1 makes it easy for you to figure out how to call instance methods. Each time you come across a new instance method, read the pop-up documentation in Xcode first, as you just did, to see what the method does. Then refer to the steps outlined in **Table 5.1** to figure out how to call it.

Let's see how that process works now with the **stringByAppendingPathExtension:** method.

1. Let's create a playground where we can test our code. To do this, select

File > New > Playground... from the Xcode menu.

2. In the New Playground dialog's **Name** box, enter **CallingMethods**. Make sure the **Platform** is set to **iOS** and click **Next**.

3. In the Save dialog, select the Documents folder, or any other folder where you want to start the playground, and then click **Create**.

4. Delete the "Hello playground" line of code from the playground.

Table 5.1 Steps for Calling an Instance Method

1. Create the object on which you are calling the method.

2. If there is a return value:

   - Create a variable or constant to hold the return value (you can name it whatever you want).

   - Type " = " to store the return value in the variable

3. Type the name of the variable that holds a reference to the object you are calling the method on.

4. Type a period, and then, the name of the method to be called.

5. Type a left parenthesis "(".

6. If there are any arguments

   - Type the first argument value.

   - If there is a second argument, press **tab** to accept the parameter name and colon, then type the argument value.

   - Do the same for any additional arguments.

7. Type a right parenthesis ")" to complete the statement.

Follow these instructions, which mirror each step in **Table 5.1**:

1. **Create the object on which you are calling the method.**

We want to create a string object containing a file name without an extension, so add the following code in place of the line of code you just deleted:

```
var fileName = "MyImage"
```

This line creates a **String** variable named **fileName** that contains a file name. This completes the first step.

2. **If there is a return value, create a variable or constant to hold the return value.**

    The **stringByAppendingPathExtension:** method returns a **String** value (Figure 5.7), so you need to create a variable or constant to hold the value, and then type the assignment operator " = " with a space before and after the equal sign. Let's add the following code that create a constant, since we don't expect the value to be changed afterwards:

```
let fullFileName =
```

Since Swift has type inference, it's not required that we specify the type of the constant.

3. **Type the name of the variable that holds a reference to the object you are calling the method on.**

    Type the **fileName** variable, which holds a reference to the string object:

```
    let fullFileName = fileName
```

4. **Type a period, and then, the name of the method to be called.**

    Type a period and **stringByAppendingPathExtension:**

```
let fullFileName =
 fileName.stringByAppendingPathExtension:
```

5. **Type a left parenthesis "(".**

```
let fullFileName =
 fileName.stringByAppendingPathExtension(
```

6. **If there are any arguments, type the first argument value.**

This method accepts a single **String** argument, so enter the value in double quotes ("jpg"):

```
let fullFileName =
  fileName.stringByAppendingPathExtension("jpg"
```

7. **Type a right parenthesis ")" to complete the statement.**

```
let fullFileName =
fileName.stringByAppendingPathExtension("jpg")
```

That's it. You have completed a call to an instance method! In the Results sidebar on the right side of the playground, you can see the value in the **fullFileName** is "**MyImage.jpg**" (Figure 5.8).

```
var fileName = "MyImage"                          "MyImage"
let fullFileName = fileName.                       {Some "MyImage.jpg"}
    stringByAppendingPathExtension("jpg")
```

*Figure 5.8 The **fullFileName** variable's value is "MyImage.jpg".*

To review, as Figure 5.9 shows, this line of code calls the **stringByAppendingPathExtension** method on the **fileName** object. The method executes and returns the "MyImage.jpg" string, which is then stored in the **fullFileName** string variable.

*Figure 5.9 The **stringByAppendingPathExtension:** method is called on the **filename** object, which returns "MyImage.jpg".*

If a method accepts more than one argument, the argument name and a colon come before the additional argument values. For example:

```
var paddedString =
   myString.stringByPaddingToLength(10,
   withString: ".", startingAtIndex: 0)
```

This method accepts three arguments. For the first argument, the value **10** is passed by itself. For the second argument, the **withString:** argument name is specified along with the value "**.**". For the third argument, the **startingAtIndex:** argument name is specified, followed by the value **0**.

Calling Type Methods

You learned earlier that you can call methods on objects created from a class, and you can also call certain methods on the class itself. Methods that belong to a class are called *type methods*.

Let's use the **UIColor** class to demonstrate how to call a type method. The **UIColor** class has a variety of methods for working with colors, such as **redColor**, **blackColor**, **blueColor**, and so on.

The **UIColor** Class Reference documentation (Figure 5.10) provides information about the **redColor** method.

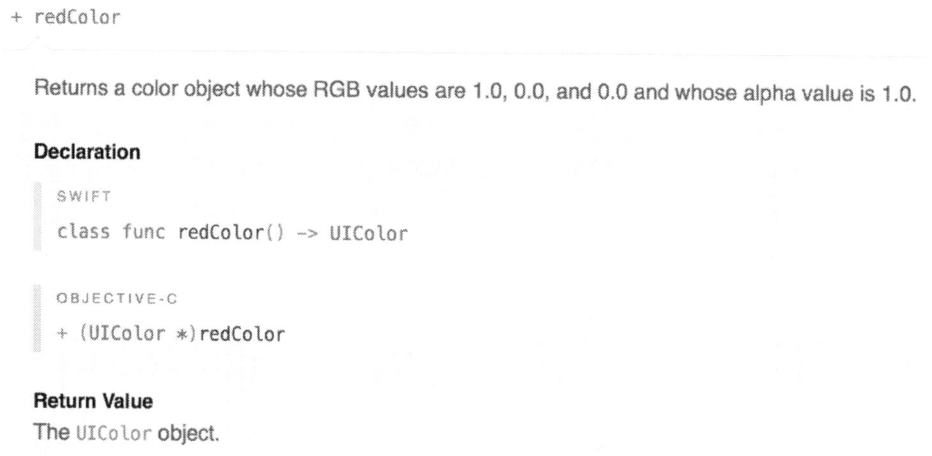

+ redColor

Returns a color object whose RGB values are 1.0, 0.0, and 0.0 and whose alpha value is 1.0.

Declaration

```
SWIFT
class func redColor() -> UIColor
```

```
OBJECTIVE-C
+ (UIColor *)redColor
```

Return Value
The UIColor object.

*Figure 5.10 The **redColor** documentation.*

The **redColor** method description states:

> *Returns a color object whose RGB values are 1.0, 0.0, and 0.0 and whose alpha value is 1.0.*

Under the **Declaration** section, the documentation shows both the Swift and Objective-C syntax. The Swift declaration begins with the keyword **class**, indicating this is a class, or type method.

Even though you are learning Swift, it's good to know a little Objective-C syntax since you will encounter it in Apple's documentation and in older code samples. In Objective-C, when the first character is a plus (+) sign, it indicates this is a *type* method.

This means you can follow the instructions in **Table 5.2** to determine how to call this type method.

Table 5.2 Steps for Calling a Type Method

1. If there is a return value:

    -   Create a variable to hold the return value (you can name it whatever you want).

    -   Type " = " to store the return value in the variable.

2. Type the name of the class you are sending the message to.

3. Type a period and then the name of the method to be called.

4. Type a left parenthesis "(".

5. If there are any arguments

    -   Type the first argument value.

    -   If there is a second argument, press **tab** to accept the parameter name and colon, then type the argument value.

    -   Do the same for any additional arguments.

6. Type a right parenthesis ")" to complete the statement.

As you might imagine, calling a type method takes one less step, because you don't need to create an instance of the class.

Let's follow these steps now.

1. **If there is a return value, create a variable to hold the return value.**

According to the documentation, the method returns a value of type **UIColor**.

Add the following code to the playground that creates a constant to hold a **UIColor** return value, and then type " = " to store the return value in the variable:

```
let redColor =
```

2. **Type the name of the class you are sending the message to.**

```
let redColor = UIColor
```

3. **Type a period, and then the name of the method to be called.**

```
let redColor = UIColor.redColor
```

4. **Type a left parenthesis.**

```
let redColor = UIColor.redColor(
```

5. **If there are any arguments, type the first argument value.**

This method doesn't accept any arguments, so we can skip this step.

6. **Type a right parenthesis to complete the statement.**

```
let redColor = UIColor.redColor()
```

That's it! You have successfully created a line of code that calls a type method. In the Results sidebar, you can see the RGB (red, green, blue) values of the red color (Figure 5.11).

```
let redColor = UIColor.redColor()          ██ r 1.0 g 0.0 b 0.0 a 1.0
```

*Figure 5.11 The RGB value of the **redColor** object.*

In review, as Figure 5.12 shows, you are calling the redColor method on the **UIColor** class. The UIColor class returns a **UIColor** object, whose RGB value is 1.0, 0.0, 0.0 (red).

*Figure 5.12 The **redColor** method is called on the **UIColor** class and it returns a **UIColor** object.*

Now you can refer back to **Table 5.1** for the steps in calling an instance method and to **Table 5.2** for the steps in calling a type method.

Summary

Here are the steps for calling an instance method:

1. Create the object on which you are calling the method.

2. If there is a return value:

    •   Create a variable or constant to hold the return value (you can name it whatever you want).

    •   Type " = " to store the return value in the variable

3. Type the name of the variable that holds a reference to the object you are calling the method on.

4. Type a period, and then, the name of the method to be called.

5. Type a left parenthesis "(".

6. If there are any arguments

    •   Type the first argument value.

    •   If there is a second argument, press **tab** to accept the parameter name and colon, then type the argument value.

    •   Do the same for any additional arguments.

7. Type a right parenthesis ")" to complete the statement.

Here are the steps for calling a type method:

1. If there is a return value:

    - Create a variable to hold the return value (you can name it whatever you want).

    - Type " = " to store the return value in the variable.

2. Type the name of the class you are sending the message to.

3. Type a period and then the name of the method to be called.

4. Type a left parenthesis "(".

5. If there are any arguments

    - Type the first argument value.

    - If there is a second argument, press **tab** to accept the parameter name and colon, then type the argument value.

    - Do the same for any additional arguments.

6. Type a right parenthesis ")" to complete the statement.

- Here is an example of calling an instance method:

    ```
    let fullFileName =
    fileName.stringByAppendingPathExtension("jpg")
    ```

- Here is an example of calling a type method:

    ```
    let redColor = UIColor.redColor()
    ```

- An *argument* is a piece of data passed to a method.

- A *parameter* is part of the method declaration that dictates the number and type of arguments passed to the method.

Exercise 5.1

In this exercise, you will use what you have learned in this chapter about figuring out how to call a method.

1. The **NSString** class, and by extension the Swift **String** class, has a **stringByReplacingOccurrencesOfString: withString:** method, which is documented this way:

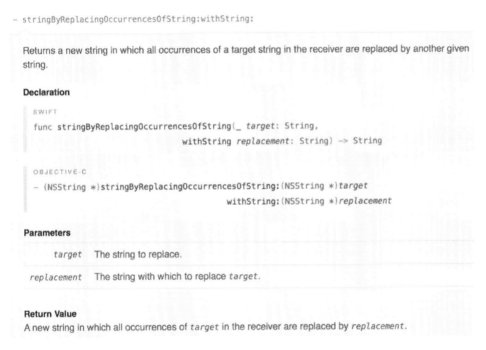

2. In the SwiftDemo project, you currently have the following string in the **viewDidLoad** method of the **ViewController.swift** class:

```
self.lblDemo.text = myString.stringByAppendingString(" is
for me")
```

3. Below the line that uses **stringByReplacingOccurrencesOfString: withString**: add another line of code to replace the string "me" with the string "everyone". Store the resulting value back into the **lblDemo** object's **text** property.

4. Run the app in the Simulator to make sure the text has changed.

Solution Movie 5.1

To see a video providing the solution for this exercise, you can enter the link below in your Web browser to see each step performed for you.

Movie 5.1

http://www.iOSAppsForNonProgrammers.com/B4M51.html

Chapter 6: Creating Objects From Classes

Earlier you learned that objects are created from class "blueprints" that define the object's attributes and behavior. In this chapter, you will learn how to create objects from Apple's Cocoa Touch Framework classes.

Along the way, you are also going to learn a little more about properties and be introduced to functions, constants, and enumerations.

Sections in This Chapter

1. Creating an Instance of a Class

2. Multiple Initializer Methods

3. More About Properties

4. Introducing Functions

5. Introducing Constants and Enumerations

6. Adding the Text Field to the View

7. Functions vs. Methods

8. Summary

9. Exercise 6.1

10. Solution Movie 6.1

In the previous chapter, you created a string object by storing a string into a variable like this:

```
var myString: String = "Swift"
```

This doesn't look much like creating an object from a class, does it? In fact, this is not the usual way to create an object.

In *Chapter 2: Understanding Classes and Objects*, you learned that you can create an instance of a text field class visually by dragging a text field class icon from the library to the design surface (Figure 2.4). Now you will see that you can also create a text field object by writing code. This is something you often need to do in your apps, so it's a good skill to master.

Creating an Instance of a Class

The simplest way to create an instance (object) of a class is to type the name of the class followed by empty parentheses. Let's give it a try.

1. Open the **SwiftDemo** project in Xcode if it's not already open.

2. Select the **ViewController.swift** file in the Project Navigator.

3. In a new empty line under the code you added to the **viewDidLoad** method in the last chapter, add the following line of code:

```
var textField = UITextField()
```

This code calls **UITextField's *initializer*,**method, indicated by the empty parentheses. This method returns a fully initialized object that has all its properties set to default values, and performs any other setup the object needs. In this example, the initialized object is stored into the **textField** variable.

Note that when creating instances of the Cocoa Touch Framework classes (still written in Objective-C), you don't need to call the **alloc** method. Swift takes care of this for you.

Multiple Initializer Methods

Often, a class has more than one initializer method to choose from. To see an example of this:

1. Place your cursor between the open and closed parentheses at the end of the code you just added:

```
var textField = UITextField(|)
```

2. Press the **escape** key for a list of three initializer methods to choose from (Figure 6.1). You used the first method that accepts no arguments in the code that you just entered, but you can also choose the **coder** or **frame** initializer method to pass additional arguments).

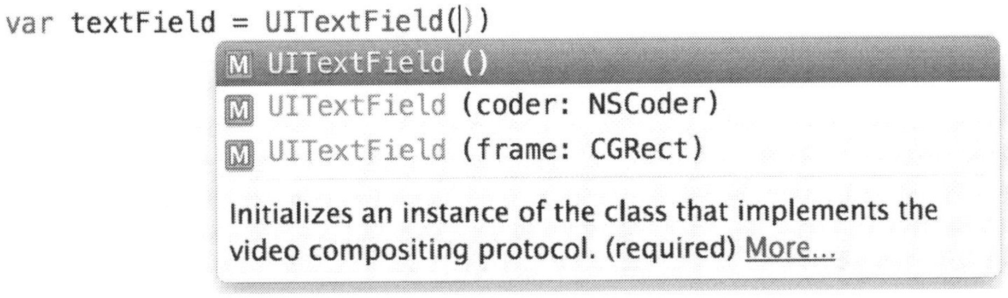

```
var textField = UITextField(|))
```

Figure 6.1 UITextField initializer methods

Typically, the extra arguments you pass are used to provide additional initialization data. Apple's Cocoa Touch Framework documentation provides details for each argument. As you enter code later in this chapter, you will use a variety of initializer methods.

More About Properties

Earlier, you learned that classes not only have methods, but also properties. Follow these instructions to set the text field's **placeholder** property.

1. Move your cursor to the end of the line of code you just created, press **return** to create a new empty line, and type **textField** followed by a period. This brings up a list of properties for the **textField** object as you see in Figure 6.2.

```
        var textField = UITextField()
        textField.delegate
                      Void decodeRestorableStateWithCoder(coder: NSCoder)
        Ⓜ            Void decreaseSize(sender: AnyObject!)
        Ⓥ  [NSObject : AnyObject]! defaultTextAttributes
        Ⓥ      UITextFieldDelegate! delegate
        Ⓜ            Void delete(sender: AnyObject!)
        Ⓜ            Void deleteBackward()
        Ⓥ         String! description
        Ⓜ            Void dictationRecognitionFailed!()
```
The layer's delegate object. More...

Figure 6.2 Code Completion provides a list of object properties.

When accessing object properties, you just type a period after the object name, and then the name of the property. If the list disappears, press the **escape** key to display it again.

2. Select the **placeholder** property from the list. To do this, use the scroll bar on the far right of the popup, use the up/down arrow keys, or just start typing the name of the property to narrow down the list. In either case, when the **placeholder** property is selected in the list, press **return** to have Xcode complete the name for you. Afterward, finish the line of code as shown here:

```
textField.placeholder = "First Name"
```

This line of code stores the string "First Name" in the **textField** object's **placeholder** property. When you run the app later on, you will see what the **placeholder** property does for you.

Introducing Functions

Now you are going to use what you have learned so far to write code that adds the text field to the user interface at run time. On the way, you are going to learn about Swift *functions*.

Normally, you add a text field to a user interface in Xcode by dragging a text field from the Object Library and positioning and sizing it on the design surface. When you are adding a text field in code, you specify its size and position using its **frame** property. A *frame* is a rectangle that specifies the text field's position on the user interface (in x and y coordinates) as well as its width and height.

1. Create a new line of code by pressing **return** after the code that you just entered, and then type the following:

```
textField.frame = CGRectMake
```

2. Typing this brings up a Code Completion list. Select the first item in the Code Completion list and then press **return**; then, you should see the code shown in Figure 6.3.

```
CGRectMake( x: CGFloat ,  y: CGFloat , width: CGFloat ,  height: CGFloat )
```

Figure 6.3 Code completion for the CGRect function

3. The code you've typed so far assigns a value to the text field's **frame** property. But what about the code to the right of the equal sign? This is something new. **CGRectMake** is a *function*, not a method. A function is a lot like a method; it groups together one or more lines of code that perform a task. However, *unlike* a method, a function is not attached to an object or a class. It's stand-alone, or "free floating."

4. Notice that Xcode's Code Completion guides you to enter x and y coordinates as well as a width and a height.

   - To enter the **x** coordinate (which specifies how far the text field is placed from the left side of the view), enter the number **20**.

   - To enter the **y** coordinate (which indicates how far down from the top of the view to place the text field), press **tab** and enter **70**.

   - Press **tab** again and enter **280** for the **width**.

   - Press **tab** again and enter **31** for the **height**.

   - Finally, press the right arrow key to have Xcode automatically add a closing parenthesis.

The complete line of code should look like Figure 6.4.

```
textField.frame = CGRectMake(20, 70, 280, 31)
```

*Figure 6.4 Using the **CGRectMake** function*

I have chosen numbers that I know will place the text field in a good location with an appropriate size on the iPhone.

Note: When using functions such as **CGRectMake** to specify coordinates and size, the numbers represent points rather than actual pixels on the screen. One point is not necessarily equal to one pixel. It's a relative number whose actual size is not important. At run time, the point size is translated to the correct number of pixels based on the device's screen resolution. This allows you to write code that works on any iOS device without worrying about its screen resolution.

Introducing Constants and Enumerations

By default, a text field added to the user interface in code doesn't have a border, so you need to add another line of code that sets the border style. To do this:

1. Add a new empty line, and then type the following partial line of code:

```
textField.border
```

As soon as you type this, Code Completion displays the popup shown in Figure 6.5.

*Figure 6.5 Selecting a text field's **borderStyle** property*

Code Completion suggests you are looking for one of two properties. Use the up/down arrow keys to select the **borderStyle** property. Before continuing, notice the pop-up indicating that the property is of type **UITextBorderStyle**. This is worth noting, because it is an indicator of the type of value that you are expected to store in this property.

2. Press **return** to select the **borderStyle** property, and then continue typing the following partial code:

```
textField.borderStyle = UITextB
```

This displays the Code Completion suggestion shown in Figure 6.6.

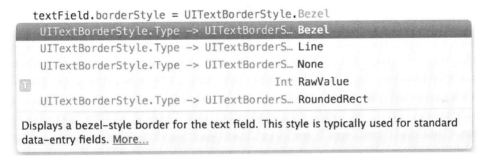

*Figure 6.6 Code Completion suggest **UITextBorderStyle**.*

Press **tab** or **return** to accept **UITextBorderStyle**.

3. Now type a period. This displays the list of choices shown in Figure 6.7.

*Figure 6.7 **UITextBorderStyle** options*

Notice that all the choices in the list have **UITextBorderStyle** listed on the left. This is the property type specified in the pop-up in the previous step. Each item listed is a different border style that you can specify for the text field. Each of these four options is a constant predefined in the Cocoa Touch Framework.

In contrast with variables, constants are just that—constant. Their values don't change. Sometimes constants are stand-alone, but, as in this case, they are often grouped together with other related constants known as an ***enumeration***. This means you can select any one of these styles when setting a text field's **borderStyle** property.

4. Select **RoundedRect**, and the completed line of code should look like Figure 6.8.

```
textField.borderStyle = UITextBorderStyle.RoundedRect
```

Figure 6.8 The completed code that sets the text field's border style

Because there are many different constants and enumerations in the Cocoa Touch Framework, this section is a great introduction to the concept. *Chapter 14: Comments, Constants and Enumerations* teaches you more about these.

Adding the Text Field to the View

Now you're ready to write code that adds the text field to the view.

1. Add the following line of code immediately after the border style code you just entered:

```
self.view.addSubview(textField)
```

   In this code, you are calling a method on the **self.view** object, where **self** refers to the view controller and **view** is the area in the user interface you want to add the text field to. The method being called on the view is **addSubView**, and the argument being passed is the new **textField** object.

   Effectively, this message tells the view, "Add this text field to yourself."

   All iOS user-interface controls are subclasses of the **UIView** class, and are therefore a kind of view. That's why the method **addSubview** is used here.

2. Before running the app, look at the code you have entered so far. It should look like this:

```
var textField = UITextField()
textField.placeholder = "First Name"
textField.frame = CGRectMake(20, 70, 280, 31)
textField.borderStyle =
UITextBorderStyle.RoundedRect
self.view.addSubview(textField)
```

   In review, the first line of code creates a new text field object from the **UITextField** class. After that, the code sets the **placeholder** property, the **frame** property (for size and position), and the **borderStyle** property. The last line of code adds the text field to the view. Adding a user-interface control to the view using code is also known as adding it ***programmatically***.

3. Now run the app by pressing the **Run** button in Xcode. You should see the text field displayed below the label (Figure 6.9). (If you finished Exercise 5.1, the label text will be set to "Swift is for Everyone".)

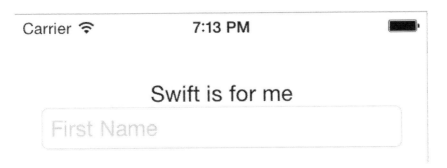

Figure 6.9 The text field at run time

You can see the **placeholder** text (First Name) is displayed in light gray. This gives the user a clue about the information they are expected to enter. As soon as the user types the first character, the **placeholder** text disappears. If you click in the text field, a keyboard pops up in the Simulator. You can use the Simulator keyboard or your computer keyboard to enter a value in the text field.

4. Take a moment again to feel the thrill of success!

5. Go back to Xcode and click the **Stop** button.

Now you have learned some basics of using Apple's Cocoa Touch classes, it's time to create your own classes in the next chapter.

Functions vs. Methods

In its Swift documentation, Apple blurs the line a bit in defining the terms *function* and *method*. In fact, when you declare a method, you use the **func** keyword! Let's get our definitions straight.

A **function** is a standalone group of statements *defined outside of a type*.

A **method** is a group of statements *defined within a type*.

Although you *can* create your own standalone functions in Swift, in most cases you shouldn't. Why?

When you create an iOS app, you are creating an API (application programming interface) that you and possibly others will work with over a period of years. When creating your API, your goal is to create a set of classes with a well-balanced load of responsibilities that is easy to learn, use, and extend (Figure 6.10).

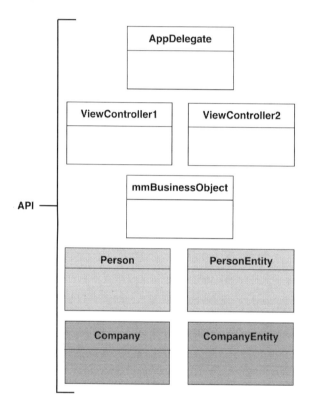

Figure 6.10 Creating your app's API

One measure of "easy to learn" is discoverability. How easy is it to discover all the things your API can do? This is where object-orientation can really help.

With object-oriented programming, you create a set of classes containing related functionality. For example, all the code that has something to do with a company goes in the **Company** class. All the code that has something to do with people goes in the **Person** class, and so on. When you discover a class in the API, you discover a whole world of related functionality.

In contrast, functions are standalone. When you discover a function in an API, you only discover one piece of functionality.

The one exception to the rule is if you have functionality you want to apply across multiple unrelated classes. In this case it may make sense to create a function rather than a method.

You can find examples of this type of function in Appendix A: Swift's Free Functions.

Summary

In this chapter, you learned the following important information about creating objects, calling functions, and using constants and enumerations:

- You use initializer methods to create an object from a class.

- An object may have more than one initializer method that takes additional arguments. Typically, the extra arguments you pass are used to provide additional initialization data.

- A function is a lot like a method. It groups together one or more lines of code that perform a task. However, unlike a method, a function is *not* attached to an object or a class.

- Constants are values that do not change.

- An enumeration is a group of related constants.

- You can create user-interface controls in code and then add them to a view using the view's **addSubView** method. This is known as adding a control *programmatically*.

- A **function** is a standalone group of statements *defined outside of a type*, that performs a specific task.

- A **method** is a group of statements *associated with a type* that performs a specific task.

- You should favor creating methods rather than functions. The one exception to the rule is if you have functionality you want to apply across multiple unrelated classes.

Exercise 6.1

In this exercise, create a new label object from the **UILabel** class and add it to the view using code, as you did with the text field object in this chapter. When you're finished, your app should look like Figure 6.11 (if you do the extra credit).

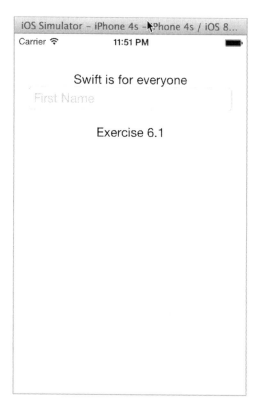

Figure 6.11 The completed scene

Here are the basic steps:

1. Create a new label object from the **UILabel** class.

2. Set the **text** property of the label to "Exercise 6.1."

3. Add the label to the view at the following coordinates and the specified size:

    *   x = 20, y = 120

- width = 280, height = 21

4. Note that labels don't have a **borderStyle** property.

5. Add the label to the view using code.

6. For extra credit, center the text of the label horizontally so it's in the middle of the view rather than aligned to the left.

Hint: Google "UILabel center text horizontally Swift". The results you find on www.StackOverflow.com are often best because participants vote for the best answer (the best answer has a green check mark next to it).

Solution Movie 6.1

To see a video providing the solution for this exercise, you can enter the link below in your Web browser to see each step performed for you.

Movie 6.1

http://www.iOSAppsForNonProgrammers.com/B4M61.html

Chapter 7: Creating Custom Classes

So far, everything you have done has used Cocoa Touch Framework classes. You have learned to:

- Create objects from a class.

- Set an object property.

- Call an object method.

- Call a type method.

Now it's time to learn how to create your own classes.

Sections in This Chapter

1. *Declaring Classes*

2. *Declaring Properties*

3. *Declaring Methods*

4. *Instance Methods*

5. *Type Methods*

6. *Adding Methods to the Calculator Class*

7. *Optional Parameters*

8. *Variadic Parameters*

9. *Constant and Variable Parameters*

10. *In-Out Parameters*

11. *Summary*

12. *Exercise 7.1*

Solution Movie 7.1

In this chapter, you are going to create a new **Calculator** class from scratch. The **Calculator** class will perform addition, subtraction, multiplication, and division. This is a non-visual class that can be used behind the scenes to perform important functionality. Afterward, you will write code that tests this class's functionality.

Declaring Classes

1. Open the **SwiftDemo** sample project.

2. In the Project Navigator on the left side of the Xcode window, select the **SwiftDemo** group (Figure 7.1) so the new file will be added beneath this group.

Figure 7.1 New files are added to the selected group.

3. From the **File** menu, select **New > File...** to launch the New File dialog (Figure 7.2). On the left side of the dialog are two sections—**iOS** and **OS X**. This is because you can use Xcode to create both iOS and Mac OS X desktop applications. However, when creating iOS Apps, make sure you select items in the **iOS** section.

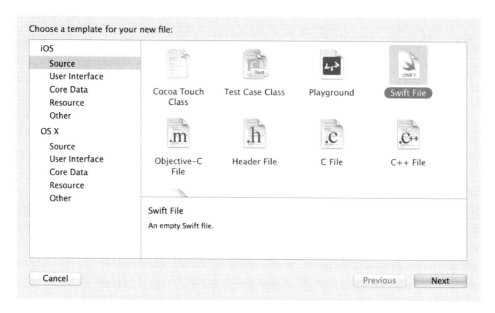

*Figure 7.2 Make sure to select items in the **iOS** section.*

4. Under **iOS**, select **Source** to display the associated file templates. On the right side of the dialog, select the **Swift File** template and then click **Next**.

5. In the Save dialog's **Class** box (Figure 7.3), enter **Calculator.swift** as the name of the file you're creating.

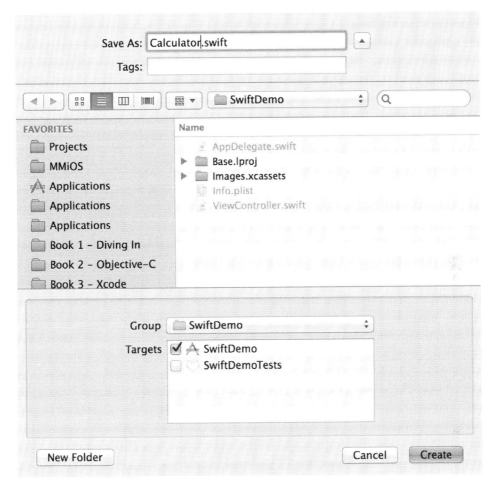

*Figure 7.3 Specify **Calculator.swift** as the name of the file.*

This dialog lets you specify where to store the new file. The default location, your project's main folder, is a good choice, so click **Create**.

6. Afterward, the Project Navigator contains the new **Calculator.swift** file as in Figure 7.4.

*Figure 7.4 The new **Calculator.swift** file*

7. The new code file is also displayed in the Code Editor as Figure 7.5 illustrates.

```
//
//  Calculator.swift
//  SwiftDemo
//
//  Created by Kevin McNeish
//  Copyright (c) 2014 Oak Leaf Enterprises, Inc.
//

import Foundation
```

*Figure 7.5 The new **Calculator.swift** code file*

The **import Foundation** statement gives the new code file access to Apple's standard development library, needed in most code files. You will learn more about import statements in *Chapter 17: Access Control*.

Note: When you add new files to a project, they are added below the last item in the currently selected group. If you prefer, you can simply drag and drop them to another location in the list of files.

8. Now let's declare a **Calculator** class in this code file. To do this, add the following code below the import statement:

```
import Foundation

class Calculator {

}
```

The **class** keyword indicates the beginning of a class definition. The word **Calculator** indicates the name of the class. The beginning and ending curly braces mark the beginning and end of the declaration of the class members (i.e. properties and methods). Since we haven't declared any members yet, nothing is between the curly braces.

In this example, we haven't declared a superclass for our new **Calculator** class and that's perfectly fine. Figure 7.6 shows an example of declaring a class and specifying its superclass. You just add a colon after the class name and then the name of the superclass.

Figure 7.6 Specifying the superclass of a class

Note that class names always begin with an uppercase letter, and then the first letter of each word in a compound word is capitalized—for example, **InvoiceDetail** and **PatientHistory**. This is called *Pascal case*. Also, class names should be singular, so you would have a **Customer** class, *not* a **Customers** class.

Declaring Properties

Next, you're going to declare a property named **total** in the **Calculator** class. You need this property because all the methods you add to the class need to act on the **total** value by adding to it, subtracting from it, multiplying it, and so on.

Before we do that, let's get a little background on properties in Swift.

- Properties are normally associated with an instance of a class (an object) but there are also type properties that are associated with the class itself (just as there are instance and type methods.)

- Property names are **camel-cased**, meaning the first letter is always in lower case, and the first letter of each word in a compound word is uppercased (like a camel's head and its humps). For example, the property

100

names **firstName** and **emailAddress** are both camel cased.

- **Stored properties** are the most common type of property. They store a constant or variable value.

- **Computed properties** do not store a value but are typically used to retrieve and manipulate values from other properties. For example, a **fullName** property may join **firstName** and **lastName** properties to compute its value.

You will learn much more about properties in *Chapter 9: Advanced Properties*.

Adding a Property to the Calculator

Although you have created local variables inside methods before, this is the first time you have created a property, so I'll provide detailed instructions.

1. In the Project Navigator, select the **Calculator.swift** code file. Add the following property declaration:

```
class Calculator {

    var total : Double = 0.0
}
```

2. Here are some important things to note:

   - The property is declared between curly braces.

   - A property can be accessed from within any method in the class it is declared in.

   - The property's name is **total** and its type is **Double**. The **Double** data type represents floating point numbers. A floating point number gets its name from the decimal point that can "float," or be placed anywhere in a number (for example, 1.234, or 12.34 or 123.4). So a **Double** type is perfect for the **total** property.

   - A default value of **0.0** is assigned to the property when an instance of the **Calculator** class is first created. If a property always has the same default value, it's best to set it this way so the initialization of the property is more closely tied to the declaration of the property, which makes your code more obvious!

- If you assign a default value to a property as we have done here, you do not need to specify the property type.

- A property declaration has a syntax very similar to that of a variable declaration.

Declaring Methods

Earlier, you learned how to call methods on an object created from a Cocoa Touch class. Now, you will learn how to declare methods in your own class. Let's cover a few ground rules first.

- You declare a method between the opening and closing curly braces of the class it belongs to.

- In Swift, method names are camel cased.

Instance Methods

You may recall there are two main types of methods—*instance methods* and *type methods*. We will cover instance methods first, but note that the syntax of declaring type methods is very similar.

Declaring a Simple Method

The following code shows the simplest method declaration:

```
func clear() {

    // Do something
}
```

Some important things to note:

- The method declaration is between the opening and closing curly braces of the class it belongs to.

- A method declaration begins with the keyword **func**.

- The name of this method is **clear**.

- This method accepts no parameters and returns no value.

- This method currently doesn't do anything. You need to put code in place of the "Do something" comment.

- An instance method has access to all other methods declared in the same class.

Declaring a Method With a Return Value

When you declare a method that returns a value, you add the symbol -> (a hyphen and a right angle bracket) after the method's parentheses followed by the type of the return value. For example:

```
func getTotal() -> Double {

   // Return a double value
}
```

Some important things to note:

- The -> symbol is also referred to as a *return arrow*.

- This method returns a value of type **Double**.

- If you don't add code to this method to actually return a value of type **Double**, then you will get an error when you build your project.

Declaring a Method With Parameters

Here is an example of a method that accepts a single parameter:

```
func addToTotal(value: Double)
{
   // Add the specified value to the total
}
```

Note the following:

- Parameters are placed between the parentheses that follow the method name.

- You specify a name for the parameter followed by a colon and its type.

Here is a method with multiple parameters:

```
func multiply(value: Double, times: Double) -> Double
{
    // Multiply the two values and return the result
}
```

Note the following:

- Multiple parameters are separated by a comma.

- This method accepts two parameters of type **Double** and returns a value of type **Double**.

- The name of the first parameter is **value** and the name of the second parameter is **times**.

Local and External Parameter Names

In Swift, parameters can have a local name (used within the method) and an external name (used when calling the method).

By default, Swift gives the first parameter name in a method a local name only and subsequent parameters both local and external names. This makes method calls easier to read. For example, here is how you would call the multiply method from the previous section:

```
calculator.multiply(5, times: 10)
```

You can read this method call as "Multiply 5 times 10."

However, *within* the multiply method, you would refer to the first parameter as **value**. For example:

```
func multiply(value: Double, times: Double) -> Double
{
    return value * times;
}
```

Although the parameter name **times** works well when calling the method, it doesn't work as well *within* the method, which would say "value times times".

Fortunately, Swift allows you to specify different local and external names for a parameter. For example:

```
func multiply(a: Double, times b: Double) -> Double
{
    return a * b;
}
```

In this method declaration, the second parameter's external name is **times** and its internal **b**. This makes the code far more readable within the method.

Changing the Default Parameter Name Behavior

If you would prefer to give the first parameter in your method both an external and internal name, you can prefix the parameter name with a hash symbol, and Swift will create an external parameter name that is the same as the internal parameter name. For example, if you insert a hash tag before the first parameter name:

```
func multiply(#a: Double, times b: Double) -> Double
{
    return a * b;
}
```

Then you call the method like this:

```
calculator.multiply(a:5, times: 10)
```

If you would like the first parameter to have different internal and external names, then simply specify both names in the method declaration, just as you do when declaring multiple parameters.

If you do not want to provide an external parameter name for the second or subsequent parameters, use an underscore character as an explicit parameter name. For example, when you declare the second parameter with an underscore:

```
func multiply(a: Double, _ b: Double) -> Double
{
    return a * b;
}
```

This allows you to call the method without including the parameter name:

```
calculator.multiply(5, 10)
```

Type Methods

Declaring a type method (a method that is called directly on a class, rather than on an instance of a class) is very similar to declaring an instance method. The main difference is that you add the class keyword at the beginning of the method declaration as shown here:

```
class MyClass {

    class func myFunction()
    {

    }
}
```

To call a class method, you reference the class name rather than an instance of the class. For example:

```
MyClass.myFunction()
```

Here are some key points to note about type methods:

- Within a type method the keyword **self** refers to the class itself, not an instance of the class.

- Type methods can call other type methods and access type properties defined on the same class without specifying the type name.

- One of the most common uses for type methods is as a factory method to create instances of the class.

Adding Methods to the Calculator Class

Now that you know the basic ground rules of declaring methods, it's time to create some methods of your own. You will start by making the **Calculator** class functional by adding methods that clear the running total, add, subtract, multiply, and divide.

1. Add the following method declaration below the **total** property declaration:

```
class Calculator {

    var total : Double = 0.0

    // Clears the calculator's running total
    func clear() {

        self.total = 0.0
    }
}
```

Important things to note:

- The name of the method is **clear** and it returns no value and accepts no parameters.

- The method's code is contained between opening and closing curly braces.

- The keyword **self** is used to reference the property. This is not a requirement for properties, but I recommend that you use it because you can tell at a glance that you are accessing a property, not a local variable.

- A comment at the beginning of the method describes what the method does!

2. Now let's add a few more methods *after* the declaration of the **clear** method and *before* the closing curly brace of the class:

```
class Calculator {

    var total : Double = 0.0

    // Clears the calculator's running total
    func clear() {

        self.total = 0.0
    }

    // Adds the value to the total
    func addToTotal(value: Double) -> Double
    {
```

```
        self.total += value
        return self.total
    }

    // Subtracts the value from the total
    func subtractFromTotal(value: Double) -> Double
    {
        self.total -= value
        return self.total
    }

    // Multiplies the value by the total
    func multiplyByTotal(value: Double) -> Double
    {
        self.total *= value
        return self.total
    }

    // Divides the value into the total
    func divideIntoTotal(value: Double) -> Double
    {
        self.total /= value
        return self.total
    }
}
```

These methods add new functionality to the **Calculator** class for adding, subtracting, multiplying and dividing values against the running total. Notice the camel casing of each method name. Each method returns a **Double** value. Each method has a **Double** parameter that accepts the value being added, subtracted, multiplied, or divided into the running total.

Notice that each method declaration has a comment, so anyone reading your code file can easily determine what each method does.

This is the first time you have seen the +=, -=, *= and /= operators. These are *compound assignment operators*. Each of these operators is shorthand for performing two operations. For example, the += operator adds the **value** parameter to the **total** property, and then stores the result back into the **total** property. As I'm sure you can guess, -= performs subtraction, *= performs multiplication, and /= performs division, and each stores the resulting value back into the variable. After performing the operation, the methods return the new running total.

3. This is a great time to make sure that your project has no errors or warnings. Press **Command+B** to build the project and make sure there are no errors or warnings before moving on.

All the methods you have created in the **Calculator** are accessible from any other class within this project. There are times when you should make a method private to the class, so no other code outside the class file can see it, or make a method public to code outside the project it is declared in. You will learn how to do this in *Chapter 17: Access Control*.

Optional Parameters

You can declare a parameter as optional (meaning, it can be omitted when calling the method) by assigning it a default value when declaring the method. For example:

```
func setInitialValue(value: Double = 0.0)
{
        self.total = value
}
```

This method accepts a single parameter named **value**. It's optional, because a default value of **0.0** has been declared for the parameter. This means when you call the method, you can pass a single argument:

```
calculator.setInitialValue(value: 123.45)
```

Or pass no arguments:

```
calculator.setInitialValue()
```

If you call this method without passing an argument, the parameter's value defaults to **0.0**.

When declaring a method, you should always place optional parameters at the end of the parameter list. This makes the order of parameters in method calls consistent, and helps avoid confusion!

Xcode's Code Completion currently doesn't indicate if a parameter is optional, so there's no way to tell if it's optional without reading the method's documentation.

Optional Parameter External Names

Swift provides a default external parameter name for optional parameters, if none is provided. Providing external names is a best practice, because it makes the purpose of the argument clear when a value is provided in a method call.

Variadic Parameters

Swift's variadic parameters allow you to pass zero or more values of a specific type. You declare a variadic parameter by adding three periods after the parameter type. For example, here is a method that accepts a single variadic parameter named **numbers**, of type **Double**:

```
func addNumbers(numbers: Double...) -> Double
{
      for number in numbers {
          self.total += number
      }
      return self.total
}
```

You can pass any number of **Double** values to the method like this:

```
self.calculator.addNumbers(1.1, 2.2, 3.3)
```

Within the method, the variadic parameter is presented as an array (you will learn more about arrays in *Chapter 10: Arrays & Other Collections*). If you don't pass any values to the method, the variadic parameter is an empty array of the specified type.

Some rules regarding variadic parameters:

- A function or method can only have one variadic parameter.

- A variadic parameter must always be last in the parameter list.

- If a function or method has one or more optional parameters, place the variadic parameter at the end of the list.

Constant and Variable Parameters

By default, parameter values are constants, meaning you can't change the value of the parameter within the body of the method. This is a good default, because usually you don't need to change a parameter's value.

If you try to change the value of the parameter in the following method, you will get a compiler error:

```
func addToTotal(value: Double) -> Double
{
        value += 1
        self.total += value
        return self.total
}
```

In situations where you need to change the parameter value (this should be rare), you can declare it as a variable. For example:

```
func addToTotal(var value: Double) -> Double
{
}
```

Changes you make to the parameter value are contained within the method. This means the code that passes a value into this method does not have its value changed.

In-Out Parameters

If you want to make a change to a parameter and also have its value changed in the code that calls the method, you can declare it as an in-out parameter. To do this, add the **inout** keyword before the parameter name:

```
func addToTotal(inout value: Double) -> Double
{
}
```

Again, you should rarely need to change the value of a parameter, and even more rarely need to have the changed value flow back to the calling code.

One example where in-out parameters can be useful in methods that change values in multiple collections. For example, Swift has a **swap()** function that swaps two items in a collection at the specified positions.

To pass an argument to a function that accepts an in-out parameter, you preface the argument with an ampersand. For example:

```
swap(&deck[index], &deck[r])
```

You will see this swap() function and in-out parameter in action in *Chapter 23: Understanding Closures.*

Some rules regarding in-out parameters:

- You can only pass a variable (not a constant or literal) as an argument for an in-out parameter.

- In-out parameters cannot have default values.

- You cannot mark an in-out variable as **var** or **let**.

- Variadic parameters cannot be marked as **inout**.

Summary

In this chapter you learned how to create your own custom classes. Here are the main points to remember:

Declaring Classes

- The **import Foundation** statement gives the new code file access to Apple's standard development library needed in most code files.

- Class names are Pascal cased with the first character uppercased and the first letter of each word in a compound word uppercased.

- The **class** keyword indicates the beginning of a class definition. The word **Calculator** indicates the class's name. The beginning and ending curly braces mark the beginning and end of the declaration of the class members (i.e. properties and methods).

```
class Calculator {

}
```

- Specifying a class's superclass is not required.

- To specify a class's superclass, just add a colon after the class name and then the name of the superclass:

```
class        class
keyword      name                superclass
  |            |                     |

class ViewController: UIViewController {

}
```

- You declare a type method by placing the keyword **class** in front of the method declaration.

Declaring Properties

- Properties are normally associated with an instance of a class (an object) but there are also type properties that are associated with the class itself (just as there are instance and type methods).

- Property names are camel cased.

- *Stored properties* are the most common type of property. They store a constant or variable value.

- *Computed properties* do not store a value but are typically used to retrieve and manipulate values from other properties. For example, a **fullName** property may join **firstName** and **lastName** properties to compute its value.

- If a property always has the same default value, it's best to set it this way so the initialization of the property is more closely tied to the declaration of the property, which makes your code more obvious!

- If you assign a default value to a property when you declare it, you do not need to specify the type of the property.

Declaring Methods

- You declare a method between the opening and closing curly braces of the class it belongs to.

- In Swift, method names are *camel cased*.

- Here is an example of declaring a method with no parameters or return value:

```
func clear() {

    // Do something
}
```

- Here is an example of declaring a method that accepts a single parameter:

```
func addToTotal(value: Double)
{
    // Add the specified value to the total
}
```

- Here is an example of a method that accepts a parameter and returns a value:

```
func multiply(a: Double, b: Double) -> Double
{
    // Multiply the two values and return the result
}
```

- A method is declared between the opening and closing curly braces of the class it belongs to.

- A method declaration begins with the keyword **func**.

- An instance method has access to all other methods declared in the same class.

- When you declare a method that returns a value, you add the symbol -> (a hyphen and a right angle bracket) after the method's parentheses followed by the type of the return value.

- Parameters are placed between the parentheses that follow the method name.

- You specify a name for the parameter followed by a colon and its type.

- Multiple parameters are separated by a comma.

- Parameters can have a local name (used within the method) and an external name (used when calling the method).

- By default, Swift gives the first parameter name in a method a local name only and subsequent parameters both local and external names.

- If you would prefer to give the first parameter in your method both external and internal names, you can prefix the parameter name with a hash symbol, and Swift will create an external parameter name that is the same as the internal parameter name.

- If you would like the first parameter to have different internal and external names, you can simply specify both names in the method declaration, just as you do when declaring multiple parameters.

- If you do not want to provide an external parameter name for the second or subsequent parameters, you can use an underscore character as an explicit parameter name.

Optional Parameters

- You can declare a parameter as optional by assigning it a default value when declaring the method. For example:

```
func setInitialValue(value: Double = 0.0)
{
        self.total = value
}
```

- When calling a method with an optional parameter, you can pass nothing, or a value of the parameter's type.

- When declaring a method, you should always place optional parameters at the end of the parameter list.

Variadic Parameters

- Swift's variadic parameters allow you to pass zero or more values of a specific type.

- You declare a variadic parameter by adding three periods after the parameter type. For example:

```
func addNumbers(numbers: Double...) -> Double
{
        for number in numbers {
        self.total += number
        }
        return self.total
}
```

- You can pass any number of values of the specified type to a method with a variadic parameter.

- Within the method, the variadic parameter is presented as an array. If you don't pass any values to the method, the variadic parameter is an empty array of the specified type.

- A function or method can only have one variadic parameter.

- A variadic parameter must always be last in the parameter list.

- If a function or method has one or more optional parameters, place the variadic parameter at the end of the list.

Constant and Variable Parameters

- By default, parameter values are constants. This means that you can't change the value of the parameter within the body of the method.

- If you try to change the value of a constant parameter, you will get a compiler error.

- In situations where you need to change the parameter value (this should be rare), you can declare it as a variable. For example:

```
func addToTotal(var value: Double) -> Double
{
}
```

- Changes you make to the parameter value are contained within the method.

In-Out Parameters

- If you want to make a change to a parameter and also have its value changed in the code that calls the method, you can declare it as an in-out parameter.

- To declare an in-out parameter, add the **inout** keyword before the parameter name:

```
func addToTotal(inout value: Double) -> Double
{
}
```

- To pass an argument to a function that accepts an in-out parameter, you preface the argument with an ampersand. For example:

```
swap(&deck[index], &deck[r])
```

- You can only pass a variable (not a constant or literal) as an argument for an in-out parameter.

- In-out parameters cannot have default values.

- You cannot mark an in-out variable as **var** or **let**.

- Variadic parameters cannot be marked as **inout**.

Exercise 7.1

In a playground, create a class named **Thermometer**. Add an instance method named **fahrenheitToCelsius** that accepts a Fahrenheit value and returns the equivalent value in Celsius. Add a second instance method named **celsiusToFahrenheit** that performs the opposite conversion.

Here are the basic steps:

1. Create a playground named **Thermometer.playground**.

2. Add code that declares a class named **Thermometer**.

3. Add the **fahrenheitToCelsisus** method to the class. This method should accept a parameter of type **Double** and return a value of type **Double**. To

convert from Fahrenheit to Celsius, subtract 32 and multiply by 5/9.

4. Add the **celsiusToFahrenheit** method to the class. It should accept a parameter of type **Double** and return a value of type **Double**. To convert from Celsius to Fahrenheit, multiply by 9, divide by 5, and add 32.

5. Add code to the playground that tests each method.

Solution Movie 7.1

To see a video providing the solution for this exercise, you can enter the link below in your Web browser to see each step performed for you.

Movie 7.1

http://www.iOSAppsForNonProgrammers.com/B4M71.html

Chapter 8: Unit Testing Your Code

Whenever you create a new class, or add a new method to an existing class, a best practice is to step through the code you have written in Xcode to make sure everything is working properly. In this chapter, you will learn some basic skills for testing your code using Xcode's debugging tools. As you step through the code, you will also gain a deeper understanding of how Swift works!

Sections in This Chapter

Why There Are So Many Bad Apps

In addition to creating apps, clients also ask me to evaluate their software development teams and the apps they write.

As you might imagine, I see the good, the bad, and the ugly. Most are in the "ugly" category. To improve badly written software, I must first improve the development team's culture before they can begin creating high-quality apps.

If you are new to programming, this book series teaches you best practices out of the gate. If you have some programming experience, I hope this chapter and the rest of this series influence your app development practices so you can build apps that are:

- Well-designed

- Stable

- Easily adaptable to change

One of the critical tasks in achieving this is to test the code you write.

Why Test Your Code?

Unfortunately, most app developers do not test their code. At best, they will write code and then run it in the Simulator. If it appears to work properly, they move on. The problem with this approach is that many bugs in your code are not readily apparent when you simply run the app.

The only way to truly test your code is to step through it line by line *immediately after writing it*. I stress this point, because this is when you most fully understand your intentions in the code you have written. If you wait several days or weeks, you will forget the nuances of what you expect from a method that you have written.

I guarantee you will be amazed at how many bugs you find when you step through your code line by line.

Why Create Unit Tests?

Software is like a waterbed. If you push down in one spot, it pops up in another. If you make a change in one area of your app, how do you know it hasn't affected another area? In short, you don't know.

However, if you create a set of tests that automatically puts the core logic of your app through its paces, you are far more certain that you have not introduced new bugs.

Unit testing is a method for testing individual units (usually a single method) of your app to make sure your app is ready to be released.

Although some developers write their unit tests before writing their methods, it's much easier for new programmers to create the unit tests afterwards.

Apple has done much to improve Xcode's ability to test your code. In fact, you may have noticed that when you create a new project, Xcode automatically adds a group to your project that contains a class you can use to create unit tests for your app (Figure 8.1). Let's get started!

Figure 8.1 Unit testing class in the Project Navigator

Setting Up the Test Project

The **Calculator** class is *very* basic, but it provides a good example of how you can implement unit tests in Xcode. Let's start by setting up the test project.

1. Open the **SwiftDemo** sample project.

2. In the Project Navigator, expand the **SwiftDemoTests** group and select the **SwiftDemoTests.swift** code file. This opens the file in the Code Editor (Figure 8.2).

```
import XCTest

class SwiftDemoTests: XCTestCase {

    override func setUp() {
        super.setUp()
        // Put setup code here. This method is called before
            the invocation of each test method in the class.
    }

    override func tearDown() {
        // Put teardown code here. This method is called after
            the invocation of each test method in the class.
        super.tearDown()
    }

    func testExample() {
        // This is an example of a functional test case.
        XCTAssert(true, "Pass")
    }

    func testPerformanceExample() {
        // This is an example of a performance test case.
        self.measureBlock() {
            // Put the code you want to measure the time of
                here.
        }
    }
}
```

Figure 8.2 The SwiftDemoTests.swift code file

Some important points to note:

- This code file imports **XCTest**, which provides access to Xcode's testing framework.

- The **SwiftDemoTests** class is a subclass of the **XCTestCase** class. This is a requirement for unit testing in Xcode.

- The **testExample** method is intended to show you how to test the functionality of your code, although there is no real test code in this method.

- The **testPerformanceExample** method is intended to show you how to test your code's performance. You just place the code you want to test between the curly braces (typically a call to a method on one of your objects), and Xcode will run the test 10 times and afterward display the average execution time and standard deviation.

- When you run your unit tests, a brand new instance of the **SwiftDemoTests** class is created for each test. So, for example, if you have three test methods, **SwiftDemoTests** is created three times, once for each test.

- The **setUp** method is called before each test method is run, and the **tearDown** method is called after each test method has completed.

3. Since these test methods are just examples, let's delete them. To do this, click to the left of the **testExample** method, hold your mouse button down and drag to the bottom of the **testPerformanceExample** method (Figure 8.3). With both methods selected, press the **delete** key.

```swift
func testExample() {
    // This is an example of a functional test case.
    XCTAssert(true, "Pass")
}

func testPerformanceExample() {
    // This is an example of a performance test case.
    self.measureBlock() {
        // Put the code you want to measure the time of
            here.
    }
}
}
```

Figure 8.3 Select both example methods.

4. Since we are going to create several test methods for the **Calculator** class, let's add a property to the test class that can hold a reference to a **Calculator** object so we can access it from any test method. To do this, add the following code to the top of the **SwiftDemoTests** class:

```swift
class SwiftDemoTests: XCTestCase {

    var calculator = Calculator()
```

Note: You will get an error as soon as you enter this code, but ignore it for now!

This code declares the **calculator** property and initializes it by creating an instance of the **Calculator** class and storing it in the property. Since Xcode creates a new instance of the **SwiftDemoTests** class for each unit test, this **Calculator** object will be created anew each time a test is run.

5. Let's take a closer look at the error you're getting. If you click on the red error icon to the left of the property, you will see the **Use of unresolved identifier 'Calculator'** error shown in Figure 8.4.

```
class SwiftDemoTests: XCTestCase {

    var calculator = Calculator()   ① Use of unresolved identifier 'Calculator'
```

Figure 8.4 You should see this compiler error.

This means the **SwiftDemoTests** class doesn't know anything about the **Calculator** class. Why is that? To answer this question, you need to learn about Xcode targets.

In the Project Navigator, expand the **Products** group and you will see the two items shown in Figure 8.5. Xcode produces these two output files (targets) from the files in your project. It generates **SwiftDemo.app** when you are running the app on a device or in the Simulator. It generates **SwiftDemoTests.xctests** when you are running your app's unit tests.

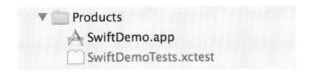

*Figure 8.5 There are two items in the **Products** group.*

For the final piece of the puzzle, go back to the Project Navigator and select the **Calculator.swift** file. Next, go to the File Inspector on the right side of the Xcode window and check out the **Target Membership** section (Figure 8.6).

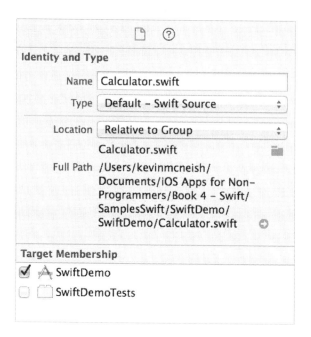

*Figure 8.6 The **Calculator.swift** file's target membership*

Notice that the **Calculator.swift** file is a member of **SwiftDemo**, but not a member of **SwiftDemoTests**. This means that when the **SwiftDemoTests** target is built, the **Calculator** class is not included. This explains why the **SwiftDemoTests** class doesn't recognize it.

6. To fix this problem, select the **SwiftDemoTests** check box. Next, select **Product > Test** from the menu (or press **Command+U**). When you do this, Xcode builds the unit test target and now that the Calculator class is included in the target, the error goes away. The Simulator is also launched when you run the tests, but you can ignore it since we are only testing the **Calculator** class, not the entire app.

Adding the Test Code

Now you're ready to add some tests to the unit test class.

1. Select the **SwiftDemoTests.swift** code file in the Project Navigator, and then add the following code directly below the **tearDown** method and before the ending curly brace (note that some longer lines of code are broken into two lines, which is perfectly legal in Swift):

```
func testAddToTotal() {
    var currentTotal =
```

```
            self.calculator.addToTotal(10);
        XCTAssertEqual(currentTotal, 10)
    }

    func testSubtractFromTotal() {
        var currentTotal =
            self.calculator.subtractFromTotal(6)
        XCTAssertEqual(currentTotal, -6)
    }

    func testMultiplyTimesTotal() {
        var currentTotal =
            self.calculator.addToTotal(9)
        currentTotal =
            self.calculator.multiplyByTotal(5)
        XCTAssertEqual(currentTotal, 45)
    }

    func testDivideIntoTotal() {
        var currentTotal =
            self.calculator.addToTotal(99)
        currentTotal =
            self.calculator.divideIntoTotal(11)
        XCTAssertEqual(currentTotal, 9)
    }

    func testClear() {
    var currentTotal =
            self.calculator.addToTotal(11)
        self.calculator.clear()
        XCTAssertEqual(calculator.total, 0)
    }

}
```

2. This code has five different methods for testing each function of the **Calculator** class (add, subtract, multiply, divide, and clear.) Each test method performs a math function by calling a method on the Calculator object. Afterward, the method's return value is passed to the **XCTAssertEqual** function. This function compares the returned value against the correct value. If they are not equal, the function generates a failure. Notice each method begins with the word **test**, which is a requirement.

The **XCTest** framework provides many other tests you can perform. For a complete list, check out Apple's help topic *Writing Test Classes and Methods.*

Working With the Test Navigator

Now let's examine our new tests in Xcode's Test Navigator. To do this, go to the Navigator toolbar on the left side of the Xcode window and click the fifth button from the left (Figure 8.7). Afterward, expand the **SwiftDemoTests** node and you should see the five tests that you added to the test class code file (if you don't see these tests, try typing **Command+B** to build the project.)

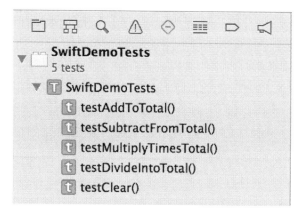

Figure 8.7 The Test Navigator

If you hover your mouse pointer over the blue **SwiftDemoTests** node, you will see a circular run button (Figure 8.8). Don't click this button just yet; when you are ready to, it will run all the unit tests.

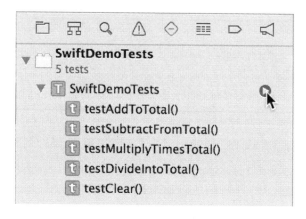

Figure 8.8 Running all unit tests

To run a single test, just hover your mouse pointer over the test and click the run button that appears to the right of the test.

Stepping Through the Code

For a closer look at how the unit test code works, pause execution when the Calculator test code is executed. To do this, add a **breakpoint** in the code. For now you just need to know that a breakpoint allows you to temporarily pause execution and examine the value of variables, properties, and so on. Let's start with the **addToTotal** test method.

1. Select the **SwiftDemoTests.swift** file in the Project Navigator.

2. Click in the gutter to the left of the first line of code in the **addToTotal** method. This adds the breakpoint indicator as in Figure 8.9.

```
func testAddToTotal() {

    var currentTotal = self.calculator.addToTotal(10);
    XCTAssertEqual(currentTotal, 10)
}

func testSubtractFromTotal() {
```

Figure 8.9 Creating a breakpoint

3. Go to the Test Navigator, hover your mouse over the **testAddToTotal** method and then click the **Run** button that appears to the right of the method. This launches the Simulator, and then Xcode displays the message shown in Figure 8.10 to indicate that it has paused execution at the breakpoint.

```
func testAddToTotal() {

    var currentTotal = self.calculator.addToTotal(10);
    XCTAssertEqual(currentTotal, 10)        Thread 1: breakpoint 2.1
}
```

Figure 8.10 The breakpoint is hit!

4. The Debug area should automatically be displayed at the bottom of the Xcode window as in Figure 8.11. The Debug area comprises the Variables View on the left and the Console on the right. If you don't see one of these panels, you can show it by clicking the corresponding button in the bottom-right corner of the Debug area.

Figure 8.11 The Debug area

5. In the bottom-left corner of the Debug area, if **Auto** is not selected, click
    on the control and select **Auto** from the pop-up list.

    The Variables View displays a list of variables accessible in the method
    that is currently executing—in this case, the **self** and **currentTotal**
    variables. As you can see, **currentTotal** is set to **Nan** (Not a Number).
    The Console displays the progress of the unit tests so far. It indicates that
    testAddToTotal has started.

6. At the top of the Debug area are toolbar buttons that allow you to control
    app execution (Figure 8.12).

Figure 8.12 The Debug toolbar

The buttons from left to right:

•   **Hide / Show** the Debug area

•   **Toggle global breakpoint state** turns all of the breakpoints in your
    app on and off.

•   **Continue program execution** causes execution to continue to the
    next breakpoint or, if there is no other breakpoint, resume execution
    of the app.

•   **Step over** allows you to step over the current line of code without
    examining it further.

- **Step into** allows you to step into a method (if any) for the current line of code.

- **Step out** allows you to step out of the current method and break on the next line of code outside the method.

- **Simulate location** allows you to select from a list of major cities throughout the world. When you select a city, your app reports that city as your current location.

To learn what a button does, just hover your mouse pointer over the button and Xcode displays a popup describing the button.

7. Click the **Step into** button to step into the calculator's **addToTotal()** method. Since you are stepping through code one line at a time, execution stops on the first line of code in the **addToTotal()** method (Figure 8.13).

```
// Adds the value to the total
func addToTotal(value: Double) -> Double
{
    self.total += value          Thread 1: step in
    return self.total
}
```

*Figure 8.13 Stepping into the **addToTotal()** method*

8. If you look in the Variables View on the left side of the Debug area, you can see the **value** parameter is set to **10** (Figure 8.14). That's because we passed **10** to this method in our unit test. If you expand the **self** node, you can see the **total** property is set to **0**.

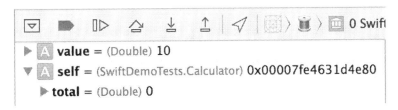

*Figure 8.14 **value** is set to **10** and **total** is **0**.*

You may have noticed that when the first breakpoint was hit, the Navigator pane switched from the Test Navigator to the Debug Navigator (Figure 8.15).

Figure 8.15 The Debug Navigator

The Debug Navigator displays important information such as CPU, Memory, Disk, and Network usage. It also shows the current **call stack** of your app—the list of methods called at run time from the beginning of the program until the execution of the current line of code.

In Figure 8.15 under the **Thread 1** node, you can see the highlight bar indicates that execution is paused on line **0**, which is the **addToTotal()** method of the **Calculator** object. Just below line **0** is line **1**. This is the previous line of code to execute (the **SwiftDemoTests.addToTotal** method.) If you click on line **1**, the Code Editor switches to the associated line of code so you can examine it.

This is extremely useful when debugging your app. It allows you to see which lines of code were executed to bring you to the current line of code.

9. If you clicked on a different line of code in the Debug Navigator, click on line **0** to select it again.

10. Now click the **Step over** button to execute the first line of code in the **addToTotal** method. You should see that the **total** property is set to **10**,

because we just executed a line of code that added the **value** parameter's value to the **total** property (Figure 8.16).

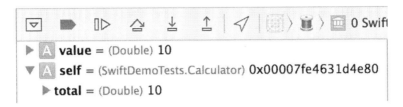

*Figure 8.16 The **total** property is set to **10**.*

11. Click either the **Step over** or **Step out** button. Both buttons have the same effect of returning you to the unit test method (Figure 8.17) because you are on the last line of code in this method.

```
    func testAddToTotal() {

        var currentTotal = self.calculator.addToTotal(10);
        XCTAssertEqual(currentTotal, 10)          Thread 1: step in
    }
```

*Figure 8.17 Back in the **testAddToTotal()** method*

12. Press the **Step over** button. This takes the value returned from the **addToTotal** method and stores it in the **currentTotal** variable. Looking in the Variables View, you'll see the **currentTotal** variable's value is now **10** as in Figure 8.18.

*Figure 8.18 **currentTotal** is now set to **10**.*

Control has now been passed to the last line of code in the unit test method (Figure 8.19).

```
    func testAddToTotal() {

        var currentTotal = self.calculator.addToTotal(10);
        XCTAssertEqual(currentTotal, 10)          Thread 1: step over
    }
```

Figure 8.19 Waiting on the last line of code in the unit test

13. Click the **Continue** button to finish the execution of the unit test. After a few seconds you will see an Xcode popup indicating success (Figure 8.20).

Figure 8.20 The test succeeded!

14. In the Navigator toolbar, click the fifth button from the left to reselect the Test Navigator. You should see a green check mark next to the test indicating it has passed (Figure 8.21). A red **x** is displayed next to any failed tests.

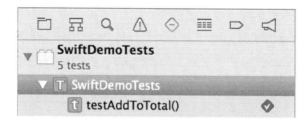

Figure 8.21 The green check mark indicates that the test has passed.

I recommend setting other breakpoints in other tests and stepping through the code, examining the values of variables and properties until you get a feel for how to step through code in the debugger.

As you continue to make changes to your code, you should run all your app's unit tests to make sure your changes haven't introduced bugs into your app. Once you have stepped through a method line by line in the debugger, you can run all the tests without breakpoints by clicking the run button next to the first node in the Test Navigator or by selecting **Product > Test** from the Xcode menu.

So there you have it! You have created your first class and tested it in the iOS Simulator.

Deleting and Disabling Breakpoints

Before moving on, now is a great time to learn how to delete and disable breakpoints. When you no longer need a particular breakpoint, you can delete it, completely removing it from your source code. To keep a break point around, but temporarily deactivate it, you can choose to disable it.

To delete or disable a single breakpoint, all you have to do is right-click (or **Control+Click**) the breakpoint in the gutter to the left of the Code editor and select **Delete Breakpoint** or **Disable Breakpoint** from the shortcut menu (Figure 8.22).

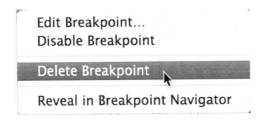

Figure 8.22 The breakpoint shortcut menu

If you would like to temporarily disable or enable all breakpoints, just click the **Breakpoints** button in the toolbar at the top of the Debug area, which toggles the breakpoints between enabled and disabled.

Since we will be using the **SwiftDemo** project in the next chapter, let's delete all the breakpoints that you have currently set in the project. The easiest way to do that is to use Xcode's Breakpoint navigator.

1. Go to the Navigation toolbar in the upper-left corner of Xcode and click the **Breakpoint navigator** toolbar button (the second button from the right), which displays all of the breakpoints in the current project as in Figure 8.23.

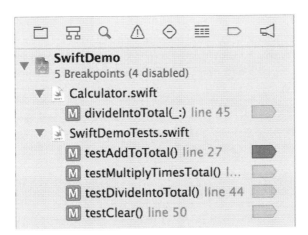

Figure 8.23 The Breakpoint Navigator

2. To delete all breakpoints, right-click the first node labeled **SwiftDemo** and select **Delete Breakpoints** from the shortcut menu.

3. To redisplay the Project Navigator, simply click the button on the far left in the Navigator toolbar.

Summary

- The only way to truly test your code is to step through it line by line *immediately after you have written it.*

- Creating a set of tests that automatically puts the core logic of your app through its paces, means you can be far more certain you have not introduced new bugs as you change your app.

- *Unit testing* is a method for testing individual units (usually a single method) of your app to make sure your app is ready to be released.

- When you create a new project, Xcode automatically adds a group to your project that contains a class you can use to create unit tests for your app.

- All test methods are required to begin with the word **test**.

- Xcode's Test Navigator lists all unit tests in your project and allows you to run a single test or all tests.

- A *breakpoint* allows you to temporarily pause execution and examine the values of variables, properties, and so on.

- When you are debugging your app, the Variables View displays a list of variables accessible in the method that is currently executing, and the Console displays the progress of the unit tests so far.

- The Debug toolbar provides various options for stepping through your code.

- The Debug Navigator displays important information such as CPU, Memory, Disk, and Network usage. It also shows the current *call stack—* the list of methods called at run time from the beginning of program until the execution of the current line of code.

- The Test Navigator displays a green check mark next to tests that have passed, and a red **x** next to any tests that have failed.

- To delete or disable a single breakpoint, all you have to do is right-click (or **Control+Click**) the breakpoint in the gutter to the left of the Code editor and select **Delete Breakpoint** or **Disable Breakpoint** from the shortcut menu.

- If you would like to temporarily disable or enable all breakpoints, just click the **Breakpoints** button in the toolbar at the top of the Debug area.

- You can also use the Breakpoint Navigator to manage your app's breakpoints.

Chapter 9: Advanced Properties

Earlier, you learned that properties describe a class's attributes, or characteristics. Now it's time to learn more about creating properties for your own custom classes.

Sections in This Chapter

Stored Properties

Earlier, you learned, *stored properties* hold a value associated with an instance of a class or the class itself. They can be either *variable* stored properties whose value can change or *constant* stored properties whose value does not change.

Let's try our hand at creating both types of stored properties. We'll work with the **PropertiesDemo** project found in this book's sample code.

1. Launch Xcode and select **File > Open** from the menu (or press **Command+O**.)

2. Navigate to where you have stored this book's sample code on your computer (in the **Documents\Samples** folder by default). Expand the **PropertiesDemo** folder and double-click the **PropertiesDemo.xcodeproj** file to open the project.

3. Select the **MemberEntity.swift** code file in the Project Navigator, and you will see the following class declaration:

```
class MemberEntity {


}
```

This **MemberEntity** class will be used to represent someone who is a member of our app's user base.

4. Add the following property declaration to the class:

```
class MemberEntity {

    var firstName : String
}
```

This code declares a property named **firstName** of type **String**. You will see an error as soon as you finish typing this line of code. Clicking on the red error icon in the gutter to the left of the class declaration, you will see the error detail popup (Figure 9.1).

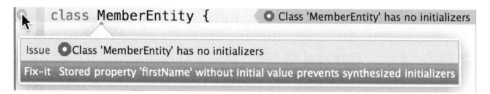

Figure 9.1 Click the error icon to see error detail.

The first line of the error popup states an Issue: **Class 'MemberEntity' has no initializers**. You are getting this warning because Swift requires that all properties have an initial value. You can set an initial value for a property in one of two main ways:

- Create an initializer method for the class and within that method store an initial value into the property.

- Store a default value into the property on the same line of code that declares the property.

Which option should you choose? If the initial value of a property is always the same, you should set a default value directly in the property declaration. This is a better choice, because it ties the default value more directly to the declaration of the property. This makes the intent of your code clearer.

5. Notice the highlighted **Fix-It** option in Figure 9.1. The associated message indicates that the firstName property is causing a problem. Go ahead and double-click the **Fix-It** option in the popup. This changes the code to the following:

```
class MemberEntity {

    var firstName : String = ""
}
```

This code sets the default value of the **firstName** property to an empty string and the error goes away. This points to another benefit of setting default values in the property declaration—it enables Swift to infer the type of the property from the default value.

Remember learning about declaring variables back in Chapter 3? Swift has
something called *type inference* that allows it to examine a value in the
context it is used and infer, or figure out, the type of the value.

6. In practical terms, this means that you can delete the type from the
    property declaration. Let's do that now, and while you're at it, let's add a
    lastName property:

```
class MemberEntity {

    var firstName = ""
        var lastName = ""
}
```

You will learn more about setting property values in initializer methods in
Chapter 16: Initializers.

7. Now let's add a constant stored property to the class:

```
class MemberEntity {

    let passwordRetries = 3

    var firstName = ""
    var lastName = ""
}
```

The **firstName** and **lastName** properties can change for each
MemberEntity, but the number of password retries is the same for all
members, so we can declare it as a constant stored property.

Computed Properties

As you have learned, unlike stored properties, *computed properties* don't
actually hold a value. Rather, they retrieve and set other property values
indirectly.

For example, add the following computed property to the MemberEntity
class:

```
class MemberEntity {

    let passwordRetries = 3
```

```
var firstName = ""
var lastName = ""
var fullName : String {
    get {
        return self.firstName + " " + self.lastName
    }
}
}
```

The **fullName** property is a computed property that combines the **firstName** and **fullName** properties, and adds a space between them.

Some important things to note:

- The type of a computed property must be explicitly declared, which is why the **fullName** property is declared to be of type **String**.

- Computed properties can have a **get** method that returns the calculated value of the property and a **set method** that takes the specified value and saves it in multiple stored properties.

- It's common for a computed property to have a **get** method, but no **set** method, making it read only.

- You must declare computed properties with the **var** keyword rather than the **let** keyword, because their value is not fixed.

- You can simplify the declaration of a read-only computed property by removing the **get** and inner curly braces. For example:

```
var fullName : String {
    return self.firstName + " " + self.lastName
}
```

Let's create a unit test so you can see how stored and computed properties work at run time.

1. First, change the **fullName** property declaration as shown above in the **MemberEntity** class.

2. Expand the **PropertiesDemoTests** group in the Project Navigator and

then click on the **PropertiesDemoTests.swift** file to select it.

3. Add the following unit test method before the closing curly brace of the PropertiesDemoTests class:

```
func testComputedProperty()
{
    var memberEntity = MemberEntity()
    memberEntity.firstName = "Kevin"
    memberEntity.lastName = "McNeish"
    var fullName = memberEntity.fullName
    XCTAssertEqual(fullName, "Kevin McNeish")
}
}
```

Here is the big picture of what this code does:

- Creates an instance of the **MemberEntity** class and stores it in the **memberEntity** variable.

- Stores my first and last name in the **firstName** and **lastName** properties of the **MemberEntity** object.

- Gets the value of the **fullName** property and stores it in the **fullName** variable.

- Checks to make sure the full name is correct.

4. Press **Command+B** to build the project. This checks to see if you have any errors in the code you just entered, and also adds the new test to the Test Navigator.

5. Let's run the test now and see how this all works at run time. Set a breakpoint on the first line of code in the **testComputedProperty** method by clicking in the gutter to the left of the code as in Figure 9.2.

```
    func testComputedProperty() {

        let memberEntity = MemberEntity()
        memberEntity.firstName = "Kevin"
        memberEntity.lastName = "McNeish"
        var fullName = memberEntity.fullName
        XCTAssertEqual(fullName, "Kevin McNeish")
    }
}
```

Figure 9.2 Set a breakpoint on the first line of code.

6. Next, go to the Test Navigator by clicking the fifth button from the left in the Navigator toolbar. Expand the **PropertiesDemoTests** node, and then run the test by clicking the Run button to the right of the **testComputedProperty()** method (Figure 9.3).

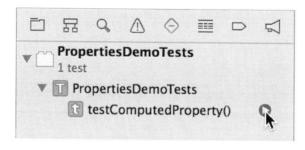

*Figure 9.3 Run the **testComputedProperty()** test.*

This causes you to hit the breakpoint as shown in Figure 9.4. Now let's step through the code.

```
    func testComputedProperty() {

        var memberEntity = MemberEntity()    Thread 1: breakpoint 1.1
        memberEntity.firstName = "Kevin"
        memberEntity.lastName = "McNeish"
        var fullName = memberEntity.fullName
        XCTAssertEqual(fullName, "Kevin McNeish")
    }
```

Figure 9.4 The breakpoint is hit.

7. This first line of code creates an instance of the **MemberEntity** class. In the Debug toolbar, click the **Step into** button to so see how this object gets initialized.

As Figure 9.5 shows, when an instance of the **MemberEntity** class is created, the properties are all set to their default values.

```
class MemberEntity {

    let passwordRetries = 3                    Thread 1: step in

    var firstName = ""
    var lastName = ""
    var fullName : String {
        return self.firstName + " " + self.lastName
    }
}
```

*Figure 9.5 The **MemberEntity** object initialization*

8. Click **Step over** three times and you will see all the properties in the class get set to their default values. If you go to the Variables View and expand the self variable, you will see that all three properties are now set to their initial values (Figure 9.6).

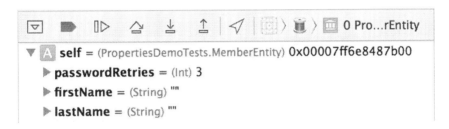

*Figure 9.6 The **MemberEntity** object's properties are initialized.*

9. Now click the **Step out** button to step out of the **MemberEntity** initialization. This takes you back to the **testComputedProperty** unit test method.

10. Click **Step over** to go to the second line of code in the test method (Figure 9.7). When you execute this line of code in the next step, it will store **Kevin** in the **firstName** property.

```
func testComputedProperty() {

    var memberEntity = MemberEntity()
    memberEntity.firstName = "Kevin"   Thread 1: step over
    memberEntity.lastName = "McNeish"
    var fullName = memberEntity.fullName
    XCTAssertEqual(fullName, "Kevin McNeish")
}
```

*Figure 9.7 Getting ready to set the **firstName** property*

11. Press the **Step into** button. This takes you to the **firstName** property

(Figure 9.8).

```
class MemberEntity {

    let passwordRetries = 3

    var firstName = ""                              Thread 1: step in
    var lastName = ""
    var fullName : String {
        return self.firstName + " " + self.lastName
    }
}
```

*Figure 9.8 Storing **Kevin** in the **firstName** property*

12. Although it may look as if you're going to store an empty string into the **firstName** property again, if you expand the **self** variable in the Variables View you can see that that **firstName** is set to **Kevin**. (Figure 9.9). Also, notice the **value** variable, which is also set to **Kevin**. Swift automatically creates this variable when you store a value into a property.

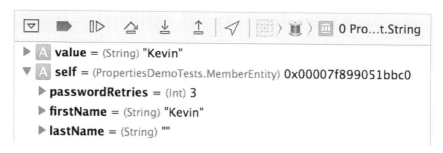

*Figure 9.9 The **firstName** property is set to **Kevin**.*

13. Click the **Step out** button again to go back to the unit test method.

14. Click **Step into** again to see the **lastName** property get set and then click **Step out** again to go back to the unit test method.

15. Now you're ready to run the third line of code in the unit test method that retrieves the value of the **fullName** property (Figure 9.10).

```
func testComputedProperty() {

    var memberEntity = MemberEntity()
    memberEntity.firstName = "Kevin"
    memberEntity.lastName = "McNeish"
    var fullName = memberEntity.fullName   Thread 1: step
    XCTAssertEqual(fullName, "Kevin McNeish")
}

}
```

*Figure 9.10 Getting the **fullName** property value*

16. Click the **Step into** button and execution will pause on the **fullName** property's **get** method (Figure 9.11). This demonstrates that when you access the value of a computed property its associated get method automatically fires.

```
class MemberEntity {

    let passwordRetries = 3

    var firstName = ""
    var lastName = ""
    var fullName : String {
        return self.firstName + " " + self.lastName
    }                                          Thread 1: step in
}
```

*Figure 9.11 Running the **fullName get** method*

17. Click the **Step out** button and execution will pause on the code that stores the **fullName** property value into the **fullName** variable. Click **Step over** and you can see that the value of the **fullName** variable in the Variables View is set properly as shown in Figure 9.12.

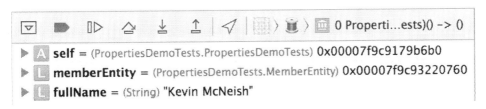

*Figure 9.12 The **fullName** computed property value was retrieved successfully.*

18. When you click the Continue button, you should see that the unit test has passed successfully.

I hope this has given you a better understanding of how stored and computed properties work at run time.

Type Properties

All the properties you have created so far are instance properties—meaning they belong to instances (objects) that you create of the class. Each instance has its own copy of the properties along with their own values. This allows instances to have different values for properties such as **firstName** and **lastName**.

Swift also has *type properties*. These are properties that belong to the class itself rather than to any instance of that class. No matter how many instances you have, there is only ever one copy of a type property.

You can use type properties where you need a value to be the same for all instances of a type. A great example is the **passwordRetries** property you created in the previous section. Although we declared it as an instance property, since the number of retries doesn't change for each member, we can declare it as a type property instead. To do this, just add the class keyword at the beginning of the property declaration:

```
class let passwordRetries = 3
```

Now that the **passwordRetries** is a type property, you access it by referencing the class. For example:

```
let retries = MemberEntity.passwordRetries
```

Lazy Stored Properties

At times, you may want to defer the initialization of a variable until it is first accessed in code. Swift provides the *lazy stored properties* to fill this need.

If you add the **lazy** modifier to a property declaration, its in-line initialization code is not executed until the property is first accessed by another line of code. This is particularly useful in situations where the initialization code is creating an object that takes a while to create. For example, take the following code:

```
class ViewController: UIViewController {

    lazy var webCalculator = WebCalculator()

    override func viewDidLoad() {
        super.viewDidLoad()
        // Do any additional setup after loading the view
    }

    func useWebCalculator() {

        webCalculator.clear()

    }
}
```

The **webCalculator** property is initialized by creating an instance of the **WebCalculator** class. As its name suggests, the WebCalculator is an online calculator and requires some processing time to access.

Normally, the **webCalculator** property would be initialized as soon as its parent **ViewController** class is created. However, since it has the **lazy** modifier, it's not created until the code in the **useWebCalculator** method first accesses the **webCalculator** property.

Lazy modifiers are a great feature of Swift! In other programming languages, I have to write several lines of code to accomplish the same thing. In Swift, I just specify the **lazy** modifier and I'm done!

Property Observers

Swift has an advanced feature known as ***property observers*** that allows you to perform an action when the value of a property is changed.

You can create property observers on stored properties you declare in your custom classes, or on stored or computed properties you inherit from a superclass.

Using property observers on computed properties you declare in your own class doesn't make sense, because you can already write code to respond to changes in the property's value within the ***setter*** method.

There are two main types of property observers:

- **willSet** observers fire immediately *before* a property value is set.

- **didSet** observers fire immediately *after* a property value has been set.

Let's check out an example that demonstrates how to use property observers.

1. Launch Xcode and select **File > Open** from the menu (or press **Command+O.**)

2. Navigate to where you have stored this book's sample code on your computer (in the **Documents\Samples** folder by default). Expand the **PropertyObserverDemo** folder and double-click the **PropertyObserverDemo.xcodeproj** file to open the project.

3. Select the **Main.Storyboard** file in the Project Navigator and you will see the scene shown in Figure 9.13.

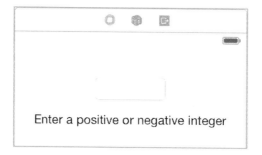

*Figure 9.13 The main scene in the **PropertyObserverDemo** project*

At run time, if you enter a positive integer in the text field, it replaces the **Enter a positive or negative integer** label text with the number you entered and in black. If you enter a negative integer, it shows the number in red. Let's give it a try.

4. Click Xcode's Run button and when the app appears in the Simulator, enter a negative integer (no decimal points) into the text field and press **return**. It should display that number in red as in Figure 9.14.

Figure 9.14 Negative numbers are displayed in red.

5. Now try entering a positive integer value and the number should be displayed in black.

6. Let's see how this works under the hood. Go back to Xcode and click the Stop button. Next, in the Project Navigator, select the **mmUILabel.swift** file, which contains the following class declaration:

```swift
class mmUILabel: UILabel {

    override var text: String? {
        didSet {
            if let integerValue = text?.toInt()
            {
                if integerValue >= 0
                {
                    self.textColor = UIColor.blackColor()
                }
                else
                {
                    self.textColor = UIColor.redColor()
                }
            }
        }
    }

    required init(coder aDecoder: NSCoder) {
        super.init(coder: aDecoder)
    }
}
```

This class is a custom subclass of the Cocoa Touch **UILabel** class. The first block of code is an override of the **text** property. The highlighted code is an observer for the **text** property. **didSet** observers are automatically fired *after* the value of the associated property is set. As you learned earlier, you can also create a **willSet** observer that fires immediately *before* the property value is set.

You may not understand everything that's going on in this method, since it includes some Swift features we haven't discussed yet in this book, but here is the gist of what this method does:

- The observer checks to see if the value stored in the **text** property is an integer.

- If the value is an integer, the observer checks if the value is greater than or equal to zero. If it is, the label color is set to black. If it isn't, the label color is set to red.

- If the value stored in the text property is *not* an integer, the label color isn't changed and the value is simply stored in the label's **text** property.

Here are some important things to consider regarding property observers:

- In a **willSet** observer, the value of the property being set is passed to the method in a constant parameter named **newValue**. You can change the name of this parameter by specifying it within parentheses. For example, the following **willSet** declaration names the parameter **myNewValue**:

```
override var text: String? {

    willSet(myNewValue) {
        // Do something
    }
}
```

- The default parameter name for **didSet** is **oldValue**, which you can also choose to rename.

- Property observers are called even if the new property value is the same as the old property value.

- Property observers do not fire when a property is first initialized by means of a default value or an initializer method!

- If you change the value of the property you are observing within the **didSet** method, the **didSet** method will fire again, which has the potential to create an infinite loop!

Summary

Here are key points to remember regarding properties:

Stored Properties

- *Stored properties* hold a value associated with an instance of a class or the class itself. They can be either *variable* stored properties whose value can change or *constant* stored properties whose value does not change.

  Here is an example of a variable stored property:

```
class MemberEntity {

    var firstName = ""
}
```

- There are two main ways you can set an initial value:

  1. Create an initializer method for the class and within that method store an initial value into the property.

  2. Store a default value into the property on the same line of code that declares the property.

- If the initial value of a property is always the same, you should set a default value directly in the property declaration.

- When you set a default value in a property's declaration, it enables Swift to infer the type of the property from the default value.

Computed Properties

- Unlike stored properties, computed properties don't actually hold a value. Rather, they retrieve and set other property values indirectly.

- The type of a computed property must be explicitly declared.

- Computed properties can have a **get** method that returns the calculated value of the property and a **set method** that takes the specified value and saves it in multiple stored properties.

- It's common for a computed property to have a **get** method but no **set** method, making it read only. Here is an example of a read-only property:

```
class MemberEntity {

    var firstName = ""
    var lastName = ""
    var fullName : String {
    get {
        return self.firstName + " " + self.lastName
        }
    }
}
```

- You can simplify the declaration of a read-only computed property by removing the **get** and inner curly braces. For example:

```
    var fullName : String {
        return self.firstName + " " + self.lastName
    }
```

- You must declare computed properties with the **var** keyword rather than the **let** keyword, because their value is not fixed.

Type Properties

- *Type properties* belong to the class itself rather than to any instance of that class. No matter how many instances you have, there is only ever one copy of a type property.

- You can use type properties where you need a value to be the same for all instances of a type.

- To declare a type property, just add the **class** keyword at the beginning of the property declaration:

```
class let passwordRetries = 3
```

Lazy Stored Properties

- If you add the **lazy** modifier to a property declaration, its in-line initialization code is not executed until the property is first accessed by another line of code.

- Lazy properties are useful in situations where the initialization code is creating an object that takes a while to create.

Property Observers

- Swift has an advanced feature known as property observers that allows you to perform an action when the value of a property is changed.

- You can create property observers on stored properties you declare in your custom classes, or on stored or computed properties you inherit from a superclass.

- It doesn't make sense to use property observers on computed properties you declare in your own class, because you can already write code to respond to changes in the property's value within the setter method.

- There are two main types of property observers:

  1. **willSet** observers fire immediately *before* a property value is set.

  2. **didSet** observers fire immediately *after* a property value has been set.

- In a **willSet** observer, the value of the property being set is passed to the method in a constant parameter named **newValue**. You can change the name of this parameter by specifying it within parentheses.

- The default parameter name for **didSet** is **oldValue**, which you can also choose to rename.

- Property observers are called even if the new property value is the same as the old property value.

- Property observers do not fire when a property is first initialized by means of a default value or an initializer method!

- If you change the value of the property you are observing within the **didSet** method, the **didSet** method will fire again, which has the potential to create an infinite loop!

Exercise 9.1

1. Create an **Invoice** class with **subtotal** and **taxRate** stored properties. Create a **grandTotal** computed property that returns the grand total as a string, formatted for currency.

2. Create a new playground called **Invoice.playground**.

3. In the playground, create a new class named **Invoice**.

4. Add a stored property named **subTotal** of type **Double**, initialized to **0.0**.

5. Add a second stored property named **taxRate** of type **Double** and set its initial value to **0.053** (or if you prefer, your local tax rate).

6. Created a read-only computed property named **grandTotal** that calculates the value of the **subTotal** plus tax (based on the **taxRate**) and returns it formatted for the local currency.

   Use the **NSNumberFormatter** class and set its **numberStyle** property to format the number as a currency string.

7. Add code to the playground to test the class.

Solution Movie 9.1

To see a video providing the solution for this exercise, you can enter the link below in your Web browser to see each step performed for you.

Movie 9.1

http://www.iOSAppsForNonProgrammers.com/B4M91.html

Chapter 10: Arrays & Other Collections

Now that you have a basic understanding of classes and objects, it's time to discuss an easier topic—arrays and other collections. These are *very* important, because all the lists of information your app displays come from some type of collection. This chapter introduces the different collections available, so you can make smart decisions about which collection to use in different situations.

Sections in This Chapter

1. *What Is a Collection?*

2. *Enumerating a Collection*

3. *Examining the CollectionsDemo Sample Project*

4. *Swift's Array Class*

5. *Swift's Dictionary Class*

6. *Mutable and Immutable Collections*

7. *Structures*

8. *Working With Tuples*

9. *Multidimensional Arrays*

10. *Creating Custom Collections*

11. *Summary*

12. *Exercise 10.1*

13. *Solution Movie 10.1*

What Is a Collection?

Maybe the word "***collection***," makes you think of stamp or coin collections. This is a good metaphor for collections in Swift, because collections give you a way to group related objects together.

All the variables and properties you have worked with so far have held a single value (such as an integer, Boolean (Bool), or a single object). In contrast, Swift and collection classes allow you to group multiple items into a single collection. Swift's primary collection classes in are:

- Array

- Dictionary

The Cocoa Touch Framework primary collection classes are:

- NSArray

- NSMutableArray

- NSDictionary

- NSMutableDictionary

- NSSet

- NSMutableSet

The newer Swift collection classes have great features that make them easy to use and help you avoid common bugs in your code. In contrast, the older Cocoa Touch collections have been around a long time and have a little extra functionality. It's perfectly fine to use a mix of Swift and Cocoa Touch collection classes in your apps. To learn more about Cocoa Touch collection classes, check out Book 2: Flying With Objective-C.

Often, collections are used in iOS Apps to create lists. For example, you can have a collection of strings used as a list of songs, or an array of images used to display album covers. In Swift, items in a collection must be of the same type and most of the time this is exactly what you need. However, this isn't a restriction in the Cocoa Touch collection classes, where each member of the collection be of a different type.

Enumerating a Collection

You can enumerate, or loop through the items in a collection by using one of Swift's looping statements, discussed in *Chapter 11: Looping Statements*. You can also enumerate a collection using a more advanced feature known as closures. For more information, see *Chapter 23: Understanding Closures*.

Examining the CollectionsDemo Sample Project

There's nothing quite like a live sample to help you understand a new topic. The **CollectionsDemo** sample project provides examples of a variety of Swift and Cocoa Touch collections.

1. If you have another project open, close it by selecting **File** > **Close Project** from the Xcode menu.

2. Open the **CollectionsDemo** project by selecting **File** > **Open...** from the Xcode menu. In the **Open** dialog, navigate to the folder where you have stored this book's sample code. Expand the **CollectionsDemo** folder, select the **CollectionsDemo.xcodeproj** file and then click **Open**.

3. In the Project Navigator, click the gray triangle to the left of the **CollectionsDemo** node to expand it, then the gray arrow to the left of the **CollectionsDemo** sub-node to expand it, and finally select the **Main.storyboard** file. You should see the very simple view in Figure 10.1, which contains a label and a *picker view*.

*Figure 10.1 The scene in the **CollectionsDemo** project*

4. Click Xcode's **Run** button to see this simple app run in the iOS Simulator. Notice it looks a little different when you run it. Rather than list California cities in the picker view, it lists several names as in Figure 10.2.

*Figure 10.2 The **CollectionsDemo** project at run time*

5. Where are these names coming from? To find out, go back to Xcode and click the **Stop** button. Select the **ViewController.swift** code file in the Project Navigator and scroll to the top of the window.

   Notice the instance variable declaration of type **Array** called **names**.

```
var names: Array<String> = ["Jordan", "Timothy",
"Alexander", "Mia", "Luca"]
```

The **names** array is used to fill the picker view. Let's look at the **Array** class to see how it works.

Swift's Array Class

The **Array** class is one of the most basic kinds of Swift collections. Declaring an **Array** variable a little different than declaring other variables. Notice the **<String>** declaration after the **Array** type. This specifies that the names array can only contain items of type **String**. In fact, if you try to add a different type of item you get a compiler error. For example, adding an integer to the end of the list of items:

```
var names: Array<String> = ["Jordan", "Timothy", "Alexander",
"Mia", "Luca", 1]
```

would cause the compiler error Type 'String' does not conform to protocol 'IntegerLiteralConvertible'.

Initializing an Array

To initialize an **Array** with a set of values, specify the values between square brackets and separated by commas as shown in the **ViewController.swift** code file.

When you initialize an array in this way, Swift can infer the type of items contained in the array so you don't need to explicitly declare it. This means you could declare the array like this:

```
var names = ["Jordan", "Timothy", "Alexander",
        "Mia", "Luca"]
```

These literal string values are the source of the names you saw in the picker view at run time.

You can also initialize an array from values stored in variables, constants, and properties:

```
var name1 = "Mia"
var name2 = "Luca"
var names = [name1, name2]
```

To initialize an empty array, specify the type of the array in square brackets followed by parentheses:

```
var ages = [Int]()
```

To initialize an array with a given number of elements all set to the same value, use this **Array** initializer:

```
var a = Array(count: 10, repeatedValue: 0.0)
```

Getting the Number of Items in an Array

To find out how many items are in an **Array** you can access its **count** property. If you scroll down a little farther in the **ViewController** code file to the **pickerView:numberOfRowsInComponent:** method, you can see the **count** property in use. This method tells the picker view how many items to display in its list:

```
func pickerView(pickerView: UIPickerView,
numberOfRowsInComponent component: Int) -> Int {

    return names.count
}
```

To test if an array is empty, check to see if its **count** is equal to zero or check its **isEmpty** property:

```
let arrayIsEmpty = names.isEmpty
```

Referencing Items in an Array by Index

In Swift, collections are zero-based. This means the first item in the collection is item zero, the second is item one, and so on. This takes a little getting used to, since items in the real world are usually numbered starting with "1." (Some hotels use this numbering scheme by calling the ground floor "zero" and the next floor "one").

An *index* references an item by its numeric position in the collection. You can get an item from an **Array** by placing the index number between square brackets. This is known as *subscript syntax*.

Let's check out an example that uses subscript syntax to reference items in an array and display them in the UI. First, run the app in the Simulator by pressing the **Run** button in Xcode. Select different items in the list by clicking on them; you should see the label text change to the name you have selected.

Let's find out how this magic works. Go back to Xcode, scroll to the **pickerView:didSelectRow:inComponent** method in the **ViewController** code file:

```
func pickerView(pickerView: UIPickerView,
        didSelectRow row: Int,
        inComponent component: Int) {
```

```
        self.lblDemo.text = names[row]
}
```

This is the code that sets the label text from the currently selected item. Let's look at the order of events when an item is selected in the picker view with the help of the following image:

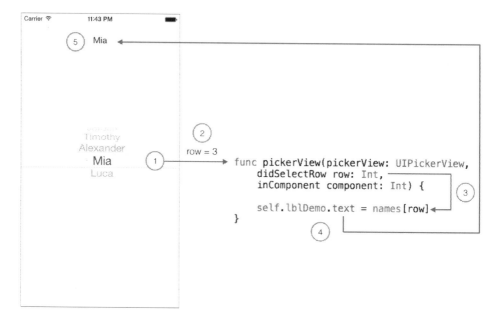

1. An item is selected in the picker view.

2. The **pickerView:didSelectRow:inComponent** method in the view controller is called by the picker view, passing the selected row number (in this case, 3).

3. The **row** number is used as an index to retrieve the third name string in the array.

4. The name string is stored in the label's **text** property.

5. The name is displayed in the label on the view.

Finding the Index of an Item in an Array

Swift has a **find()** function you can use to find a particular item in an Array. For example:

```
var names = ["Jordan", "Timothy", "Alexander", "Mia", "Luca"]

var itemNumber : Int? = find(self.names, "Luca")
```

The **find()** function accepts an array as its first parameter and the value you are searching for as a second parameter. If it finds the item you're looking for, it returns the index number of that item (4, in this case). Otherwise, it returns a nil, which is why **Int?** is the return value type.

You can also search an array for more complex objects:

```
var memberEntity1 = member.createEntity()
var memberEntity2 = member.createEntity()
var members: Array<NSManagedObject> =
        [memberEntity1, memberEntity2];

var index = find(members, memberEntity2)
```

In the first two lines of code, two **memberEntity** objects are created. In the third line, a new **members** array is created and the **memberEntity** objects are added to the array.

The fourth line of code performs the search with Swift's **find()** function. The first argument passed to the function is the **members** array (the array you want find() to search.) The second argument is the **memberEntity2** object (the object you're searching for.) The **find()** function locates the **memberEntity2** object as the second item in the array and returns a 1 for the object index. That's because arrays are zero-based, so the first item is 0, and the second is 1.

Getting the First and Last Array Items

You can get the first item in an array by referencing item 0, or the last item in an array by creating an index that is **count** (the number of items in the array) minus one. However, Swift provides the **firstItem** and **lastItem** methods, making this much easier.

The following code gets the first item in an array and then the last item in an array:

```
var firstItem = names.first
var lastItem = names.last
```

Adding Items to an Array

After an array is created, you can add more items to the array using the array's **append** and **insert** methods. Let's give it a try.

1. In the **CollectionsDemo** project select the **ViewController.swift** file in the Project Navigator.

2. Add the following code to the **viewDidLoad** method, right after the call to **super.viewDidLoad**:

```
override func viewDidLoad() {

        super.viewDidLoad()
        names.append("Ryan")
```

The **append** method adds the specified item to the bottom of the array.

3. Click the Run button. When the app appears in the Simulator, scroll to the bottom and you should see **Ryan** appear at the bottom of the list (Figure 10.3).

Figure 10.3 The newly added array item

You can append multiple items to an array using the addition assignment (+=) operator. For example:

```
names += ["Brendan", "Patrick"]
```

4. Now let's give the **insert** method a try. The **insert** method accepts a second argument that specifies the index, or location where you want to add the new item. Add the following code beneath the line of code you just

added.

```
names.append("Ryan")
names.insert("Markus", atIndex: 0)
```

This code adds **Markus** to position **0**, which is the first position of the array.

5. Click the Run button. When the app appears in the Simulator, you should see **Markus** at the top of the list (Figure 10.4).

Figure 10.4 The newly inserted array item

Changing Existing Array Items

Change an existing item in an array using subscript syntax. For example, the following code replaces the first item in the **names** array:

```
names[0] = "Sharlene"
```

You can also replace multiple items by specifying a range. For example, the following code replaces the second and third items (item 1 is the second item and item 2 is the third item).

```
names[1...2] = ["Randy", "Josh"]
```

Removing Array Items

Four methods are available for removing items from an array.

1. **removeLast** removes the last item from an array and returns the removed item. First, check to see if there are any items in the array (count > 0), otherwise you will get a runtime error.

```
if names.count > 0
{
        let removedName = names.removeLast()
}
```

2. **removeAtIndex** removes the item at the specified index and returns the removed item. It's an error if the index of the item you are removing is higher than the number of items in the array, so at a bare minimum you can make the following check:

```
var index = 1
if index < names.count
{
    let removedName = names.removeAtIndex(index)
}
```

3. **removeRange** removes the items in the specified range, but doesn't return the removed items. If either the starting or ending range is greater than the number of items in the array, it will create an error.

```
let removedName = names.removeRange(1...2)
```

4. **removeAllItems** clears all items from an array, but doesn't return the removed items. This method accepts a Boolean **keepCapacity** argument that allows you to specify if you want to keep the capacity (the amount of memory allocated) for the array. If you plan to immediately add items back into the array, it makes sense to pass **true**, otherwise, you should pass **false**.

```
names.removeAll(keepCapacity: false)
```

Combining Arrays

You can combine two or more arrays to produce a single array. The following code combines the **yourFamily** and **myFamily** arrays to create the **ourFamily** array:

```
var ourFamily = yourFamily + myFamily
```

As you might guess, when arrays are combined, both must contain members of the same type.

Reversing the Order of Array Items

If you ever need to reverse the order of items in an array, Swift's array class makes it easy by providing a **reverse** method that returns an array with all items in reverse order from the source array. For example:

```
var reverseNames = names.reverse()
```

Swift's Dictionary Class

Arrays are great for simple collections, but at times you need a little more. It's easy to find a simple string object in an array, but what if you need to find a specific item in a collection of more complex objects? For example, what if you have a collection of Customer objects, each uniquely identified by a Customer ID, and you want to search for a particular object by that unique ID? A dictionary can help.

Each dictionary item (called an *entry*) has a *key* and a *value*. The key is used to uniquely identify the entry, and the value is the item itself. In the example of a Customer object, the Customer ID is the key, and the Customer object is the value. Swift's **Dictionary** class provides you with all the basic functionality of a dictionary.

Unordered Collections

Unlike the **Array** class where items have a specific order, the **Dictionary** class is an unordered collection, meaning the **Dictionary** items are in no particular order.

Why would you want a collection to be unordered? Internally, the items in an unordered collection are arranged for fast access to individual elements. This allows you to have a **Dictionary** with many items in it, but still quickly access individual items by their key.

The DictionaryDemo Project

To see a live example of how a dictionary works, let's look at the **DictionaryDemo** project that displays a list of country codes in a picker view. When the user selects a country from the picker, the two-character country code is used as a key in the dictionary to look up the corresponding country name, which is displayed in the label at the top of the view.

1. If you have another project open, close it by selecting **File > Close Project** from the Xcode menu.

2. Open the **DictionaryDemo** project by selecting **File > Open...** from the Xcode menu. In the **Open** dialog, navigate to the folder where you have

this book's sample code. Expand the **DictionaryDemo** folder. Select the **DictionaryDemo.xcodeproj** file, and then click the **Open** button.

3. Run the project by clicking the **Run** button in Xcode. The app should look like Figure 10.5.

Figure 10.5 The Dictionary in action

4. Select a country, and notice that the two-character country code is displayed at the top of the view.

5. Go back to Xcode, and then press the **Stop** button.

Let's look at the code to see how the dictionary is used to display this information.

Initializing a Dictionary

In the Project Navigator, select the **ViewController.swift** file. Then, in the Code Editor, scroll to the top of the code file. Notice the **countries** property:

```
var countries: Dictionary<String, String> =
        ["AT": "Austria",
        "BG": "Bulgaria",
        "CH": "Switzerland",
        "DE": "Germany"]
```

This code declares a property named **countries** that is a **Dictionary** with keys and values of type **String**. Here is the syntax for declaring a **Dictionary** type:

```
Dictionary<KeyType, ValueType>
```

KeyType specifies the type of the Dictionary's *keys*, and **ValueType** specifies the type of the Dictionary's *values*. In our example, country codes are the Dictionary's keys and the names of countries are the Dictionary's values. Both are Strings.

As shown in the code sample above, you can initialize a **Dictionary** with a *dictionary literal*, which is a list of **key: value** pairs separated by commas, between square brackets.

As is true with arrays, you don't need to specify the type of a Dictionary when you initialize it. You can just let Swift infer the type based on the values you use to initialize it. This means you could declare the Dictionary like this:

```
var countries =
        ["AT": "Austria",
        "BG": "Bulgaria",
        "CH": "Switzerland",
        "DE": "Germany"]
```

You can initialize an empty **Dictionary** like this:

```
var topTenList = Dictionary<Int, String>()
```

This code declares a Dictionary named **topTenList** with Integer keys and String values.

You can also initialize an array with variable, property and constant values.

Getting the Number of Items in a Dictionary

To find out how many items are in a **Dictionary** (each key-value pair is counted as a single item), you can access its **count** property. For example, scroll down in the ViewController.swift file and you will see the **pickerView:numberOfRowsInComponent** method:

```
func pickerView(pickerView: UIPickerView,
numberOfRowsInComponent component: Int) -> Int {
```

```
        return countries.count
}
```

Remember, this method tells the picker view how many items it needs to display.

To test if a Dictionary is empty, check if its **count** is equal to zero or check its **isEmpty** property:

```
let dictionaryIsEmpty = countries.isEmpty
```

Referencing Items in a Dictionary

You can't reference an item in a **Dictionary** by its numeric position the way you can in an Array, because Dictionaries are unordered collections with items in no particular order. Rather, you use a *key* to find a particular item in a **Dictionary**. For example, the following code uses subscript syntax to pass the "CH" code to the countries dictionary to retrieve the associated country name:

```
var country: String? = countries["CH"]
```

Although I didn't need to specify the type of the **country** variable, I did so to show you how a nullable string is returned from the **countries** array. Before reading the next paragraph, see if you can figure out why a nullable string is returned.

Ready for the answer? It's because you can pass in a key that doesn't exist in the **Dictionary**, and in that case, the Dictionary returns **nil**

Getting a List of Keys and Values

Swift Dictionaries have a **keys** property that contains a list of all keys in the **Dictionary** and a **values** property that contains a list of all the values in the **Dictionary**.

The keys and values properties are both of the same type—a **LazyBidirectionalCollection**. This is a more complex collection that you can easily iterate using a **for** loop (discussed in the next chapter). If you want to convert this complex collection into a simple array, you can do so as shown in the **viewDidLoad** method near the top of the **ViewController.swift** code file:

```
override func viewDidLoad() {
        super.viewDidLoad()

        keys = Array(countries.keys)
```

This code passes the **countries.keys** collection to the initializer of the **Array** class and it returns a simple **Array** containing the keys. Let's take a closer look at how this **keys** array is used in conjunction with the **countries** Dictionary to fill the picker view and respond to selections.

1. Looking back at Figure 10.5, you can see the picker view contains the key values (country code) and the label displays the associated country value.

2. When the picker view is first created, it calls the **pickerView: titleForRow:forComponent:** method once for each row in the picker view to get the title of each row:

```
func pickerView(pickerView: UIPickerView, titleForRow row: Int,
forComponent component: Int) -> String! {
        return keys[row]
}
```

This method determines the title for the row by passing the row number to the **keys** array, which returns the corresponding country name.

3. When the user selects an item in the picker view, the **pickerView: didSelectRow:InComponent:** method gets executed, which in turn calls the **setLabelTextFromRow:** method:

```
func pickerView(pickerView: UIPickerView, didSelectRow row:
Int, inComponent component: Int) {
        self.setLabelTextFromRow(row)
}

func setLabelTextFromRow(row: Int)
{
        var key = keys[row]
        var country = countries[key]
        self.lblDemo.text = country
}
```

In the **setLabelTextFromRow:** method, the first line of code passes the row number to the **keys** array, which returns the corresponding country code.

In the second line of code, the key (country code) is passed to the **countries** Dictionary, which returns the corresponding country name.

In the third line of code, the country name is stored in the **text** property of the **lblDemo** label.

I made the code in this method a bit verbose so you can easily understand what's going on. Ultimately, you can condense the three lines down to this single line of code:

```
self.lblDemo.text = countries[keys[row]]
```

Adding Items to a Dictionary

After a Dictionary is created, you can add more key-value pairs to it with subscript syntax by specifying a key that doesn't already exist. For example:

```
countries["EG"] = "Egypt"
```

This adds a new **EG: Egypt** key-value pair to the countries **Dictionary**.

Changing Existing Dictionary Items

Change the value of an existing **Dictionary** item using subscript syntax by specifying an existing key. For example, the following code changes the value associated with the **CH** key to **China** (although it really isn't China):

```
countries["CH"] = "China"
```

You can also use a Dictionary's **updateValue** method to update an existing item. This option provides a bit more information, because the method returns the old value of the key-value pair. This lets you check if an update has taken place, because the method returns **nil** if it can't find the specified key. Here's an example:

```
let oldValue: String? =
      countries.updateValue("China", forKey: "CH")
```

In this case, the **updateValue** method would return "Switzerland" as the old value.

Removing Dictionary Items

Use the **removeValueForKey** method to remove an item from a **Dictionary**. For example:

```
var oldValue = countries.removeValueForKey("CH")
```

The **removeValueForKey** method returns the value it just removed, or if the key isn't found, it returns **nil**.

The **removeAll** method removes all key-value pairs from the **Dictionary**. This method accepts a Boolean **keepCapacity** argument that allows you to specify if you want to keep the **Dictionary's** capacity.

Mutable and Immutable Collections

When you assign a collection to a variable, it is *mutable*, meaning it can be changed. However, if you assign a collection to a constant, the collection is *immutable*, meaning it cannot be changed.

Immutable means different things for Arrays and Dictionaries. You can change the content or individual items in an immutable array, but cannot change its size by adding and removing items. In contrast, you can't change the size or content of an immutable **Dictionary**.

Structures

Although not really a collection, Swift *structures* allow you to group values together. Structures allow you to group multiple items as a single unit. For example, SAT college admission scores typically have three numeric scores: writing, mathematics, and critical reading. You could store these in three different integer variables, but since they are related, it's best to store them as a group.

You worked with structures earlier in this book. The **CGRectMake** function returns a **CGRect** rectangle, a structure containing four floating point members—**x** and **y** coordinates as well as **height** and **width** values.

Comparing Structures and Classes

Swift's structures and classes are more similar than in other programming languages. However, classes have some important capabilities that structures do not:

- Inheritance (the ability to create subclasses)

- Checking the type of a class at run time

- A Deinitialization method for cleanup purposes

- Possible multiple references to a class instance.

The last item in the list points to a key difference between structures and classes. Structures are *value types* and classes are *reference types*.

In practical terms, a value type is copied when it is assigned to a variable or constant or passed to a method or function. In contrast, when a reference type is assigned to a variable or constant or is passed to a method or function, a reference to the original object is passed, rather than passing a copy.

Declaring a Structure

Declaring a structure is similar to declaring a class, except you use the **struct** keyword. For example, you can declare a structure that combines three scores and is called **SATScores**. For example:

```
struct SATScores {

    var writing: Int = 0
    var math: Int = 0
    var reading: Int = 0
}
```

This code declares a structure named **SATScores** with three members of type integer named **writing**, **math**, and **reading**. Because you have created a new data type called **SATScores**, you can declare variables to be of this new type. For example:

```
var scores : SATScores = SATScores()
```

This code declares a variable named **scores** of type **SATScores**. In the same way you can declare variables of type integer, string, and BOOL, you can also declare variables of type **SATScores**.

Accessing Members of a Structure

You access members of a structure using dot syntax. For example:

```
scores.math = 515
scores.reading = 501
scores.writing = 493
```

You can also initialize members of a structure with values separated by commas:

```
var scores : SATScores =
  SATScores(writing: 493, math: 515, reading: 501)
```

Choosing Between Structures and Classes

A structure is a good choice if you need a simple way to group several related values. However, if you also need inheritance, or if the properties you need to add to the class or structure are reference types, creating a class is a better choice.

Working With Tuples

Swift's *tuples* provide a way to create a group of related values. Unlike arrays and dictionaries, a tuple can contain values of different types. Tuples are particularly useful in returning multiple values from a method.

Let's look at an example that demonstrates how tuples can be used in your apps.

1. If you have another project open, close it by selecting **File > Close Project** from the Xcode menu.

2. Select **File > Open...** from the Xcode menu, and in the **Open** dialog, navigate to the folder where you have stored this book's sample code. Expand the **TuplesDemo** folder, select the **TuplesDemo.xcodeproj** file and then click **Open**.

3. Let's run the project to get an overview of what the app does. Click Xcode's

176

Run button, and when the app appears in the Simulator, you should see the scene shown in Figure 10.6.

*Figure 10.6 The **TuplesDemo** main scene*

This is a very simple app that allows you to add new Locations to the app's database using Core Data.

4. Without entering a location name, click the **Add Location** button. You should see an alert saying you must enter a location name (Figure 10.7).

*Figure 10.7 The **TuplesDemo** required fields alert*

5. Click **OK** to close the alert. Now enter a **Location Name** (e.g. Los Angeles, Paris, Beijing) and click **Add Location** again. You should see

the alert shown in Figure 10.8 indicating the location was successfully saved to the database.

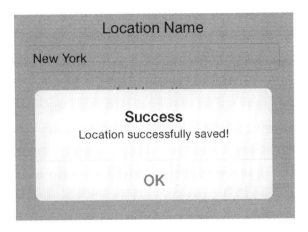

Figure 10.8 The location was successfully saved!

6. Go back to Xcode and click **Stop**. Let's look at the code that uses tuples to make all this happen.

7. Expand the **Business Layer** group and select the **mmBusinessObject.swift** file in the Project Navigator. Near the top of the file, check out the **saveEntity** method declaration:

```
func saveEntity(entity: NSManagedObject) ->
        (state: SaveState, message: String?)
{
```

8. Take a close look at the return value:

```
(state: SaveState, message: String?)
```

This declaration tells you that the **saveEntity** method returns a tuple containing two named return values. The first is named **state** and its type is **SaveState**. The second is named **message** and its type is **String?**.

SaveState is an enumeration declared at the top of the **mmBusinessObject.swift** code file:

```
enum SaveState {
    case Error, RulesBroken, SaveComplete
}
```

You will learn much more about enumerations in *Chapter 14: Comments, Constants, and Enumerations*, but for now you just need to know the **SaveState** enumeration contains three possible values reflecting three possible outcomes of saving the entity to the database:

- **Error** - An error occurred.

- **RulesBroken** - A business rule was broken (usually a required field is left empty.)

- **SaveComplete** - The entity was successfully saved.

We *could* just return the **SaveState** value from this method, but we can create a better interface for the **mmBusinessObject** class by also returning a message that contains a further explanation of what happened. That's where tuples come to the rescue!

9. Notice there are two variables at the top of the **saveEntity** method. The **saveState** variable stores the result of the **saveEntity** operation, and the **saveMessage** variable contains any message we want to return from this method.

```
func saveEntity(entity: NSManagedObject) ->
        (save: SaveState, message: String?)
{
        var saveState: SaveState
        var saveMessage: String?
```

The code beneath the variables is a bit complex and includes nested **if** statements. You will learn more about if statements in *Chapter 12: Conditional Statements*, but for now you just need to know these two variables get set based on the result of the save operation.

10. Now look at the **return** statement at the bottom of the method:

```
return (state: saveState, message: saveMessage)
```

To create a named tuple return value, specify the name, a colon and the value. Separate the values with a comma and place the return values within parentheses.

Note that you can name the values in a Swift tuple. This make them far more useful than in other languages where you can't do this. You're not required to name the tuple values, but naming them makes your code far more readable and intuitive.

11. Let's see how the tuple return values are handled. Click **ViewController.swift** in the Project Navigator.

12. Check out the third line of code in the **addLocation** method:

```
// Save the entity
var result: (state: SaveState, message: String?) =
      self.location.saveEntity(locationEntity)
```

Notice the type of the **result** variable is the same as the type returned from the **saveEntity** method. It's a tuple! Since each tuple value is named, the purpose of each value is crystal clear.

I included the **result** variable's type so you can more clearly understand the code. However, you can remove the type declaration and Swift will figure it out for you using type inference.

The rest of the code uses a **switch** statement to perform actions and display messages based on the values in the tuple. In *Chapter 12: Conditional Statements* you will gain a greater understanding of how **switch** statements work.

For now, here are some ground rules for tuples:

- The values contained in a tuple can be of any type.

- Any number of values can be in a tuple, although more than two or three becomes cumbersome.

- You can decompose the values contained in a tuple into individual variables or constants:

```
let (state, message) = result
```

- If you only need one of the tuple's values, you can use an underscore to ignore the other values:

```
let (state, _) = result
```

- You can also access the values in a tuple using a numeric index:

```
let state = result.0
```

```
let message = result.1
```

- It's best to name the values in the tuple and then access the values using those names:

```
var result: (state: SaveState, msg: String?) =
        self.location.saveEntity(locationEntity)
let state = result.state
let message = result.msg
```

Multidimensional Arrays

You can create arrays with more than one dimension. In Swift, you effectively create an "array of arrays" where each member of an array contains a reference to another array. For example, in Figure 10.9, each element in the array on the left references a second array on the right containing three elements.

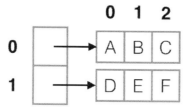

Figure 10.9 A two-dimensional array

You declare a multidimensional array by nesting pairs of square brackets.

For example, this code declares a two-dimensional integer array:

```
var array2D: [[Int]]
```

You initialize an empty multidimensional array like this:

```
var array2D: [[Int]] = [[Int]]()
```

The two-dimension string array in Figure 10.9 is sized and initialized like this:

```
var array2D:[[String]] = [["A","B","C"],["D","E","F"]]
```

You reference items in a multidimensional array using two sets of square brackets. The first set of brackets references the outer array, and the second set the inner array. For example, given the array in Figure 10.9:

- `array2D[0][1]` references the letter "B".

- `array2D[1][0]` references the letter "D".

- `array2D[1]` references the entire array "D, E, F".

Creating Custom Collections

Swift's collection classes serve most needs for your iOS apps. However, in special cases, you may want to declare your own collection class. This requires the use of Swift's subscripts.

Let's see how we can use subscripts to create a **Chessboard** class that allows us to access individual squares on the board.

Figure 10.10 shows a chessboard with slightly modified algebraic notation—a common notation used to record a game of chess.

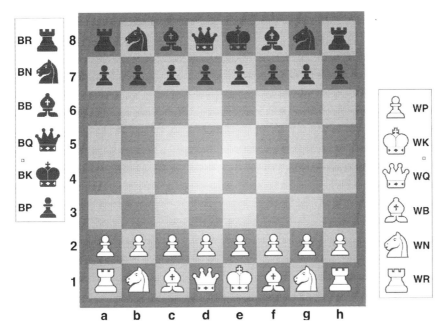

Figure 10.10 A chessboard with algebraic notation

The rows on the board are numbered **1** through **8**, and the columns **a** through **h**. Each chess piece has a two-character designation. Black pieces begin with the letter **B** and white with the letter **W**. The second letter specifies the type of pieces: **R**=Rook, **N**=Knight, **B**=Bishop, **Q**=Queen, **K**=King, **P**=Pawn.

To reference a specific square on the chessboard, you use a two-character notation comprising column/row. For example, the square at the bottom-left corner of the board is **a1**. The square at the top-right corner is **h8**.

To model this column/row notation, we can create a custom subscript for a **Chessboard** class and use this in combination with a two-dimensional string array. This allows us to reference a square like this:

```
chessBoard["a1"]
```

Subscript Syntax

Here is the syntax for declaring a subscript in Swift:

```
subscript(index: Type) -> Type {

    get {
    // Code that returns value
    }
    set {
    // Code that sets value
    }
}
```

This syntax is similar to computed properties. You begin the declaration with the **subscript** keyword, followed by one or more input parameters that accept the value(s) used to retrieve a specific item from the collection. Next, you specify the return type, which is the type of the value returned from the collection.

The **get** method is executed when retrieving a value from the collection, and the **set** method is executed when storing an item into the collection. You can create a read-only collection by leaving out the **set** method.

The Chessboard Sample

Let's take a look at sample code that demonstrates two subscripts in action.

1. Select **File > Open...** from the Xcode menu. In the **Open** dialog, navigate to the folder where you have stored this book's sample code.

2. Expand the **Subscripts** folder, select the **Subscripts.playground** file and then click **Open**.

At the top of the playground, a **Chessboard** class is declared. This class has a two-dimensional string array named **board** that models the squares on a chessboard. It contains an array of eight elements, representing the rows on a chessboard. Each row element contains another array of eight elements that represent the columns on a chessboard:

```
class ChessBoard {

    var board:[[String]] =
      [["WR","WN","WB","WQ","WK","WB","WN","WR"],
       ["WP","WP","WP","WP","WP","WP","WP","WP"],
       ["","","","","","","",""],
       ["","","","","","","",""],
       ["","","","","","","",""],
       ["","","","","","","",""],
       ["BP","BP","BP","BP","BP","BP","WP","BP"],
       ["BR","BN","BB","BQ","BK","BB","BN","BR"]]
```

The **board** array is initialized with chess pieces located on squares as at the start of a game (Figure 10.10).

The **Chessboard** class also has two dictionaries:

```
let rows: Dictionary<String, Int> =
  ["a":0,"b":1,"c":2,"d":3,"e":4,"f":5,"g":6,"h":7]

let columns: Dictionary<String, Int> =
  ["1":0,"2":1,"3":2,"4":3,"5":4,"6":5,"7":6,"8":7]
```

The **rows** dictionary accepts a row letter and returns the corresponding row number. The **columns** dictionary accepts a column string, and returns the corresponding column number. We *could* dispose of the **columns** array and just perform a simple math calculation to determine the column number. But, for the sake of discoverability, I chose to use a similar methodology for both rows and columns (choosing clarity over cleverness.)

Next in the playground is the first subscript declaration:

```
subscript(square: String) -> String? {

        get {
            var piece: String? = nil

            // Make sure there are two characters
```

```
    if countElements(square) == 2
    {
    // Convert to lowercase
    let sq = square.lowercaseString

    // Get the row character
    let index = advance(sq.startIndex, 1)
    var rowChar = sq.substringToIndex(index)

    // Convert row character to a row number
    if let rowNumber = rows[rowChar]
    {
        // Get the column character
        var columnChar =
            square.substringFromIndex(index)

        // Convert column character to a column #
        if let columnNumber = columns[columnChar] {
            // Get the piece at the row/column
            piece = board[columnNumber][rowNumber]
        }
    }
    }
    return piece
}
}
```

This subscript accepts a **String** parameter (the column/row pair) and returns an optional **String** (the chess piece). The return value must be optional, because you can pass in an invalid column/row (such as **z9**) in which case the subscript returns **nil**.

The subscript's **get** method (*getter*) takes the first character in the string and retrieves the corresponding row number from the **rows** dictionary. It then takes the second character in the string and retrieves the corresponding column number from the **columns** dictionary. If either the row or column is not found in the dictionary, the getter returns **nil**.

If the column and row numbers are valid, they are used to retrieve the chess piece that is on the corresponding square in the two-dimensional **board** array:

```
piece = board[columnNumber][rowNumber]
```

This chess piece is then returned from the getter.

To try out this subscript, at the bottom of the playground, try entering different column/row pairs. For example, Figure 10.11 shows the results of typing two valid and one invalid column/row pairs.

```
board["a1"]                        {Some "WR"}
board["h8"]                        {Some "BR"}
board["g9"]                        nil
```

Figure 10.11 Testing the first subscript

Look further down in the playground to see the second subscript declared for the **Chessboard** class:

```
// Gets piece on specified row/column (e.g. "C",7)
subscript(row: Character, column: Int) -> String? {
      get {
          var piece: String? = nil

          // Convert row character to a row number
          if let rowNumber = rows[String(row)] {

              // Convert column to a column number
              if let columnNumber = columns[String(column)] {
                  piece = board[column - 1][rowNumber]
              }
          }
          return piece

      }
}
```

This subscript accepts a **row** parameter of type **Character** and a **column** parameter of type **Int** (for example, "C",7), and returns the chess piece as an optional **String**. Subscripts can accept any number and type of input parameters and return any type.

At the bottom of the playground, try different **row, column** combinations as in Figure 10.12.

```
board["a",1]                       {Some "WR"}
board["h",8]                       {Some "BR"}
board["g",9]                       nil
```

Figure 10.12 Testing the second subscript

This subscript needs less error-checking code because the input parameters are more strictly defined. However, it's less natural to use, because you have to pass each character separately rather than using the more familiar row/column combination of the first subscript.

I added this second subscript to show you how to accept multiple parameters. Ultimately, I would choose the first subscript in a real-world app because, even though I had to initially write a little more code, it produced a class with a more intuitive interface.

Summary

In this chapter, you learned these principles regarding Swift collections:

- A **collection** is a grouping of one or more related objects. Swift collection classes such as **Array** and **Dictionary** allow you to group multiple items into a single collection.

- It's perfectly fine to use a mix of Swift and Cocoa Touch collection classes in your apps.

The Array Class

- The **Array** class is one of the most basic kinds of Swift collections. You can declare an array like this:

```
var names: Array<String> = ["Jordan",
  "Timothy", "Alexander", "Mia", "Luca"]
```

- Swift infers the type of items contained in the array so you don't need to explicitly declare it. This means you could declare the array like this:

```
var names = ["Jordan", "Timothy", "Alexander",
    "Mia", "Luca"]
```

- To initialize an empty array, you specify the type of the array in square brackets followed by parentheses:

```
var ages = [Int]()
```

- To initialize an array with a given number of elements all set to the same value, use this initializer:

```
var a = Array(count: 10, repeatedValue: 0.0)
```

- To find out how many items are in an **Array**, you can access its **count** property.

- To test if an array is empty, check if its **count** is equal to zero or you can check its **isEmpty** property.

- In Swift, collections are zero-based. This means the first item in the collection is item zero, the second is item one, and so on.

- An index references an item by its numeric position in the collection. You can get an item from an **Array** by placing the index number between square brackets. This is known as *subscript syntax.*

- Swift has a **find()** function you can use to find a particular item in an Array. For example:

```
var itemNumber : Int? = find(self.names, "Luca")
```

- Swift provides **firstItem** and **lastItem** methods that make it easy to get the first and last item in an array.

- You can add a new item to the end of an array using the array's append method:

```
names.append("Ryan")
```

- You can append multiple items to an array using the addition assignment (+=) operator:

```
names += ["Brendan", "Patrick"]
```

- You can add items at a specific index of an array using its **insert** method:

```
names.insert("Markus", atIndex: 0)
```

- You can change an existing item in array using subscript syntax:

```
names[0] = "Sharlene"
```

- Four methods are available for removing items from an array:

  1. **removeLast** removes the last item from an array and returns the removed item.

  2. **removeAtIndex** removes the item at the specified index and returns the removed item.

  3. **removeRange** removes the items in the specified range, but doesn't return the removed items.

  4. **removeAllItems** clears all items from an array, but doesn't return the removed items. This method accepts a Boolean **keepCapacity** argument that allows you to specify if you want to keep the capacity (the amount of memory allocated) for the array.

- Swift's array class has a **reverse** method that returns an array with all items in reverse order from the source array.

The Dictionary Class

- A Dictionary is a collection of key-value pairs. The key is used to uniquely identify the entry, and the value is the item itself.

- The **Dictionary** class is an ***unordered collection***, meaning the **Dictionary** items are in no particular order.

- Here is the syntax for declaring a **Dictionary** type:

```
Dictionary<KeyType, ValueType>
```

- You initialize a dictionary by specifying the key and value pairs of each member separated by commas and within square brackets:

```
var countries: Dictionary<String, String> =
        ["AT": "Austria",
        "BG": "Bulgaria",
        "CH": "Switzerland",
        "DE": "Germany"]
```

- You don't need to specify the type of a Dictionary when you initialize it. You can just let Swift infer the type based on the values you use to initialize it.

- You can initialize an empty **Dictionary** like this:

```
var topTenList = Dictionary<Int, String>()
```

- To test if a Dictionary is empty, check its **isEmpty** property.

- You use a *key* to find a particular item in a **Dictionary**. For example:

```
var country: String? = countries["CH"]
```

- Swift Dictionaries have a **keys** property containing a list of all keys in the **Dictionary** and a **values** property containing a list of all the values in the **Dictionary**.

- After you create a Dictionary, you can add more key-value pairs to it with subscript syntax by specifying a key that doesn't already exist. For example:

```
countries["EG"] = "Egypt"
```

- Change the value of an existing **Dictionary** item using subscript syntax by specifying an existing key. For example:

```
countries["CH"] = "China"
```

- Use the **removeValueForKey** method to remove an item from a Dictionary. For example:

```
var oldValue =
      countries.removeValueForKey("CH")
```

The **removeValueForKey** method returns the value it just removed, or if the key wasn't found, it returns **nil**.

- The **removeAll** method removes all key-value pairs from the **Dictionary**. This method accepts a Boolean **keepCapacity** argument that allows you to specify if you want to keep the **Dictionary's** capacity.

- When you assign a collection to a variable, it is *mutable*, meaning that it can be changed. However, if you assign a collection to a constant, the collection is immutable, meaning it cannot be changed.

- *Immutable* means different things for Arrays and Dictionaries. You can change the content or individual items in an immutable array, but cannot change its size by adding and removing items. In contrast, you can't change the size or content of an immutable **Dictionary**.

Structures

- Although not really a collection, Swift structures allow you to group multiple items as a single unit.

- Declaring a structure is similar to declaring a class, except you use the **struct** keyword. For example, declare a structure that combines three scores and is called **SATScores**. For example:

```
struct SATScores {
    var writing: Int = 0
    var math: Int = 0
    var reading: Int = 0
}
```

- Classes have some important capabilities that structures do not:

  - Inheritance (the ability to create subclasses)

  - Checking the type of a class at run time

  - A Deinitialization method for cleanup purposes

  - Possible multiple references to a class instance.

- Structures are *value types* and classes are *reference types*.

- You access members of a structure using dot syntax. For example:

```
scores.math = 515
scores.reading = 501
scores.writing = 493
```

- Initialize members of a structure with values separated by commas:

```
var scores : SATScores =
  SATScores(writing:493, math:515, reading:501)
```

- A structure is a good choice if you need a simple way to group several related values. However, if you also need inheritance, or if the properties you need to add to the class or structure are reference types, creating a class is a better choice.

Tuples

- Tuples provide a way to create a group of related values that can be of different types. They are particularly useful in returning multiple values from a method.

- To declare a return type that is a tuple, just place the data types in parentheses, separated by a comma:

```
func saveEntity(entity: NSManagedObject) ->
        (SaveState, String?)
```

- To create a tuple return value, separate the values by a comma and place them within parentheses:

```
return (state, saveMessage)
```

- The values contained in a tuple can be of any type.

- Any number of values can be in a tuple, although more than two or three becomes cumbersome.

- You can decompose the values contained in a tuple into individual variables or constants:

```
let (state, message) = result
```

- If you only need one of the tuple's values you can use an underscore to ignore the other values:

```
let (state, _) = result
```

- You can also access the values in a tuple using a numeric index:

```
let state = result.0
let message = result.1
```

- A better approach is to name the values in the tuple and then access them using those names:

```
var result: (state: SaveState, msg: String?) =
        self.location.saveEntity(locationEntity)

let state = result.state
let message = result.msg
```

Multidimensional Arrays

- You can create arrays with more than one dimension. In Swift, you effectively create an "array of arrays" where each member of an array, contains a reference to another array.

- You declare a multidimensional array by nesting pairs of square brackets. For example:

```
var array2D: [[Int]]
```

- You initialize empty multidimensional arrays like this:

```
var array2D: [[Int]] = [[Int]]()
```

- You can create and initialize a two-dimensional string array like this:

```
var a2D:[[String]] = [["A","B","C"],["D","E","F"]]
```

- You reference items in a multidimensional array using two sets of square brackets. The first set of brackets references the outer array, and the second set the inner array. For example:

```
array2D[0][1]
```

Subscripts for Your Custom Types

- In most cases, Swift's collection classes will serve all your needs for your iOS apps. However, in special cases, you may want to declare your own collection class, which requires the use of Swift's subscripts.

- Here is the syntax for declaring a subscript in Swift:

```
subscript(index: Type) -> Type {

    get {
        // Code that returns value
    }
    get {
        // Code that sets value
    }
}
```

The syntax is similar to computed properties. You begin the declaration with the **subscript** keyword, followed by one or more input parameters that accept the value(s) used to retrieve a specific item from the collection. Next, you specify the return type, which is the type of the value returned from the collection.

- A subscript's **get** method is executed when retrieving a value from the collection, and its **set** method is executed when storing an item into the collection.

- You can create a read-only collection by leaving out the **set** method.

- Subscripts can accept any number and type of input parameters and return any type.

Exercise 10.1

In this exercise, you perform one of the most common tasks associated with collections—displaying a list.

1. In the **CollectionsDemo** project, add a new class named **Continent**.

2. Add an instance method to the **Continent** class named **getAllContinents** that returns an array of all continents (Africa, Antarctica, Asia, Australia, Europe, North America, South America).

3. In the **ViewController** class, add a **continent** property to hold a reference to a **Continent** object.

4. In the **ViewController** class, add a **continents** array to hold the list of continents returned from the **getAllContinents** method.

5. In the **viewDidLoad** method, add code to call the continent object's

getAllContinents method and store the result in the **continents** array.

6. Change the **ViewController** class to display the list of continents. This requires changes to these methods:

- **viewDidLoad**

- **pickerView:numberOfRowsInComponent:**

- **pickerView:titleForRow:forComponent:**

- **pickerView:didSelectRow:inComponent:**

Solution Movie 10.1

To see a video providing the solution for this exercise, you can enter the link below in your Web browser to see each step performed for you.

Movie 10.1

http://www.iOSAppsForNonProgrammers.com/B4M101.html

Chapter 11: Looping Statements

Sometimes, we need to loop through all of the items in a collection. Swift has a few looping statements that let you do just that. In fact, you can use looping statements to repeatedly execute a set of code for a wide variety of purposes. You will also get more hands-on experience with Xcode's playgrounds.

Sections in This Chapter

Creating a New Playground

Let's create a playground we can use to experiment with Swift's looping statements.

1. Select **File** > **New** > **Playground** in the Xcode menu.

2. In the Create Playground dialog, set the **Name** to **LoopingStatements**, and the **Platform** to **iOS** as Figure 11.1 shows.

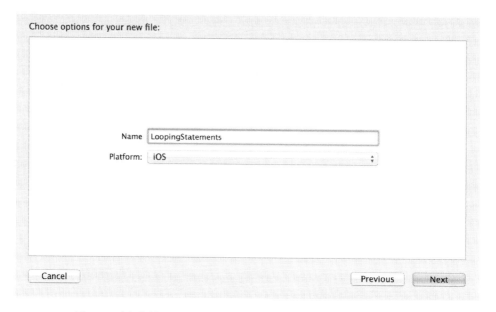

Choose options for your new file:

Name   LoopingStatements

Platform: iOS

Cancel   Previous   Next

*Figure 11.1 Name the playground **LoopingStatements***

3. In the **Name** box, enter **LoopingStatements**, and in the **Platform** box, enter **iOS**. Then, click **Next**.

4. In the Save dialog, select the folder where you want to save the playground (I like to use the **Documents** folder), and then click **Create**.

   Now, you should now see a new playground.

5. Delete the following line of code from the left side of the playground:

   ```
   var str = "Hello, playground"
   ```

6. Now let's display the Assistant Editor at the bottom of the playground. In the Xcode menu, select **View** > **Assistant Editor** > **Assistant Editors on Bottom**.

Now you're ready to learn about looping statements!

Swift's Looping Statements

The primary looping statements in Swift are:

- **for-condition-increment** loop

- **for-in** loop

- **while** loop

- **do-while** loop

Let's take a close look at each of these loops.

for-condition-increment Loop

In Swift, there are two different **for** loops you can use to repeat the execution of a block of code.

Here is the syntax of the **for-condition-increment** loop:

```
for initialization; condition; increment
{
        statements
}
```

This type of **for** statement is typically used to loop a specified number of times.

- The *initialization* expression executes before the first iteration of the **for** loop is run. Normally, it is used to initialize an index variable that specifies the current item number.

- The loop **condition** is tested at the top of the **for** loop before each iteration to determine if another iteration should be executed.

- The *statements* between curly braces are executed.

- The loop *increment* is executed at the bottom of the **for** loop after each iteration. It's normally used to increment the index variable created in the initialization expression. Although this is less common, you can also decrement the index to go backward through a loop, or even loop through every other item by setting the increment statement to **index += 2**.

Follow these steps to see a **for-condition-increment** loop in action:

1. Add the following code below the **import** statement in the playground. It creates an array of colors:

```
var colors = ["Red", "Orange", "Yellow",
  "Green", "Blue", "Indigo", "Violet"]
```

   As soon as you do this, you can see the items in the array displayed in the Results sidebar on the right.

2. Add the following code below the array declaration:

```
for var index = 0; index < colors.count; index++ {

   println("For loop color: \(colors[index])")
}
```

3. When you finish entering this code, the text **(7 times)** appears in the Result sidebar on the right. This indicates that this loop ran seven times—once for each item in the **colors** array.

With the help of the image below, let's look at this code in the order it runs in:

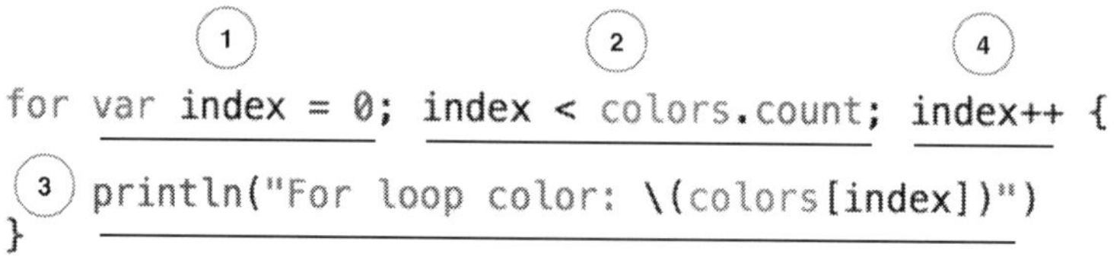

Here's a plain-text description of the animation:

1. The *initialization* expression executes just once right before the first iteration of the loop. In this example, it creates an integer variable named **index** and sets its value to zero.

2. The loop *condition* check runs next. In this example, it checks to see if the **index** is less than the number of items in the **colors** array. If it's less, the statements between the curly braces are executed. Otherwise, the loop is exited, and the next line of code after the loop is executed.

3. The code between the **for** statement's curly braces runs next. The **println** statement uses the **index** to retrieve an object from the **colors** array. The first time through, the **index** is set to zero; the next time through, it's set to one, and so on. In *Chapter 13: Working With Strings,* you'll learn more about the special notation in the **println** command that inserts the color from the array into the string.

4. The loop *expression* increments the **index** variable at the end of the loop, and then control goes back to step 2, where the loop condition is checked again.

Let's go back to the playground for a closer look at the **for-condition-increment** loop.

1. Hover your mouse pointer to the right of the **(7 times)** result in the Results sidebar and click the Value History button (Figure 11.2).

*Figure 11.2 Click the **Value History** button.*

This displays the Console Output panel at the bottom of the playground (Figure 11.3).

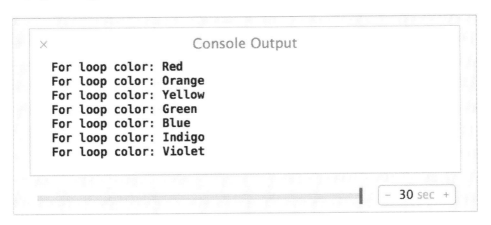

Figure 11.3 The Console Output panel

You can see the Console displays the output of the **println** statement for each iteration of the **for** loop, which worked exactly as it should!

for-in Loop

The second type of Swift **for** loop is called the **for-in** loop, designed especially for looping through collections.

The **for-in** loop doesn't require that you keep track of either the number of items in the collection or the current index number. The loop is automatically executed once for each item in the collection.

Here is the syntax of the **for-in** statement:

```
for item in collection {

        statements
}
```

In a **for-in** loop:

- *item* represents a single item in the collection.

- *collection* specifies the collection containing the items that you want to loop through.

- *statements* represents the statements enclosed in curly braces executed for each iteration of the loop.

To see the **for-in** loop in action, follow these steps:

1. Add the following code below the **for-condition-increment** loop you created in the previous section:

```
for color in colors {
    println("For-in loop color \(color)")
}
```

This code is much simpler than the **for-condition-increment** loop! In each of the **for-in** loop's iterations, the next item is automatically retrieved from the **colors** array and stored in the **color** variable for you, and then the code between the curly braces executes. This continues until the statements for all items in the collection are executed.

2. In the Console Output panel at the bottom of the playground, you can see the output of the **for-in** loop (Figure 11.4) in addition to the output of the previous **for** loop.

```
                    Console Output
 ×
 For loop color: Red
 For loop color: Orange
 For loop color: Yellow
 For loop color: Green
 For loop color: Blue
 For loop color: Indigo
 For loop color: Violet
 For-in loop color Red
 For-in loop color Orange
 For-in loop color Yellow
 For-in loop color Green
 For-in loop color Blue
 For-in loop color Indigo
 For-in loop color Violet
```

*Figure 11.4 The **for-in** loop output*

When using the **for-in** loop, never change the collection you are iterating over by adding or removing items. If you change the collection, you will get an error at run time!

If you need both the index number and value of each array item, you can use Swift's **enumerate()** function. For example:

```
for (index, color) in enumerate(colors) {
    println("Color \(index) - \(color)")
}
```

The **enumerate()** function returns a tuple containing the index number and value of the current array item. This **for-in** loop produces the Console Output in Figure 11.5.

```
                    Console Output
 ×
 Color 0 - Red
 Color 1 - Orange
 Color 2 - Yellow
 Color 3 - Green
 Color 4 - Blue
 Color 5 - Indigo
 Color 6 - Violet
```

*Figure 11.5 The **for-in** loop with **enumerate()** output*

Using the Range Operators

You can use Swift's range operators along with the **for-in** loop to iterate over a range of numbers.

For example, add the following code to the playground:

```
for index in 0...6 {
    println("For-in loop color: \(colors[index])")
}
```

This code uses Swift's closed range operator (**...**) to iterate a range of numbers from 0 to 6 inclusive.

However, to make this code less brittle, you should use Swift's half-open range operator (**..<**) along with the **colors** array's **count** property:

```
for index in 0..<colors.count {
    println("For-in loop color: \(colors[index])")
}
```

In this example, the half-open range operator (**..<**) defines a range that runs from 0 to 7 (the value of **colors.count**) but does not include 7. This is very useful for zero-based collections.

In both examples, **index** is a constant whose value is initially set to 0. With each iteration of the loop the **index** value is updated to the next number in the range and the statement between curly braces is executed until the end of the range is reached.

Notice the **index** constant is implicitly declared without the need for a **let** declaration. You can give the constant any name you want. However, if you don't need to use the index value in the body of the **for-in** loop, you can replace it with an underscore:

```
for _ in 0..<colors.count {
```

In many situations, you can use this simpler **for-in** loop to replace the **for-condition-increment** loop. The **for-in** loop in this example can replace this equivalent **for-condition-increment** loop:

```
for var index = 0; index < colors.count; index++ {
```

```
    println("For loop color: \(colors[index])")
}
```

As you can see, the **for-in** version of the loop is much simpler and easier to read.

while Loop

The **while** loop provides another way to loop through a set of statements. Here is the syntax of the **while** loop:

```
while condition {
        statements
}
```

The *expression* is evaluated at the top of the loop for every iteration. If it evaluates to true, the *statements* are executed; otherwise, the loop exits and passes control to the next statement after the closing curly brace.

To see the while statement in action, follow these steps:

1. Add the following **while** loop below the **for-in** loop you created in the previous section:

   ```
   var index = 0
   while index < colors.count {

       println("While loop color: \(colors[index])")
        index++
   }
   ```

   The first line of code creates an integer variable named **index** and initializes it to zero before the **while** loop begins. As each iteration of the loop starts, the condition checks to see if the **index** is less than the number of items in the **names** array. If it is, the **println** statement executes. Otherwise, the **while** loop is exited.

2. Look in the Console Output pane, and you should see the "While loop color" items displayed there.

If you are thinking you could have used a **for** loop in this situation, you are right! Ultimately, you can use a **for** loop in place of a **while** loop and vice versa.

do-while Loop

The Swift **do-while** loop provides another looping option with a twist—the condition that determines if the associated statements should be executed is checked at the *bottom* rather than *top* of the loop. This means the statements always run at least once.

Here is the syntax of the do statement:

```
do {
        statements
} while ( expression )
```

When the **do** loop is first executed, the statements within curly braces are executed unconditionally. At the bottom of the loop, the expression is evaluated. If it evaluates to **true**, the loop is executed again. If it evaluates to **false**, execution passes to the statement immediately after the **do** statement.

Let's see how the **do-while** statement works.

1. Add the following code to the playground directly below the **while** loop you created in the previous section:

    ```
    var doIndex = 0
    do {
        println("Do-while color: \(colors[doIndex])")
        doIndex++
    } while doIndex < colors.count
    ```

2. Now you should see the "Do-while color" items displayed in the Console Output pane.

Avoiding Infinite Loops

An infinite loop is a looping statement that continues forever. You can inadvertently create an infinite loop if the condition checked at the beginning or end of the loop never evaluates to **false**. To see this in action, go back to the **do-while** loop you just created and comment out the line that increments **doIndex** as shown here:

```
var doIndex = 0
do {
    println("Do-while color: \" \(colors[doIndex])")
```

```
//doIndex++
} while doIndex < colors.count
```

Looking in the Results sidebar, you'll see the number of times the loop has run increasing dramatically!

The reason for the infinite loop is that **doIndex** is always set to zero—it's never incremented in the **while** loop, so it is always less than the value of **colors.count**. To fix the problem, just delete the two forward slashes, which uncomments the line and causes the **doIndex** value to increment again.

Summary

for-condition-increment Loop

- The **for-condition-increment** loop is typically used to loop a specified number of times.

- An example of a **for** loop:

```
for var index = 0; index < colors.count; index++ {

    println("For loop color: \(colors[index])")
}
```

- The *initialization* expression (**var index = 0**) executes before the first iteration of the **for** loop is run. Normally it is used to initialize an index variable that specifies the current item number.

- The loop *condition* (**index < colors.count**) is tested at the top of the **for** loop before each iteration to determine if another iteration should be executed.

- If the condition is met, the *statements* between curly braces are executed.

- The loop *increment* (**index++**) is executed at the bottom of the **for** loop after each iteration. It's normally used to increment the index variable created in the initialization expression.

for-in Loop

- An example of a for-in loop:

```
for color in colors {
    println("For-in loop color \(color)")
}
```

The **for-in** loop doesn't require you to keep track of either the number of items in the collection or the current index number. The loop is automatically executed once for each item in a collection.

- In each **for-in** loop iteration, the next item is automatically retrieved from the array and stored in the variable for you (the **color** variable in this example). Afterward, the code between the curly braces executes. This continues until the statements have been executed for all items in the collection.

- If you need both the index number and value of each array item, you can use Swift's **enumerate()** function:

```
for (index, color) in enumerate(colors) {
    println("Color \(index) - \(color)")
}
```

for-in Loop With Range Operators

- You can use Swift's range operators along with the **for-in** loop to iterate over a range of numbers. For example, this code uses the closed range operator:

```
for i in 0...6 {
    println("For-in loop color: \(colors[i])")
}
```

- You can use Swift's half-open range operator (..<) along with an array's **count** property:

```
for i in 0..<colors.count {
    println("For-in loop color: \(colors[i])")
}
```

In this example, the half-open range operator defines a range that runs from 0 to the array's **count** value, but does not include the **count** value.

- In a for-in loop that uses a range operator, **i** is a constant whose value is initially set to 0. With each iteration of the loop the value of **i** is updated to the next number in the range. The statements between curly braces are executed until the end of the range is reached.

- In a for-in loop that uses a range operator, the **i** constant is implicitly declared without the need for a **let** declaration. (You can give the constant any name you want.)

- If you don't use the index value in the body of the **for-in** loop, you can replace it with an underscore:

```
for _ in 0..<colors.count {
```

- In many situations, you can use this simpler **for-in** loop with a range operator to replace the **for-condition-increment** loop.

while Loop

- An example of a **while** loop:

```
var index = 0
while index < colors.count {
  println("While loop color: \(colors[index])")
  index++
}
```
As each loop iteration starts, the condition is checked. If the condition is **true**, the statements between curly braces are executed. If the condition is **false**, the while loop is exited.

do-while Loop

- An example of a **do-while** loop:

```
var doIndex = 0
do {
  println("Do-while color: " \(colors[doIndex])")
  doIndex++
} while doIndex < colors.count
```

The condition that determines if the statements should be executed is checked at the bottom rather than top of the loop. This means the statements always run at least once.

Infinite Loops

- To avoid infinite loops, make sure the condition in your loop eventually evaluates to **false**. This usually means making sure the index value gets incremented.

Exercise 11.1

In this exercise you will use what you have learned about looping statements to work with items in an array.

1. Create a playground named **Looping.playground**.

2. In the playground, create a variable named **iOSDevices** that holds a **String** array of iOS device categories: iPhone, iPad, iPod Touch

3. Use a **for-in** loop and a **println()** statement to display each item in the array. (To see the results of the **println()** statement, select **View > Assistant Editor > Show Assistant Editor** from the Xcode menu.)

4. Use a **for-in** loop with range operators and a **println()** statement to display each item in the array.

5. Use a **for-in** loop with Swift's **enumerate()** function and a **println()** statement to display each item in the array, prefixed by item number, starting with **1**.

Solution Movie 11.1

To see a video providing the solution for this exercise, you can enter the link below in your Web browser to see each step performed for you.

Movie 11.1

http://www.iOSAppsForNonProgrammers.com/B4M111.html

Chapter 12: Conditional Statements

Conditional statements are a core programming concept you need to master before writing any real-world apps. Conditions allow you execute one set of code under one condition and one or more sets of code under other conditions. This chapter gives you real-world examples of conditional statements that will help you fully grasp the concepts.

Sections in This Chapter

The Sample Code

Looking at conditional statements in the context of an app is the best way to learn about them, so let's dive right into this chapter's sample code project.

1. If you have another project open, close it by selecting **File > Close Project** from the Xcode menu.

2. Open the **ConditionalStatementsDemo** project by selecting **File > Open...** from the Xcode menu. In the **Open** dialog, navigate to the folder where you have stored this book's sample code. Drill down into the **ConditionalStatementsDemo** folder, select the **ConditionalStatementsDemo.xcodeproj** file, and then click **Open**.

3. In the Project Navigator, click the gray triangle to the left of the **ConditionalStatementsDemo** node to expand it, and then click the gray arrow to the left of the **ConditionalStatements** sub node to expand it, and finally select the **Main.storyboard** file. You will see the view displayed in Figure 12.1. This is a very simple view containing a label, a picker view, and a switch control with another label.

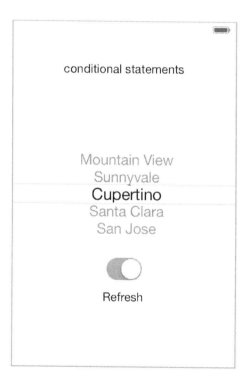

Figure 12.1 The ConditionalStatementsDemo scene

4. Click Xcode's **Run** button to see this simple app run in the iOS Simulator. Notice it looks a little different when you run it. Rather than listing California cities in the picker view, it lists two options—**Upper Case** and **Lower Case** (Figure 12.2).

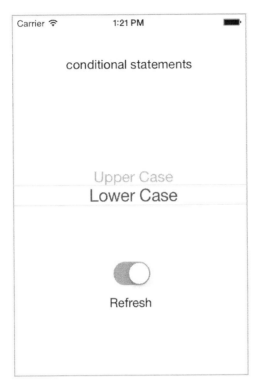

Figure 12.2 The picker view at run time

For now, note that selecting any option in the picker view or changing the setting of the **Refresh** switch has no effect.

5. Go back to Xcode and click the **Stop** button. In the Project Navigator, select the **ViewController.swift** file. Notice the **@IBOutlet** property declarations at the top of the code window:

```
@IBOutlet weak var lblDemo: UILabel!
@IBOutlet weak var pckOptions: UIPickerView!
@IBOutlet weak var swtRefresh: UISwitch!
```

The **lblDemo** property references the label at the top of the view; **pckOptions** references the picker view; and **swtRefresh** references the switch control.

6. Below the **@IBOutlet** declarations, notice a declaration for an array property named **choices**.

```
var choices = ["Upper Case", "Lower Case"]
```

The code initializes the **choices** array with the two options that you saw at run time: "Upper Case" and "Lower Case."

Check out the last line of code in the viewDidLoad method:

```
self.pckOptions.selectRow(1, inComponent: 0,
        animated: false)
```

This code sets the default selection in the picker view to the second item in the **choices** array (remember, collections are zero-based, so the number 1 indicates the second item in the collection) using the picker view's **selectRow:inComponent:animated:** method.

Three other methods of interest are associated with the picker view:

1. The **pickerView:numberOfRowsInComponent:** method is called automatically by the picker view when it first loads items into its list. This method returns the **count** of items in the **choices** array.

2. The **pickerView:titleForRow:forComponent:** method is used at run time to get the title, or text to be displayed for each item. It is automatically called once for each row in the **choices** array.

3. The **pickerView:didSelectRow:inComponent:** method is called automatically when the user selects an item from the list. The second parameter, **row**, specifies the row the user has selected.

This third method is the main method of interest because the code in this method reacts to the user's selection.

if Statements

Swift's **if** statement allows you to run one or more lines of code if a particular condition is **true**. The **if** statement has the following syntax:

```
if condition {

        // statements to be executed

}
```

When creating an **if** statement, you first type **if**, and then enter an expression to be evaluated, and follow it with the code to be executed (if the evaluated expression is true) within curly braces. If it's not already open, in Xcode, open the **ConditionalStatements** project.

1. Go to the **pickerView:didSelectRow:InComponent:** method, and enter this code on an empty line between the method's curly braces:

    ```
    if row == 0 {
    ```

2. Press the **return** key and Xcode automatically adds a closing curly brace and places the cursor on the empty line between the curly braces:

    ```
    if row == 0 {

    }
    ```

3. Enter the following code between the curly braces:

    ```
    func pickerView(pickerView: UIPickerView,
        didSelectRow row: Int,
        inComponent component: Int) {

        if row == 0 {
            self.lblDemo.text =
                self.lblDemo.text?.uppercaseString
        }
    }
    ```

This method's code does the following:

*   It uses an **if** statement to see if the currently selected row is zero.

*   If the row is zero, it calls the **uppercaseString** method on the label's **text** object, converting the text string to uppercase.

*   It stores the uppercased return value back into the label's **text** property.

4. Add a breakpoint on the **if** statement by clicking to the left of it in the gutter (Figure 12.3).

```
func pickerView(pickerView: UIPickerView,
    didSelectRow row: Int, inComponent
    component: Int) {

    if row == 0 {

        self.lblDemo.text =
            self.lblDemo.text?.uppercaseString
    }
}
```

Figure 12.3 Set a breakpoint on the if statement.

5. Next, press the **Run** button to run the app in the Simulator. Select **Upper Case** in the picker view and you will hit the breakpoint (Figure 12.4).

```
func pickerView(pickerView: UIPickerView,
    didSelectRow row: Int, inComponent
    component: Int) {

    if row == 0 {                    Thread 1: breakpoint 1.1

        self.lblDemo.text =
            self.lblDemo.text?.uppercaseString
    }
}
```

Figure 12.4 The breakpoint is hit.

6. Looking at the **row** variable in the Variables View, you can see it's set to zero; the row number you selected in the picker view (Figure 12.5).

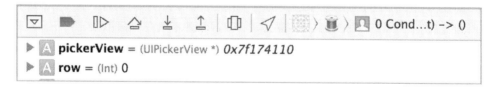

Figure 12.5 The row variable is zero.

7. Click the **Step over** button in the Debug toolbar. Since the condition is **true** (**row** == **o**), the code between the curly braces executes (Figure 12.6).

```
if row == 0 {

    self.lblDemo.text =
        self.lblDemo.text?.uppercaseString
    }                              Thread 1: step over
```

Figure 12.6 The code between curly braces executes.

8. Press **Continue**. You should see the label text uppercased in the Simulator (Figure 12.7).

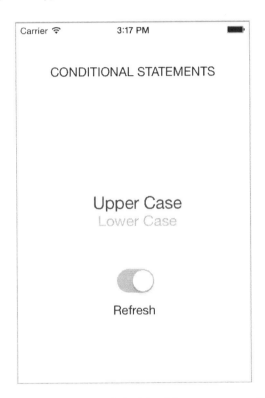

Figure 12.7 The label text is uppercased!

If you click the **Lower Case** option in the picker view, notice that the item gets selected, but the label text doesn't change. This requires a code change that you will make in this section.

9. To stop the app running in the Simulator, go back to Xcode and press the **Stop** button.

if else Statements

To perform an alternate set of code in an **if** statement, add an **else** statement. Here is the syntax of the **if else** statement:

```
if condition {
        statements
}
else {
        alternate statements
}
```

If the condition in the **if** statement evaluates to **true**, the first set of code is executed; if it evaluates to **false**, the **else** alternate statements are executed. To see the **if else** statement in action, follow these steps:

1. If it's not already open, in Xcode, open the **ConditionalStatements** project.

2. Add the following **else** statement to the **if** statement:

```
if row == 0 {

        self.lblDemo.text =
        self.lblDemo.text?.uppercaseString
}
else {
        self.lblDemo.text =
        self.lblDemo.text?.lowercaseString
}
```

3. Disable the first breakpoint by clicking on it, and then add a second breakpoint to the **else** statement (Figure 12.8).

*Figure 12.8 Set a breakpoint on the **else** statement.*

4. Next, click the **Run** button to run the app in the Simulator. After the app is displayed, select the **Upper Case** option from the list to see the label text displayed in upper case. Next, by selecting the **Lower Case** option from the picker view, you will hit the breakpoint (Figure 12.9).

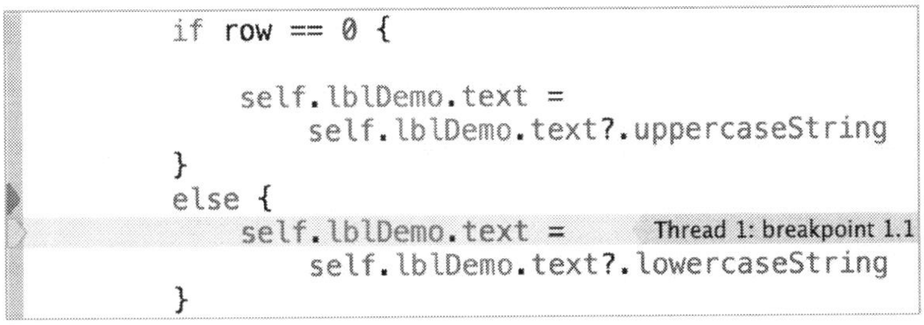

if row == 0 {
self.lblDemo.text =
self.lblDemo.text?.uppercaseString
}
else {
self.lblDemo.text =
Thread 1: breakpoint 1.1
self.lblDemo.text?.lowercaseString
}

*Figure 12.9 The **else** breakpoint is hit.*

5. Looking at the **row** variable in the Variables View, you can see it is set to **1** (Figure 12.10).

0...()
pickerView = (UIPickerView *) 0x7a2803d0
row = (Int) 1

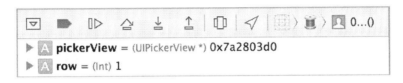

*Figure 12.10 The **row** variable is set to 1.*

Since the row is **1**, the condition (**row == 0**) evaluates to **false**, and the **else** statement is executed as evidenced by your breakpoint being hit.

6. Press the **Continue** button and see that the label text is now lowercased (Figure 12.11).

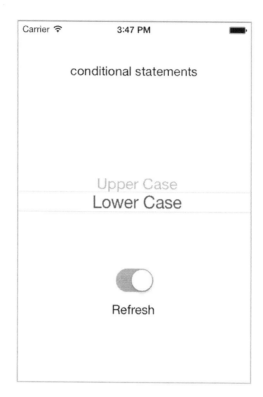

Figure 12.11 The label text is lowercased.

7. Go back to Xcode and press **Stop** to stop the app running in the Simulator.

Now let's see how to handle three picker view options.

else if Statements

In Swift (and other programming languages), it's common to check two different conditions and provide three alternate sets of code to be executed based on these conditions.

This is where the **else if** statement comes in handy. Here is the syntax of the **else if** statement:

```
if condition 1 {

    statements executed on first condition
}
else if condition 2 {

    statements executed on second condition
```

```
}
else {
    statements executed otherwise
}
```

If the first condition is **true**, then the first set of statements is executed. If the second condition is **true**, the second set of statements is executed. If neither condition is **true**, the third set of statements is executed.

1. If it's not already open, in Xcode, open the **ConditionalStatements** project.

2. Next, go to the **viewDidLoad** method and add a third option, **Capitalized**, to the list of choices:

   ```
   var choices = ["Upper Case", "Lower Case",
           "Capitalized"]
   ```

3. Go to the **pickerView:didSelectRow:inComponent:** method and change the code to the following:

   ```
   if row == 0 {

           self.lblDemo.text =
           self.lblDemo.text?.uppercaseString
   }
   else if row == 1 {
           self.lblDemo.text =
           self.lblDemo.text?.lowercaseString
   }
   else {
           self.lblDemo.text =
           self.lblDemo.text?.capitalizedString
   }
   ```

   Note the addition of **if (row == 1)** as well as the new **else** statement at the end.

4. Before running this code, delete the old breakpoints (just right-click and select **Delete breakpoint** from the shortcut menu) and add the breakpoints shown in Figure 12.12.

```
if row == 0 {

    self.lblDemo.text =
        self.lblDemo.text?.uppercaseString
}
else if row == 1 {
    self.lblDemo.text =
        self.lblDemo.text?.lowercaseString
}
else {
    self.lblDemo.text =
        self.lblDemo.text?.capitalizedString
}
```

Figure 12.12 Set three new breakpoints.

5. Click the **Run** button in Xcode and see the new **Capitalized** option in the picker view (Figure 12.13).

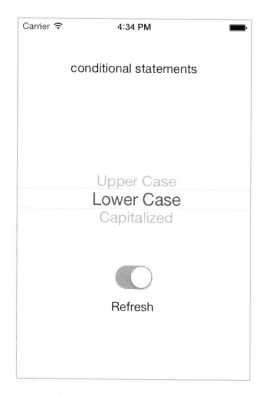

*Figure 12.13 The new **Capitalized** option*

6. Select **Capitalized**, and you will hit your new breakpoint (Figure 12.14).

```
if row == 0 {                          Thread 1: breakpoint 1.1
        self.lblDemo.text =
            self.lblDemo.text?.uppercaseString
}
else if row == 1 {
        self.lblDemo.text =
            self.lblDemo.text?.lowercaseString
}
else {
        self.lblDemo.text =
            self.lblDemo.text?.capitalizedString
}
```

Figure 12.14 The first breakpoint is hit.

7. Looking at the **row** variable in the Variables View, you can see it is set to **2**. This means the first and second conditions, which check for **row** == **0** and **row** == **1**, will evaluate to **false** and their associated code will not be executed. Only the code in the final **else** statement will be executed.

8. Click the **Step over** button. This causes execution to jump to the second condition to be evaluated (Figure 12.15).

```
if row == 0 {
        self.lblDemo.text =
            self.lblDemo.text?.uppercaseString
}
else if row == 1 {                     Thread 1: breakpoint 2.1
        self.lblDemo.text =
            self.lblDemo.text?.lowercaseString
}
else {
        self.lblDemo.text =
            self.lblDemo.text?.capitalizedString
}
```

Figure 12.15 The second breakpoint is hit.

9. Since this condition also evaluates to **false**, click **Step over** again and execution jumps to the statements bracketed within the final **else** statement (Figure 12.16).

```
if row == 0 {

    self.lblDemo.text =
        self.lblDemo.text?.uppercaseString
}
else if row == 1 {
    self.lblDemo.text =
        self.lblDemo.text?.lowercaseString
}
else {
    self.lblDemo.text =
        self.lblDemo.text?.capitalizedString
}
```
Thread 1: step over

*Figure 12.16 The final **else** statement is executed.*

10. Click **Continue**, and you can see in the Simulator that the label text has changed. The first letter of each word is capitalized and all other characters are lowercased (Figure 12.17).

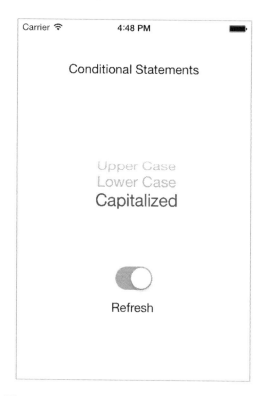

Figure 12.17 The label text is capitalized.

11. Press **Stop** to stop the app running in the Simulator.

Nested if Statements

So far, we have ignored the **Refresh** switch at the bottom of the view. When the **Refresh** switch is **On**, the label text should be refreshed whenever the user makes a new selection. If the switch is **Off**, the label text should not change when the user makes a new selection.

Here, you will learn how to handle this situation with nested **if** statements.

Although it's a bit more complex, it's very common to nest one set of **if** statements inside another.

```
if condition 1 {

    statements to be executed

    if condition 2 {

        statements to be executed

    }
}
```

This is exactly what you need to handle the situation of deciding whether to refresh the label.

1. Open the **ConditionalStatements** project.

2. Go back to the **if** statements you just entered and, right before the first **if**, add the following partially complete **if** statement:

```
if self.swtRefresh.on
{

}
if row == 0 {
        self.lblDemo.text =
        self.lblDemo.text?.uppercaseString
}
else if row == 1 {
        self.lblDemo.text =
        self.lblDemo.text?.lowercaseString
}
else {
        self.lblDemo.text =
```

```
            self.lblDemo.text?.capitalizedString
}
```

Within the condition of this new **if** statement, the switch's **on** property is checked.

3. Since you only want the label to be refreshed when the switch is on, select all the old **if** statements by clicking, holding the mouse button down, then dragging your mouse as Figure 12.18 shows.

```
if row == 0 {

    self.lblDemo.text =
        self.lblDemo.text?.uppercaseString
}
else if row == 1 {
    self.lblDemo.text =
        self.lblDemo.text?.lowercaseString
}
else {
    self.lblDemo.text =
        self.lblDemo.text?.capitalizedString
}
```

*Figure 12.18 Select all of the old **if** statement code.*

4. Next, type **Command+X** to cut these lines of code from the source code file, and then click on the blank line between the curly braces of the new **if** statement.

5. Now type **Command+V** to paste these lines inside the new **if** statement. Afterward, add a breakpoint at the top of the new code (Figure 12.19).

```
if self.swtRefresh.on
{
    if row == 0 {

        self.lblDemo.text =
            self.lblDemo.text?.
                uppercaseString
    }
    else if row == 1 {
        self.lblDemo.text =
            self.lblDemo.text?.
                lowercaseString
    }
    else {
        self.lblDemo.text =
            self.lblDemo.text?.
                capitalizedString
    }
}
```

Figure 12.19 Set a breakpoint on the new if statement.

6. Click **Run** to run the new code in the Simulator. Leave the **Refresh** switch **On**, and then select **Upper Case** from the picker view. You will hit your breakpoint on the outer **if** statement (Figure 12.20).

```
if self.swtRefresh.on          Thread 1: breakpoint
{
    if row == 0 {

        self.lblDemo.text =
            self.lblDemo.text?.
                uppercaseString
    }
    else if row == 1 {
        self.lblDemo.text =
            self.lblDemo.text?.
                lowercaseString
    }
    else {
        self.lblDemo.text =
            self.lblDemo.text?.
                capitalizedString
    }
}
```

Figure 12.20 The breakpoint on the new if statement is hit.

7. The outer **if** statement condition is evaluated first. Since the switch is on, the **on** property is set to **true** and the nested code executes. To see this, click the **Step over** button, and execution should move to the nested **if** statement. Click **Continue** and see the label text uppercased.

8. Next, click on the **Refresh** switch to turn it off, and then select another option in the picker view. Again, you should hit the outer **if** statement, which checks to see if the switch is on. Click **Step over**, and you will see execution jump over the nested **if** statements and go to the bottom of the method (Figure 12.21). This is exactly as it should be.

```
if self.swtRefresh.on
{
    if row == 0 {

        self.lblDemo.text =
            self.lblDemo.text?.
                uppercaseString
    }
    else if row == 1 {
        self.lblDemo.text =
            self.lblDemo.text?.
                lowercaseString
    }
    else {
        self.lblDemo.text =
            self.lblDemo.text?.
                capitalizedString
    }
}
}                                          Thread 1: step over
```

Figure 12.21 Execution moves to the bottom of the method.

9. Press **Continue** in the Debug area, and you will see the label text is unchanged. Now click the **Refresh** switch to turn it back on. Select an option in the picker view, and you will hit the outer **if** statement again. Click **Continue**, and you will see the label text is now updating again.

10. Press Xcode's **Stop** button to stop the app running in the Simulator.

Compound Comparisons

Before moving on from **if** statements, you need to learn about **compound comparisons**. A compound comparison allows you to perform multiple tests in a single condition.

For example, if you want to check the value of an IQ (intelligence quotient) to see if it falls within the gifted range (130-139), you can create a compound comparison something like this:

```
if iq >= 130 && iq <= 139 {
```

```
    // statements to be executed
}
```

This compound comparison checks two conditions. First, it checks to see if the value of **iq** is greater than or equal to 130, and then checks to see if the value of **iq** is less than or equal to 139.

You are most likely familiar with the greater than or equal to (>=) and the less than or equal to (<=) operators, but you may not be familiar with the Swift **AND** operator (**&&**). A compound condition is only **true** if both comparisons are **true**. So, if the value of **iq** is 140, the first check in the condition is **true**; but because the second check in the condition is **false**, the entire condition is **false**.

Here is another example of a compound comparison that uses the Swift OR operator (||):

```
if iq < 20 || iq > 140 {

    // statements to be executed
}
```

In this code sample, the value of the **iq** variable is checked to see if it is extreme on either scale—less than 20 *or* greater than 140.

When using the **OR** operator in a compound condition, the condition is **true** if either comparison is **true**. So, if the value of **iq** is 19 and the first check is **true**, the entire compound condition is **true**. If the value of **iq** is 141, the first check is **false**, but the second check is **true**, then the entire compound condition is **true**. If the value of **iq** is anything between 20 and 140, both checks evaluate to **false** and, therefore, the entire condition is **false**.

Note that you can combine multiple comparisons in a single condition. For example:

```
if iq < 20 || (iq >= 130 && iq <= 139) || iq > 140 {
    // statements to be executed
}
```

In this code, there are two **OR** conditions and one **AND** condition. For clarity, parentheses have been added to the middle condition. You can create endless combinations of these conditional checks.

switch Statements

In writing an app, there are many times when you need to check to see if a value is one of several different values—just as you did with the **iq** variable in the previous section.

Rather than using the **if** statement, which can become difficult to read when comparing several values, you can use the **switch** statement. The **switch** statement has the following syntax:

```
switch expression {
     case value1:
        // statements to be executed
     case value2:
        // statements to be executed
     case value3:
        // statements to be executed
     default:
        // statements to be executed
}
```

When a **switch** statement executes at run time, the value of the *expression* at the top of the **switch** is evaluated. The value of the expression is then compared against each **case** value until a match is found. If no match is found, the statements in the **default** case are executed.

The **switch** statement ground rules:

- A **switch** statement must provide cases for every possible value. If it's not feasible to provide a **case** for every value, you can provide a default "catch all" **case** to cover any values not covered in other cases.

- **switch** statements to do not automatically fall through to the next case as with other languages.

- The **switch** statement's expression can be of any type that implements the **Comparable** protocol (see *Swift Standard Library Reference: Comparable* for details). This means you can now test on the basic data types including strings!

- Each **case** must contain at least one line of code, meaning you can't have empty cases. Multiple matches for a single case can be checked in a single case and separated by commas. For example:

```
switch myValue {
case 0, 1:
    println("case 0, 1")
case 2:
    println("case 2")
case 3:
    println("case 3")
default:
    println("default")
}
```

- You can check a value's inclusion in a range:

```
case 0...2:
    println("case 0...10")
```

Let's create a live example of how the **switch** statement works.

1. If it's not already open, in Xcode, open the **ConditionalStatements** project.

2. Comment out the **if** statements you have created so far. To do this, select all the code in the **pickerView:didSelectRow:inComponent:** method, and then press the **Command+/** (forward slash) (Figure 12.22).

```
//          if self.swtRefresh.on
//          {
//              if row == 0 {
//                  self.lblDemo.text =
//                  self.lblDemo.text?.uppercaseString
//              }
//              else if row == 1 {
//                  self.lblDemo.text =
//                  self.lblDemo.text?.lowercaseString
//              }
//              else {
//                  self.lblDemo.text =
//                  self.lblDemo.text?.capitalizedString
//              }
//          }
```

Figure 12.22 Comment out the **if** *statements.*

3. In the **pickerView:didSelectRow:inComponent:** method, below the

commented **if** statements, add the following code:

```
switch row {
case 0:
        self.lblDemo.text =
        self.lblDemo.text?.uppercaseString
case 1:
        self.lblDemo.text =
        self.lblDemo.text?.lowercaseString
case 2:
        self.lblDemo.text =
        self.lblDemo.text?.capitalizedString
default:
        break
}
```

Let's look at this code in the order it runs in with the help of the following image:

1. The value of the **row** variable is evaluated.

2. The value is compared against each **case** value until a match is found, and then the statements associated with that **case** are executed.

3. Execution continues with the next line of code after the ending curly brace of the **case** statement.

Now let's see how the case statement works at run time:

1. Click the **Run** button in Xcode to see whether this works the same way as the **if** statements it replaced. The real point is that the **switch** statement

is much easier to write and understand. As an app developer, you can take pride in writing code that is easily understood.

2. Press the **Stop** button to stop the app running in the Simulator.

break Statement

Since Swift's **switch** statements do not automatically fall through to the next **case**, you don't normally need to use a **break** statement. However, you can use the **break** statement when you don't want to do anything in a particular **case**.

For example, the **switch** statement you created in the previous section had a **break** statement in its **default** case. That's because we only needed to take an action if the value was 0, 1, or 2.

fallthrough Statement

If you want a particular **case** to fall through to the next **case**, just add the **fallthrough** statement:

```
switch row {
    case 1:
    // Do something
    fallthrough
    case 2:
    // Both case 1 and case 2 do this
    default:
    break
}
```

In this example, **case 1** does something and then unconditionally falls through to **case 2** to do something else, even though **row** is not equal to **2**.

Tuples

In a switch statement, you easily test multiple values in a tuple. Let's look at a live example of this.

1. If you have another project open, close it by selecting **File > Close Project** from the Xcode menu.

2. Select **File > Open...** from the Xcode menu, and in the **Open** dialog,

navigate to the folder where you have stored this book's sample code. Expand the **TupleDemo** folder, select the **TupleDemo.xcodeproj** file and then click **Open**.

3. Select the **ViewController.swift** file in the Project Navigator. Check out this code from the **addLocation** method:

```
// Save the entity
var result: (state: SaveState, message: String?) =
    self.location.saveEntity(locationEntity)
```

4. This code calls the **saveEntity** method of the **Location** business object and stores the return value in the **result** variable. You can see the return value is a tuple that contains two values, one of type **SaveState** and the other of type **String?**:

```
var result: (state: SaveState, message: String?)
```

You may remember learning in *Chapter 10: Arrays & Other Collections* that **SaveState** is an enumeration with three possible values.

The **switch** is able to test both values in the tuple in its **case** statements. I have condensed the code here so it's easier to see the different cases:

```
switch result {

case (SaveState.Error, let message):

    // Check the results

case (SaveState.RulesBroken, let message):

    // Check the results

case (SaveState.SaveComplete, let message):

    // Check the results
```

5. Some important things to note:

    •   The **switch** is on the **result** variable, which contains the tuple value.

    •   Each **case** receives both values in the tuple—the **SaveState** enumerated value as well as the optional string.

- Each case stores the optional string value in a constant named **message**:

```
case (SaveState.Error, let message):
```

This allows the statements associated with each case to access the string value via the **let** constant. This is known as ***value binding***.

where Clause

You can use the **switch** statement's **where** clause if you need more complex evaluation of **switch** values. For example:

```
switch iq {

case let i where i <= 69:
    println("Extremely Low")
case (70...79):
    println("Well below average")
case (80...89):
    println("Low average")
case (90...109):
    println("Average")
case (110...119):
    println("High Average")
case (120...129):
    println("Superior")
case let i where i >= 130:
    println("Very superior")
default:
    break;
}
```

In both first and last **case** statements of this **switch**, the value of **iq** is stored in a placeholder constant named **i**, and the **where** clause is used to perform a test on the value.

Ternary Conditional Operator

One other conditional statement to discuss is the *ternary conditional operator.*

Because it takes two operators, this statement is a bit of an oddity. Here is its basic syntax:

```
condition ? expression1 : expression2
```

When this line of code executes, the *condition* is evaluated first. If the condition evaluates to **true**, *expression1* is evaluated and its result becomes the result of the entire operation. If the condition evaluates to **false**, *expression 2* is evaluated and *its* result becomes the result of the entire operation instead.

If that seems confusing, this example should help:

```
var goodGrade: Bool = ( grade > 85 ) ? true : false
```

In this code sample, the condition **(grade > 85)** is evaluated first. If it's **true**, the value **true** is stored in the **goodGrade** variable. If it's **false**, the value **false** is stored in the **goodGrade** variable.

Summary

Here is an overview of conditional statements in Swift:

if Statements

- Swift's **if** statement allows you to run one or more lines of code if a condition is true.

- An example of an if statement:

```
if row == 0 {
    self.lblDemo.text =
        self.lblDemo.text?.uppercaseString
}
```

In this example, if the condition **(row == 0)** is **true**, then the statement between the curly braces is executed. If the condition is **false**, the statement is not executed.

if else Statements

- An **if else** statement allows you to run one of two different sets of statements.

- An example of an **if else** statement:

```
if row == 0 {
    self.lblDemo.text =
        self.lblDemo.text?.uppercaseString
}
else {
    self.lblDemo.text =
    self.lblDemo.text?.lowercaseString
}
```

In this example, if the condition in the **if** statement **(row == 0)** evaluates to **true**, the code between the first set of curly braces is executed. If it evaluates to **false**, the **else** alternate statement is executed.

else if Statements

- An **else if** statement allows you to check two different conditions and to provide three alternate sets of code to be executed based on these conditions.

- An example of an **else if** statement:

```
if row == 0 {

    self.lblDemo.text =
    self.lblDemo.text?.uppercaseString
}
else if row == 1 {
    self.lblDemo.text =
    self.lblDemo.text?.lowercaseString
}
else {
    self.lblDemo.text =
        self.lblDemo.text?.capitalizedString
}
```

In this example, if the first condition **(row == 0)** is **true**, the code between the first set of curly braces is executed. If the second condition **(row == 1)** is **true**, the code between the second set of curly braces is executed. If neither condition is **true**, code between the third set of curly braces is executed.

Nested if Statements

- In Swift, you can nest one set of **if** statements inside another. An example of a nested **if** statement:

```
if self.swtRefresh.on
{
    if row == 0 {
        self.lblDemo.text =
        self.lblDemo.text?.uppercaseString
    }
    else if row == 1 {
        self.lblDemo.text =
        self.lblDemo.text?.lowercaseString
    }
    else {
        self.lblDemo.text =
        self.lblDemo.text?.capitalizedString
    }

}
```

In this example, the outer **if** statement condition **(self.swtRefresh.on)** is evaluated first. If it's **true**, the nested **if** statement is executed. If it's **false**, the nested **if** statement is NOT executed.

Compound Comparisons

- A compound comparison allows you to perform multiple tests in a single condition. An example of a compound comparison:

```
if iq >= 130 && iq <= 139 {

    // statements to be executed
}
```

In this example, the compound comparison checks two conditions. First, it checks to see if the value of **iq** is greater than or equal to **130**, *and* then it checks to see if the value of **iq** is less than or equal to **139**.

- When the Swift **AND** operator (**&&**) is used in a compound condition, the condition is only **true** if both comparisons are **true**.

- When using the **OR** operator in a compound condition, the condition is **true** if either comparison is **true**.

- You can combine multiple comparisons in a single condition. For clarity, you can add parentheses to conditions:

```
if iq < 20 || (iq >= 130 && iq <= 139) || iq > 140 {
    // statements to be executed
}
```

switch Statements

- Rather than using the **if** statement, which can be difficult to read when comparing several values, use the **switch** statement, which makes your code much easier to read. An example of a **switch** statement:

```
switch row {
case 0:
        self.lblDemo.text =
        self.lblDemo.text?.uppercaseString
case 1:
        self.lblDemo.text =
        self.lblDemo.text?.lowercaseString
case 2:
        self.lblDemo.text =
        self.lblDemo.text?.capitalizedString
default:
        break;
}
```

- When a **switch** statement executes at run time, the value of the expression at the top of the **switch** is evaluated. The value of the expression is then compared against each **case** value until a match is found. If no match is found, the statements in the **default** case are executed.

- A **switch** statement must provide cases for every possible value. If it's not feasible to provide a **case** for every value, you can provide a default "catch all" **case** to cover any values not covered in other cases.

- **switch** statements to do not automatically fall through to the next case as with other languages.

- The **switch** statement's expression can be of any type that implements the **Comparable** protocol. This means you can now test on the basic data types including strings!

- Each **case** must contain at least one line of code, meaning you can't have empty cases. Multiple matches for a single case can be checked in a single case and separated by commas. For example:

```
switch myValue {
case 0, 1:
    println("case 0, 1")
case 2:
    println("case 2")
case 3:
    println("case 3")
default:
    println("default")
}
```

- You can check a value's inclusion in a range:

```
case 0...2:
    println("case 0...2")
```

- If you *do* want the same statements executed for different values, you can list multiple **cases** before the statements to be executed.

- In a **switch** statement, you easily test multiple values of a tuple.

- When a **switch** evaluates a tuple, each **case** receives all values in the tuple.

- In a **switch** statement, a **case** can store the value being tested in a constant or variable. For example:

```
case (SaveState.Error, let message):
```

This allows the statements associated with each case to access the value via the constant or variable. This is known as value binding.

- You can use the **switch** statement's **where** clause if you need more complex evaluation of **switch** values. For example:

```
switch iq {

case let i where i <= 69:
    println("Extremely Low")
case (70...79):
    println("Well below average")
case (80...89):
    println("Low average")
case (90...109):
    println("Average")
case (110...119):
    println("High Average")
case (120...129):
    println("Superior")
case let i where i >= 130:
    println("Very superior")
default:
    break
}
```

Ternary Conditional Operator

- The ternary conditional operator allows you to check a condition and to perform one of two expressions based on the result.

- An example of the conditional operator:

```
var goodGrade: Bool = ( grade > 85 ) ?
    true : false
```

In this code sample, the condition **(grade > 85)** is evaluated first. If it's **true**, the value **true** is stored in the **goodGrade** variable. If it's **false**, the value **false** is stored in the **goodGrade** variable.

Exercise 12.1

In this exercise you will put into practice what you have learned about conditional statements.

1. Create a playground called **Conditional.playground**.

2. Create a variable named **month** and initialize it to **0**.

3. Create a variable named **quarter** and initialize it to an empty string.

4. Create a **switch** statement that checks the **month** number and if it's 1, 2, or 3, sets the **quarter** variable to the string "First quarter", and so on for the second, third and fourth quarters.

Solution Movie 12.1

To see a video providing the solution for this exercise, you can enter the link below in your Web browser to see each step performed for you.

Movie 12.1

http://www.iOSAppsForNonProgrammers.com/B4M121.html

Chapter 13: Working With Strings

In creating apps, you work with a lot of character strings—so often that strings deserve their own chapter. You have already learned many of the basics of strings, but this chapter goes a bit deeper and even teaches you how to make your app's strings multi-lingual.

Sections in This Chapter

1. Strings and Characters

2. Empty Strings

3. Counting Characters

4. Converting Values to String

5. Converting Strings to Integer Values

6. Converting Strings to Other Numeric Types

7. Getting a Substring from a String

8. Removing All Occurrences of a String

9. Trimming White Space From a String

10. Concatenating Strings and Characters

11. Comparing Strings

12. Special Escaped Characters

13. Summary

14. Exercise 13.1

15. Solution Movie 13.1

Strings and Characters

Strings and **Characters** are two distinct data types in Swift. A **String** represents a collection of characters.

Here is a **String** declaration:

```
var s: String = "This is a string"
```

Earlier, you learned that you don't need to explicitly declare the type of the variable or constant when you are assigning an initial value, since Swift's type inference can figure out the type for you.

Character types can only hold a single character:

```
var c: Character = "c"
```

The **Character** type is an exception to the type inference rule. If you want the **Character** type, you must explicitly specify it. Otherwise, Swift will declare it as a **String**.

Empty Strings

To create an empty string value, you can either assign an empty string to a variable:

```
var myString = ""
```

Or you can create a new **String** object and store it in the variable:

```
var myString = String()
```

You can test if a string is empty by checking its **IsEmpty** Boolean property:

```
if myString.isEmpty {
    println("It's empty!")
}
```

Counting Characters

Use the global **countElements()** function to count the number of characters in a string. Let's try this in a playground.

1. If you already have a playground, feel free to use it. Otherwise, to create a

new playground, go to the Xcode menu and select **File > New > Playground**.

2. In the Create Playground dialog set the **Name** to **StringsPlayground**, the **Platform** to **iOS**, and then click **Next**. In the Save dialog, choose a folder to save your playground and then click **Create**.

   If you prefer, you can delete the sample line of code from the playground to start with a clean slate.

3. Enter the following code in the playground:

```
var chrCount = countElements("Three Blind Mice")
```

The Results sidebar will show a count of **16**.

The **countElements()** function returns the correct number of characters even when the string contains emoji (picture) characters, even though these characters take up twice the space of a regular character or more. This is more accurate than **NSString's length** property, which is called **utf16count** when accessed on a Swift string.

To see an example of this, check out the code entered into a playground in Figure 13.1.

```
let cat: String = "\u{1F638}"    "😸"
countElements(cat)               1
cat.utf16Count                   2
```

*Figure 13.1 **countElements()** reports the correct number of characters.*

The first line of code stores the Unicode character for a smiling cat into the **cat** string.

The second line of code uses Swift's **countElements** function to count the number of characters and accurately report **1** character.

The third line of code uses the **utf16Count** property and reports **2** characters, because it's counting the number of 16-bit units taken up by the character rather than the actual number of characters.

Be aware that if you are working with particularly long strings (many thousands of characters) the **countElements** function must do quite a bit of processing, because it needs to iterate through each character in the string to get a correct character count.

Converting Values to String

Swift has a feature known as ***string interpolation*** that allows you to build a string from a mix of string literals, variables, constants, and expressions. All you have to do is place the values you want to convert inside parentheses and prefixed by a backslash.

Try adding the following code to the playground:

```
var count = 10
let message = "There are \(count) students."
```

When you do this, you should see the text shown in Figure 13.2 on the Results sidebar on the right.

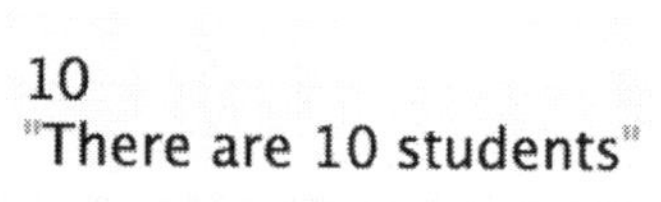

```
10
"There are 10 students"
```

Figure 13.2 String interpolation in action!

You can see the **count** variable value of **10** was converted to string and inserted into the **message** string.

This works great for all Swift's basic data types, including Boolean. For example, add the following code to the playground:

```
var isTrue = true
let msg2 = "My Aim Is \(isTrue)"
```

Swift converts the Boolean value true into the text "true" and inserts it into the string (Figure 13.3).

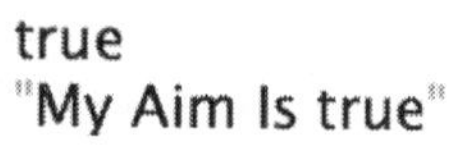

```
true
"My Aim Is true"
```

Figure 13.3 String interpolation with Boolean values

Converting Strings to Integer Values

Converting a Swift String to an integer value is as easy as calling a string's **toInt** method. Try entering the following code in the playground:

```
var intValue = "10".toInt()
```

The Results sidebar shows that **toInt()** converts the string value into an optional Integer value. Why an *optional* Integer value? There's no guarantee the string contains a valid Integer value. If it doesn't, **toInt()** returns a **nil**. To see this in action, change the code you just entered by adding the letter "b" to the string literal:

```
var intValue = "10b".toInt()
```

When you add the "b" the Results sidebar shows the result is **nil**.

Converting String to Other Numeric Types

If you need to convert a string to a numeric type other than integer (double, float, etc.) you need the help of the Cocoa Touch Framework's **NSString** class. Basically, you need to convert the Swift **String** to an **NSString** and then you will have access to all **NSString's** conversion capabilities.

For example, add the following code to the playground:

```
var s = "10.0"
var doubleValue = (s as NSString).doubleValue
```

The first line of code creates a Swift **String** initialized to "10.0".

When the second line of code executes, the code within the parentheses is evaluated first:

```
var doubleValue = (s as NSString).doubleValue
```

This code converts the Swift **String** stored in the **s** variable into an **NSString** using Swift's **as** operator. (You will learn more about the **as** operator in *Chapter 18: Data Types & Conversions*.)

The next code to be evaluated is the **doubleValue** property:

```
var doubleValue = (s as NSString).doubleValue
```

doubleValue is a property of **NSString** objects. Since the code within the parentheses converts the Swift String object to an **NSString** object, you can now access any property or method of an **NSString** object.

Some other conversion methods you can access the same way:

```
// Convert to a float value
var floatValue = (s as NSString).floatValue

// Convert to a boolean value
var boolValue = ("true" as NSString).boolValue
```

If the string you are converting does not contain a valid numeric string of the specified type, these **NSString** properties will return 0.0 rather than **nil**.

The **boolValue** method returns **true** if the first character is **Y, y, T, t**, or a number 1-9. Otherwise, it returns **false**.

Getting a Substring From a String

You typically use index numbers to get a substring from a string (the first character is index 0, the second character index 1, and so on). However, because Swift stores strings in a special way, you can't use a simple integer index to access a character in a Swift string. You must build an index specifically for the string you are working with. Let's give it a try.

1. Enter the following string in the playground:

    ```
    var s = "Waiting for Apple Watch"
    ```

    In this exercise, we want to get the substring "Apple Watch" out of this string.

2. Now you need to build a **String.Index** type using Swift's **advance()** function. Just pass the starting index of the string and the desired character position:

    ```
    let index = advance(s.startIndex, 12)
    ```

3. Now you can use this index in the String object's **substringFromIndex** method:

    ```
    var sub = s.substringFromIndex(index)
    ```

As Figure 13.4 shows, **substringFromIndex** returns a substring starting at the specified index all the way to the end of the string, returning the string "Apple Watch".

```
var s = "Waiting for Apple Watch"        "Waiting for Apple Watch"
let index = advance(s.startIndex, 12)    12
var sub = s.substringFromIndex(index)    "Apple Watch"
```

*Figure 13.4 Using the **substringFromIndex** method*

Alternately, you can use the **subStringToIndex** to get a substring that starts at the beginning of the string and ends at the specified index.

For example, the code in Figure 13.5 gets the substring "Waiting" from the string using the **substringToIndex** method.

```
var s = "Waiting for Apple Watch"        "Waiting for Apple Watch"
let index = advance(s.startIndex, 7)     7
var sub = s.substringToIndex(index)      "Waiting"
```

*Figure 13.5 Using the **substringToIndex** method*

If you want to pull a substring out of the middle of a string, you need a starting and ending index as Figure 13.6 illustrates.

```
var s = "Waiting for Apple Watch"               "Waiting for Apple Watch"
let start = advance(s.startIndex, 12)           12
let end = advance(start, 4)                     16
var sub = s.substringWithRange(start...end)     "Apple"
```

*Figure 13.6 Using the **substringWithRange** method*

Removing All Occurrences of a String

Sometimes you need to remove all occurrences of a character (or sequence of characters) from a string. The **stringByReplacingOccurrencesOfString:** method is just right for this job. In Figure 13.7, the question mark is removed from the "Swift is great?" string, making "Swift is great" a statement rather than a question!

```
let s = "Swift is Great?"              "Swift is Great?"
let s1 = s.stringByReplacingOccurrencesOfString("?",   "Swift is Great"
    withString: "")
```

Figure 13.7 Removing all occurrences of a string

Trimming White Space From a String

Another common task is removing spaces from the beginning and end of a string. To do this, you can use the **stringByTrimmingCharactersInSet:** method. As Figure 13.8 shows, you must pass **NSCharacterSet. whiteSpaceCharacterSet()** as an argument and all spaces are trimmed from the beginning and end of the string.

```
let s1 = "  iPhone 6 Plus    "          "  iPhone 6 Plus   "
let s2 = s1.stringByTrimmingCharactersInSet    "iPhone 6 Plus"
    (NSCharacterSet.whitespaceCharacterSet())
```

Figure 13.8 Removing white space from a string

If you also want to remove "new line" characters from the string (the **\n** character combination in a string creates a new line, so that subsequent characters are displayed on the next line), use the character set in Figure 13.9.

```
let s1 = "  iPhone 6 Plus    "
let s2 = s1.stringByTrimmingCharactersInSet
    (NSCharacterSet.whitespaceAndNewlineCharacterSet())
```

Figure 13.9 Removing white space and new lines

Concatenating Strings

String and values can be concatenated (joined) together using the addition operator (+):

```
let string1 = "Hello"
let string2 = "World"

var stringResult = string1 + " " + string2
// stringResult = "Hello World"
```

You can also append a **String** to an existing **String** using the += operator:

```
var string1 = "Hello"
let string2 = "?"
string1 += string2 // string1 = "Hello?"
```

You can't use the + or += operators to add a **Character** type to a **String**, but you can use the append method:

```
var s = "Swift"
var c: Character = "!"
s.append(c)
```

Comparing Strings

You can use several methods to compare two Swift strings.

Testing String Equality

Two strings are considered equal if they have the same characters in the same order. You can test for string equality using the == operator. For example, in Figure 13.10, string **s1** and **s2** are equal.

```
let s1 = "One Infinite Loop"    "One Infinite Loop"
let s2 = "One Infinite Loop"    "One Infinite Loop"

if s1 == s2 {
    // Strings are equal
}
```

Figure 13.10 Comparing two strings

Comparing String Prefix and Suffix

You can check if a string has a particular prefix using the **hasPrefix** property of the Swift **String** class (Figure 13.11).

```
let s1 = "Apple TV"              "Apple TV"

if s1.hasPrefix("Apple") {
    // It has the prefix
}
```

Figure 13.11 Checking a string's prefix

You can check if a string has a particular suffix using the **hasSuffix** property of the Swift **String** class (Figure 13.12).

```
let s1 = "www.apple.com"        "www.apple.com"

if s1.hasSuffix(".com") {
    // It has the suffix
}
```

Figure 13.12 Checking a string's suffix

Checking If a String Contains Another String

Use the **rangeOfString** method to determine if one string contains another string. In Figure 13.13, the **if** statement condition checks for the string "OS" in the string "Mac OS X", and as you see in the Results sidebar, the string is found.

```
let s = "Mac OS X"                "Mac OS X"
if s.rangeOfString("OS") != nil {
    println("String found!")      "String found!"
}
else {
    println("String not found!")
}
```

Figure 13.13 Checking if one string contains another

Special Escaped Characters

The backslash (\) character has special meaning in a Swift string literal. It indicates that the character following it should be treated differently. Here is the list of special escaped characters and their meaning:

- \0 (null character)

- \\ (backslash)

- \t (horizontal tab)

- \n (line feed)

- \r (carriage return)

- \" (double quote)

- \' (single quote)

- \xnn (Single-byte Unicode **scalars** (primitive data types that contain only a single value) where nn is two hexadecimal digits)

- \unnnn (Two-byte Unicode scalars where nnnn is four hexadecimal digits

- \Unnnnnnnn (Four-byte Unicode scalars where nnnnnnnn is eight hexadecimal digits

Here is an example of adding tabs between numbers:

```
println("1\t2\t3")   // Outputs: 1    2    3
```

You can add any number of special escaped characters to a single string.

Multi-Lingual Support

You can often expand your user base by offering your app in multiple languages. The term **localize** is used in iOS and other software platforms to describe the process of translating and adapting your app to different cultures, countries, regions, or groups of people. This section isn't an exhaustive discussion of localization, but simply addresses how to make sure the strings in your app can be translated to other languages.

Not every string in your app needs to be localized, but any string displayed to the user interface should be made localizable. So far, all the samples in this book have used hard-coded strings. For example:

```
lblDemo.text = "screen"
```

This code always stores the text "screen" to the label's **text** property regardless of the user's language setting on his or her iOS device (specified in the **Settings** app under **General > International > Language**).

Rather than hard-coding strings in your app, use the **NSLocalizedString()** function instead.

The simplest form of this function accepts two arguments:

- **key** - The text *string* you want to display

- **comment** - A description of the text you want to display

Here is the same line of code used as an example above but modified to use the **NSLocalizedString()** function instead:

```
lblDemo.text = NSLocalizedString("screen",
    comment: "An iOS display")
```

When this function executes at run time, it checks to see if a translation of the text "screen" has been provided for the user's current language. If it has, the *translated string* is returned from the function. If no translation has been provided, the text "screen" is returned from the function.

This means you don't have to translate your app strings until you have finished creating your app. Then, you can decide which languages you want to support and translate your app into those languages.

In this example, the comment "An iOS display" describes the "screen" text string. In this case, the comment is important, because the English word screen has multiple meanings. It could mean the screen on your iPhone or it could mean "to examine something closely," as when you are screened at airport security. Providing a meaningful comment helps translators produce accurate localizations of your App's strings!

Summary

Here is a review of string manipulation in Swift:

Strings and Characters

- **Strings** and **Characters** are two distinct data types in Swift. A **String** represents a collection of characters.

- Here is a **String** declaration:

  ```
  var s = "This is a string"
  ```

- **Character** types can only hold a single character:

  ```
  var c: Character = "c"
  ```

- The **Character** type is an exception to the type inference rule. If you want the **Character** type, you must explicitly specify it. Otherwise, Swift will declare it as a **String**.

Empty Strings

- To create an empty string value, either assign an empty string to a variable:

```
var myString = ""
```

Or create a new **String** object and store it in the variable:

```
var myString = String()
```

- You can test if a string is empty by checking its **IsEmpty** Boolean property:

```
if myString.isEmpty {
    // It's empty!!
}
```

Counting Characters

- You can use the global **countElements()** function to count the number of characters in a string. For example:

```
var chrCount = countElements("Three Blind Mice")
```

Converting Values to String

- Swift has a feature known as *string interpolation* that allows you to build a string from a mix of string literals, variables, constants, and expressions:

```
var count = 10
let message = "There are \(count) students."
```

Converting Strings to Integers

- Converting a Swift String to an integer value is as easy as calling a string's **toInt()** method:

```
var intValue = "10".toInt()
```

Converting String to Other Numeric Types

- If you need to convert a string to a numeric type other than integer (double, float, etc.) you need the help of the Cocoa Touch Framework's **NSString** class. You need to convert the Swift **String** to an **NSString** and then you will have access to all of **NSString's** conversion capabilities:

```
var s = "10.0"
var doubleValue = (s as NSString).doubleValue
```

Getting a Substring From a String

- Because Swift stores strings in a special way, you can't use a simple integer index to access a character in a Swift string. You must build an index specifically for the string you are working with:

```
var s = "Waiting for Apple Watch"
let index = advance(s.startIndex, 12)
var sub = s.substringFromIndex(index)
```

Removing All Occurrences of a String

- The **stringByReplacingOccurrencesOfString:** method allows you to remove all occurrences of one string from another string:

```
let s = "Swift is Great?"
let s1 =
    s.stringByReplacingOccurrencesOfString("?",
    withString: "")
```

Trimming White Space From a String

- To remove spaces from the beginning and end of a string, use the **stringByTrimmingCharactersInSet:** method, passing **whiteSpaceCharacterSet()** as an argument:

```
let s1 = "   iPhone Plus   "
let s2 = s1.stringByTrimmingCharactersInSet(NSCharacterSet.
    whitespaceCharacterSet())
```

- If you also want to remove "new line" characters from the string in addition to white space, use the **whiteSpaceAndNewLineCharacterSet()**.

Concatenating Strings

- **String** and values can be concatenated (joined) together using the addition operator (+):

```
var stringResult =
        string1 + " " + string2
```

- You can also append a **String** or to an existing **String** using the += operator:

```
string1 += string2
```

Comparing Strings

- Two strings are considered equal if they have the same characters in the same order. Test for string equality using the == operator:

```
let s1 = "One Infinite Loop"
let s2 = "One Infinite Loop"

if s1 == s2 {
    // Strings are equal
}
```

- Test if a string has a particular prefix using the **hasPrefix** property of the Swift **String** class:

```
let s1 = "Apple TV"

if s1.hasPrefix("Apple") {
    // It has the prefix
}
```

- Test if a string has a particular suffix using the **hasSuffix** property of the Swift **String** class:

```
let s1 = "www.apple.com"

if s1.hasSuffix(".com") {
    // It has the suffix
}
```

- Test if one string contains another string using the **rangeOfString** method of the Swift **String** class:

```
let s = "Mac OS X"
if s.rangeOfString("S") != nil {
        // Found the string!
}
```

- Rather than hard-coding strings in your app, you can use the **NSLocalizedString()** function instead:

```
lblDemo.text = NSLocalizedString("screen",
    comment: "An iOS display")
```

Exercise 13.1

In this exercise, you will put into practice several techniques you have learned for working with strings.

1. Create a new playground named **Strings.playground**.

2. Add a **String** variable named **s** to the playground and initialize it to "Learning Swift is fun".

3. Add a **Character** variable named **c** to the playground and initialize it to "!"

4. Append the **Character** in variable **c** to the **String** in variable **s**.

5. Create a variable named **count**. Determine the number of characters in string **s** and store it in **count**.

6. Append the value in the count variable to the end of the string **s**, so the final string reads "Learning Swift is fun - *n* characters", where **n** is the character count.

7. Remove "Learning " from the beginning of the string in the **s** variable.

Solution Movie 13.1

To see a video providing the solution for this exercise, you can enter the link below in your Web browser to see each step performed for you.

Movie 13.1

http://www.iOSAppsForNonProgrammers.com/B4M131.html

Chapter 14: Comments, Constants, & Enumerations

Here, you will learn more about adding quality comments to your code—something you will thank yourself for many times over. You will also learn why and how you should declare your own constants and learn to use Swift's powerful enumerations in your iOS Apps.

Sections in This Chapter

Commenting Your Code

Commenting your code is important. It allows others to quickly look at your code and understand what it does. Comments also help when you come back to your code several months later to try to figure out what's going and how it works. A well-written comment can save you time and speed you along to the fun part—writing code.

Some of the most important comments that you create are those describing the methods in your classes. Here you can provide a succinct comment on what each method does in a way that is easier than looking at the **method signature** (the name of the method and the number of and type of its parameters, not including the return type) to figure it out.

Comments in Swift come in two forms. Earlier, you saw the single line comment, which looks like this:

```
// This is a single line comment
```

When the compiler sees the two forward slashes indicating a comment, it ignores all other characters on that line. You can also create a comment on the same line as a Swift statement. For example:

```
return true   // We are on an iPad!
```

You can also create multi-line comments by placing "/*" at the beginning of the comment line and "*/" after the last comment line. For example:

```
/*    Here is a multi-line comment
      Here is the second line
      And the third line */
```

Good Comments and Bad Comments

What's the difference between a good comment and a bad comment? Here's an example of a bad comment:

```
count++;   // increment the count
```

This comment is unnecessary, because it's painfully obvious what the code does. Reading the comment takes longer than reading the code!

Here's an example of a good comment:

```
// The persistent store coordinator for the application. This
implementation creates and returns a coordinator, having added
the store for the application to it. This property is optional
since there are legitimate error conditions that could cause
the creation of the store to fail.

var coordinator: NSPersistentStoreCoordinator? =
   NSPersistentStoreCoordinator(managedObjectModel:
   self.managedObjectModel)
```

This comment and code are added to your project if you add Core Data when you create your project. The comments provide an overview of the purpose and initialization of the Persistent Store Coordinator that would be difficult to derive by examining the code.

Remember: create comments when you need them; do *not* create comments when you don't need them.

Using Constants

Earlier, you learned about declaring and using constants, but here, I am devoting a special section to the subject to ensure you understand the bigger picture of how constants can and should be used in your app's code base.

To review, *constants* are similar to variables in providing a place in memory where a value can be stored. The difference is a constant's value cannot be changed once it is assigned—that's what makes it a constant. To declare a constant, you use the **let** keyword:

```
let maxAllowedDigits = 10
```

When to Use Constants

Apple has placed a stronger-than-usual emphasis on the use of constants in your Swift code. Developers typically create variables far more often than constants. They tend to use constants in the following situations:

- **When a value is used repeatedly throughout an app** - Rather than hard-coding or manually entering the same value each time, you declare a constant once in your code and refer to that constant instead. That way, if you ever need to change the value, you can change it in one place, instead of scouring your code for the hard-coded value.

- **To avoid "magic numbers"** - Rather than entering numeric values in your code, it's best to create constants with meaningful names. For example, the following code uses an integer, and it's not obvious why the number **10** is used, making it a "magic number":

```
if value < 10
```

In contrast, if you use a well-named constant, it can explain the context for the number. For example, the following code lets you know you are comparing against the maximum allowed digits:

```
if value < maxAllowedDigits
```

Use Constants When You Can; Variables When You Must

In its Swift documentation, Apple offers this advice:

> *If a stored value in your code is not going to change, always declare it as a constant with the let keyword. Use variables only for storing values that need to be able to change.*

When of the best reasons to use constants, is because Swift is better able to optimize your code when it knows what isn't going to change! In addition, using constants makes the intent of your code clearer. When a value is declared as a constant, you know it will not change. If you declare a value as a variable, you are indicating the value can potentially change. This helps make your code more self-evident.

This advice is summed up in the phrase "use constants where you can, variables where you must."

Constant Scope

If you only need a constant in a single class, you can declare the constant in the class file. Constants are typically declared near the top of the code file where you declare your instance variables.

If you want to use certain constants throughout your project, you can declare them as global constants. You will learn more about how to do this in *Chapter 17: Access Control.*

Creating Your Own Enumerations

Earlier, you learned that an *enumeration*, or enum, is a group of related constants. Although you have used enumerations, you haven't created your own. In this section you are going to do just that.

Swift's enumerations are extremely powerful. They can have computed properties, instance methods and initializers. In addition, you can enhance them with extensions and protocols. However, they cannot be subclassed.

Currently, the **Calculator** class you created earlier in this book performs five operations—add, subtract, multiply, divide, and clear. This is a great place to create an enumeration that specifies all the possible operations. An enumeration will help document the available operations to anyone using the **Calculator** class. And, as you will see, it also allows you to create methods that accept an argument specifying the current operation.

A **Calculator** class has been added to the **AdvancedSwiftDemo** sample code project for use in this and the next few chapters. Follow the steps below to enhance this **Calculator** class by creating an enumeration that declares all its operations:

1. If you have another project open, close it by selecting **File** > **Close Project** from the Xcode menu.

2. Open the **AdvancedSwiftDemo** project located in a subfolder where you have saved this book's sample code.

3. Expand the **AdvancedSwiftDemo** node in the Project Navigator and then expand the **AdvancedSwiftDemo** sub node.

4. In the Project Navigator, select the **Calculator.swift** file and add the following enumeration declaration above the **class** declaration:

```
enum Operation {
    case Add
    case Subtract
    case Multiply
    case Divide
    case Clear
}
```

This code declares an enumeration named **Operation**, containing five members: **Add**, **Subtract**, **Multiply**, **Divide**, and **Clear**. Each **case** statement declares a separate member of the enumeration.

You can also declare an enumeration using a single **case** statement and list the members of the enumeration separated by commas:

```
enum Operation {

    case Add, Subtract, Multiply, Divide, Clear
}
```

Use Pascal case to declare both the enumeration name and the names of its members. Also, the name of the enumeration and its members should be singular rather than plural (**Operation**, not **Operations**).

Unlike enumerations in other programming languages, the members of a Swift enumeration are not automatically assigned an integer value.

When you reference an enumeration in code, you specify the enumeration name, followed by a period, and then the member name. For example:

```
var currentOperation = Operation.Add
```

If a variable or constant is specified to be the type of an enumeration, you can leave out the enumeration name and simply reference the enumeration member with a period prefix. For example, in the following code, the **op** variable is typed as an **Operation** enumeration, so you can leave the **Operation** prefix off and simply reference the .**Add** member:

```
var op: Operation = .Add
```

In the next section, you'll see this comes in handy when you're evaluating enumerations in **switch** statements.

Enumerations and Switch Statements

The use of enumerations and **switch** statements goes hand in hand. This is because a **switch** statement allows you to check for all possible enumeration values and perform an action on each.

Xcode's Code Completion comes in handy when creating a **switch** on an enumeration. As Figure 14.1 shows, Code Completion shows a list of all the members of the enumeration you can pick from.

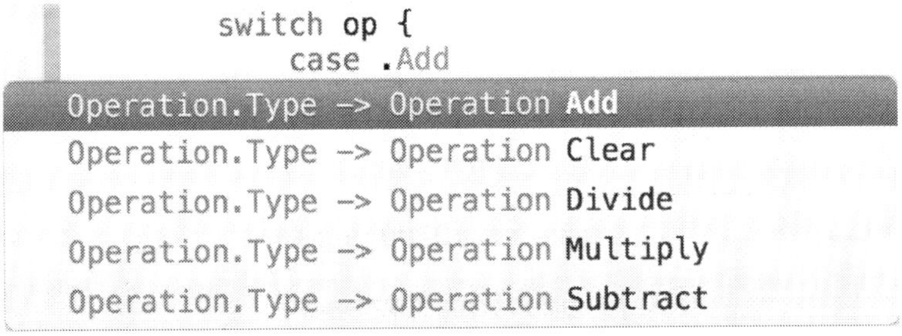

```
          switch op {
               case .Add
    Operation.Type -> Operation Add
    Operation.Type -> Operation Clear
    Operation.Type -> Operation Divide
    Operation.Type -> Operation Multiply
    Operation.Type -> Operation Subtract
```

Figure 14.1 Code Completion for enumerations

Here is a **switch** statement that evaluates a variable of type **Operation** and provides a **case** for each member of the enumeration:

```
switch op {

case .Add:
        println("Add")
case .Subtract:
        println("Subtract")
case .Multiply:
        println("Multiply")
case .Divide:
        println("Divide")
case .Clear:
        println("Clear")
}
```

Notice the use of the abbreviated **.member** notation in each **case**.

Enumeration Raw Values

At times, you may want to associate a value, such as a string, with each member of an enumeration. This functionality is built into enumerations as *raw values*.

When declaring raw values for an enumeration, you add a colon after the enumeration name followed by the type of the raw values (they must all be of the same type). Then you specify the raw value for each member.

For example, the following enumeration specifies a string value for each member:

```
enum Operation: String {
    case Add = "+"
    case Subtract = "-"
    case Multiply = "*"
    case Divide = "/"
    case Clear = "C"
}
```

You can access the raw value of an enumeration member by accessing its **rawValue** property. For example, the following code gets a "+" string from the **Add** member's **rawValue** property:

```
let opString: String = Operation.Add.rawValue
```

Going the other way, when you declare enumerations with raw values, the enumeration automatically receives an initializer that accepts a parameter named **rawValue** of the raw value type and returns an enumeration member or **nil**. For example, the following code gets the **Operation.Add** member by passing a plus sign string argument to the **rawValue**: initializer:

```
let op: Operation? = Operation(rawValue: "+")
```

Notice the return type of the initializer is optional (as the question mark indicates). This is because the initializer returns **nil** if you specify a string that isn't defined in the enumeration.

Some rules governing raw values:

- All raw values must be of the same type

- Raw values can be strings, characters, or any integer or floating point number type.

- Within an enumeration, each raw value must be unique.

- Integer raw values auto-increment if no value is specified for some of the enumeration members. So if you declare the raw value of a member as 1, if you don't specify otherwise, the raw value of the next member is 2.

Enumeration Associated Values

In Swift, enumerations also have an advanced feature that allows you to store *associated values* with enumeration members. In concept, this is similar to raw values, but a bit different. It allows you to store additional custom information with each member, and allows the information to change each time you use the member.

For example, the following code declares a **UniqueIdentifier** enumeration that has **UUID** (Universally Unique Identifier) and **AutoIncrement** members:

```
enum UniqueIdentifier
{
    case UUID(String)

    case AutoIncrement(Int)
}
```

The **UUID** member can have an associated **String** value and the **AutoIncrement** member can have an associated **Int** (Integer) value. This enumeration might be used in a situation where you are creating a bridge between two apps—one app that stores unique identifiers as UUID values and one that stores unique identifiers as integers.

Note that the **UniqueIdentifier** enumeration declaration doesn't specify the value of each member the way you do when you specify raw values. Rather, it simply declares the type of the value associated with each member.

This allows you to declare a variable to be of type **UniqueIdentifier**, and store either an **Int** or **UUID** value in the variable. For example:

```
var uniqueID: UniqueIdentifier
uniqueID = UniqueIdentifier.AutoIncrement(541709628)
uniqueID = UniqueIdentifier.UUID("22F66-7287-4D7E-BDB3")
```

Then, you can use a **switch** statement to check for both the **.UUID** and the **.AutoIncrement** values:

```
switch uniqueID {

case .UUID(let uuid):
      println("UUID: \(uuid)");

case .AutoIncrement(let autoInc):
      println("AutoIncrement: \(autoInc)")
}
```

In a **switch** statement, the associated value of each member can be extracted as a constant (using the **let** keyword) or a variable (using the **var** keyword.) These values are then accessible in the body of the case statement as seen in the **println**() commands.

In addition to the features already mentioned, enumerations can also have the following advanced features:

- Computed properties

- Instance methods

- Initializers to provide an initial member value

- Conformance to protocols

Using Type Aliases

Swift has a feature known as *type aliases* that allow you to assign a different name to an existing class. This can be useful in situations where a different name can help clear up its purpose in a particular context.

For example:

```
typealias CoreDataWrapper = mmBusinessObject
```

This code creates a **CoreDataWrapper** type alias for the **mmBusinessObject** class. Now you can use the type **CoreDataWrapper** name in any place where you would normally use **mmBusinessObject**.

Summary

The key points in this chapter:

Comments

- Create single-line comments by using two forward slashes:

```
// This is a single line comment
```

- Create multi-line comments by placing "/*" at the beginning of the comment line and "*/" after the last comment line. For example:

```
/*   Here is a multi-line comment
     Here is the second line
     And the third line */
```

Constants

- Constants are similar to variables in providing a place in memory where a value can be stored. The difference is a constant's value cannot be changed once it is assigned.

- To declare a constant, you use the **let** keyword:

```
let maxAllowedDigits = 10
```

- Constants are useful where you use a specific value repeatedly throughout your app.

- You should declare constants rather than use "magic numbers."

- If a value will not change, declare it as a constant. If it has the potential to change, declare it as a variable.

- Use constants when you can, and variables when you must.

Enumerations

- You declare an enumeration like this:

```
enum Operation {
    case Add
    case Subtract
    case Multiply
    case Divide
    case Clear
}
```

Each **case** statement declares a separate member of the enumeration.

- You can also declare an enumeration using a single **case** statement and list the members of the enumeration separated by commas:

```
enum Operation {

    case Add, Subtract, Multiply, Divide, Clear
}
```

- You should use Pascal case to declare both the enumeration name and the names of its members. Also, the names of the enumeration and its members should be singular rather than plural.

- Swift's enumerations can have computed properties, instance methods and initializers. In addition, you can enhance them with extensions and protocols. However, they cannot be subclassed.

- The use of enumerations and **switch** statements goes hand in hand, because a **switch** statement allows you to check all the possible enumeration values and perform an action on each.

- If a variable or constant is specified to be the type of an enumeration, you can leave out the enumeration name and simply reference the enumeration member with a period prefix. For example:

```
var op: Operation = .Add
```

- You can associate a value, such as a string, with each member of an enumeration using *raw values*.

- When declaring raw values, add a colon after the enumeration name followed by the type of the raw values (they must all be of the same type). Then specify the raw value for each member.

```
enum Operation: String {
    case Add = "+"
    case Subtract = "-"
    case Multiply = "*"
    case Divide = "/"
    case Clear = "C"
}
```

- You can access the raw value of an enumeration member by accessing its **rawValue** property. For example, the following code gets a "+" string from the **Add** member's **rawValue** property:

```
let opString: String = Operation.Add.rawValue
```

- When you declare enumerations with raw values, the enumeration automatically receives an initializer that accepts a parameter named **rawValue** of the raw value type and returns an enumeration member or **nil**. For example:

```
let op: Operation? = Operation(rawValue: "+")
```

- Here are some rules governing raw values:

  - All raw values must be of the same type.

  - Raw values can be strings, characters, or any integer or floating point number type.

  - Within an enumeration, each raw value must be unique.

  - Integer raw values auto-increment if no value is specified for some of the enumeration members.

- In Swift, enumerations also have an advanced feature that allows you to store *associated values* with enumeration members. In concept, this is similar to raw values, but a bit different. It allows you to store additional custom information with each member, and allows the information to change each time you use the member.

- As an example of associated values, the following code declares a **UniqueIdentifier** enumeration that has **UUID** (Universally Unique Identifier) and **AutoIncrement** members:

```
enum UniqueIdentifier
{
    case UUID(String)

    case AutoIncrement(Int)
}
```

This declaration doesn't specify the *value* of each member the way you do when you specify raw values. Rather, it simply declares the *type* of the value associated with each member. The **UUID** member can have an associated **String** value and the **AutoIncrement** member can have an associated **Int** (Integer) value.

- Enumerations can also have the following features:

  - Computed properties

  - Instance methods

  - Initializers to provide an initial member value

  - Conformance to protocols

- *Type aliases* allow you to assign a different name to an existing class.

Exercise 14.1

In this exercise you will use what you have learned about enumerations to improve the sample code you created in Exercise 12.1.

1. Open **Conditional.playground**.

2. Add an enumeration named **Month** at the top of the code file below the **import** statement that contains a list of months from January through December.

3. Initialize the **month** variable to **January**.

4. Change the **cases** in the **switch** statement to use the new **Month** enumeration.

5. Change the **month** variable to different months to make sure the new **switch** statement works properly.

Solution Movie 14.1

To see a video providing the solution for this exercise, you can enter the link below in your Web browser to see each step performed for you.

Movie 14.1

http://www.iOSAppsForNonProgrammers.com/B4M141.html

Chapter 15: Inheritance & Polymorphism

You've already learned a bit about inheritance. In this chapter, you're going to be diving deeper and getting a fuller picture of how inheritance works in Swift, and how you can use it to create iOS apps that are easy to extend when you need to add new functionality. Along the way, you will also learn about the important concept of polymorphism!

Sections in This Chapter

1. *Understanding Inheritance*

2. *Overriding Methods*

3. *Overriding Properties*

4. *Preventing Overriding*

5. *Polymorphism*

6. *Summary*

7. *Exercise 15.1*

8. *Solution Movie 15.1*

Understanding Inheritance

Earlier, you learned the basics of Swift *inheritance* but now you are going to dive in a bit deeper and see live examples of inheritance at work.

First, let's refresh your memory: inheritance allows you to create new classes based on other classes. Figure 15.1 shows a **ScientificCalculator** class subclassed from a **Calculator** class. In this relationship, **Calculator** is the *superclass* and **ScientificCalculator** is the *subclass*.

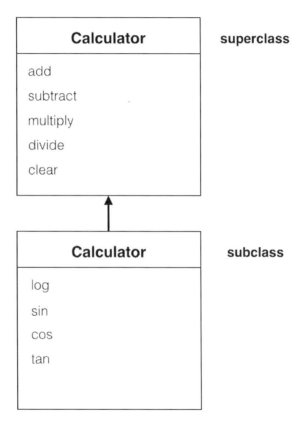

*Figure 15.1 **ScientificCalculator** is a subclass of **Calculator**.*

Specifying a superclass is optional, but you can specify a superclass in the class declaration:

```
class ScientificCalculator : Calculator {
```

A class with no superclass is known as a ***base class***.

The beauty of inheritance is that you don't have to create every class from scratch. You can create a subclass from an existing class, inherit all its properties and methods and extend it to suit your needs.

In this example, the **ScientificCalculator** inherits all the functionality of its **Calculator** superclass, including **add**, **subtract**, **multiply**, **divide**, and **clear** methods. You don't have to rewrite these methods for the **ScientificCalculator** class. They are simply inherited. Then, you can add methods in the **ScientificCalculator** class—such as **log**, **sin**, **cos**, and **tan**—that extend its functionality and specialize it.

Overriding Methods

At times, you may need to *override* a method or property inherited from a superclass. To override an inherited member, declare a new implementation of that member in a class file and mark it with the **override** keyword.

Overriding an inherited member allows you to:

- *Extend* the superclass member by doing something additional in the subclass

- *Override* the superclass member by doing something completely different in the subclass

To access a superclass member such as a property or method, use the **super.** prefix followed by the member name you are overriding.

Let's check out an example of inheritance.

1. Open the **AdvancedSwiftDemo** project.

2. In the Project Navigator, drill down into the **AdvancedSwiftDemo** node to see the **Calculator** and **ScientificCalculator** classes.

3. Select the **Calculator.swift** code file in the Project Navigator and take note of the **clear** method in the **Calculator** superclass:

```
func clear () {

        self.total = 0.0
    }
```

4. Select the **ScientificCalculator.swift** file to see that it is a subclass of the **Calculator** class:

```
class ScientificCalculator : Calculator
```

5. Notice there is also a **clear** method that is inherited from the **Calculator** class:

```
override func clear() {
        super.clear()
        self.memory = 0.0
    }
```

This method *overrides* the **clear** method in the **Calculator** superclass. Remember, you override an inherited method by adding a method with the same signature in the subclass and marking it with the **override** keyword, as shown above.

In the first line of code is a call to **super.clear**, which calls the **clear** method in the **Calculator** superclass. This is very common. When overriding a method, you often make a call to the superclass method in addition to the custom code that you have added. This allows you to extend the existing functionality of the method because you are still running the method in the superclass, and you are doing something extra in the subclass.

When the method is executed in the subclass:

*   First, a call is made to the **Calculator** superclass **clear** method that clears the **total** property.

*   Execution moves to the **ScientificCalculator** subclass **clear** method and the **memory** property is cleared.

To see this at run time:

1. Expand the **AdvancedSwiftDemoTests** node in the Project Navigator and then select the **AdvancedSwiftDemoTests.swift** code file.

2. Add the following test method before the closing curly brace of the class:

```
func testScientificCalculatorClear() {
    var calc = ScientificCalculator()
    calc.clear()
}
}
```

Although not a true unit test, this code creates an instance of the
ScientificCalculator class and then calls the object's **clear** method so
we can see how this works at run time.

3. Next, set a breakpoint on the first line of code in the new test method by
   clicking in the gutter to the left (Figure 15.2).

```
func testScientificCalculatorClear() {

    var calc = ScientificCalculator()
    calc.clear()
}
}
```

Figure 15.2 Set a breakpoint.

4. Press **Command+B** to build the project.

5. In the Navigator toolbar on the left side of the Xcode window, click the
   fifth button from the left to select the Test Navigator and then click the
   run button to the right of the **testScientificCalculatorClear()** test
   method (Figure 15.3).

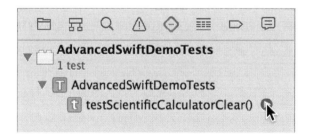

*Figure 15.3 Run the **testScientificCalculatorClear** test.*

This causes you to hit the breakpoint in the test method (Figure 15.4). As
you can see, the code that creates an instance of the
ScientificCalculator class is waiting to be executed.

```
func testScientificCalculatorClear() {

    var calc = ScientificCalculator()
    calc.clear()
}
```

Figure 15.4 The breakpoint is hit.

6. In the Debug toolbar at the bottom of the Xcode window, click the **Step into** button to execute this line of code. This begins the creation of the object and takes you to the initialization of the **ScientificCalculator's memory** property (Figure 15.5).

```
class ScientificCalculator : Calculator {

    var memory: Double = 0.0
```

*Figure 15.5 Initializing the **memory** property*

7. Press the **Step into** button twice. This takes you to the initialization of the **Calculator** class's **total** property (Figure 15.6).

```
class Calculator {

    var total: Double = 0.0
```

*Figure 15.6 Initializing the **total** property*

8. Click the **Step out** button and you will be returned to the first line of the test method. Press **Step over** and the initialized **ScientificCalculator** object that is returned by calling **ScientificCalculator()** is stored in the **calc** variable (Figure 15.7).

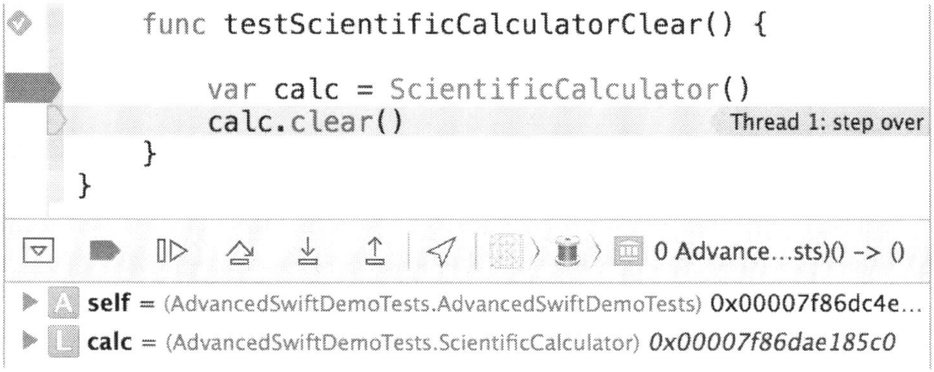

```
func testScientificCalculatorClear() {

    var calc = ScientificCalculator()
    calc.clear()                            Thread 1: step over
}
}
```

▽ ▶ ‖▷ ⌂ ↧ ↑ ⊿ ⧉ 〉 🗑 〉 🔲 0 Advance...sts)() -> ()

▶ A **self** = (AdvancedSwiftDemoTests.AdvancedSwiftDemoTests) 0x00007f86dc4e...
▶ L **calc** = (AdvancedSwiftDemoTests.ScientificCalculator) *0x00007f86dae185c0*

*Figure 15.7 The **ScientificCalculator** object is created.*

9. With a fully initialized **ScientificCalculator** object, you're ready to run its **clear** method. Click the **Step into** button twice and you will be taken to the first line of code in the **ScientificCalculator** object's **clear** method (Figure 15.8).

```
class ScientificCalculator : Calculator {

    var memory: Double = 0.0

    override func clear() {
        super.clear()
        self.memory = 0.0
    }
```

*Figure 15.8 Running the **ScientificCalculator** object's **clear** method*

10. The code that calls the superclass **clear** method is waiting to be executed. Click the **Step into** button twice and execution is taken to the Calculator's **clear** method, which is getting ready to store **0.0** in its **total** property (Figure 15.9).

```
class Calculator {

    var total: Double = 0.0

    func clear () {

        self.total = 0.0
    }
```

*Figure 15.9 Running the Calculator's **clear** method*

11. Click the **Step out** button and you will be taken back to the **ScientificCalculator** object's **clear** method, which is waiting to execute the line of code that stores **0.0** in the **memory** property (Figure 15.10).

```
class ScientificCalculator : Calculator {

    var memory: Double = 0.0

    override func clear() {
        super.clear()
        self.memory = 0.0
    }
```

*Figure 15.10 Getting ready to clear the **memory** property*

12. Click **Step out** and then **Step over** and execution will move to the end of the test method (Figure 15.11).

```
func testScientificCalculatorClear() {

    var calc = ScientificCalculator()
    calc.clear()
}                                        Thi
```

*Figure 15.11 Back in the **test** method*

13. Click the **Continue** button in the Debug toolbar to finish running the test, and then click the **Stop** button.

A few additional notes on overriding—when you override a method, you can choose to add custom code *before* the call to **super**, or *after* the call to **super** (or both). For example:

```
override func clear() {

    // Custom subclass code

    super.clear()

    // More custom subclass code
}
```

Also, if you eliminate the call to the superclass method, you *completely* override the code in the superclass, because that code never executes. It's more common to *extend* a method by including the call to **super**.

Overriding Properties

Although it's more common to override methods, there may be times you want to override properties of a superclass to add new functionality to the subclass.

Let's look at step-by-step instructions to see how it's done.

1. Start by creating a new playground. Select **File > New > Playground...** from Xcode's menu.

2. In the Create Playground dialog, change the name to

InheritancePlayground. Make sure the Platform is set to iOS, and then click **Next**.

3. In the Save dialog, select a folder to save the playground and then click **Create**.

4. Delete the "Hello, playground" sample code at the top of the playground.

5. Add the following code to the playground that declares a **PatientEntity** class has three properties:

```
class PatientEntity {

    var firstName = "Kevin"
    var lastName = "McNeish"
    var SSN = "123-45-6789"
}
```

This **PatientEntity** class contains a social security number, which is sensitive information. Add the following code below the closing curly brace of the class declaration:

```
var p = PatientEntity()
p.SSN
```

This code creates an instance of the **PatientEntity** class and then accesses its **SSN** property. This displays the information shown in Figure 15.12 in the Results sidebar.

```
var p = PatientEntity()    {firstName "Kevin" lastName "McNeish"
p.SSN                       "123-45-6789"
```

*Figure 15.12 The **PatientEntity** social security number*

In most cases, people viewing this patient's information shouldn't be able to see their full social security number. So let's create a more secure subclass.

6. Add the following code to the playground below the code you just added:

```
class PatientSecureEntity: PatientEntity {

    override var SSN: String {
```

```
    get {
    let index = advance(super.SSN.startIndex,7)
    var ss = super.SSN.substringFromIndex(index)
    return "***-**-\(ss)"
    }

    set {
    super.SSN = newValue
    }
  }
}
```

PatientSecureEntity is a subclass of **PatientEntity** and overrides the inherited **SSN** property. Some important things to note about this code:

- To override a property, you use the **override** keyword and then you *must* specify both the name and type of the property. This helps the compiler verify that you are overriding the correct property.

- In the **PatientEntity** superclass, the **SSN** property is a stored property. In Swift, you can override any property, whether it's stored or computed.

- The code in the **get** method fires whenever the **SSN** property is accessed. This code returns a series of asterisks and dashes followed by the last four digits of the social security number.

- In the **get** method, you can access the property's value using the syntax **super.propertyName**.

- If the superclass declares a property as read-write, you must provide both **get** and **set** methods in the subclass. However, if the superclass declares a read-only property, you can make it read-write in the subclass.

- If you declare a **set** method in the subclass, you must also declare a **get** method. If you don't want to do anything in the **get** method, just return **super.propertyName**.

- The code in the **set** method gets fired when a value is stored in the property. As the sample code shows, you can access the value being saved to the property using the **newValue** argument.

7. Now add the following code below the **PatientSecureEntity** to test the property overload:

```
var ps = PatientSecureEntity()
ps.SSN
```

This code creates an instance of **PatientSecureEntity** and then accesses its **SSN** property. This displays the information in Figure 15.13 in the Results side bar.

```
{{firstName "Kevin" lastName "McNeish" SSN "123-45-6789"}}
"***-**-6789"
```

*Figure 15.13 The **PatientSecureEntity** SSN*

Although the first line in the Results side bar shows the internal state of the **SSN** property, anyone referencing the **SSN** property in code will see only the last four digits as shown in the second line.

8. You can effectively create a read-only property by not adding any code to the **set** method. Since this is the secure version of the entity, you may not want to allow change to the patient's social security number. Let's make sure it' can't be changed. Comment out the code in the **set** method as shown here:

```
set {
        //super.SSN = newValue
}
```

9. Now let's see what happens if we try to assign a value to the **PatientSecureEntity** object's **SSN** property. Add the following code below the code you added in the previous step:

```
ps.SSN = "987-65-4321"
```

Check out the Results side bar and you will see the value of the **SSN** property has not changed!

Preventing Overriding

At times, you may want to prevent someone from overriding a member of a class or an entire class. Do this by using the **final** modifier.

For example, if you don't want anyone overriding the **SSN** property of the **PatientSecureEntity** class, you can mark it with the **final** modifier like this:

```
override final var SSN: String {
```

You can prevent the entire class from being overridden by marking it as **final**:

```
final class PatientSecure : Patient {
```

And here is a method marked as **final**:

```
final func log(value:Double) -> Double {
```

Polymorphism

Polymorphism is one of object-oriented programming's core principles, and you really need to understand it well to write the most effective code.

So far, whenever you have declared a variable of a particular type, you have always stored an object of that exact same type into the variable. For example, the following code declares a variable of type **UITextField**, and then creates an instance of **UITextField** and stores it in the **textField** variable:

```
var textField = UITextField()
```

No surprises here. However, in Swift, when you declare a variable of a particular type, it can also hold a reference to any *subclass* of that type. For example, take the class hierarchy shown in Figure 15.14, which shows **UITextField**, **UIButton**, and **UISlider**, just a few of the subclasses of the **UIControl** class.

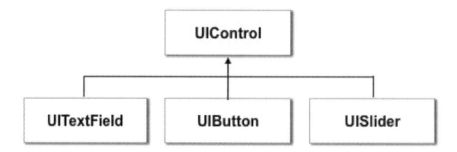

Figure 15.14 When you declare a variable of a particular type, it can hold a reference to any subclass of that type.

The word "polymorphism" means "many forms," and in this example you can see the **UIControl** class can take many different forms—a text field, a button, or a switch.

Given this hierarchy, you can declare a variable of type **UIControl** and then store a reference to the **UITextField**, **UIButton** or **UISwitch** object in this variable:

```
var control: UIControl
control = UITextField()
control = UIButton()
control = UISwitch()
```

Polymorphism allows you to write more generic code that works with families of objects, rather than writing code for a specific class. In this example, regardless of which class you ***instantiate*** (create an instance of), you can access all the properties and methods declared in the **UIControl** class that are inherited by all the subclasses.

For example, the **UIControl** class has an **enabled** property, so you can write the following line of code:

```
control.enabled = true;
```

The **UIControl** class also has an **isFirstResponder** method, so you can call the following method on the control object:

```
if control.isFirstResponder() {
        // Do something
}
```

Over time, as you write more iOS apps, you will find plenty of uses for polymorphism in building generalized code and class libraries that can be reused in many different apps.

Summary

- Inheritance allows you to create new classes that are based on other classes. For example, in the relationship shown here, **Calculator** is the *superclass* and **ScientificCalculator** is the *subclass*.

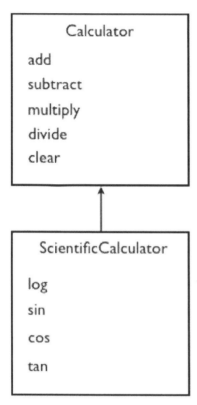

- A superclass is optional, but you can specify a superclass in the declaration of a class:

```
class ScientificCalculator : Calculator {
```

- A class with no superclass is known as a *base class*.

- To override an inherited member, you declare a new implementation of that member in a class file and mark it with the **override** keyword. For example:

```
override func clear() {
        super.clear()
        self.memory = 0.0
}
```

- To access a superclass member such as a property or method, you use the **super.** prefix followed by the member name you are overriding.

- Overriding an inherited member allows you to:

    - *Extend* the superclass member by doing something additional in the subclass and

    - *Override* the superclass member by doing something completely different in the subclass.

Overriding Methods

- When you override a method, you can choose to add custom code *before* the call to **super**, or *after* the call to **super** (or both). For example:

```
override func clear() {

    // Custom subclass code

    super.clear()

    // More custom subclass code
}
```

- If you eliminate the call to the superclass method, you *completely* override the code in the superclass, because that code never executes.

Overriding Properties

- Here is an example of overriding a property:

```
class PatientSecureEntity: PatientEntity {

    override var SSN: String {

      get {
      let index = advance(super.SSN.startIndex,7)
      var ss = super.SSN.substringFromIndex(index)
```

```
            return "***-**-\(ss)"
        }

        set {
        super.SSN = newValue
        }
    }
}
```

- To override a property, you use the **override** keyword and then you *must* specify both the name and type of the property. This helps the compiler verify that you are overriding the correct property.

- In the **PatientEntity** superclass, the **SSN** property is a stored property. In Swift, you can override any property, whether it's stored or computed.

- The code in the **get** method fires whenever the **SSN** property is accessed. This code returns a series of asterisks and dashes followed by the last four digits of the social security number.

- In the **get** method, you can access the property's value using the syntax **super.propertyName**.

- If the superclass declares a property as read-write, you must provide both a **get** and **set** method in the subclass. However, if the superclass declares a read-only property, you can make it read-write in the subclass.

- If you declare a **set** method in the subclass, you must also declare a **get** method. If you don't want to do anything in the **get** method, just return **super.propertyName**.

- The code in the **set** method gets fired when a value is stored in the property. You can access the value that is being saved to the property by means of the **newValue** argument.

- You can effectively create a read-only property by not adding any code to the **set** method.

Preventing Overriding

- Prevent a class member or an entire class from being overridden using the

final modifier.

- Here is an example of the **final** modifier on a method:

```
override final var SSN: String {
```

- Prevent the entire class from being overridden by marking it as **final**:

```
final class PatientSecure : Patient {
```
- Here is a method marked as **final**:

```
final func log(value:Double) -> Double {
```

Polymorphism

- In Swift, when you declare a variable of a particular type, it can also hold a reference to any *subclass* of that type.

- Since **UITextField**, **UIButton**, and **UISwitch** are all subclasses of **UIControl**, you can declare a variable of type **UIControl** and store a reference to any of these subclasses in that variable:

```
var control: UIControl
control = UITextField()
control = UIButton()
control = UISwitch()
```

- The word "polymorphism" means "many forms". For example the **UIControl** class can take many different forms—a text field, a button, or a switch.

- Polymorphism allows you to write more generic code that works with families of objects, rather than only with a specific class.

Exercise 15.1

In this exercise, you will test what you have learned about inheritance to create a subclass and override an inherited property and method.

1. Create a playground named **Inheritance.playground**.

2. Declare a **Person** class with **firstName** and **lastName** properties

initialized to an empty string.

3. Declare a **fullName** computed property that returns the **firstName** and **lastName** separated by a space.

4. Declare a **Patient** class as a subclass of **Person**.

5. Declare a **patientID** property in the **Patient** class and initialize it to an empty string.

6. Override the inherited **fullName** property and return **lastName** uppercased and **firstName** separated by a comma and space (LAST, First).

7. Let's test the inherited property. In the **Person** class, set the **firstName** property to "Jane" and the **lastName** property to "Doe".

8. Add code to the playground that instantiates the **Person** and **Patient** classes and checks their **fullName** properties.

9. In the **Person** class, add a **String** array property named **brokenRules** and initialize it to an empty string array.

10. Add the following method to the **Person** class:

```
func checkRequiredValues() -> [String] {

    if self.firstName.isEmpty {
        self.brokenRules.append("First Name")
    }
    if self.lastName.isEmpty {
        self.brokenRules.append("Last Name")
    }
    return self.brokenRules
}
```

11. In the **Patient** class, override the **checkRequiredValues** method. Within the method, call the superclass method, and then check if the **patientID** property is empty. If so, add "Patient ID" to the **brokenRules** array, and then return the array from the method.

12. In the **Person** class, set **lastName** to an empty string.

13. Add code to the bottom of the playground that calls the **checkRequiredValues** method on the **Person** and **Patient** objects.

Solution Movie 15.1

To see a video providing the solution for this exercise, you can enter the link below in your Web browser to see each step performed for you.

Movie 15.1

http://www.iOSAppsForNonProgrammers.com/B4M151.html

Chapter 16: Initializers

Learning to properly use initializers in Swift can be daunting at first. Swift's requirement that all stored properties be initialized introduces challenges for the app developer. This chapter gives you hands-on experience on how best to implement initializers for your custom classes.

Sections in This Chapter

Creating Initializers for Your Custom Classes

When you create your own custom classes in Swift, make sure new objects instantiated from your custom class are properly initialized (ready to be used). This usually involves making sure all stored properties have an initial value, as well as any other specialized setup your class may require.

In Swift, all stored properties must be initialized. They are not allowed to be in an unknown state. There are two main ways to store an initial value in a property:

1. **In the property declaration** - For example:

```
class Calculator {

    var total: Double = 0.0
```

2. **In an initializer** - For example:

```
class Calculator {

    var total: Double

    // Initializer
    init() {
        self.total = 0.0
    }
```

Where the initial value of the property is always the same, choose the first option and initialize the value in the property declaration. This closely links the initialization of the property with its declaration, making your code more intuitive.

Where the initial value of a property changes, use an initializer instead. For example, if you want to display the total from the last time the Calculator was used, you could read it from a database on the local device. In that scenario, it makes sense to set the **total** property's initial value in an initializer:

```
class Calculator {

    var total: Double
```

```
init() {

    // Get last total value
    self.total = Calculator.getPreviousTotal()
}
```

Initialization and Type Inference

If you store an initial value in a property's declaration, you don't need to specify the type of the property, because Swift can figure out—or infer—its type based on the type of the value you are storing in the property.

However, if you set the initial value of a property in an initializer, you must specify the property's type when you declare it.

Declaring Initializers

Some basic rules governing initializers:

- Initializers in Swift are always named **init**.

- You don't use the **func** keyword when declaring an initializer.

- Initializers do not return a value.

- You can create several initializers for a single class that accept different parameters.

- If your class has a superclass, you must call one of its *designated initializers* from your custom initializer (more on that in just a bit).

Initializer Parameters

You can create multiple initializer methods for your custom classes that provide consumers of your class a variety of ways to initialize objects.

If you have a class that requires specific properties to be set by the app developer before it can be used, you should create one or more initializers that allow those values to be passed in on initialization. This helps make your class self-documenting and is a best practice.

To help you better understand how initializers work, let's create a **Translator** class whose purpose is to translate phrases from one language to another (this will just be a mockup). First, we will create the class with no initializers, and then we will improve it by adding an initializer with parameters.

1. In Xcode, open the project located in the folder where you have stored this book's sample code.

2. Right-click the **InitializerDemo** group and then select **New File...** from the popup menu.

3. On the left side of the Create File dialog under the **iOS** section, select **Source**.

4. On the right side of the dialog, select the **Swift File** template, and then click **Next**.

5. In the Save File dialog, change the **Name** of the file to **Translator.swift**, and then click the **Create** button. This adds the **Translator.swift** file to the project.

6. Add the following enumeration declaration at the top of the file below the **import Foundation** statement:

```
import Foundation

enum Language {
    case Arabic, Bengali, English, Hindi,
        Japanese, Chinese, Portuguese, Spanish
}
```

This enumeration declares all the languages the **Translator** class supports.

7. Now add the following class declaration below the enumeration declaration:

```
class Translator {
    var fromLanguage : Language? = nil
    var toLanguage : Language? = nil
}
```

In this example, the **Translator** class's main purpose is to translate phrases from one language to another. It can't perform any translations without knowing the "from" and "to" languages.

However, the **fromLanguage** and **toLanguage** properties are marked as optional. From a practical perspective, these values are anything *but* optional! **Note:** You don't need to explicitly set optional properties to **nil**, but I did this to get around a bug with the Swift compiler!

8. Let's try to create an instance of this class from a unit test. With the **Translator.swift** file selected in the Project Navigator, go to the File Inspector (the first button on the left in the Inspector toolbar) and select the **InitializerDemoTests** check box. Remember, this makes the class accessible to the unit test project.

9. Expand the **InitializerDemoTests** group in the Project Navigator, and select the **InitializerDemoTests.swift** file.

10. Add the following test method to the bottom of the code file above the closing curly brace of the class:

```
    func testTranslator()
    {
    var t = Translator()
    t.fromLanguage = Language.English
    t.toLanguage = Language.Chinese
    }
}
```

This is a bad design for the Translator class. It requires the developer to figure out that the **fromLanguage** and **toLanguage** properties must be set before the **Translator** object can be used.

Let's create a better class design.

1. Go back to the **Translator** class and remove **? = nil** from the **fromLanguage** and **toLanguage** properties to indicate they are not

optional. Afterward, add the initializer as shown here:

```
class Translator {
    var fromLanguage : Language
    var toLanguage : Language

    init(from: Language, to: Language)
    {
        self.fromLanguage = from
        self.toLanguage = to
    }
}
```

This class now has a single initializer with **from** and **to** parameters of type **Language**.

2. Press **Command+B** to build the project. You should now have one compiler error. To see what's causing the problem, select the **InitializerDemoTests.swift** file in the Project Navigator and you should see the error shown in Figure 16.1.

```
func testTranslator()
{
    var t = Translator()  ① Missing argument for parameter 'from' in call
    t.fromLanguage = Language.English
    t.toLanguage = Language.Chinese
}
```

Figure 16.1 The "Missing argument" compiler error

The complete text of the error states, "**Missing argument from parameter 'from' in call.**" Why are you getting this error?

If you don't specify a custom initializer for a class, behind the scenes, the Swift compiler adds a default initializer to the class that accepts no parameters. However, if you create a custom initializer, it no longer adds the default initializer. That's why the code in the unit test that tries to use this default initializer fails.

In our example, this is exactly what we want! We want to force developers to pass the two necessary **Language** values when they create an instance of a class. Let's change the code to do that now.

3. First, delete all the code inside the **testTranslator** method. Afterwards,

add the following code:

```
func testTranslator()
{
        var t = Translator(
}
```

When you type the left parenthesis, Code Completion pops up offering the option shown in Figure 16.2.

```
func testTranslator()
{
    var t = Translator(from:  Language , to:  Language )
}              M Translator (from: Language, to: Language)
```

Figure 16.2 Code Completion for the custom initializer

This makes it abundantly clear to a developer that they must specify the "from" and "to" languages when creating an instance of the **Translator** class.

4. With the Code Completion template displayed (if it's not visible, press **escape** to redisplay it), press **tab** to move to the **from** placeholder and type **Language.English**. Press **tab** a second time to move to the **to** placeholder and enter **Language.Chinese**. Afterward, press the right arrow key to have Swift auto-fill the closing parenthesis for you. When you're finished, your code should look like this:

```
func testTranslator()
{
        var t = Translator(from: Language.English,
        to: Language.Chinese)
}
```

You can see that Code Completion inserts the parameter names into the method call. This is mandatory. If you leave out these parameter names, you will get a compiler error! Press **Command+B** and you should compile successfully.

Again, this is not a true unit test, but I wanted you to experience calling different types of initializers.

Local and External Parameter Names

Local and external parameter names work a little differently for initializers than for regular methods.

Since an initializer is always called **init**, you don't have the luxury of creating an initializer name that includes a description of the first parameter. Because of this, Swift provides an automatic external name that is the same as the local name for every parameter that you declare, as Figure 16.2 shows.

If you want to declare an external name different from the local name, use the same syntax as with regular Swift methods. For example, the following code declares a different external name for the **from** and **to** local parameter names (don't add these to your sample code):

```
init(fromLanguage from: Language,
        toLanguage to: Language)
{
    self.fromLanguage = from
    self.toLanguage = to
}
```

In this example, declaring external parameter names changes the names of the parameters when you call the initializer as in Figure 16.3.

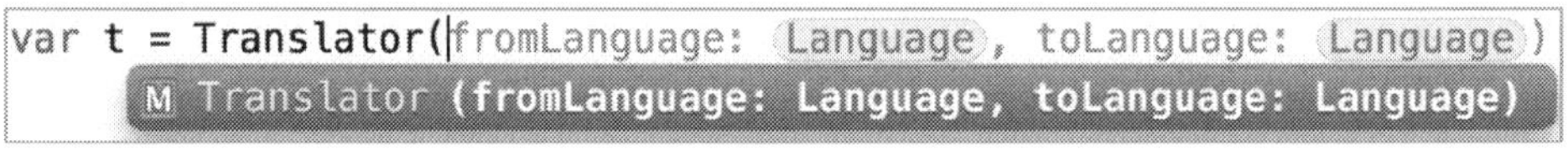

Figure 16.3 The new external names in action

If you don't want to provide an external name for a parameter, simply insert an underscore before the local parameter name. For example (don't add this to your sample code):

```
init(_ from: Language, _ to: Language)
{
    self.fromLanguage = from
    self.toLanguage = to
}
```

Designated & Convenience Initializers

Swift supports two main types of initializers—designated and convenience initializers. Let's take a closer look at each so you can learn how best to initialize your custom classes.

Designated Initializers

A ***designated initializer*** is the main initializer for a class. It initializes all properties declared in the class, and is responsible for calling an initializer in its superclass (if it has is a superclass).

For example, in the **Translator** class, **init:from:to:** is the designated initializer, because it initializes both the properties that are declared in the class.

Here is the syntax of a designated initializer:

```
init(parameters)
{
    statements
}
```

Every class must have at least one designated initializer. You can have more than one, but its more common to have just one.

Convenience Initializers

A ***convenience initializer*** is a secondary class initializer that typically accepts fewer parameters than the designated initializer, but then calls the designated initializer with defaults set for some of the parameters. Convenience initializers are optional, but they often make it easier for your classes to be instantiated.

Here is the syntax of a convenience initializer:

```
convenience init(parameters)
{
    statements
}
```

Let's create a convenience initializer so you can more clearly understand how they work.

1. Select the **Translator.swift** file in the Project Navigator.

2. Add the following initializer to the **Translator** class:

```
class Translator {
    var fromLanguage : Language
    var toLanguage : Language

    init(from: Language, to: Language)
    {
        self.fromLanguage = from
        self.toLanguage = to
    }

    convenience init(toLanguage: Language)
    {
        self.init(from: Language.English,
        to: toLanguage)
    }
}
```

Some important points to note:

• The **convenience** keyword is used to mark the method as a convenience initializer.

• The convenience initializer calls the designated initializer in the same class, passing a default **Language.English** value as the first parameter and passing through its own **toLanguage** parameter as the second parameter.

• This convenience initializer allows you to instantiate the class by passing only one parameter to the initializer. For example:

```
var t = Translator(toLanguage: Language.German)
```

• When you instantiate an instance of the class, Code Completion now shows both initializers (Figure 16.4).

```
var t = Translator(toLanguage: Language )
    M  Translator (from: Language, to: Language)
    M  Translator (toLanguage: Language)
```

Figure 16.4 Multiple initializers in Code Completion

Initializer Chaining

Initializer chaining occurs when one initializer calls another in the same class or in its superclass. In Apple's Swift documentation, three rules are listed that govern initializer chaining.

These rules can be boiled down to one **Golden Rule of Initializer Chaining**:

> *When you instantiate an object, a designated initializer must be executed in every class in the inheritance chain.*

For an example of this, check out the classes shown in Figure 16.5. **ScientificCalculator** is a subclass of **Calculator**, which in turn is a subclass of **BusinessObject**. The Golden Rule dictates that when you instantiate an instance of the **ScientificCalculator** class, the designated initializer of each class (shown in bold) must be executed. Figure 16.5 shows one possible initializer chaining path, but regardless of the path, *a designated initializer must be executed in every class in the inheritance chain.*

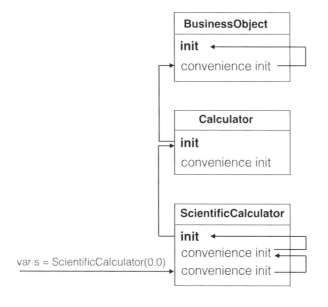

Figure 16.5 Initializer chaining in action

Now let's take a look at Apple's three rules and see how they are really enforcing the one Golden Rule.

1. *Designated initializers must call a designated initializer from their immediate superclass* - If you skip a level of inheritance, then you break the Golden Rule, because one of the designated initializers in the inheritance chain wouldn't be called.

2. *Convenience initializers must call another initializer available in the same class* - If a convenience initializer called an initializer in a different class or didn't call another initializer in the same class, the designated initializer in that class would not be executed, breaking the Golden Rule.

3. *Convenience initializers must ultimately end up calling a designated initializer* - If this rule is broken, then the designated initializer in the same class as the convenience initializer would not be executed.

Two-Phase Initialization

Swift's class initialization occurs in two phases. Figure 16.6 demonstrates these two phases when you instantiate an instance of the **Translator** class that is a subclass of the **BusinessObject** class (we'll change things in just a bit so that it is). Here are the basic steps:

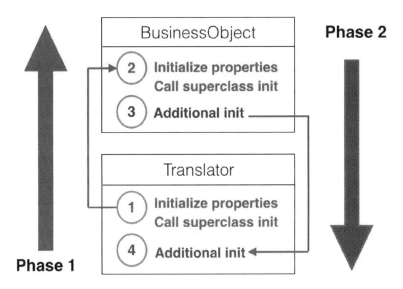

Figure 16.6 Two-phase initialization

1. The **Translator** object's initializer is executed and its properties are

initialized.

2. The **Translator** object calls up to the superclass initializer and the **BusinessObject** properties are initialized.

3. The **BusinessObject's** initializer can optionally perform additional initialization including referencing self and calling instance methods.

4. Execution is transferred back to the **Translator** object's initializer, which can optionally perform additional initialization.

To help you fully understand how this two-phase initialization works, let's make the **Translator** class a subclass of **BusinessObject** and see how this affects its initialization.

1. In the **InitializerDemo** project, select the **BusinessObject.swift** file in the Project Navigator.

2. Notice the **BusinessObject** class has a **dbName** and an **entityClassName** property as well as a single designated initializer that accepts a **dbName** parameter:

```
class BusinessObject
{
    var dbName : String
    var entityClassName : String = ""

    init(dbName: String)
    {
        self.dbName = dbName
    }
}
```

3. Select the **Translator.swift** file in the Project Navigator. It has **fromLanguage** and **toLanguage** properties as well as a designated initializer and convenience initializer:

```
class Translator {

    var fromLanguage : Language
    var toLanguage : Language

    init(from: Language, to: Language)
    {
```

```
        self.fromLanguage = from
        self.toLanguage = to
}

    convenience init(toLanguage: Language)
    {
        self.init(from: Language.English,
            to: toLanguage)
    }
```

4. Now let's create the inheritance relationship shown in Figure 16.7.

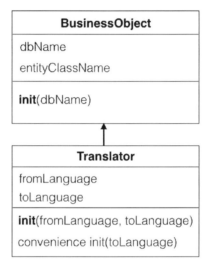

*Figure 16.7 **BusinessObject** and **Translator** classes*

Add the following superclass declaration to the **Translator** class:

```
class Translator: BusinessObject {
```

As soon as you specify this relationship, you're going to get a compiler error that states, "Super.init isn't called before returning from init." To fix this problem, go to the **Translator** class's designated initializer and add the following call to the superclass initializer:

```
init(from: Language, to: Language)
{
        self.fromLanguage = from
        self.toLanguage = to

        super.init(dbName: "InitializerDemo")
}
```

This code calls the **BusinessObject** class's designated initializer, passing a value for the **dbName** parameter.

5. Press **Command+B** and you should build successfully.

Initializer Safety Checks

Four basic safety checks performed by the Swift compiler ensure Swift's two-phase initialization is properly set up in your custom classes.

Let's look at each of these checks in the context of the **Translator** and **BusinessObject** relationship you have just set up.

Safety Check 1: *A designated initializer must ensure that all of the properties introduced by its class are initialized before it delegates up to a superclass initializer.*

The **Translator** class currently initializes both of its properties before it makes a call to **super.init**. If you comment out the code that initializes the **toLanguage** property (don't do this in your sample code), the compiler enforce Safety Check 1 as shown in Figure 16.8.

```
class Translator : BusinessObject {

    var fromLanguage : Language
    var toLanguage : Language

    init(from: Language, to: Language)
    {
        self.fromLanguage = from
        //self.toLanguage = to

        super.init(dbName: "InitializerDemo")
    }                ● Property 'self.toLanguage' not initialized at super.init call
```

*Figure 16.8 Calling **super.init** before initializing properties*

Safety Check 2: *A designated initializer must delegate up to a superclass initializer before assigning a value to an inherited property.*

The **Translator** class inherits the **entityClassName** property from the **BusinessObject** class. If you try to set the value of this property in the Translator's initializer before making a call to **super.init**, you will see the compiler enforce Safety Check 2 (Figure 16.9).

```
class Translator : BusinessObject {

    var fromLanguage : Language
    var toLanguage : Language

    init(from: Language, to: Language)
    {
        self.fromLanguage = from
        self.toLanguage = to
        self.entityClassName = "TranslatorEntity"
           ⓘ Use of property 'entityClassName' in base object before super.init initializes it
        super.init(dbName: "InitializerDemo")
    }
}
```

*Figure 16.9 Initializing an inherited property before calling **super.init***

Safety Check 3: *A convenience initializer must delegate to another initializer before assigning a value to any property (including properties defined by the same class).*

If you add code to the **Translator** object's convenience initializer that sets the value of the **fromLanguage** property before calling the designated initializer, you will see the compiler enforce Safety Check 3 as Figure 16.10 illustrates.

```
convenience init(toLanguage: Language)
{
    self.fromLanguage = Language.English
              ⓘ Use of 'self' in delegating initializer before self.init is called
    self.init(from: Language.English, to: toLanguage)
}
```

Figure 16.10 A convenience initializer assigning a value to a property before calling another initializer

Safety Check 4: *An initializer cannot call any instance methods, read the values of any instance properties, or refer to **self** as a value until after the first phase of initialization is complete.*

Add the following convenience initializer and instance method to the **Translator** class (keep the other initializers):

```
convenience init()
{
    self.init(toLanguage: Language.English)
```

```
          var languages = self.getLastUsedLanguages()

          self.fromLanguage = languages.from
          self.toLanguage = languages.to
}

func getLastUsedLanguages() -> (from:Language,
          to:Language)
{
          // Mimic reading from the database
          return (Language.English, Language.Spanish)
}
```

This convenience initializer first calls **self.init**, and then calls the
getLastUsedLanguages instance method, which reads the previously used
from/to languages from a local database (we're just mimicking that here)
returning the languages in a tuple. The initializer then stores those values in
the **fromLanguage** and **toLanguage** properties.

If you move the call to the instance method above the call to **self.init**, you
would see the compiler enforce Safety Check 4 as Figure 16.11 illustrates.

```
convenience init()
{
     var languages = self.getLastUsedLanguages()
          🛈 Use of 'self' in delegating initializer before self.init is called
     self.init(toLanguage: Language.English)

     self.fromLanguage = languages.from
     self.toLanguage = languages.to
}
```

*Figure 16.11 Calling an instance method before the first initialization phase is
complete*

At times, you can get around this limitation by calling a class method rather
than an instance method. To see this demonstrated, remove the
convenience keyword from the initializer that accepts no parameters to
make it a designated initializer, add the **class** keyword to the
getLastUsedLanguages method, and change the code in the initializer as
shown here:

```
init()
{
     var languages = Translator.getLastUsedLanguages()
```

```
    self.fromLanguage = languages.from
    self.toLanguage = languages.to

    super.init(dbName: "InitializerDemo")
}

class func getLastUsedLanguages() -> (from:Language,
to:Language)
{
    // Mimic reading from the database
    return (Language.English, Language.Spanish)
}
```

This gives the **Translator** class two designated initializers (which is perfectly legal) and allows the initializer to set the values of the **fromLanguage** and **toLanguage** properties in phase 1 of initialization rather than waiting for phase 2.

Initializer Inheritance

Unlike regular methods, Swift initializers are only inherited by a subclass under specific conditions.

Let's try a hands-on example so you fully understand how this works. Since you are already familiar with the **Translator** class and its initializers, let's create a subclass of **Translator** to see how initializer inheritance works.

1. In the **InheritanceDemo** project in Xcode, right-click the **Translator.swift** file in the Project Navigator and select **New File...** from the menu.

2. On the left side of the New File dialog under the **iOS** section, select **Source**. On the right side of the dialog, select **Swift File**, and then click **Next**.

3. In the Save File dialog, change the **Name** of the file to **Subtranslator.swift** and click the **Create** button. This adds the new code file to the Project Navigator.

4. Add the following class declaration with no superclass specified to the **Subtranslator.swift** file:

```
class Subtranslator {

}
```

5. With the **Subtranslator.swift** file selected in the Project Navigator, go to the File Inspector (the first button on the left in the Inspector toolbar) and select the **InitializerDemoTests** check box.

6. Select the **InitializerDemoTests.swift** file in the Project Navigator and add the following test method before the closing curly brace of the class:

```
func testInitializerInheritance()
{
    var st = Subtranslator()
}

}
```

When you type the opening parenthesis to invoke the **Subtranslator** initializer, notice there is only one initializer shown in Code Completion (Figure 16.12). This is the default initializer Swift provides when you don't declare any initializers for a class.

Figure 16.12 The default initializer

Let's see what happens when we make **Subtranslator** a subclass of the **Translator** class.

1. Add the following code to the **Subtranslator.swift** file's class definition:

```
class Subtranslator: Translator {

}
```

2. Press **Command+B** to build the project.

3. Go back to the **InitializerDemoTests.swift** file and delete the parentheses in the code that creates an instance of the **Subtranslator** class. Afterward, add the opening parentheses back in and you will see the list of initializer methods shown in Figure 16.13 (due to a bug in Xcode, you may not see all the initializers in Code Completion, but you can still use them).

```
func testInitializerInheritance()
{
    var st = Subtranslator(|)
         M  Subtranslator ()
         M  Subtranslator (from: Language, to: Language)
         M     Translator (toLanguage: Language)
}
```

Figure 16.13 Inherited initializers

The first two initializers in the list are designated initializers inherited from the **Translator** class. This is because of Swift's first rule of initializer inheritance:

Rule 1: *If your subclass doesn't define any designated initializers, it automatically inherits all its superclass-designated initializers.*

We didn't declare any initializers in the **Subtranslator** class, so it inherited the designated initializers from the **Translator** class.

The third initializer in the Code Completion list shown in Figure 16.13 is a convenience initializer. This initializer is also inherited from the **Translator** class because of Swift's second rule of initializer inheritance.

Rule 2: *If your subclass provides an implementation of all of its superclass designated initializers—either by inheriting them as according to rule 1, or by providing a custom implementation as part of its definition—then it automatically inherits all the superclass convenience initializers.*

The **Subtranslator** class inherited all of the **Translator** class's designated initializers, so it also inherited its convenience initializer.

Now let's see what happens if we declare a designated initializer in the **Subtranslator** subclass.

1. In the **Subtranslator.swift** file, add the following property and designated initializer:

```
class Subtranslator: Translator {

    var limit: Int32 = 0

    init(translationLimit: Int32) {

        self.limit = translationLimit
        super.init()
    }
}
```

2. Go back to the **InitializerDemoTests.swift** file and delete the parentheses in the code that creates an instance of the **Subtranslator** class. Afterward, add the opening parenthesis back in and you will see the list of initializer methods shown in Figure 16.14.

```
func testInitializerInheritance()
{
    var st = Subtranslator(translationLimit  Int32 )
}
          M  Subtranslator (translationLimit: Int32)
```

Figure 16.14 No initializers are inherited.

According to the rules of initializer inheritance, the **Subtranslator** class no longer inherits any initializers from the **Translator** class, because it declares its own designated initializer.

Let's change the **Subtranslator** designated initializer to a convenience initializer and see what happens.

1. In the **Subtranslator.swift** code file, change the initializer to the following code:

```
convenience init(translationLimit: Int32) {

        self.init()
        self.limit = translationLimit
}
```

2. Now go back to the **InitializerDemoTests.swift** code file, delete the parentheses, add the opening parenthesis back in and you will see the list of initializers shown in Figure 16.15 (again, due to a bug in Xcode, you may not see all the initializers in the Code Completion list, but you can use them in your app's code).

```
func testInitializerInheritance()
{
    var st = Subtranslator()
}       M  Subtranslator ()
        M  Subtranslator (from: Language, to: Language)
        M      Translator (toLanguage: Language)
        M  Subtranslator (translationLimit: Int32)
```

Figure 16.15 The inherited initializers are back!

From this, we learn that if a subclass only declares convenience initializers, it inherits all its superclass initializers.

3. Delete the partial code you added to the test method.

Overriding Initializers

As with regular Swift methods, if you override an initializer from a superclass, you use the **override** keyword and declare an initializer with the same parameters and types. Let's give it a try.

1. In the **Subtranslator.swift** code file, add the following initializer overrides:

```
override init(from: Language, to: Language)
{
        super.init(from: from, to: to)
}

override init()
{
        super.init()
}
```

These initializers override the designated initializers in the **Translator** superclass.

2. Go back to the **InitalizerDemoTests.swift** file and check out the initializers that now appearing in the Code Completion list (Figure 16.16).

```
func testInitializerInheritance()
{
    var st = Subtranslator()
}
       M Subtranslator ()
       M Subtranslator (from: Language, to: Language)
       M    Translator (toLanguage: Language)
       M Subtranslator (translationLimit: Int32)
```

Figure 16.16 Still inheriting the convenience initializers when manually overriding the designated initializers

You can see the **Subtranslator** class still inherits the convenience initializers when it manually overrides the **Translator** class's designated initializers.

Another point about overriding initializers is that a class can override a designated initializer and make it a convenience initializer instead. Doing this still allows the subclass to inherit the superclass convenience initializers.

Required Initializers

When you specify a *required initializer*, it must be implemented in all subclasses. You add the **required** modifier to an initializer to indicate that it is required:

```
class Translator {

    required init()
    {
    }
}
```

When you implement a required initializer in a subclass, you specify the **required** keyword to indicate that subclasses lower in the inheritance chain are also required to implement the initializer. Note that you don't use the **override** keyword when providing an implementation of a required initializer:

```
class Subtranslator: Translator {

    required init() {

        super.init()
    }
}
```

If a subclass automatically inherits a required initializer from its superclass, you don't need to explicitly declare one in the subclass.

Optional Properties & Constants

Optional properties automatically receive a value of **nil** during initialization. You should declare a property as optional if it's allowed to have no value during initialization or at some later point. For example:

```
var middleName: String?
```

Constant property values can be set during initialization, but they must have a definite value by the time the initialization process is complete. Constant values can only be set by the class they are declared in. This means you can't modify the value of a constant property in a subclass.

Failable Initializers

Apple introduced sweeping changes to initializers in Swift 1.1, including a number of breaking changes (meaning, code that compiled properly in Swift 1.0, produced compiler errors in Swift 1.1).

In Swift 1.0, there were two ways to create a new instance of a particular type:

1. Call an initializer

2. Call a *factory method*

A factory method is a method that creates an object. For example, in Swift 1.0, you could create a new **NSDate** object initialized to the current date by calling the **today** factory method on the **NSDate** class:

```
let today = NSDate.today()
```

As another example, in Swift 1.0, enumerations had a **fromRaw** factory method that returned an optional enum member for the specified raw value:

```
let op: Operation? = Operation.fromRaw("+")
```

In Swift 1.1, most factory methods have been replaced by initializers, because as Apple states, it "simplifies the language by eliminating the confusion and duplication between initializers and factory methods."

So for example, the **today** method in the **NSDate** class has been replaced by an initializer that accepts no arguments:

```
let today = NSDate()
```

The **fromRaw** factory method has been replaced by an initializer that accepts a parameter named **rawValue** and returns an enumeration member or **nil**:

```
let op: Operation? = Operation(rawValue: "+")
```

The initializer in this example returns **nil** if you specify a string that isn't defined in the enumeration.

In Swift 1.0, initializers could not return **nil** values. To enable this functionality in Swift 1.1, Apple introduced *failable initializers*. A failable initializer returns an object if the initialization succeeds, or a **nil** if it doesn't. A regular initializer cannot return a **nil**.

When to Create Failable Initializers

In Swift, you can create failable initializers for your own custom classes. However, you should use this feature sparingly. In most cases your initializers should succeed. They should only fail if the primary information the class needs in order to function properly is not provided.

The **UIImage** class is a good example of properly using a failable initializer:

```
let img = UIImage(contentsOfFile: "Image.png")
```

This initializer accepts a single String argument that specifies the name of an image file. If the image file exists, the initializer returns an object. Otherwise, it returns **nil**.

Declaring Failable Initializers

You declare a failable initializer by adding a question mark after the **init** keyword. For example:

```
class mmBusinessObject {

    var dbName: String?

    init?(dbName: String) {

        if dbName.isEmpty {
            return nil
        }
        self.dbName = dbName
    }
}
```

This initializer accepts a single **dbName** string argument that specifies the database associated with the business object. Calling the initializer with a database name returns an instance of the class. Calling the initializer with an empty string returns **nil**.

You indicate the point of failure in an initializer by writing **return nil**. This is somewhat confusing since Swift initializers do not directly return a value. In fact, if initialization succeeds, there is no statement that returns an instance from the initializer. Ultimately, the act of calling an initializer returns an object:

```
let employee = Employee()
```

However, the new instance is not returned directly from the initializer.

Failable Initializer Rules

- You can't declare a failable and non-failable initializer with the same parameter names and types.

- Structures and enumerations can trigger a failure at any point in the initialization process.

- A class can only trigger a failure after it initializes all stored properties it introduces, and any required initialization delegation has taken place.

- A failable initializer can call another failable initializer in the same type, or in its superclass.

- A failable initializer can also delegate to a non-failable initializer.

- A non-failable initializer cannot delegate to a failable initializer.

- Enumerations with raw values automatically receive an initializer that accepts a parameter named **rawValue** and returns an enumeration member or **nil**.

- You can override a failable initializer in a subclass.

- You can override a failable initializer with a non-failable initializer, which allows you to create a subclass that can't fail initialization even though its superclass can.

- You can't override a non-failable initializer with a failable initializer.

The init! Failable Initializer

You can create an initializer that returns an implicitly unwrapped optional instance by adding an exclamation mark (rather than a question mark) after the **init** keyword. For example:

```
class ABusinessObject: mmBusinessObject {

    init!() {
        super.init(dbName: "MyDBCName")
    }
}
```

In this example, **ABusinessObject** calls its superclass's failable initializer, passing the name of a database. This means initialization never fails. It makes sense to mark **ABusinessObject's** initializer as implicitly unwrapped so you don't have to deal with optional values when creating an instance of **ABusinessObject** or its subclasses.

Some rules regarding **init!** failable initializer:

- You can delegate from **init?** to **init!**

- You can delegate from **init!** to **init?**

- You can delegate from **init** to **init!**, but you will get a runtime error if the **init!** initializer fails.

- You can override from **init?** to **init!**

- You can override from **init!** to **init?**

Summary

Key points to remember about Swift initializers.

- All non-optional stored properties must be initialized. They are not allowed to be in an unknown state.

- There are two main ways to store an initial value in a property:

    1. **In the property declaration** - For example:

    ```
    class Calculator {

        var total: Double = 0.0
    ```

    2. **In an initializer** - For example:

    ```
    class Calculator {

        var total: Double

        // Initializer
        init() {
            self.total = 0.0
        }
    ```

- Where the initial value of the property is always the same, you should choose the first option and initialize the value in the property declaration. This closely links the initialization of the property with its declaration, making your code more intuitive.

- Where the initial value of a property changes, you should use an initializer instead.

- If you store an initial value in a property's declaration, you don't need to specify the type of the property, because Swift can infer it from the type of the value you are storing in the property.

- If you set the initial value of a property in an initializer, you must specify the property's type when you declare it.

- Some basic rules governing initializers:

  - Initializers in Swift are always named **init**.

  - You don't use the **func** keyword when declaring an initializer.

  - Initializers do not return a value.

  - You can create several initializers for a single class that accept different parameters.

  - If your class has a superclass, you must call one of its ***designated initializers*** from your custom initializer.

- You can create multiple initializer methods for your custom classes that provide consumers of your class a variety of ways to initialize objects.

- *Best Practice*: If a class requires specific properties to be set by the app developer before it can be used, you should create one or more initializers that allow those values to be passed in on initialization.

- If you don't specify a custom initializer for a class, behind the scenes, the Swift compiler adds a default initializer to the class that accepts no parameters. However, if you create a custom initializer, it no longer adds the default initializer.

- Swift provides an automatic external name that is the same as the local name for every parameter you declare.

Designated & Convenience Initializers

- Swift supports two main types of initializers—designated and convenience initializers.

- A *designated initializer* is the main initializer for a class. It initializes all properties declared in the class, and is responsible for calling an initializer in its superclass (if it has a superclass).

- Here is the syntax of a designated initializer:

```
init(parameters)
{
        statements
}
```

- Every class must have at least one designated initializer.

Initializer Chaining

- **The Golden Rule of Initializer Chaining**: When you instantiate an object, a designated initializer must be executed in every class in the inheritance chain.

- This Golden Rule encompasses Apple's three rules of initializer chaining:

  1. *Designated initializers must call a designated initializer from their immediate superclass.*

  2. *Convenience initializers must call another initializer available in the same class.*

  3. *Convenience initializers must ultimately end up calling a designated initializer.*

Two-Phase Initialization

- Swift's initialization takes place in two phases:

- In phase 1, starting with the class you instantiated and working up the inheritance chain, each class initializes the properties it declares.

- In phase 2, starting with the class at the top of the inheritance hierarchy, each class can perform additional initialization including referencing **self** and calling instance methods.

Initializer Safety Checks

- Four basic safety checks are performed by the Swift compiler to make sure Swift's two-phase initialization is set up properly in your custom classes.

  - **Safety Check 1:** *A designated initializer must ensure that all of the properties introduced by its class are initialized before it delegates up to a superclass initializer.*

    ```
    init(from: Language, to: Language)
    {
        self.fromLanguage = from
        self.toLanguage = to

        super.init(dbName: "InitializerDemo")
    }
    ```

  - **Safety Check 2:** A designated initializer must delegate up to a superclass initializer before assigning a value to an inherited property.

    ```
    init(from: Language, to: Language)
    {
        self.fromLanguage = from
        self.toLanguage = to

        super.init(dbName: "InitializerDemo")

        self.myInheritedProperty = true
    }
    ```

  - **Safety Check 3:** A convenience initializer must delegate to another initializer before assigning a value to any property (including properties defined by the same class).

    ```
    convenience init(toLanguage: Language)
    {
      self.init(from: Language.English,
          to: toLanguage)

      self.myProperty = true
    }
    ```

  - **Safety Check 4:** An initializer cannot call any instance methods, read the values of any instance properties, or refer to self as a value until after the first phase of initialization is complete.

```
convenience init()
{
  self.init(toLanguage: Language.English)

  var languages = self.getLastUsedLanguages()
}
```

Initializer Inheritance

- Unlike regular methods, in Swift, initializers are only inherited by a subclass under specific conditions as defined in the following rules:

  - **Rule 1:** If your subclass doesn't define any designated initializers, it automatically inherits all its superclass-designated initializers.

  - **Rule 2:** If your subclass provides an implementation of all of its superclass-designated initializers—either by inheriting them as according to rule 1, or by providing a custom implementation as part of its definition—then it automatically inherits all the superclass convenience initializers.

Overriding Initializers

- As with regular Swift methods, if you override an initializer from a superclass, you use the **override** keyword and declare an initializer with the same parameters and types.

- A subclass still inherits convenience initializers when it manually overrides the superclass's designated initializers.

- A class can override a designated initializer and make it a convenience initializer instead. Doing this still allows the subclass to inherit the superclass convenience initializers.

Required Initializers

- A *required initializer* must be implemented in all subclasses. You add the **required** modifier to an initializer to indicate that it is required:

```
class Translator {

    required init()
    {
    }
}
```

- When you implement a required initializer in a subclass, you specify the **required** keyword to indicate that subclasses lower in the inheritance chain are also required to implement the required initializer:

```
class Subtranslator: Translator {

    required init() {

        super.init()
    }
}
```

- If a subclass automatically inherits a required initializer from its superclass, you don't need to explicitly declare one in the subclass.

Optional Properties & Constants

- Optional properties automatically receive a value of **nil** during initialization.

- Constant property values can be set during initialization, but they must have a definite value by the time the initialization process is complete.

- Constant values can only be set by the class they are declared in. This means you can't modify the value of a constant property in a subclass.

Failable Initializers

- A failable initializer returns an object if the initialization succeeds, or a **nil** if it doesn't.

- Initializers should only fail if the primary information the class needs in order to function properly is not provided.

- You declare a failable initializer by adding a question mark after the **init** keyword. For example:

```
class mmBusinessObject {

    var dbName: String?

    init?(dbName: String) {

        if dbName.isEmpty {
            return nil
        }
        self.dbName = dbName
    }
}
```

- You indicate the point of failure in an initializer by writing **return nil**.

- You can't declare a failable and non-failable initializer with the same parameter names and types.

- Structures and enumerations can trigger a failure at any point in the initialization process.

- A class can only trigger a failure after it initializes all stored properties it introduces, and any required initialization delegation has taken place.

- A failable initializer can call another failable initializer in the same type, or in its superclass.

- A failable initializer can also delegate to a non-failable initializer.

- A non-failable initializer cannot delegate to a failable initializer.

- Enumerations with raw values automatically receive an initializer that accepts a parameter named **rawValue** and returns an enumeration member or **nil**.

- You can override a failable initializer in a subclass.

- You can override a failable initializer with a non-failable initializer, which allows you to create a subclass that can't fail initialization even though its superclass can.

- You can't override a non-failable initializer with a failable initializer.

- You can create an initializer that returns an implicitly unwrapped optional instance by adding an exclamation mark (rather than a question mark) after the **init** keyword. For example:

```
class ABusinessObject: mmBusinessObject {

    init!() {
        super.init(dbName: "MyDBCName")
    }
}
```

- Some rules regarding **init!** failable initializer:

  - You can delegate from **init?** to **init!**

  - You can delegate from **init!** to **init?**

  - You can delegate from **init** to **init!**, but you will get a runtime error if the **init!** initializer fails.

  - You can override from **init?** to **init!**

  - You can override from **init!** to **init?**

Exercise 16.1

In this exercise, you will apply what you have learned about initializers to enhance the sample code you created in Exercise 15.1.

1. Open the **Inheritance.playground**.

2. In the **Person** class, add a designated initializer that accepts **firstName** and **lastName** parameters and stores these values into the corresponding properties.

3. In the **Person** class, add a convenience initializer that accepts no parameters and calls the designated initializer.

4. In the **Patient** class, add a designated initializer that accepts **patientID**, **firstName** and **lastName** parameters.

5. In the **Patient** class, add a convenience initializer that accepts no parameters and calls the designated initializer.

6. Change the code at the bottom of the playground to use the new designated initializers to create instances of the **Person** and **Patient** classes.

Solution Movie 16.1

To see a video providing the solution for this exercise, you can enter the link below in your Web browser to see each step performed for you.

Movie 16.1

http://www.iOSAppsForNonProgrammers.com/B4M161.html

Chapter 17: Access Control

Access control is one of the late-breaking features added to the Swift language. It allows you to specify the parts of your code you want to make public, and the parts you want to hide. It's an important tool in creating easy-to-use, and easy-to-understand interfaces.

Sections in This Chapter

1. *Targets and Modules*

2. *Access Levels*

3. *Access Control Modifiers*

4. *Types, Members, and Access Levels*

5. *Inheritance and Access Control*

6. *Summary*

Targets and Modules

In Xcode, your source code files are assigned to different targets. A typical Xcode project has two targets—one for your main app file, and one for unit tests. To see the targets in a project, click the first node in the Project Navigator. This displays the Project Editor with a Project and Targets list on the left. (If you don't see this list, click the small square highlighted in Figure 17.1.)

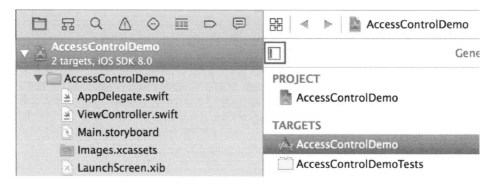

Figure 17.1 Xcode's targets

By default, all the files in the Project Navigator and any new files you add to the project are part of the main app target. The only file that is part of the unit test target is the unit test code file under the "Tests" group.

Remember, to see which target a particular file belongs to, select it in the Project Navigator, go to the File Inspector, and look under the **Target Membership** section (Figure 17.2).

Figure 17.2 Viewing a file's Target Membership

By default, all the code in a project belonging to the same target is also part of a single module.

In Swift, by default, all the code that is part of the same module can access all other code in that module. This is a vast improvement over Objective-C where you could only reference another class in the same project by importing its header file—a real speed bump when teaching beginners how to write code.

If you are building a single, stand-alone app, this level of access control may work well for most of the code you write. However, there are typically a number of places where it's best to change this default access level.

Access Levels

There are three access levels in Swift (Figure 17.3).

Public access

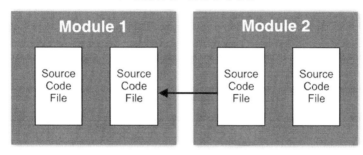

Internal access

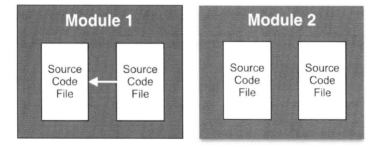

Private access

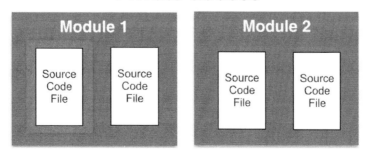

Figure 17.3 Swift's code access levels

1. **Public** - Allows access to code within the same module, or to another module that imports the module the code is declared in.

2. **Internal** - Allows access to code in the same module, but not to any other module. This Swift's default access level.

3. **Private** - Restricts access to the source file the code is declared in. Although it's typical to have a single class, structure, enum, etc. defined in a source code file, you can declare more than one per file.

Access Control Modifiers

You use the **public**, **internal**, and **private** modifiers to specify the access level of your code. For example, here are the modifiers used to declare access to classes:

```
public class MyPublicClass {}
internal class MyInternalClass {}
private class MyPrivateClass {}
```

Here are the modifiers used to declare access to members of a class:

```
public var myPublicProperty = 0
internal let myInternalConstant = 1
private func MyPrivateMethod() {}
```

Again, if you don't specify an access modifier, the default access level for your code is **internal**.

Class Access Level

Let's get a hands-on look at class access level.

1. Open the **AccessControlDemo** project located in the folder where you have downloaded this book's sample code.

2. As the Project Navigator shows, there are three classes you are going to use to check out how access levels work with classes; **PublicNote**, **InternalNote**, and **PrivateNote** (Figure 17.4).

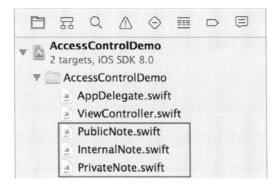

Figure 17.4 The "class access level" demo classes

3. If you select each of the three classes, you will see the following class declarations:

```
public class PublicNote {

    public init() {}
}

internal class InternalNote {

}

private class PrivateNote {

}
```

Keep the three different access levels depicted in Figure 17.3 in mind as we try to access these classes from these different places:

- A different module

- The same module

- The same source code file

Accessing a Public Class

Let's start by trying to access the public class from a different module.

1. In the Project Navigator, expand the **AccessControlDemoTests** group folder and select the **AccessControlDemoTests.swift** code file.

2. Add the following code to the **testExample** method:

```
func testExample() {

    var p = PublicNote()
}
```

3. Press **Command+B** to build the project. You will get a **Use of unresolved identifier 'PublicNote'** compiler error. Do you know why?

   Remember, the **PublicNote** class is in a module different from the one the unit test class is in, so we need to import the module.

4. By default, a project's module name is the same as the project name, so you need to add the **import** statement to the top of the **AccessControlDemoTests** code file:

```
import UIKit
import XCTest
import AccessControlDemo
```

5. Press **Command+B** to build the project and the compiler error will go away.

6. Now add the following code to the **testExample** method:

```
var i = InternalNote()
var pr = PrivateNote()
```

7. Press **Command+B** and both of these lines of code produce a **Use of unresolved identifier** error. That's because, as Figure 17.3 shows, you cannot access an internal or private class from a different module.

8. Go ahead and delete the last two lines of code you added in the previous step so the project compiles without error.

Now let's see how this works when we try it from the same module where the classes are declared.

1. Select the **ViewController.swift** file in the Project Navigator.

2. In the **viewDidLoad** method, add the following three lines of code:

```
override func viewDidLoad() {
    super.viewDidLoad()

        var p = PublicNote()
        var i = InternalNote()
        var n = PrivateNote()
}
```

The first two lines of code work great. That's because you can reference a **public** or **internal** class from code in the same module. However, the last line of code fails, because you can only reference a **private** class from within the same source code file where the **private** class is declared.

3. Delete the last line of code you added in the previous step, so the project compiles without error.

4. Select the **PrivateNote.swift** file in the Project Navigator, and add the following class declaration to the code file:

```
private class PrivateNote {
}

class TestNote {

    func test() {
        var pr = PrivateNote()
    }
}
```

This code compiles without an error. That's because the only way you can access a **private** class is from code that resides in the same source code file.

Class Member Access Level

Now let's see how different access levels work with *members* of a class.

1. Select the **Note.swift** file in the Project Navigator. Here's the class definition you'll find there:

```
public class Note {

    public init(){}
```

```
public func getPublicNote() -> String {

    return "This is a public note"

}

internal func getInternalNote() -> String {

    return "This is an internal note"

}

private func getPrivateNote() -> String {

    return "This note is private!"

}
}
```

This is a **public** class named **Note** that has **public**, **internal**, and **private** methods.

Let's try accessing the methods of this class from a different module.

2. Select the **AccessControlDemoTests.swift** file in the Project Navigator and add the following code to the **testExample** method. This code creates an instance of the **Note** class:

```
func testExample() {

        var p = PublicNote()
        var n = Note()

}
```

3. Add a new empty line of code and then type **n.** as in Figure 17.5.

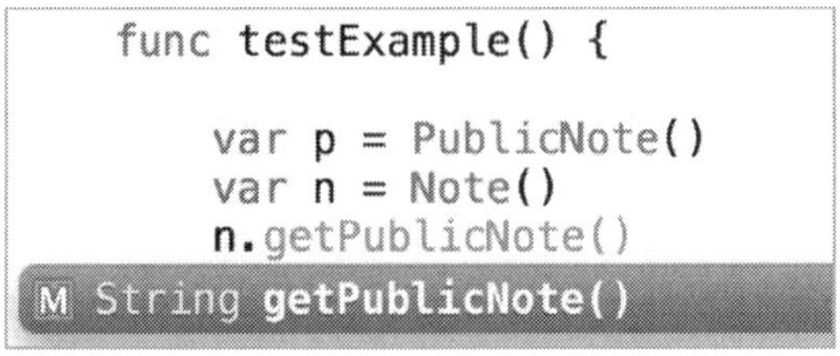

Figure 17.5 Only the public method is accessible.

Notice that the only method accessible from another module is the **public** method.

4. Delete the last few characters you entered in the previous step.

Let's see how the method access levels work when we access them from within the same module.

1. Select the **ViewController.swift** file in the Project Navigator and add the following code to the **viewDidLoad** method:

```
override func viewDidLoad() {
    super.viewDidLoad()
    var p = PublicNote()
    var i = InternalNote()
    var n = Note()
}
```

2. Add a new empty line of code and type **n.** as in Figure 17.6.

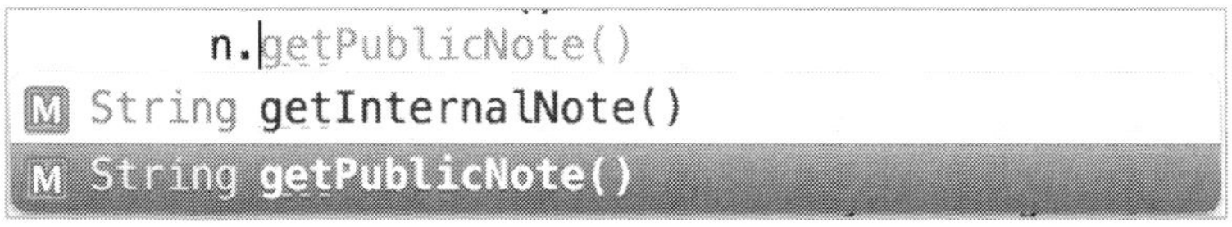

Figure 17.6 Both the public and internal methods are accessible from the same module.

Notice that both the **public** and **internal** methods are accessible from code located in the same module.

3. Delete the last few characters you entered so the project compiles again without error.

Now let's see how the method access levels work when we access them from within the same source code file.

1. Select the **Note.swift** code file in the Project Navigator.

2. Add the following class declaration at the very bottom of the **Note.swift** code file:

```
class TestMethodAccess {

    func test() {
        var n = Note()
    }
}
```

3. On a new empty line, type **n.** and you will see all three methods including the method marked as **private** as in Figure 17.7.

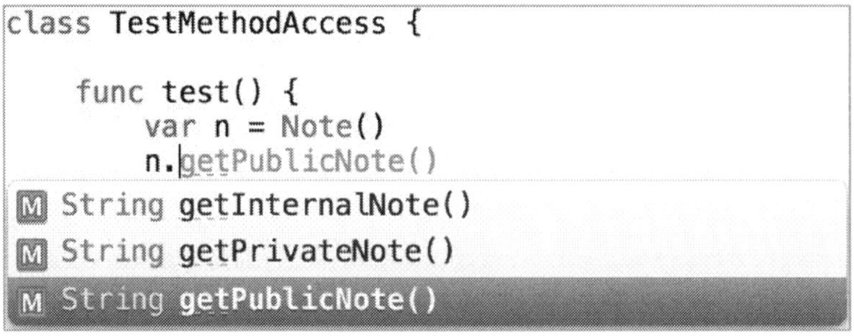

```
class TestMethodAccess {

    func test() {
        var n = Note()
        n.getPublicNote()
    M String getInternalNote()
    M String getPrivateNote()
    M String getPublicNote()
```

Figure 17.7 All three methods appear in Code Completion.

4. Remove the last few characters you typed so the project will compile again.

5. Note that you can also access the **private** method within the class it is declared in. For example, if you go to the **getPublicNote** method and type **self.** you can see that all three methods are accessible (Figure 17.8).

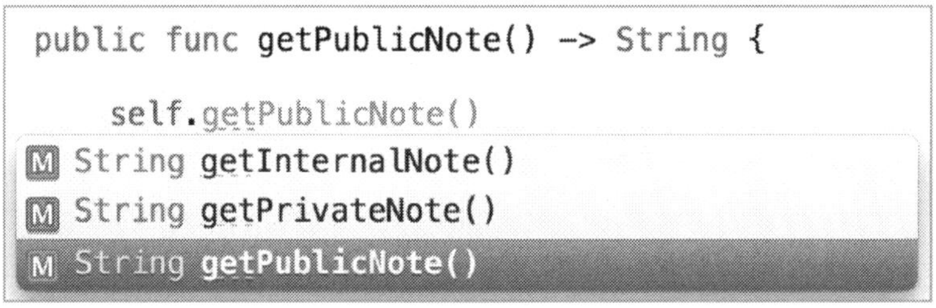

```
public func getPublicNote() -> String {

    self.getPublicNote()
    M String getInternalNote()
    M String getPrivateNote()
    M String getPublicNote()
```

*Figure 17.8 You can access a **private** member from within the class in which it is declared.*

6. If you typed **self.** in the **getPublicNote** method, delete it so the project compiles without error.

Types, Members, and Access Levels

Here are some basic rules governing how setting the access level of a class affects the access level of its members (properties, methods, initializers and subscripts).

- Setting the access level of a class to **private** sets all its members to **private** by default.

- Setting the access level of a class to **public** or **internal** (or don't specify any level, which defaults to **internal**), defaults all its members to **internal**.

Beginner developers often make the mistake of making all members of a class **public**. This is not a good approach, because it exposes members of the class that may not be useful to a consumer of the class, and in the process clutters and confuses the class interface.

In addition, if you expose too much of the inner workings of a class, you run the risk of allowing developers to use your class in ways that are unsafe and that produce tight coupling. If classes are too tightly coupled, it creates a brittle code base—when one class changes, it creates a chain reaction that forces major changes to other classes.

So Apple's approach of making the members of a **public** class **internal** by default is the right way to go. It forces you to take the extra step of adding the **public** keyword to a member, causing you to consider whether that member should be **public**.

Method and Function Access Level

In addition to the default access level it receives from its containing class, a method's access level must be set to the most restrictive access of its parameters and return values. For example:

```
private func getNotes(n: PrivateNote) -> InternalNote
{
    ...
}
```

This method has a **private** parameter type and an **internal** return type. This makes the entire method **private** and therefore it must be marked **private** as this code sample shows.

This rule also applies to functions, which do not have a containing class.

Initializer Access Level

The rules that apply to a method's default access level that it receives from its containing class also apply to initializers—**public** and **internal** classes have **internal** initializers, and **private** classes have **private** initializers by default.

Where this rule usually surprises developers is when they realize they need to create a **public** initializer for a **public** class, since its default is **internal**.

The rules that apply to method parameters also apply to initializers—their access level must be set to the most restrictive access level of their parameters.

You can manually specify an initializer's access to be the same as or equal to the access level of its containing class. The one exception is *required initializers*, which must have the same access level as the type they are contained in.

The initializer for structures is **internal** by default, unless it has any private members. In that case, it would be **private** by default. You can also manually create a **public** initializer for a structure.

Variable, Constant, Property, and Subscript Access Levels

In Swift, you can't set a variable, constant, property or subscript access level higher than the level of its type.

For example, in the following code, you must declare the **note** property as **private**, because its type, **PrivateNote** is **private**:

```
private var note = PrivateNote()
```

Getter and Setter Access Levels

Getter and setter methods are automatically assigned the same access level as the variable, constant, property or subscript they belong to.

You can manually specify a lower access level for a setter than a getter to restrict the read-write accessibility of that member. To do this, specify **private(set)** or **internal(set)** before the **var** or **subscript** declaration. For example:

```
private(set) var iNote = InternalNote()
```

Note that this works for both computed and stored properties, since Swift generates a getter and setter for a stored property behind the scenes.

Enumeration Access Level

When you specify the access level of an enumeration, all members of that enumeration are set to the same access level. You can't specify a different access level for members of the enumeration.

In addition, any raw or associated values of the enumeration must have an access level at least as high as the enumeration itself. For example, you can't have an enumeration access level of **internal** and have a raw or associated value with an access level of **private**.

Protocol Access Level

You can explicitly set the access level of a protocol when you declare it. This dictates the different levels at which a protocol can be adopted.

All protocol requirements default to the access level of the protocol itself and none can be changed to a different access level. This is even true of the **public** access level that normally defaults to **internal** for other types.

Extension Access Level

When you create an extension, the members of the extension default to the same access level as those of the type being extended.

You can manually specify an access level for an extension, which specifies a new default access level for members of the extension. From there, you can specify a different access level for individual members.

However, you can't specify an explicit access level for an extension that is being used to add protocol conformance. In that scenario, the protocol's access level provides the default access level for protocol requirements.

Generics Access Level

The access level of a generic type or function is determined by the most restrictive access level of the type or function itself and the access level of its parameters and constraints.

Tuple Access Level

You can't directly specify the access level of a tuple. Rather, a tuple's access level is determined by the most restrictive access level of the types used in that tuple. For example:

```
(PrivateNote, InternalNote)
```

This tuple contains one **private** and one **internal** type. This makes the entire tuple **private**.

Nested Type Access Level

Nested types declared within a public type have an automatic access level of **internal**. However, you can manually specify their access level as **public** or **private**.

A nested type declared within an **internal** type is **internal** by default, but can be changed to **private**.

A nested type declared within a **private** type is **private** and cannot be changed to a different access level.

Type Alias Access Level

You can specify an access level for a type alias lower than or equivalent to the access level of the type it aliases. For example, a type alias for an **internal** type can be either **internal** or **private**.

Inheritance and Access Control

One of the more interesting effects of access control is how it works with inheritance.

Inheritance and Classes

You can subclass any class your code has access to. This means:

- You can create a subclass of a **public** class from anywhere.

- You can create a subclass of an **internal** class only from within the same module.

- You can create a subclass of a **private** class only from within the same source code file.

A class does not automatically inherit its superclass access level. For example, in the following code, **SubPublicNote** does not inherit its superclass **public** access level:

```
public class PublicNote {

    public init() {}
}

class SubPublicNote: PublicNote {

}
```

If you want **SubPublicNote** to be **public**, you have to explicitly declare it. However, note that you can't specify an access level for a subclass higher than its superclass. So, for example, you can't subclass an **internal** class and make it **public**.

Inheritance and Class Members

Class members also do not automatically inherit their access level. Rather, they get their default access level based on the access level of the class they are declared in, as described earlier in the Access Levels of Types and Their Members section.

For example, in the following code, **Subnote** is subclass of **Note**, and overrides its **getPublicNote** method. This method is **internal** by default. That's because it doesn't get its default access from its superclass, but from the class in which it is declared.

```
public class Note {

public init(){}

    public func getPublicNote() -> String {
```

```
        return "This is a public note"
    }
}

public class Subnote : PublicNote {

    func getPublicNote() -> String {

        return "This is not a public note"
    }
}
```

When you override a member, you can make it more accessible in the subclass, but you can't make it less accessible. For example, in the following code **Subnote** is a subclass of **Note**. It overrides the **getPrivateNote** method and elevates its access level to **public**:

```
public class Note {

    public init(){}

    internal func getInternalNote() -> String {

        return "This is an internal note"
    }
}

public class Subnote : Note {

  public override func getInternalNote() -> String {
        return "Now this note is public"
    }
}
```

Inheritance and Protocols

If you subclass a protocol, the subclass can only have an access level as high as the protocol it inherits from.

A type can adopt a protocol that has a lower access level. For example, a public type can adopt an internal protocol. This makes the type's conformance to the protocol **internal**.

When you implement the requirements of a protocol, the requirements (such as the methods and properties) must have at least the same access level as the type's conformance to that protocol. For example, if a type conforms to a protocol with an **internal** access level, all requirements that it implements must be at least **internal**.

Summary

- By default, all the code in a project that belongs to the same target is also part of a single module.

- In Swift, by default, all of the code that is part of the same module can access all other code in that module.

- Swift has three access levels:

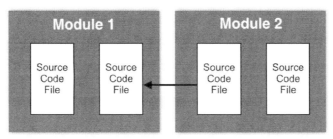

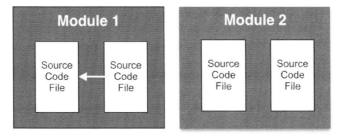

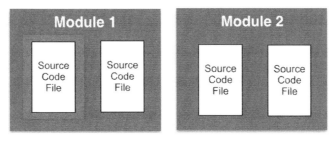

- **Public** - Allows access to code within the same module, or to another module that imports the module the code is defined in.

- **Internal** - Allows access to code in the same module, but not to any other module. This is the default access level for all code in Swift.

- **Private** - Restricts access to the source file the code is declared in. Although it's typical to have a single class, structure, enum, etc. defined in a source code file, you can declare more than one per file.

- You use the **public**, **internal**, and **private** modifiers to specify the access level of your code. Here are the modifiers used to declare access to classes:

```
public class MyPublicClass {}
internal class MyInternalClass {}
private class MyPrivateClass {}
```

Here are the modifiers used to declare access to members of a class:

```
public var myPublicProperty = 0
internal let myInternalConstant = 1
private func MyPrivateMethod() {}
```

Types, Members, and Access Levels

- Setting the access level of a class to **private** sets all of its members to **private** by default.

- Setting the access level of a class to **public** or **internal** (or don't specify any level, which defaults to internal), defaults all its members to **internal**.

- In addition to the default access level it receives from its containing class, a method's access level must be set to the most restrictive access of its parameters and return values. For example:

```
private func getNotes(n: PrivateNote) ->
      InternalNote
{
   ...
}
```

This method has a parameter type that is **private** and a return type that is **internal**. This makes the entire method **private** and, therefore, it must be marked **private** as this code sample shows.

- The rules that apply to a method's default access level that it receives from its containing class also apply to initializers—**public** and **internal** classes have **internal** initializers, and **private** classes have **private** initializers by default.

Initializers

- The rules that apply to method parameters also apply to initializers—their access level must be set to the most restrictive access level of their parameters.

- You can manually specify an initializer's access to be the same or equal to the access level of its containing class. The one exception is *required initializers*, which must have the same access level as the type in which they are contained.

- The initializer for structures is **internal** by default, unless it has any **private** members. In that case, it would be **private** by default. You can also manually create a **public** initializer for a structure.

Variables, Constants, Properties & Subscripts

- You can't set a variable, constant, property, or subscript access level higher than the access level of its type.

Getters and Setters

- Getter and setter methods are automatically assigned the same access level as the variable, constant, property or subscript they belong to.

- You can manually specify a lower access level for a setter than a getter to restrict the read-write accessibility of that member. To do this, specify **private(set)** or **internal(set)** before the **var** or **subscript** declaration. For example:

```
private(set) var iNote = InternalNote()
```

Enumerations

- When you specify the access level of an enumeration, all members of that enumeration are set to the same access level. You can't specify a different access level for members of the enumeration.

- Any raw values or associated values of the enumeration must have an access level at least as high as the enumeration itself.

Protocols

- You can explicitly set the access level of a protocol when you declare it. This dictates the levels at which a protocol can be adopted.

- All protocol requirements default to the access level of the protocol itself and none can be changed to a different access level.

Extensions

- When you create an extension, the members of the extension default to the same access level as those of the type being extended.

- You can manually specify an access level for an extension, which specifies a new default access level for members of the extension. From there, you can specify a different access level for individual members.

- You can't specify an explicit access level for an extension that is being used to add protocol conformance. In that scenario, the protocol's access level provides the default access level for protocol requirements.

Generics

- The access level of a generic type or function is determined by the most restrictive access level of the type or function itself and the access level of its parameters and constraints.

Tuples, Nested Types, and Type Aliases

- You can't directly specify the access level of a tuple. Rather, a tuple's access level is determined by the most restrictive access level of the types that are used in that tuple. For example:

```
(PrivateNote, InternalNote)
```

This tuple contains one **private** and one **internal** type. This makes the entire tuple **private**.

- Nested types declared within a public type have an automatic access level of **internal**. However you can manually specify their access levels as **public** or **private**.

- A nested type declared within an **internal** type is **internal** by default, but can be changed to **private**.

- A nested type declared within a **private** type is **private** and cannot be changed to a different access level.

- You can specify an access level for a type alias lower than or equivalent to the access level of the type it aliases. For example, a type alias for an **internal** type can be either **internal** or **private**.

Inheritance and Classes

You can subclass any class your code has access to. This means:

- You can create a subclass of a **public** class from anywhere.

- You can create a subclass of an **internal** class only from within the same module.

- You can create a subclass of a **private** class only from within the same source code file.

- A class does not automatically inherit its superclass access level.

- You can't specify an access level for a subclass higher than its superclass.

Inheritance and Class Members

- Class members do not automatically inherit their access level. Rather, they get their default access level based on the access level of the class in which they are declared.

- When you override a member, you can make it more accessible in the subclass, but you can't make it less accessible.

Inheritance and Protocols

- If you subclass a protocol, the subclass can only have an access level as high as the protocol it inherits from.

- A type can adopt a protocol that has a lower access level.

- When you implement the requirements of a protocol, the requirements (such as the methods and properties) must have at least the same access level as the type's conformance to that protocol.

Chapter 18: Data Types & Conversions

When writing code in Swift, it's important to know how to convert from one type to another whether it's basic data types such as numerics or more complex classes. In this chapter's hands-on exercises, you will learn about implicit and explicit conversions and about upcasting and downcasting.

Sections in This Chapter

Numeric Type Conversions

Swift has a variety of integer data types in a variety of sizes **Int8**, **Int16**, **Int32**, **Int64**, as well as corresponding unsigned integer types (that only contain positive values above zero). *Appendix B: Swift's Basic Data Types* lists all Swift's numeric types including integers).

Apple recommends using the **Int** data type for all general-purpose integer constants and variables, even if you know the integer value will never be negative. This is because Swift doesn't allow you to perform operations on different numeric types. For example, you can't add an **Int8** value to an **Int16** value. Using **Int** ensures that all your integers are of the same type and therefore interoperable.

However, if you decide to use some of the other numeric data types, you will run into the need to perform an ***explicit conversion*** from one numeric type to another. For example, the following code is illegal in Swift:

```
var x: Int8 = 2
var y: Int16 = 3
var z = x + y
```

Variable **x** is of type **Int8** and variable **y** is of type **Int16**. Even though these are both integer data types, Swift does not allow you to add them together. You must convert one of the data types so that they are both the same in order to perform the addition operation.

To convert the **x** variable to **Int16**, you can do the following:

```
var z = Int16(x) + y
```

All Swift's integer data types have initializers that convert from one data type to another. So this code constructs a new **Int16** value by passing the **Int8** value stored in variable **x** to the **Int16** initializer.

This conversion only works when passing in a numeric data type. If you pass in a Bool or String, for example, you would get a compiler error.

This same explicit conversion is required when you convert between integer and floating-point numeric types. For example:

```
var i: Int = 3
var f: Float = 1.4
var c = Float(i) + f
```

In this code, the integer value in variable i has to be converted to Float before it can be added to the Float value in variable **f**.

Note that then when you go the other way and convert a float value to integer, the decimal portion of the number is truncated. So, for example, converting **1.4** to an integer yields **1**.

Type Casting

Type casting is a way to treat an instance as if it were a different class in its inheritance chain. When you treat an instance as if it were a class higher up in the inheritance chain (for example, its superclass), that's called ***upcasting***. When you treat an instance as if it were a class farther down in the inheritance chain (for example, its subclass), it's called ***downcasting***.

Implicit Conversions With Upcasting

In Chapter 15's section on Polymorphism, you learned that when you declare a variable of a particular type, it can also hold a reference to any *subclass* of that type.

Let's get a hands-on look at how upcasting works given the inheritance relationship shown in Figure 18.1.

1. Open the **TypeCastingDemo** project located in a subfolder where you have stored the sample code for this book.

2. Select the **AirportEntity.swift** file in the Project Manager and you will see the following class declaration:

```
public class AirportEntity: NSManagedObject {

    @NSManaged var airportID: NSNumber
    @NSManaged var codeIATA: String
    @NSManaged var name: String
}
```

You can see this is the same **AirportEntity** class as in Figure 18.1.

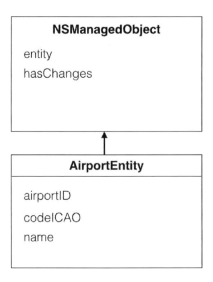

*Figure 18.1 **AirportEntity** is a subclass of **NSManagedObject**.*

3. Next, expand the **TypeCastingDemoTest** group and select the **TypeCastingDemoTests.swift** code file.

4. Add the following code to the **testExample** method:

```
func testExample() {

    var airport = Airport()

    var airportEntity: AirportEntity =
    airport.createAirportEntity()

    var managedObject: NSManagedObject =
    airportEntity
}
```

The first line of code creates a new **Airport** business object. The second line of code calls the object's **createAirportEntity** method and stores the new **AirportEntity** object in a variable of type **AirportEntity**. This is apples to apples, so no casting is necessary.

The second line of code stores the **AirportEntity** object into a variable of type **NSManagedObject**. Since **NSManagedObject** is higher up in the inheritance chain, this is upcasting. It's an ***implicit conversion*** without the need for special type-casting operators.

Figure 18.2 provides a visual representation of this code. It shows that the **managedObject** and **airportEntity** variables are actually referencing the same object.

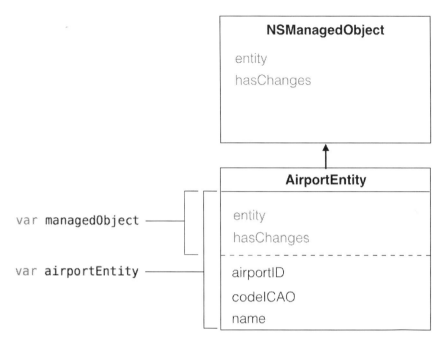

*Figure 18.2 Upcasting from **AirportEntity** to **NSManagedObject***

The **managedObject** variable treats the object as an **NSManagedObject**, so you only see the members of the **NSManagedObject** class inherited by **AirportEntity** (such as **entity** and **hasChanges**).

The **airportEntity** variable treats the object as an **AirportEntity**, so you see the properties and methods it inherits from **NSManagedObject** as well as the properties and methods it declares itself (such as **airlineID**, **codeICAO** and **name**).

Let's try this in code so you can see for yourself.

1. At the bottom of the **testExample** method, add the following code:

```
func testExample() {

    var airport = Airport()

    var airportEntity =
        airport.createAirportEntity()
```

```
var managedObject: NSManagedObject =
    airportEntity

managedObject.entity
}
```

Typing the word **entity**, you can see it comes up in Code Completion (Figure 18.3).

```
managedObject.entity
V  NSEntityDescription entity
```

The entity description of the receiver. (read-only) More...

*Figure 18.3 The **entity** property appears in Code Completion.*

2. If you delete the **.entity** portion of the code you just entered and type **.hasChanges** instead, you will see this property also appears in Code Completion.

   These properties appear because the **managedObject** variable is of type **NSManagedObject**, and these properties are declared in that class (Figure 18.2).

3. Delete the **.hasChanges** portion of the code and replace it with **.airportID**. Notice this property doesn't appear in Code Completion.

   You can try the same thing with the **codeICAO** and **name** properties. None of them appear in Code Completion, because they are declared in the **AirportEntity** class. The object is referenced from a variable of type **NSManagedObject** and is treated as such—even though it's an **AirportEntity** object behind the scenes.

4. Now let's reference the object from the **airportEntity** property. Completely delete the line of code you added in the previous step, and replace it with the following code:

```
func testExample() {

    var airport = Airport()

    var airportEntity =
```

```
        airport.createAirportEntity()

    var managedObject: NSManagedObject =
        airportEntity

    airportEntity.entity
}
```

Notice the **entity** property appears in the Code Completion list.

5. Try it with the **hasChanges** property, then the **airportID, codeICAO**, and **name** properties. All these properties appear because we are referencing the object from a variable of type **AirportEntity**, and we can therefore see all the properties that **AirportEntity** inherits, as well as the properties declared in its class definition.

Frameworks and Downcasting

When you treat an instance as if it were a class farther down in the inheritance chain (for example, as its subclass), that's called *downcasting*.

One place you will most often need to use downcasting is when you create your own framework—a custom code base that you use in your iOS projects.

Why do you need your own custom framework? So you don't have duplicate code in your iOS projects. You should avoid duplicate code, because if the code ever needs to change (it will), you don't want to have several places where it needs to change.

For example, Figure 18.4 demonstrates what happens when you create multiple projects in which you "Include Core Data." Each time you create a new project, Xcode adds the same Core Data code to each project. If you need to change this code (you will), you have multiple places to change it. For that matter, Apple keeps changing this code with new releases of iOS. So keeping up to date with the latest Core Data code means manually making changes to your older projects. This is *not* a best practice.

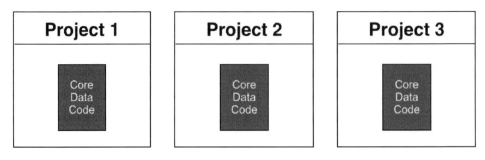

Figure 18.4 Duplicate Core Data code

Figure 18.5 depicts a much better code model. The **mmBusinessObject** class contains all the Core Data code necessary for your projects. Each project references this single **mmBusinessObject.swift** class file. If the Core Data code ever needs to change, there is only one place you need to change it.

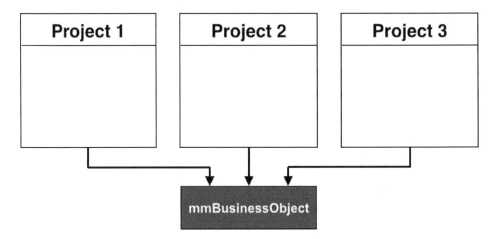

*Figure 18.5 The **mmBusinessObject** class can be referenced from multiple projects.*

Figure 18.6 depicts the inheritance relationship of classes in the **TypeCastingDemo** project.

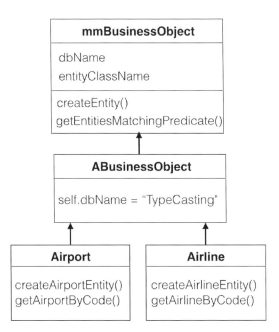

Figure 18.6 The business class inheritance hierarchy

mmBusinessObject sits at the top of the hierarchy. It contains properties and methods that retrieve and manipulate entities using Core Data.

ABusinessObject is a subclass of **mmBusinessObject**. It doesn't contain much code, but provides a place where you can add code that affects all the business classes in your project.

The **Airport** and **Airline** classes sit at the bottom of the hierarchy and inherit all the properties and methods of the **mmBusinessObject** and **ABusinessObject** classes.

The methods in **mmBusinessObject** work with instances of the **NSManagedObject** class rather than application-specific entities such as **AirportEntity** and **AirlineEntity**, which are subclasses of **NSManagedObject** (Figure 18.2). These methods need to be generic, because they need to work for all types of entities.

So when the **Airport** and **Airline** classes call methods they inherit from **mmBusinessObject** such as **createEntity** and **getEntitiesMatchingPredicate**, these methods return instances of **NSManagedObject**.

However, to do anything meaningful with these objects, the **Airport** and **Airline** classes need to convert these generic **NSManagedObject** instances to the more specific **AirportEntity** and **AirlineEntity** objects.

This is where downcasting comes into the picture.

Downcasting With **as**

Let's look at an example of how the **Airport** class uses downcasting.

1. Open the **TypeCastingDemo** project in Xcode.

2. Click the **Airport.swift** file in the Project Navigator.

3. Check out the **createAirportEntity** method:

```
public func createAirportEntity() ->
    AirportEntity {

    var entity = self.createEntity()
    return entity as AirportEntity
}
```

The first line of code makes a call to the **createEntity** method inherited from the **mmBusinessObject** class, which returns an instance of **NSManagedObject**.

4. To verify this, click on the **entity** variable, go to the Quick Help Inspector (select the button on the right in the Inspector toolbar) and it shows the **entity** variable is of type **NSManagedObject** (Figure 18.7).

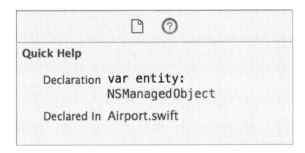

*Figure 18.7 The **entity** variable is of type **NSManagedObject**.*

The second line of code in the **createAirportEntity** method uses Swift's **as** operator to downcast the **NSManagedObject** instance to **AirportEntity**:

```
return entity as AirportEntity
```

Only use Swift's **as** operator when you are certain the object is of the type you are downcasting to. This is important because the **as** operation generates a run-time error if the downcast fails.

If you're not sure if the downcast will succeed, you can use Swift's **as?** operator. The optional form of this operator returns an optional value of the type you are downcasting to. For example:

```
var airportEntity: AirportEntity? =
          entity as? AirportEntity
```

For clarity, I have explicitly declared the **airportEntity** variable as type **AirportEntity?**. If the downcast succeeds, the variable holds a reference to the **AirportEntity** object. If it fails, the variable is set to **nil**.

Checking Type With **is**

To check if an object is of a particular type, use Swift's **is** operator. For example:

```
if managedObject is AirportEntity
{
    // Do something
}
```

If you often find yourself using the **is** operator you may want to look closely at your code's architecture to see if there is a better way to approach the problem. This better approach often involves creating a protocol that your classes can adopt. For more information, check out *Chapter 20: Mastering Protocols and Delegates*.

Working With **AnyObject** and **Any**

You learned earlier that Swift's **AnyObject** can represent an instance of any class type. **Any** is a little broader in its scope and can represent an instance not just of classes, but of any type at all (except for function types).

You should use **AnyObject** and **Any** only when you absolutely need to. It's best to use the most specific type available whenever you can. However, there are cases where **AnyObject** is the best tool for the job.

For example, when you create a new project, Xcode adds the following method to the **AppDelegate** class:

```
func application(application: UIApplication,
      didFinishLaunchingWithOptions launchOptions:
      [NSObject: AnyObject]?) -> Bool {
```

The last parameter in this method is a dictionary of type **AnyObject**. This dictionary contains information passed to the app when it is first launched. It can contain a wide variety of types such as **NSString**, **NSURL**, and **NSDictionary** based on the way the app is launched. Since there is no single type that describes all objects in the dictionary, specifying its type as **AnyObject** allows the dictionary to contain different types.

If a variable needs to hold a value that can be a class, as well as non-class types such as tuples, you can declare it to be of type **Any**. For example, the **a** variable is of type **Any** and can therefore hold a tuple or an object:

```
var a: Any = (0,"test")
a = Airport()
```

All the **AnyObject** type checking and downcasting rules also apply to **Any**. For example:

```
var a: Any = Airport()

if a is Airport
{
   var ap = a as Airport
}
```

As with **AnyObject**, a variable of type **Any** can also be optional.

Where might you encounter objects of type **AnyObject**? When creating connections between user interface controls and view controllers with Xcode's Interface Builder, you have the choice of specifying the type of the object that is passed to your action method.

For example, in Figure 18.8, an action method is being created for a segmented control's **Value Changed** event. In the Create Connection popup, you can specify the **Type** as **AnyObject** or **UISegmentedControl**.

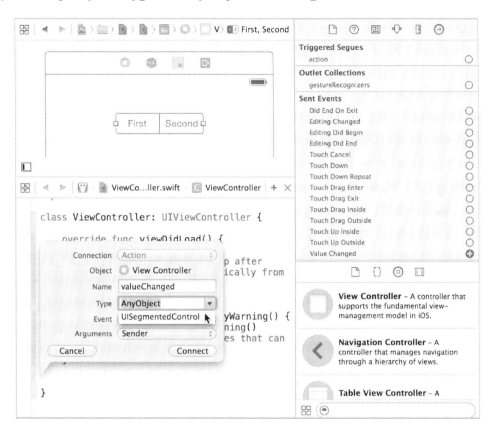

Figure 18.8 Selecting a specific type

If you set the **Type** to **AnyObject**, Xcode creates an action method that passes the segmented control as an object of type **AnyObject**. This requires you to use the **as** operator to convert it to type **UISegmentedControl**.

```
@IBAction func valueChanged(sender: AnyObject) {

    var segControl = sender as UISegmentedControl
    if segControl.selectedSegmentIndex == 1 {
        // Do something
    }
}
```

If you set the Type to **UISegmentedControl**, Xcode creates an action method that accepts a sender argument of type **UISegmentedControl**:

```
@IBAction func valueChanged(sender: UISegmentedControl) {

    if sender.selectedSegmentIndex == 1 {
        // Do something
    }
}
```

Summary

- Apple recommends using the **Int** data type for all general-purpose integer constants and variables, even if you know the integer value will never be negative.

- All Swift's integer data types have initializers that convert from one data type to another.

  ```
  var z = Int16(x) + y
  ```

- Type casting is a way to treat an instance as if it were a different class in its inheritance chain.

- When you treat an instance as if it were a class higher up in the inheritance chain (for example, its superclass), that's called *upcasting*.

- Upcasting happens implicitly, so you don't need a special operator to upcast.

- When you treat an instance as if it were a class farther down in the inheritance chain (for example, its subclass), it's called *downcasting*.

- One place you will most often need to use downcasting is when you create your own framework.

- You use Swift's **as** operator to downcast:

  ```
  return entity as AirportEntity
  ```

- You should only use Swift's **as** operator when you are certain of an object's type.

- If you're not sure if the downcast will succeed, you can use Swift's **as?**

operator. The optional form of this operator returns an optional value of the type you are downcasting to. For example:

```
var airportEntity: AirportEntity? =
        entity as? AirportEntity
```

- To check if an object is of a particular type, use Swift's **is** operator.

```
if managedObject is AirportEntity
{
    // Do something
}
```

- You should use **AnyObject** and **Any** only when you absolutely need to. It's best to use the most specific type available whenever you can.

Exercise 18.1

In this exercise, you will apply what you have learned about type conversions.

1. Create a playground named **Conversions.playground**.

2. Create a variable named **i16** of type **Int16** and initialize it to **1**.

3. Create a variable named **i32** of type **Int32** and initialize it to **2**.

4. Add the values in the **i16** and **i32** variables.

5. Create a variable named **control**, and specify its type as a class that will allow you to store an instance of **UIButton**, **UITextField**, or **UISlider** (Check Apple's documentation to figure out which type to use.)

6. Store an instance of **UITextField** in the **control** variable.

7. Create a variable named **textField** of type **UITextField**.

8. Convert the object stored in the **control** variable to **UITextField** and store it in the **textField** variable.

Solution Movie 18.1

To see a video providing the solution for this exercise, you can enter the link below in your Web browser to see each step performed for you.

Movie 18.1

http://www.iOSAppsForNonProgrammers.com/B4M181.html

Chapter 19: Object Lifetime & Memory Management

Starting with iOS 5, memory management has become far simpler. Advances in the compiler have made it easy for non-programmers to manage memory and produce high quality, stable apps.

Sections in This Chapter

An Object's Lifetime

An object "comes to life" when you first create an instance of it from a class definition. Every object you create takes up a different amount of space in memory (Figure 19.1).

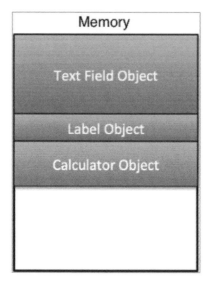

Figure 19.1 Every object you create takes up space in memory.

Each iOS app has a maximum amount of memory allocated to it, so when you are finished using an object, it should be released so the space it takes up in memory can also be released (Figure 19.2).

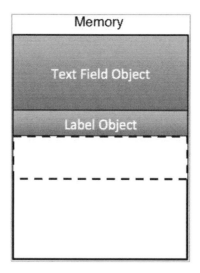

Figure 19.2 Objects must be released when no longer in use to free up available memory.

Historically, one of the biggest problems in iOS development is apps that don't release objects properly. If an app doesn't release objects as it should, the objects eventually take up too much memory and the iOS run time reacts by *killing* your app (brutal, I know!). A situation where an app continually eats up memory is also known as a ***memory leak***.

Memory Management: The Way It Was

Properly releasing unused objects requires memory management. Memory management used to be hard. In the "old days" (before October 2011), when you wanted to keep an object around, you sent it a **retain** message as in Figure 19.3.

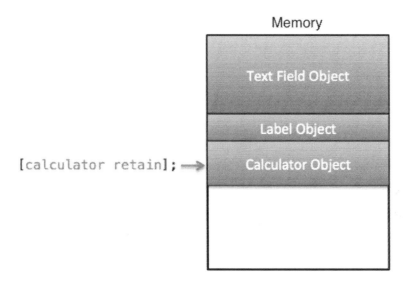

Figure 19.3 Retained objects stay in memory.

Other objects wanting to keep this same object around would each send it a **retain** message. Every time an object receives a **retain** message, its internal retain count is incremented (Figure 19.4).

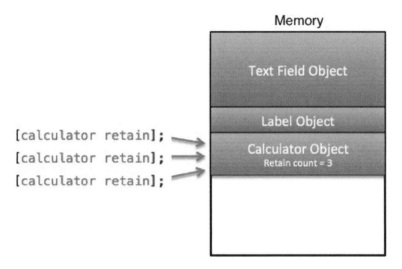

*Figure 19.4 Multiple **retain** messages sent to an object*

When you no longer needed an object, you sent it a **release** message, decrementing its retain count (Figure 19.5).

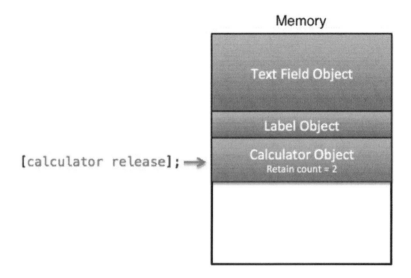

*Figure 19.5 A **release** message decrements an object's **retain** count.*

But just because one part of the app doesn't need the object any longer doesn't mean it isn't needed elsewhere. So iOS only truly releases the object from memory when its retain count is decremented to zero.

As you might imagine, it took a concerted effort to make sure a class was sent **retain** messages when appropriate, and **release** messages when necessary. Forgetting to send an object a **release** message causes its retain count to be something other than zero, meaning it will never be released. Eventually, this causes a memory leak as more and more memory is consumed.

Memory Management: The Way It Is

Fortunately, starting in iOS 5, Apple introduced the concept of ***Automatic Reference Counting***, or ***ARC***. With Automatic Reference Counting, the same principles of memory management still apply. Objects must still be sent **retain** and **release** method calls. However, rather than manually adding these method calls to the code yourself, with ARC, the compiler inserts these **retain** and **release** method calls in the compiled code for you!

So, if you no longer send **retain** method calls to an object, how do you let the compiler know you want to keep a particular object around? With ARC, all you need is a variable pointing, or holding a reference to an object to keep it alive.

Let's check out an example of ARC in action.

1. In Xcode, navigate to the folder where you downloaded this book's sample code. Expand the **MemoryManagementDemo** subfolder and double-click the **MemoryManagementDemo.xcodeproj** file.

2. Go to the Project Navigator and select the **ViewController.swift** file. Near the top of the file, you can see the **calculator** property:

```
class ViewController: UIViewController {

    var calculator = Calculator()
```

At run time when the **ViewController** loads, an instance of the **Calculator** object is created and stored in the **calculator** property. This property's reference to the **Calculator** object keeps it alive (Figure 19.6).

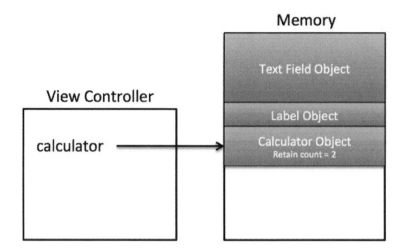

Figure 19.6 The property keeps the object alive!

Memory Management and Local Variables

To understand this concept a little better, rather than using a property, you are going to create a local variable to hold a reference to the **Calculator** object and then examine how this affects its lifetime.

1. In the **MemoryManagementDemo** project, select the **ViewController.swift** file in the Project Navigator.

2. At the top of the file, comment out the **calculator** property by placing two forward slashes in front of it:

```
//var calculator = Calculator()
```

3. Add the following code to the **viewDidLoad** method:

```
override func viewDidLoad() {

    super.viewDidLoad()
    var calculator = Calculator()
}
```

This code creates an instance of the Calculator class and stores it in a local variable.

As Figure 19.7 shows, when you declare the **calculator** variable within a method, the variable lives until the end of the method. Since the variable keeps the **Calculator** object alive, when the variable is released at the end of the method, the object is also released.

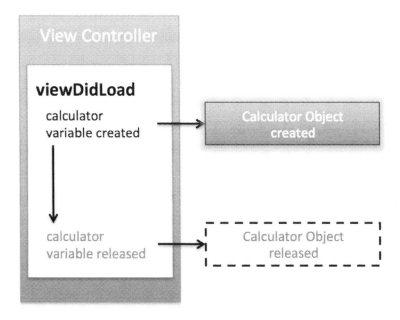

Figure 19.7 Local variables live until the method's end.

To see this demonstrated, you are going to set a breakpoint in the **Calculator** class that automatically fires when the **Calculator** object gets released.

Overriding the **deinit** Method

Every object in Swift has a **deinit** method. You never call the **deinit** method directly, but it is automatically called when the object is being released from memory.

Let's look at the **Calculator** class's **init** and **deinit** methods.

1. In the **MemoryManagementDemo** project, select the **Calculator.swift** file in the Project Navigator. Set a breakpoint on the **println** statement in the **deinit** method (Figure 19.8).

```
deinit {
    println("Deinitializing Calculator")
}
```

*Figure 19.8 Set a breakpoint in the **deinit** method.*

Remember, when the **Calculator** object is released at run time, the **deinit** method automatically fires.

2. Now let's set a breakpoint when the Calculator first gets instantiated. Select the **ViewController.swift** file in the Project Navigator, and set a breakpoint on the code that creates the **Calculator** object (Figure 19.9).

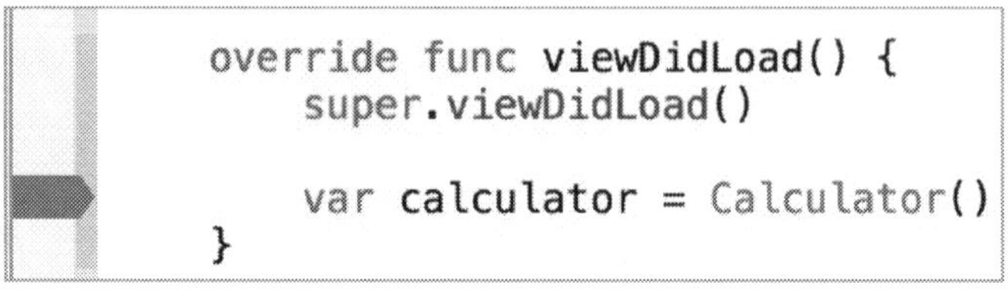

```
override func viewDidLoad() {
    super.viewDidLoad()

    var calculator = Calculator()
}
```

*Figure 19.9 Set a breakpoint on the code that creates the **Calculator** object.*

Testing the **deinit** Method

Now you're ready to test the **deinit** method and see when the **Calculator** object gets released.

1. Run the project by clicking the **Run** button in the upper-left corner of Xcode. After several seconds, you should hit the first breakpoint (Figure 19.10).

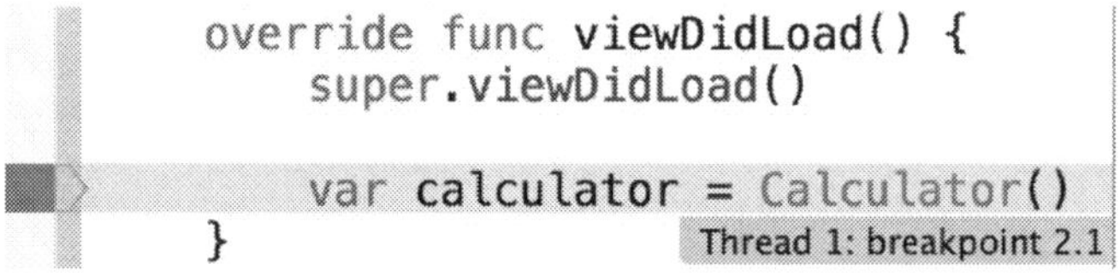

```
override func viewDidLoad() {
    super.viewDidLoad()

    var calculator = Calculator()
}                       Thread 1: breakpoint 2.1
```

Figure 19.10 The first breakpoint is hit!

2. Click the **Step over** button in the Debug toolbar to create the **Calculator** object.

As soon as you step out of the method, the **deinit** method of the **Calculator** object is executed (Figure 19.11). Why?

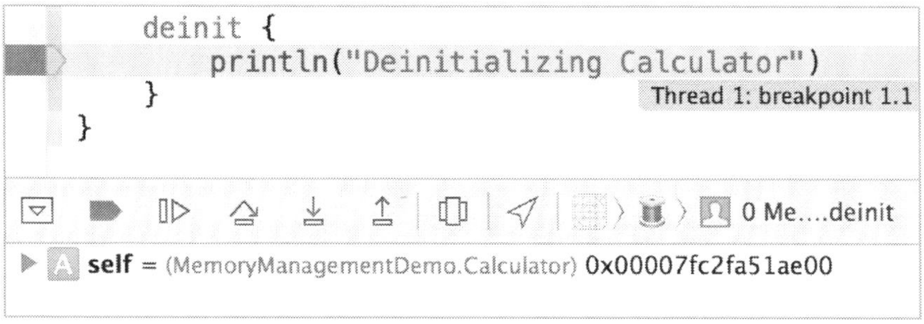

```
        deinit {
            println("Deinitializing Calculator")
        }                                    Thread 1: breakpoint 1.1
    }
```

▽ ▶ Ⅰ▷ ⏏ ↧ ↥ | ▢ | ◁ | ▦ › ▮ › 🔲 0 Me....deinit

▶ A **self** = (MemoryManagementDemo.Calculator) 0x00007fc2fa51ae00

*Figure 19.11 The **deinit** method fires.*

Immediately after the **Calculator** object is created, we reach the end of the **viewDidLoad** method and the **calculator** local variable is released. Since there are no other references to the **Calculator** object, it is also released. At this point its **deinit** method is executed, and execution stops at the breakpoint you set.

3. Go ahead and click the **Stop** button so you can set up another test case.

Memory Management and Properties

How does memory management work when referencing the **Calculator** object from a property rather than a variable? Let's give it a try.

First Attempt: Weak Property

Let's start with a **weak** property and see how that works for us. In Swift, a weak reference does not maintain a strong hold on an object, and allows ARC to release the referenced object.

1. In the **MemoryManagementDemo** project, select the **ViewController.swift** file in the Project Manager.

2. Near the top of the code file, replace the commented **calculator** property with the following property declaration:

```
class ViewController: UIViewController {

    weak var calculator: Calculator?
```

3. This code declares a weak property named **calculator** of an optional **Calculator** type. Weak properties must always be declared as optional, because they can potentially hold a **nil** value.

4. Next, replace the code in the ViewController's **viewDidLoad** method with the code shown in Figure 19.12 and set a breakpoint on the first line of code.

```
override func viewDidLoad() {
    super.viewDidLoad()

    self.calculator = Calculator()
    var total = self.calculator?.addToTotal(10)
}
```

*Figure 19.12 Add new code to **viewDidLoad**.*

The code creates a new instance of the **Calculator** class and stores it in the **calculator** property. Next, it calls the calculator's **addToTotal** method.

5. Now you are ready to see how the declaration of a **weak** property works with regard to the **Calculator** object's lifetime. Click the **Run** button and you will hit the first breakpoint on the line of code that creates the **Calculator** object (Figure 19.13).

```
override func viewDidLoad() {
    super.viewDidLoad()

    self.calculator = Calculator()  Thread 1: breakp..
    var total = self.calculator?.addToTotal(10)
}
```

Figure 19.13 The first breakpoint is hit.

6. Now click the **Step into** button in the Debug toolbar twice. This takes you to the initialization of the Calculator object (Figure 19.14).

```
class Calculator {

    var memory1: Double = 0.0
    var memory2: Double = 0.0
    var total: Double = 0.0
```

*Figure 19.14 The **Calculator** initialization*

7. Click **Step over** three times and execution moves to the **init** method (Figure 19.15).

```
init() {
    println("Initializing Calculator")
}                                        Thread 1:
```

*Figure 19.15 The Calculator's **init** method*

8. Click the **Step out** button to be taken back to the first line of code in the **viewDidLoad** method. This is where the new **Calculator** object gets stored into the **calculator** property (Figure 19.16). The next line of code calls the **addToTotal** method of the Calculator object.

```
override func viewDidLoad() {
    super.viewDidLoad()

    self.calculator = Calculator()    Thread 1: step ou
    var total = self.calculator?.addToTotal(10)
}
```

*Figure 19.16 The **Calculator** object is stored in the **calculator** property.*

9. Click the **Step over** button. You will be taken to the **Calculator** object's **deinit** method (Figure 19.17).

```
deinit {
    println("Deinitializing Calculator")
}                                          Thread 1: bre
```

*Figure 19.17 The Calculator's **deinit** is executed.*

This probably isn't what you were expecting to happen! The **Calculator** object was immediately released after it was created—and before you even had a chance to call any methods on it! Let's keep going to see what happens next.

10. Click the **Step out** button in the Debug toolbar three times. This takes you back to the **calculator** property in the **ViewController**. Click **Step over** and execution moves to the second line of code in the **viewDidLoad** method (Figure 19.18).

```
self.calculator = Calculator()
var total = self.calculator?.addToTotal(10)
```

*Figure 19.18 Getting ready to call **addToTotal***

11. Click the **Step into** button. According to the rules of optional chaining, Swift sees the **calculator** property is **nil**, so it never executes **addToTotal**.

12. Click the **Stop** button in the Xcode toolbar.

As interesting as this is, you actually do want the **Calculator** to work properly, so ultimately, marking the **calculator** property as **weak** is not a good approach, because it doesn't allow the **Calculator** object to live long enough.

IBOutlet Properties

You may have noticed another property at the top of the **ViewController** class:

```
@IBOutlet weak var lblLabel: UILabel!
```

This property is marked as **weak**. It is used to reference the label on the scene in the project's Storyboard (Figure 19.19). Let's test this property to see if it works.

*Figure 19.19 This label is referenced by the **lblLabel** property in the **ViewController** class.*

1. Select the **ViewController.swift** code file in the Project Navigator.

2. Add the following code to the **viewDidLoad** method:

```
override func viewDidLoad() {
    super.viewDidLoad()

    self.lblLabel.text = "A weak property"

    self.calculator = Calculator()
    var total = self.calculator?.addToTotal(10)
}
```

This code stores the text "A weak property" in the label's text field.

3. Click Xcode's Run button. Click the Continue button in the Debug toolbar when you hit the breakpoints you set earlier. When the app appears in the Simulator, you will see the label's text has been successfully set (Figure 19.20).

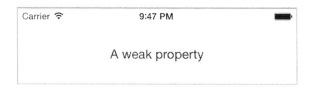

Figure 19.20 The label's text has been successfully set.

So this begs the question, "Why does the **weak** declaration work for the **lblLabel** property, but not for the calculator property?"

It works because, behind the scenes, the view in this scene automatically **retains** all objects referenced as **@IBOutlets**. Since these user-interface controls are retained by the view, you can declare them as weak because the view keeps them alive for you!

Second Attempt: Strong Property

Now you have seen that a weak property doesn't work well (other than IBOutlets), let's try a strong property.

1. If you haven't already done so, click the **Stop** button to stop the app from running.

2. Select the **ViewController.swift** file in the Project Navigator and remove the **weak** modifier:

```
weak var calculator: Calculator?
```

Swift properties are strong by default, so removing the **weak** keyword automatically makes it strong.

3. Add the **println** statement shown in Figure 19.21 to the bottom of the **viewDidLoad** method. Make sure there is still a breakpoint on the third line from the bottom that creates the **Calculator** object.

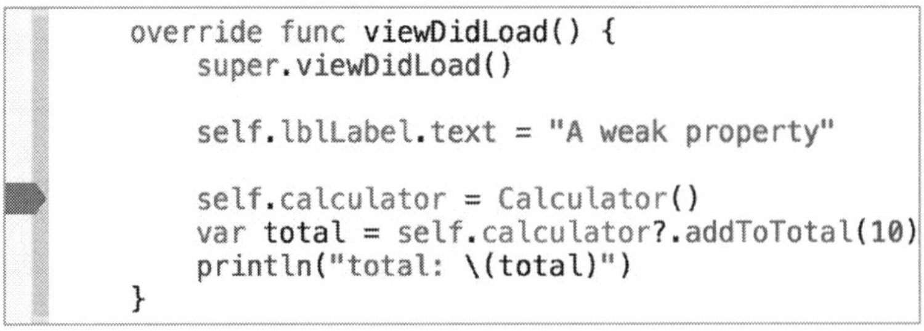

```
override func viewDidLoad() {
    super.viewDidLoad()

    self.lblLabel.text = "A weak property"

    self.calculator = Calculator()
    var total = self.calculator?.addToTotal(10)
    println("total: \(total)")
}
```

*Figure 19.21 Add a **println** statement to the bottom of the **viewDidLoad** method.*

4. Click the **Run** button to see how it works at run time. After hitting the first breakpoint where the **Calculator** object is created, click the **Step over** button twice and then hover your mouse pointer over the **total** variable. You should see it now contains the value **10** as in the Variables View in Figure 19.22.

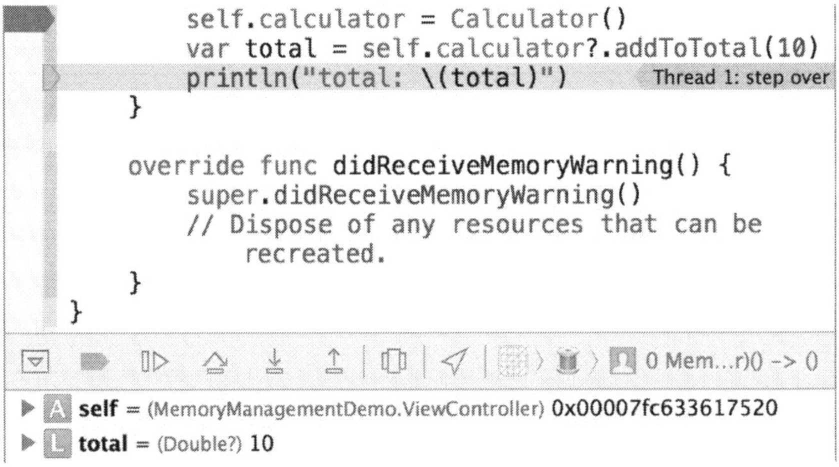

```
        self.calculator = Calculator()
        var total = self.calculator?.addToTotal(10)
        println("total: \(total)")          Thread 1: step over
    }

    override func didReceiveMemoryWarning() {
        super.didReceiveMemoryWarning()
        // Dispose of any resources that can be
            recreated.
    }
}
```

▷ A **self** = (MemoryManagementDemo.ViewController) 0x00007fc633617520
▷ L **total** = (Double?) 10

*Figure 19.22 The **total** variable's value is **10**.*

5. Press Continue in the Debug toolbar. Notice the **deinit** breakpoint doesn't get hit. This is because the **Calculator** object stays alive as long as the **calculator** property continues to hold a reference to it.

As you can see, you should use a strong property when you need the object it references to stay alive.

6. Go back to Xcode and click the **Stop** button.

Strong Reference Cycles

A circular reference, also known as a ***strong reference cycle***, occurs when two objects have a strong reference to each other, and therefore neither object can be released.

Let's look closely at a strong reference cycle so you can learn to avoid it. The sample project has code that models a relationship between a person and a rental car.

1. In the **MemoryManagementDemo** project, select the **Person.swift** code file to view the **Person** class:

```
class Person {

    var car: RentalCar?

    deinit {
        println("Person is deinitializing")
    }
}
```

2. Select the **RentalCar.swift** code file to view the **RentalCar** class:

```
class RentalCar {

    var lessee: Person?

    deinit {
        println("RentalCar is deinitializing")
    }
}
```

The **Person** class has a **car** property that can hold a reference to a **RentalCar** object, and the **RentalCar** class has a **lessee** property that can hold a reference to a **Person** object.

Notice both these classes have a **deinit** method containing a **println** statement that writes a message to the Console when the object is released.

3. Under the **MemoryManagementDemoTests** group, select the **MemoryManagementDemoTests.swift** file. Check out the

testCircularReference method:

```
func testCircularReference() {

    var person: Person? = Person()
    var car: RentalCar? = RentalCar()

    // Assign a car to a person
    person!.car = car

    // Assign a person to the car
    car!.lessee = person

    car = nil
    person = nil
}
```

Using the following image, let's take a step-by-step look at what this code does:

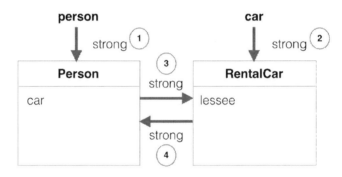

① `var person: Person? = Person()`

② `var car: RentalCar? = RentalCar()`

③ `person!.car = car`

④ `car!.lessee = person`

⑤ `car = nil`

⑥ `person = nil`

1. An instance of the **Person** class is created and a strong reference to the object is stored in the **person** variable.

2. An instance of the **RentalCar** class is created and a strong reference to the object is stored in the **car** variable.

3. A strong reference to the **RentalCar** object is stored in the **Person** object's **car** property.

4. A strong reference to the **Person** object is stored in the **RentalCar** object's **lessee** property.

5. The **car** variable is set to **nil**, clearing the reference to the **Person** object.

6. The **person** variable is set to **nil**, clearing the reference to the **RentalCar** object.

However, since the **Person** and **RentalCar** objects still hold a strong reference to each other, neither object gets released, causing a ***memory leak*** in the app. A memory leak means an app is continually eating up memory until all memory allocated to the app is eventually consumed, and the app crashes.

Let's run this test method so you can see for yourself that the objects are not being released.

1. First, let's clear the existing breakpoints in the project. To do this, click the second button from the right in the Navigator Toolbar to display the Breakpoint Navigator. Right-click the **MemoryManagementDemo** node and select **Delete Breakpoints** from the menu.

2. Next, go to the Test Navigator by clicking the fifth button from the left in the Navigator toolbar.

   Click on the **testCircularReference()** method to select it and then set a breakpoint in the first line of code in this method (Figure 19.23).

```
func testCircularReference() {

    var person: Person? = Person()
    var car: RentalCar? = RentalCar()

    // Assign a car to a person
    person!.car = car

    // Assign a person to the car
    car!.lessee = person

    car = nil
    person = nil
}
```

*Figure 19.23 Set a breakpoint in **testCircularReference**.*

3. Run the test by hovering your mouse pointer over the **testCircularReference** test and clicking the run button that appears. (If no button appears, try hovering your mouse pointer over the first node in the list instead.)

4. Click the **Step over** button until you reach the closing curly brace of the test method (Figure 19.24).

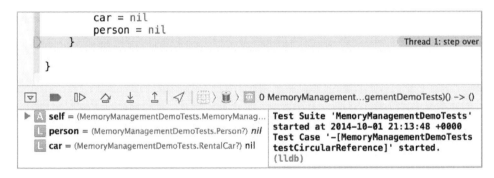

Figure 19.24 The objects are not released.

5. Notice in the Variables View that the **person** and **car** variables are **nil**. However, there is no deinitializing message in the Console, indicating the objects are still in memory. This is definitely a memory leak!

6. Click Xcode's **Stop** button.

Resolving Strong Reference Cycles

You can resolve a circular reference in one of two ways. Your first option is to change one of the strong references to a weak reference. Let's give that a try.

1. Select the **Person.swift** file in the Project Navigator.

2. Add the **weak** modifier to the **car** property:

```
class Person {

    weak var car: RentalCar?
```

3. Run the **testCircularReference** test method again. When you hit the breakpoint, keep clicking **Step over** until you hit the line of code that sets the car variable to **nil** (Figure 19.25).

```
            // Assign a person to the car
            car!.lessee = person

            car = nil
            person = nil
        }
```

*Figure 19.25 Ready to set the variables to **nil**.*

4. Click **Step over** again. The **car** variable is set to **nil** in the Variables View and the **RentalCar is deinitializing** message is shown in the Console (Figure 19.26).

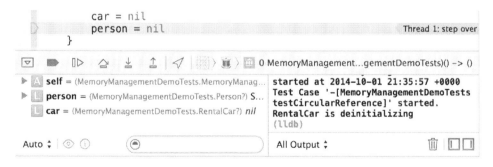

*Figure 19.26 The **RentalCar** object is released!*

5. Figure 19.27 demonstrates what happens behind the scenes when you set the **car** variable to **nil**. The gray, dotted-line arrows indicate object references that have been released.

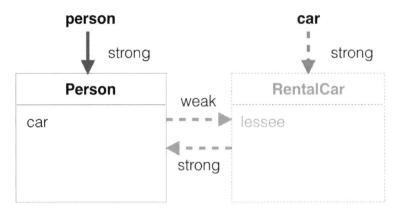

*Figure 19.27 The weak reference lets **RentalCar** be released from memory.*

When the **car** variable is set to **nil**, it releases its reference to the **RentalCar** object. Since there are no strong references to the **RentalCar** object left, (just the weak reference from the **Person** object), the **RentalCar** object is released from memory. In the process, the **RentalCar** object's strong reference to the **Person** object is also released.

6. Press **Step over** again. The **person** variable is set to **nil** in the Variables View and **Person is deinitializing** is displayed in the Console (Figure 19.28).

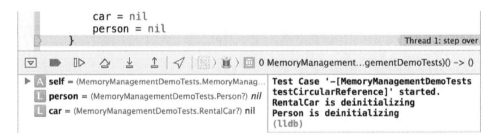

*Figure 19.28 The **Person** object is released!*

7. Figure 19.29 demonstrates what happens behind the scenes when you set the **person** variable to **nil**.

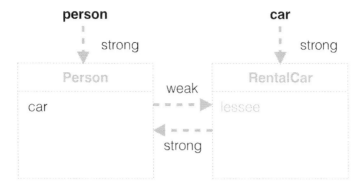

*Figure 19.29 The Person object is released when the last strong reference to it is set to **nil**.*

When the **person** variable is set to **nil**, it releases its strong reference to the **Person** object. Since there are no other strong references to the object, it's released.

8. Press the **Stop** button in Xcode.

Resolving Strong Reference Cycles With Unowned References

Your second option for avoiding strong reference cycles is to use *unowned references.*

Unowned references are similar to weak references in not keeping a strong hold on objects. The difference is that unowned references are not optional. The reference is always assumed to have a value.

1. Let's look at another example to see how they work. The sample project has code that models a relationship between a traveler and a passport.

2. In the **MemoryManagementDemo** project, select the **Traveler.swift** code file to view the **Traveler** class:

```
class Traveler {

    var passport: Passport?

    deinit {
        println("Traveler is deinitializing")
    }
}
```

3. Select the **RentalCar.swift** code file to view the **RentalCar** class:

```
class Passport {

    unowned var traveler: Traveler

    init(traveler: Traveler)
    {
        self.traveler = traveler
    }

    deinit {
        println("Passport is deinitializing")
    }
}
```

The **Traveler** class has a **passport** property that can hold a reference to a **Passport** object (Figure 19.30). The property is optional, because a **Traveler** may not always have a **Passport**.

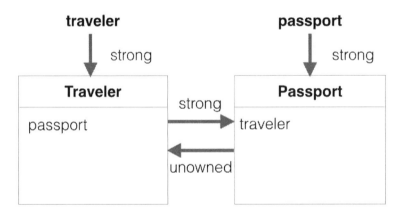

*Figure 19.30 Unowned reference from **Passport** to **Traveler***

The **Passport** class has a **traveler** property that can hold a reference to a **Traveler** object. It's marked as **unowned**, so it holds a weak reference to the **Traveler**. It's not optional, because a **Passport** always has a **Traveler** associated with it.

Both these classes have a **deinit** method containing a **println** statement that writes a message to the Console when the object is released.

4. Select the **MemoryManagementDemoTests.swift** code file and check out the **testUnownedReference** method:

```
func testUnownedReference()
{
    // Create the Traveler
    var traveler: Traveler? = Traveler()
    // Create the Passport & set the     Traveler
    var passport: Passport? =
        Passport(traveler: traveler!)

    // Associate the Passport with the Traveler
    traveler!.passport = passport

    passport = nil
    traveler = nil
}
```

The first few lines of code create the **Traveler** and **Passport** objects and establish the relationships between them as Figure 19.31 depicts.

5. The second-to-last line of code in this method sets the **passport** property to **nil**. As Figure 19.31 shows, this releases the strong reference from the passport variable. This doesn't release the **Passport** object, because the **Traveler** object still has a strong reference to it.

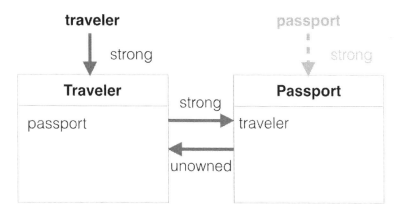

*Figure 19.31 The **passport** variable is set to **nil**.*

6. When the last line of code sets the **traveler** variable to **nil**, as depicted in Figure 19.32, it releases the strong reference to the **Traveler** object. Since there are no other strong references to the **Traveler** object, it's released. In turn, this releases the reference to the **Passport** object. Since there are no more strong references to the Passport object, it too is released.

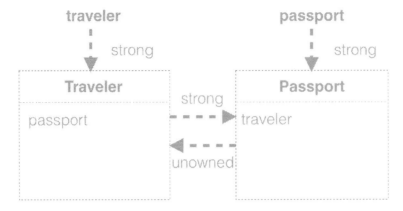

*Figure 19.32 The **traveler** variable is set to **nil**.*

Strong Reference Cycles and Closures

There are a few things to look out for when you're creating strong reference cycles with closures. In most cases you don't have to worry about this, but there are some very specific cases you need to look out for. Check out Apple's *Strong Reference Cycles for Closures* help topic for details.

Summary

Here is an overview of the key points covered in this section on memory management:

- An object "comes to life" when you first create an instance of it from a class definition.

- The "old" way of managing memory required you to:

  1. Send a **retain** message to an object to keep it alive, incrementing its retain count.

  2. Send a **release** message to indicate you no longer need an object, decrementing its retain count.

- When an object's retain count reaches zero, it is physically released from memory.

- Automatic Referencing Counting (ARC) sends the **retain** and **release** messages for you.

- With ARC, all you need to keep an object alive is to have a variable pointing to it.

- Local variables only stay alive in the method in which they are declared. This means if you create a local variable that references an object, when the method is finished executing, the variable is released, and the object it references is released.

- When referencing an object from a property, use the **weak** property accessor keyword if you don't need to hold a reference to the object (such as with **IBOutlet** properties that are retained for you).

- Weak properties must always be declared as optional, because they can potentially hold a **nil** value.

- Swift properties are strong by default, so removing the **weak** keyword automatically makes it strong. Use strong properties if you need to keep an object alive.

- A circular reference, also known as a *strong reference cycle*, occurs when two objects have a strong reference to each other, and therefore neither object can be released.

- You can resolve a circular reference in one of two ways; Your first option is to change one of the strong references to a weak reference.

- Your second option for avoiding strong reference cycles is to use *unowned references*.

- Unowned references are similar to weak references in not keeping a strong hold on objects. The difference is that unowned references are not optional. The reference is always assumed to have a value.

Exercise 19.1

In this exercise, you will apply what you have learned in this chapter to fix a strong reference cycle.

1. Open the **MemoryManagementDemo** project in Xcode.

2. Add a new class named **Employee** to the project:

```
class Employee {

    var office: Office?

    init() {}

    deinit {
        println("deinit Employee")
    }
}
```

3. Add a new class named **Office** to the project:

```
class Office {

    var employee: Employee?

    init() {}

    deinit {
        println("deinit Office")
    }
}
```

4. In the File Inspector, add the **Employee** and **Office** classes to the **MemoryManagementDemoTests** target.

5. In the **MemoryManagementDemoTests.swift** code file, add the following test method:

```
func testEmployeeOffice() {

        var employee: Employee? = Employee()
        var office: Office? = Office()

        // Assign an office to an employee
        employee?.office = office
        // Assign an employee to an office
        office?.employee = employee
```

```
            employee = nil
            office = nil
    }
```

6. Run the unit test and confirm there is a strong reference cycle between the two objects.

7. You have two options for fixing this circular reference. Choose the most appropriate, and fix the problem.

Solution Movie 19.1

To see a video providing the solution for this exercise, you can enter the link below in your Web browser to see each step performed for you.

Movie 19.1

http://www.iOSAppsForNonProgrammers.com/B4M191.html

Chapter 20: Mastering Protocols and Delegates

Protocols are a powerful, advanced tool that help make your apps easier to design and extend. They define standard behavior in classes that are not necessarily related. Protocols used together with delegates allow you to create classes with a well-balanced load of responsibilities.

Sections in This Chapter

Understanding Protocols and Delegates

Protocols are a powerful feature used throughout the Cocoa Touch Framework, so it's important to get a solid grasp of the subject. They are a great tool in helping you create apps that are easy to extend.

Outside the software world, a *protocol* is defined as:

> *The established code of behavior in any group, organization, or situation.*

This definition isn't far off the mark when it comes to Swift's protocols. They define standard behavior that can be adopted by classes, structures, and enumerations.

There are two main ways you can add common behavior to classes in Swift— class inheritance and protocols.

The left side of Figure 20.1 depicts using class inheritance to define standard behavior. Subclasses inherit the behavior defined in a superclass.

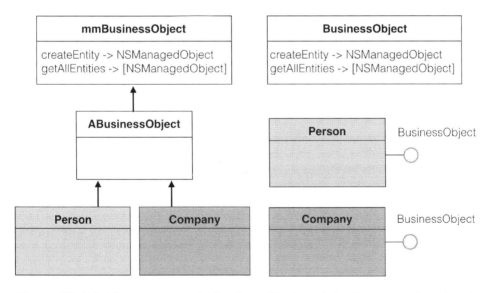

Figure 20.1 Adding common behavior with class inheritance and protocols

The right side of Figure 20.1 depicts using a protocol to define standard behavior. Classes that adopt the protocol are guaranteed to implement the behavior defined in the protocol. Protocols are a great way to add common behavior to classes not in the same inheritance chain or to enumerations and structures, which can't be subclassed.

One of the most common uses of protocols in the Cocoa Touch Framework is related to user-interface controls. In fact, you have already used a few protocols without knowing it. The **CollectionsDemo** and **ConditionalStatements** projects both use a picker view control, which requires the use of protocols.

The picker views you have seen so far contain just one component, or column. However, picker views can have multiple components, as Figure 20.2 illustrates.

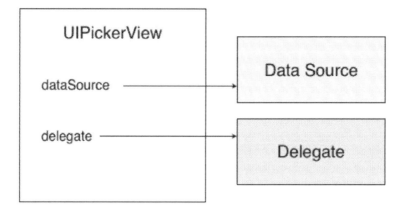

Figure 20.2 A picker view can have multiple components.

The **UIPickerView** control works together with a *data source* and a *delegate* object to fill its rows and respond to user selection. In fact, the **UIPickerView** class has both a **dataSource** and a **delegate** property containing a reference to these objects (Figure 20.3). As a bonus, when you learn how data source and delegate objects work with picker view, you are also learning how they work with other controls such as table views and collection views.

*Figure 20.3 **UIPickerView** has a data source and delegate.*

The *data source* object tells the picker view how many components, or columns, are in the picker and how many rows are in each component.

The *delegate* constructs each row in the picker view and responds to the user selecting an item. In object-oriented programming, a *delegate* is an object that performs a task for another object, which is definitely true in this case.

The beauty of the design in Figure 20.3 is that any object can act as the data source or the delegate. You store the objects you want to use in the picker view's **dataSource** and **delegate** properties, and at designated times, the picker view calls methods on the data source and delegate objects. You can even have the same object act as both data source and delegate (a common practice).

What methods does the picker view call on each of these objects? How can you guarantee the objects in the **dataSource** and **delegate** properties have the methods that the picker view needs? The answer is *protocols*.

The **UIPickerViewDataSource** protocol declares methods required by an object that acts as a data source for the picker view. In turn, the **UIPickerViewDelegate** protocol declares methods required by an object that acts as a delegate for the picker view.

UIPickerViewDataSource Protocol

The **UIPickerViewDataSource** protocol declares these methods:

Method	Description
numberOfComponentsInPickerView:	Called by the picker view when it needs the number of components
pickerView:numberOfRowsInComponent	Called by the picker view when it needs the number of rows for a specific component

Both methods in this protocol are required, so any object that wants to act as a data source for a picker view *must* implement these two methods.

UIPickerViewDelegate Protocol

None of the methods in the **UIPickerViewDelegate** protocol (shown in the following table) are "required," but your picker view won't work very well without implementing the two most commonly used methods:

- pickerView:titleForRow:forComponent:

- pickerView:didSelectRow:inComponent:

pickerView:titleForRow:forComponent: returns a title for the specified row and component. The second method, **pickerView:didSelectRow:inComponent:**, provides a place where you can put code to respond to a user selecting an item in the picker view.

Method	Description
pickerView:didSelectRow: InComponent:	Called by the picker view when the user selects a row in a component
pickerView: titleForRow:forComponent:	Called by the picker view when it needs the title (the text displayed in the picker) for a given row in a given component
pickerView:attributedTitleForRow: forComponent	Called by the picker view when it needs the styled title (the text displayed in the picker) for a given row in a given component
pickerView:viewForRow: forComponent:reusingView:	Called by the picker view when it needs to know which view to use for a given row in a given component
pickerView:rowHeightForComponent:	Called by the picker view when it needs the row height to use for drawing row content
pickerView:widthForComponent:	Called by the picker view when it needs the row width to use for drawing row content

Adopting Protocols

A class *adopts* a protocol to indicate it implements all the required methods and often some of the optional methods, too. Rather than a separate object acting as the data source and delegate, Figure 20.4 shows a common iOS convention whereby a view controller adopts both protocols for the picker view.

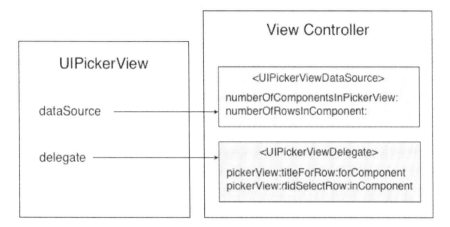

Figure 20.4 A view controller often implements UI control protocols.

A class, structure, or enumeration can declare that it adopts specific protocols. In the following code, the **ViewController** class adopts **UIPickerViewDataSource** and **UIPickerViewDelegate** protocols:

```
class ViewController: UIViewController,
  UIPickerViewDelegate, UIPickerViewDataSource {
```

The protocols adopted by a class are listed after the superclass declaration and separated by commas.

Protocols Step by Step

So you more fully grasp the use of protocols, let's write code from scratch that fills a picker view and responds to the selection of an item in the picker view.

1. Open the **ProtocolDemo** project located in a subfolder where you have stored this book's sample code.

2. In the Project Navigator, drill into the **ProtocolDemo** node and select the **Main.storyboard** file. You should see the scene displayed in Figure 20.5.

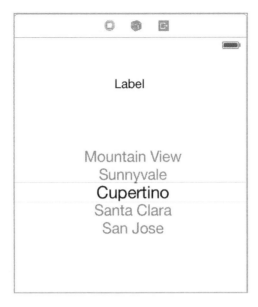

Figure 20.5 The picker view on a storyboard scene

Currently, no code in the **ViewController** class is associated with the picker view, although there are properties you can use to reference the picker view and label. There is also a **fifaWinners** array containing the last four FIFA World Cup winners, which you will use to fill the picker view.

Now you need to create a data source and delegate for the picker view. Remember, it's common for the associated view controller to act as the data source and delegate. This means it needs to adopt both the **UIPickerViewDataSource** and **UIPickerViewDelegate** protocols.

3. Select the **ViewController.swift** code file in the Project Navigator and change the class declaration to:

```
class ViewController: UIViewController,
 UIPickerViewDataSource, UIPickerViewDelegate {
```

When you add the protocols, you will immediately see a compiler error, **Type 'ViewController' does not conform to protocol 'UIPickerViewDataSource'**. This is exactly right. You have declared that the **ViewController** class implements the picker view protocols, but without adding the methods yet.

Let's get rid of this error by implementing the methods of the **UIPickerViewDataSource** protocol.

4. At the top of the **ViewController.swift** file, directly below the declaration of the **fifaWinners** array, add the following methods:

```
func numberOfComponentsInPickerView(pickerView:
    UIPickerView) -> Int {

    return 1
}

    func pickerView(pickerView: UIPickerView,
  numberOfRowsInComponent component:Int) -> Int {

    return fifaWinners.count
    }
}
```

As soon as you add this code, the error disappears, even though you haven't implemented both protocols. This is because you are not required to implement the **UIPickerViewDelegate** methods (although you will).

The **numberOfComponentsInPickerView:pickerView:** method returns **1**, because you only want one column, or component, in the picker view.

The **pickerView:numberOfRowsInComponent:** method returns the count of items in the **fifaWinners** array. Since only one component is in the picker view, the **component** parameter is ignored.

5. Now let's implement the **UIPickerViewDelegate** protocol. In the **ViewController.swift** file, directly below the methods you just added, add these two new methods:

```
func pickerView(pickerView: UIPickerView,
  titleForRow row: Int,
     forComponent component: Int) -> String! {

    return fifaWinners[row]
}

func pickerView(pickerView: UIPickerView,
```

```
        didSelectRow row: Int,
    inComponent component: Int) {

        self.lblDemo.text = fifaWinners[row]
}
```

The **pickerView:titleForRow:forComponent:** method returns the item from the **fifaWinners** array using the currently selected picker view row as an index.

The **pickerView:didSelectRow:inComponent:** method automatically executes when a user selects an item from the picker view. It gets the text of the currently selected picker view row from the **fifaWinners** array and stores it into the **text** property of the label at the top of the view.

Now you have implemented methods for both protocols, press the **Run** button to run the app in the Simulator. Oddly enough, the picker view is empty (Figure 20.6)!

Figure 20.6 The picker view is empty!

What's going on? Although you have implemented the protocols on the view controller, you haven't told the picker view which objects to use as data source and delegate. To do this, you have to set the picker view's **dataSource** and **delegate** properties.

I intentionally had you "forget" to set these properties, because this is something you will often forget to do in your day-to-day app development. Now you can see what a picker view looks like at run time when its **dataSource** and **delegate** properties are not set!

6. First, let's look at the **dataSource** and **delegate** properties. Go back to Xcode and click the **Stop** button, and select the **Main.storyboard** file in the Project Navigator.

7. Select the picker view by clicking on it.

You can view the **dataSource** and **delegate** properties in Xcode's Connections Inspector, located in the Utilities panel on the right side of the Xcode window. If Xcode's Utilities panel is not visible, click the far-right button in the **View** button group at the top of the Xcode window (the Utilities panel is visible if this button is depressed as shown in Figure 20.7).

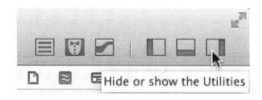

Figure 20.7 Show the Utilities panel.

In the Utilities panel, view the Connections Inspector by selecting the button on the far right (Figure 20.8).

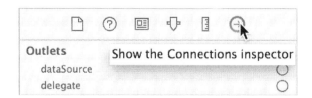

Figure 20.8 Show the Connections Inspector.

The picker view's **dataSource** and **delegate** properties are at the top of the Inspector. Notice the circles to the right of the properties. These are called *connection wells*. When they are empty, the properties are not connected to anything. Let's connect the picker view's **dataSource** and **delegate** properties to the view controller.

8. In the storyboard file, hold the **control** key down, and click the picker view. Still holding the **control** key, drag up to the **View Controller** icon in the scene dock (Figure 20.9).

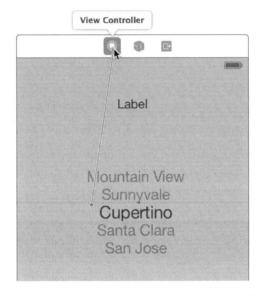

Figure 20.9 ***Control+Drag*** *to the view controller icon.*

9. When you see the View Controller popup appear, let go of the mouse button and **control** key and you will see the **Outlets** popup (Figure 20.10).

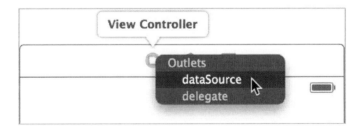

Figure 20.10 Select the ***dataSource*** *outlet.*

10. Select the **dataSource** outlet by clicking on it. You will see the small View Controller icon flash, indicating the connection has been made.

11. Next, **Control+Drag** again between the picker view and the **View Controller** icon. Notice the small white dot to the left of the **dataSource**

outlet, indicating that it has already been selected. This time, select the **delegate** outlet (Figure 20.11).

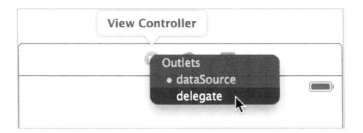

*Figure 20.11 Select the **delegate** outlet.*

Now look at the Connections Inspector and you can see both the **dataSource** and **delegate** outlets are connected to the View Controller, and the connection wells are no longer empty (Figure 20.12).

*Figure 20.12 The **dataSource** and **delegate** outlets are connected to the view controller.*

12. Let's see how these new connections work at run time. Click Xcode's **Run** button. When the app appears in the Simulator, you can see the picker view contains a list of FIFA teams (Figure 20.13).

Figure 20.13 The FIFA teams displayed at run time

13. Select an item from the list. When you do, the **pickerView:didSelectRow:inComponent:** method is automatically called and the selected item is displayed in the label's **text** property (Figure 20.14).

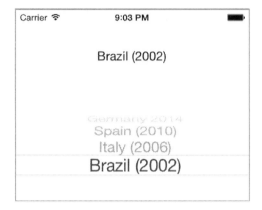

Figure 20.14 The selected team appears in the label.

The pattern of using protocols in conjunction with the picker view is a common approach you will use many times with different user-interface controls in iOS.

Declaring Your Own Protocols

At times, you may need to declare your own protocols that you want other classes to implement. Here is the syntax for declaring a protocol:

```
protocol MyProtocol {

    // Protocol definition
}
```

Protocol Methods

A protocol can specify instance and type methods that must be implemented by classes that conform to it.

You declare a protocol's methods the same way you declare them for a class, but don't include curly braces or implementation code (although the protocol itself has curly braces.)

Here is an example of an instance method that accepts a single integer parameter and returns a Boolean value:

```
protocol MyProtocol {

    func amIOld(age: Int) -> Bool
}
```

To declare a type method, use the **class** keyword. The following type method accepts no parameters and returns an integer value:

```
protocol MyProtocol {

    class func getHighScore() -> Int
}
```

Protocol Properties

A protocol can also declare instance and type properties. The protocol specifies the properties' names and types, but doesn't specify whether they must be stored or computed properties. However, a protocol must specify whether a property is read-only or read-write.

For example, the following protocol declares a read-write Boolean property named **verbose** and a read-only integer property named **numberOfRetries**:

```
protocol MyProtocol {

    var verbose: Bool {get set}
    var numberOfRetries: Int {get}
}
```

Optional Protocol Members

By default, methods and properties declared in a protocol are required—meaning any class adopting the protocol must implement them.

However, you can indicate that a particular member is optional by using the **optional** keyword in conjunction with the **@objc** attribute.

For example, the following protocol declares the **verbose** property as optional and the **numberOfRetries** property as required:

```
@objc protocol MyProtocol {

    optional var verbose: Bool {get set}
    var numberOfRetries: Int {get}
}
```

The **@objc** attribute can be used before any Swift class, method, or property. It indicates that you want to access it from Objective-C. In this case, even if you're not accessing it from Objective-C, you need to use it to mark members of your protocol as **optional**.

Checking for Protocol Conformance

At times, you may want to check if a class conforms to a particular protocol. Use Swift's **is** operator to check for conformance, and use its **as?** and **as** operators to cast to a particular protocol.

Protocols use the same syntax as checking for and casting to a type described in *Chapter 18: Data Types & Conversions*.

There are two important caveats regarding checking for protocol conformance:

1. You must mark your protocol with the **@objc** attribute (as shown in the previous section) to check it for conformance.

2. If you mark your protocol with the **@objc** attribute, you can only apply the protocol to classes—not structures or enumerations.

Protocol Inheritance

There are two aspects of protocol inheritance.

First, protocols are inherited by subclasses. If a class adopts a protocol, its subclasses automatically adopt the protocol.

The second aspect of protocol inheritance is that you can subclass and extend the protocol itself.

A protocol can inherit one or more protocols and extend those protocols even further. For example, in the following code, the **Localizable** and **Secureable** protocols are inherited by the

LocalizeableSecureableSustainable protocol, which adds its own **isSustainable** property:

```
protocol Localizable {

    var isLocalizable: Bool {get set}
}

protocol Secureable {

    var isSecureable: Bool {get set}
}

protocol LocalizableSecureableSustainable: Localizable,
Secureable {

    var isSustainable: Bool {get set}
}
```

A class that adopts **LocalizeableSecureableSustainable** must implement all members of the protocols it inherits as well as the members it declares. For example:

```
class MySuperclass: LocalizableSecureableSustainable {
    var isLocalizable: Bool = true
    var isSecureable: Bool = true
    var isSustainable: Bool = true
}
```

Protocol Composition

You can specify that a variable, property, or parameter contains types that conform to multiple protocols.

For example, the following code declares a variable named **localizeSecure** that contains types that conform to both the **Localizable** and **Secureable** protocols:

```
var localizeSecure: protocol<Localizable,Secureable>
```

Given this declaration, a type that conforms to only the **Localizable** protocol or only the **Secureable** protocol can't be stored in this variable. The type must conform to both protocols.

Note that protocol compositions do not create a new protocol. They simply declare a temporary combination of protocols.

Practical Use of Protocols

Where might you use protocols in your iOS projects? As one example, you could declare a protocol for retrieving and storing app settings:

```
protocol AppSetting {

    func getSettingForKey(key: String) -> String
    func setSetting(setting: String, forKey: String)
}
```

Multiple classes can implement this protocol and provide completely different implementations for the methods. For example, one class can read and write settings to a local file:

```
class SettingsLocalFile: AppSetting {

    func getSettingForKey(key: String) -> String {
        // Get setting from the local file
        return ""
    }

    func setSetting(setting: String, forKey: String) {
        // Store setting in a local file
    }
}
```

Another class can read and write settings to a database:

```
class SettingsDatabase: AppSetting {

    func getSettingForKey(key: String) -> String {
        // Get setting from the database
        return ""
    }

    func setSetting(setting: String, forKey: String) {
     // Store setting in a database
    }
}
```

In Figure 20.15, the lollipop shape on the right edge of each class indicates it adopts the **AppSetting** protocol.

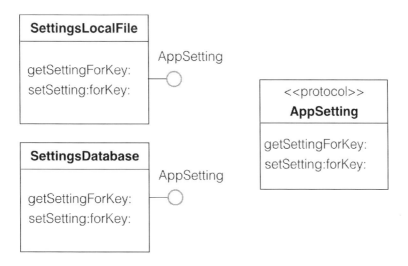

Figure 20.15 Classes implementing a protocol

A protocol declares the *signature* of methods that a class must implement to adopt the protocol, but it doesn't specify the methods' content and behavior. This provides tremendous flexibility, allowing you to easily extend your app in the future. For example, you may decide to store app settings on the web. You can create a third **SettingsInternet** class, adopt the **AppSetting** protocol, and you're ready to go!

In Swift, protocols are full-fledged types. Practically, this means you can declare a variable to be a specific protocol type, and it can store a reference to any class that adopts that protocol.

For example, the following code declares a **settings** variable of type **AppSetting** (the protocol). It then stores an instance of the **SettingsLocalFile** class in the variable, and afterward, an instance of **SettingsDatabase**:

```
var settings: AppSetting = SettingsLocalFile()
settings = SettingsDatabase()
```

If you store an instance of a class that doesn't adopt the **AppSetting** protocol, it produces a compiler error that says: **Type 'x' does not conform to protocol AppSetting**.

You can even specify a protocol as the type of an array or dictionary. For example, you can declare a protocol named **Localizable**, and then create an array of **Localizable** objects:

```
var localizableObject = Array<Localizable>()
```

You can declare a protocol in its own class file, or in the same file as a related class. For example, the **UIPickerView** class has an associated **UIPickerViewDelegate** protocol that defines the methods a delegate needs to implement. In this case, it makes sense to declare the protocol in the same file as the **UIPickerView** class.

Returning Values From View Controllers

Another practical use of protocols is returning values from one view controller to another. Let's look at an example of this.

1. Open the **iAppsReview** project located in a subfolder of the directory where you have stored this book's sample code.

2. Select **Main.storyboard** file in the Project Navigator. On the upper-right side of the storyboard are the scenes shown in Figure 20.16.

*Figure 20.16 Two scene use the **App Category** scene.*

When you tap the **App Category** row at the top of these scenes, they navigate to the **App Category** scene. When you select a category in the list and tap the **Back** button, the row at the top of the originating scene displays the selected category.

So how should the **App Category** scene pass the selected category back to the originating scene?

Let's talk about how *not* to do it first. Figure 20.17 demonstrates a poor solution to this problem. In this example, when a view controller navigates to the **AppCategoryViewController**, it stores a reference to itself in the **originatingController** property.

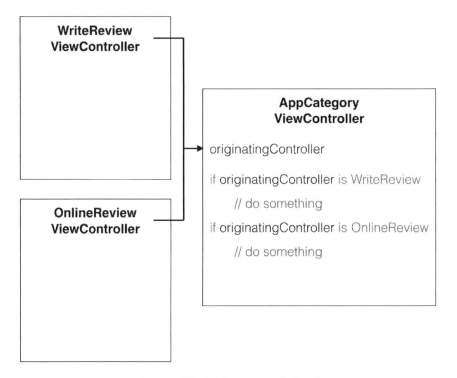

Figure 20.17 A poor solution!

When a user selects a category from the list, the **AppCategoryViewController** uses Swift's **is** operator to check the type of the originating controller. If it's **WriteReview**, then it executes one set of actions to pass back the selected category. If it's **OnlineReview**, it executes another set of actions.

When I'm performing code reviews for software companies, I see a lot of this "test the object type and perform a set of actions" approach. It's an example of tight coupling, which is *not* a good thing. The **AppCategoryViewController** knows too much about the scenes that call it. In fact, if you add a new scene to your app that needs to access the category list, you must add another **if** statement in the

AppCategoryViewController to accommodate the new scene (or maybe even convert it to a **switch** statement).

Using a protocol is a much better solution. Figure 20.18 demonstrates how a protocol can be used to elegantly solve this problem. Here are the key points as numbered in the class diagram:

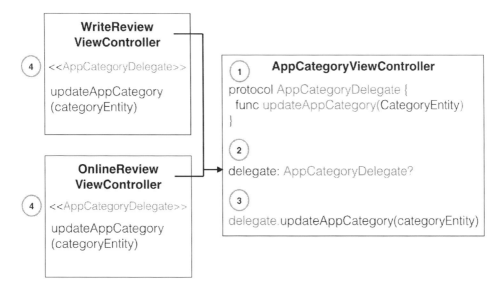

Figure 20.18 Use a protocol for a better solution.

1. The **AppCategoryViewController** class declares a protocol named **AppCategoryDelegate** that contains a single **updateAppCategory** method that all originating view controllers must implement.

2. The **AppCategoryViewController** has a **delegate** property that is the type of the **AppCategoryDelegate** protocol. Originating view controllers store a reference to themselves in this property.

3. When an app category is selected from the list, the **AppCategoryViewController** calls the **updateAppCategory** method on the view controller stored in the **delegate** property, passing the selected **CategoryEntity**.

4. The originating view controller's **updateAppCategory** method is executed, and the newly selected app category is displayed.

Figure 20.19 contains a sequence diagram that provides a step-by-step view of how the protocol works at run time.

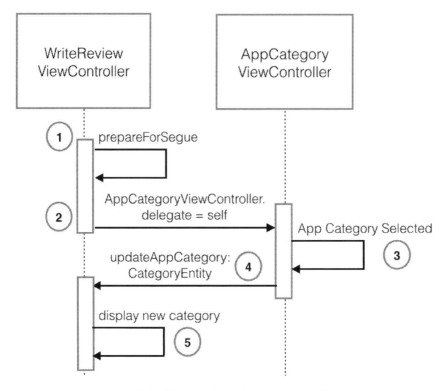

Figure 20.19 The protocol sequence diagram

1. The originating view controller's **prepareForSegue** method is called.

2. The originating view controller stores a reference to itself in the **AppCategoryViewController's delegate** property and control is passed to the **AppCategoryViewController**.

3. An app category is selected from the list.

4. The **AppCategoryViewController** calls the **updateAppCategory** method on the originating view controller, passing a reference to the selected **AppCategoryEntity**.

5. The originating view controller displays the selected app category.

Now that you have an overview of how the protocol works, let's look at the actual code that makes it all happen.

1. Select the **AppCategoryViewController.swift** file in the Project Navigator.

2. Near the top of the code file is a protocol named **AppCategoryDelegate**:

```
protocol AppCategoryDelegate {

    func updateAppCategory(appCategoryEntity:
      AppCategoryEntity)

}
```

This protocol declares an **updateAppCategory** method that all originating view controllers must implement so they can be notified when the user selects an app category from the list.

This means an originating view controller must have a method called **updateAppCategory** that accepts a parameter of type **AppCategoryEntity**.

3. Look a little farther down in the code file to see the **delegate** property:

```
class AppCategoryViewController:
    UITableViewController {

    var delegate: AppCategoryDelegate?
```

Notice its type is the **AppCategoryDelegate** protocol. An originating view controller that implements the **AppCategoryDelegate** protocol can store a reference to itself in this property.

4. Scroll to **tableView:didSelectRowAtIndexPath**. This method is called when an app category is selected at run time. Here is the last line of code in this method:

```
self.delegate?.updateAppCategory(categoryEntity)
```

This code calls the **updateAppCategory** method on the originating view controller object stored in the **delegate** property, passing the selected **AppCategoryEntity**.

5. Select the **WriteReviewViewController.swift** file in the Project Navigator. At the top of the file, this view controller adopts the **AppCategoryDelegate** protocol:

```
class WriteReviewViewController:
```

```
UITableViewController, AppCategoryDelegate {
```

6. The **prepareForSegue** method is called right before navigating to the **AppCategoryViewController**. In the last line of this method, the originating view controller stores a reference to itself in the **delegate** property of the **AppCategoryViewController**:

```
controller.delegate = self
```

7. At the bottom of the file is the implementation of the **updateAppCategory** protocol method:

```
func updateAppCategory(appCategoryEntity:
        AppCategoryEntity) {

    self.appCategoryID =
        appCategoryEntity.categoryID

    self.appCategoryCell.detailTextLabel?.text =
        appCategoryEntity.name

    self.tableView.reloadData()
}
```

This code updates the row to display the **AppCategoryEntity** passed back from the **AppCategoryViewController**.

Testing the Protocol at Run Time

Now let's step through this code at run time so you get an even clearer picture of all the moving parts.

1. In the **WriteReviewViewController** class, add a breakpoint on the last line of code in the **prepareForSegue** method (Figure 20.20).

```
        // Store a reference to this view controller in the
        // delegate property of the destination view controller
        controller.delegate = self
    }
```

*Figure 20.20 Set a breakpoint in **prepareForSegue**.*

2. Next, set a breakpoint on the first line of code in the **updateAppCategory** method (Figure 20.21).

```swift
func updateAppCategory(appCategoryEntity: AppCategoryEntity) {

    self.appCategoryID = appCategoryEntity.categoryID
    self.appCategoryCell.detailTextLabel?.text = appCategoryEntity.name
    self.tableView.reloadData()
}
```

*Figure 20.21 Set a breakpoint in **updateAppCategory**.*

3. Select the **AppCategoryViewController.swift** file in the Project Navigator. Set a breakpoint on the last line in the **tableView:didSelectRowAtIndexPath:** method (Figure 20.22).

```swift
        self.delegate?.updateAppCategory(categoryEntity)
    }
```

*Figure 20.22 Set a breakpoint in **tableView:didSelectRowAtIndexPath:**.*

4. Press Xcode's **Run** button. When the app appears in the Simulator, select the **Write a Review** option in the first screen. This takes you to the **Write Review** scene (Figure 20.23).

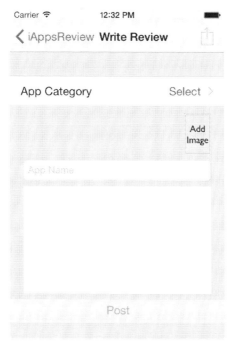

*Figure 20.23 The **Write Review** scene*

5. At the top of the scene, click on the **App Category** cell. This causes the first breakpoint to be hit (Figure 20.20) and the

WriteReviewViewController stores a reference to itself in the **AppCategoryViewController delegate** property.

6. In the Debug toolbar, press Continue. This navigates the app to the **App Category** scene (Figure 20.24).

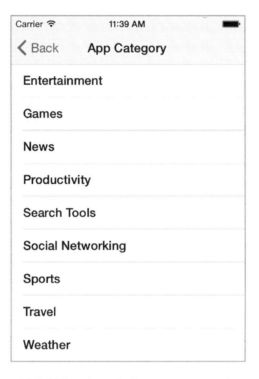

Figure 20.24 The App Category scene at run time

7. Select an app category from the list. When you do this, you hit the breakpoint in the **tableView: didSelectRowAtIndexPath** method (Figure 20.22). The **AppCategoryViewController** calls the **updateAppCategory** method on the view controller stored in its **delegate** property, passing the currently selected **AppCategoryEntity**.

8. In the Debug toolbar, click the Continue button. This takes you to the breakpoint in the originating view controller's **updateAppCategory** method (Figure 20.21). This code gets the name of the newly selected app category, stores it in the row at the top of the scene, and then tells the table view to reload its data, which refreshes the row.

9. Click Continue in the Debug toolbar. This displays the **App Category** scene with a check mark next to the newly selected app category (Figure

20.25).

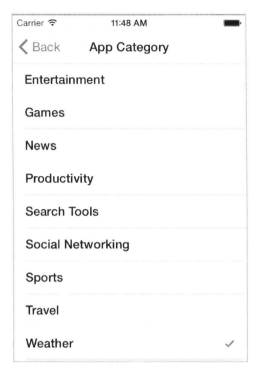

Figure 20.25 A check mark next to the selected item

10. Click the **Back** button at the top of the **App Category** scene. This takes you back to the **Write Review** scene where you can see the newly selected category displayed in the cell at the top of the screen (Figure 20.26).

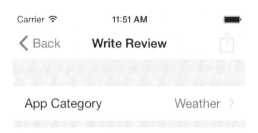

Figure 20.26 The newly selected item is displayed in the row at the top of the scene!

This is a great solution, because it's loosely coupled. The **AppCategoryViewController** knows very little about the view controllers that are calling it. In fact, the *only* thing it knows is that the view controller has a method named **updateAppCategory** that accepts an

AppCategoryEntity parameter. That's it! Now any time you have another view controller that needs to use the App Category scene, you don't have to make any changes to the **AppCategoryViewController** class. *That* is loose coupling.

This elegant solution is brought to you by Swift's protocols!

Summary

- A *protocol* is an advanced feature of Swift that allows you to define a standard set of behavior that classes, structures, and enumerations can implement.

- A *delegate* is an object that performs a task for another object.

- You can add common behavior to classes using inheritance or protocols.

- Protocols are a great way to add common behavior to classes not in the same inheritance chain or to enumerations and structures, which can't be subclassed.

Adopting Protocols

- A class *adopts* a protocol to indicate that it implements all its required properties and methods.

- The protocols adopted by a class are listed after the superclass declaration and separated by commas.

Declaring Protocols

- Here is the syntax for declaring a protocol:

```
protocol MyProtocol {

    // Protocol definition
}
```

- A protocol can specify instance and type methods that must be implemented by classes, structures, and enumerations that conform to it.

- You declare a protocol's methods the same way you declare them for a class, but don't include curly braces or implementation code:

```
protocol MyProtocol {

    func amIOld(age: Int) -> Bool
}
```

- To declare a type method, you use the **class** keyword:

```
protocol MyProtocol {

    class func getHighScore() -> Int
}
```

- A protocol can declare instance and type properties. It specifies the properties' names and types, but doesn't specify whether they must be stored or computed properties. A protocol must specify whether a property is read-only or read-write:

```
protocol MyProtocol {

    var verbose: Bool {get set}
    var numberOfRetries: Int {get}
}
```

- By default, methods and properties declared in a protocol are required— meaning any class adopting the protocol must implement them.

Optional Protocol Members

- You can indicate that a particular member is optional by using the **optional** keyword together with the **@objc** attribute:

```
@objc protocol MyProtocol {

    optional var verbose: Bool {get set}
    var numberOfRetries: Int {get}
}
```

Checking for Protocol Conformance

- You use Swift's **is** operator to check if a class conforms to a particular protocol.

- You use the **as?** and **as** operators to cast to a particular protocol.

- There are two important caveats regarding checking for protocol conformance:

    11. You must mark your protocol with **@objc** attribute (as shown in the previous section) to check it for conformance.

    12. If you mark your protocol with the **@objc** attribute, you can only apply the protocol to classes—not structures or enumerations.

Protocol Inheritance

- Protocols are inherited by subclasses. If a class adopts a protocol, its subclasses automatically adopt the protocol.

- A protocol can inherit one or more protocols and extend those protocols even further.

Protocol Composition

- You can specify that a variable, property, or parameter contains types that conform to multiple protocols. For example, the following code declares a variable named **localizeSecure** that contains types that conform to both the **Localizable** and **Secureable** protocols:

```
var localizeSecure:    protocol<Localizable,Secureable>
```

    A type that conforms to only the **Localizable** protocol or only the **Secureable** protocol can't be stored in this variable. The type must conform to both protocols.

- Protocol compositions do not create a new protocol. They simply declare a temporary combination of protocols.

Practical Use of Protocols

- One practical use of protocols is to return values from one view controller to another.

- Protocols can help eliminate tight coupling between types, making it easier to extend your app.

Exercise 20.1

Currently, the **Write Review** scene in the **iAppsReview** project allows the user to select an **App Category** and displays the selected category on the right side of its table view row (Figure 20.26). Your mission, is to change the **Online Reviews** scene to do the same.

Here are the main steps:

1. Open the **iAppsReview** project in Xcode.

2. In the **OnlineReviewsViewController** class, adopt the **AppCategoryDelegate** protocol.

3. Implement the **AppCategoryDelegate** protocol's **updateAppCategory** method in the view controller. This method needs to:

- Store the AppCategoryEntity object's name in the appCategoryCell's detailTextLabel.text property.

- Reload the table view's data.

4. In the view controller's **prepareForSegue** method, add code that stores a reference to the originating view controller in the destination view controller's **delegate** property.

Solution Movie 20.1

To see a video providing the solution for this exercise, you can enter the link below in your Web browser to see each step performed for you.

Movie 20.1

http://www.iOSAppsForNonProgrammers.com/B4M201.html

Chapter 21: The Power of Extensions

Extensions are one of Swift's best
features. Extensions allow you to
add behavior to existing classes,
including classes in the Cocoa
Touch Framework. Apple can't
add every feature you want to
their framework classes, but they
have provided a tool to allow you
to do it yourself!

Sections in This Chapter

1. *Swift's Extensions*

2. *Creating Custom Extensions*

3. *Adding Computed Properties*

4. *Adding Initializers*

5. *Adding Subscripts*

6. *Adding Nested Types*

7. *Extension Rules*

8. *Summary*

9. *Exercise 21.1*

10. *Solution Movie 21.1*

Swift's Extensions

Swift provides a powerful tool for extending classes, structures, and enumerations—***extensions***. An extension allows you to extend a type without creating a subclass. You can even extend types in the Cocoa Touch Framework!

It's better to create an extension to add functionality to a Cocoa Touch Framework class than to create a subclass, because it allows you to use the standard Cocoa Touch class throughout your app. For example, if you add an extension to the **NSURL** class, you can still use **NSURL** throughout your app. You don't have to remember to use a custom subclass in some places and **NSURL** in others.

You can add these things to a type using extensions:

- Instance and type methods

- Computed instance and computed type properties

- Initializers

- Subscripts

- Nested types

- Conformance to a protocol

This is the basic syntax for declaring an extension:

```
extension TypeToExtend {

    // New extension members and/or behavior
}
```

Creating Custom Extensions

To see how Swift extensions work, let's add a new method to Swift's **String** class.

By default, **String** has no method that tells you the number of times one string occurs in another string. For example, you may want to know how many commas are in a string. Since **String** doesn't have this method, you can add it using an extension.

I've already created an extension for you. Let's take a look.

1. Open the **ExtensionsDemo** project by selecting **File > Open...** from the Xcode menu. In the Open dialog, navigate to the folder where you have stored this book's sample code. Drill into the **ExtensionsDemo** folder, select the **ExtensionsDemo.xcodeproj** file and then click **Open**.

2. Select the **StringExtensions.swift** file in the Project Navigator to see the following extension declaration:

```
extension String {

func occurrencesOfString(aString: String) -> Int
{
    var occurrences: Int = 0
    // Set the initial range to the full string
    var range: Range<String.Index>? =
        self.startIndex..<self.endIndex

    while range != nil
    {
        // Search in the current range
        range = self.rangeOfString(aString,
                options: NSStringCompareOptions.
              CaseInsensitiveSearch,
               range: range,
               locale: nil)

        if range != nil
        {
        // String was found, move the range
        range = range!.endIndex..<self.endIndex
        // Increment the number of occurrences
        occurrences++
        }
    }
    return occurrences
}

}
```

The **extension** keyword is followed by the name of the class being extended—in this case, **String**. The extension declares an **occurrencesOfString**: method that accepts a **String** parameter named **aString**. This is the string you are searching for. The return value is an **Int** that contains the number of times **aString** is found in the string you are testing.

Within this method, **self** refers to the string object you are searching.

3. Let's see how this extension works at run time. In the Project Navigator, expand the **ExtensionsDemoTests** group and select the **ExtensionDemoTests.swift** file.

    This file contains the **testExtension** method:

    ```
    func testExtension() {

        let s = "The quick brown fox jumped over
            the lazy gray dog"
    }
    ```

4. The **StringExtensions.swift** class is not included in the unit test project's target. To verify this, type the letters **s.o** after the constant declaration:

    ```
    func testExtension() {

            let s = "The quick brown fox jumped over
            the lazy gray dog"

        s.o
    }
    ```

    The **occurrencesOfString** method doesn't appear in Code Completion, because the extension hasn't been included in the unit test target. Let's change that.

5. Select the **StringExtensions.swift** file in the Project Navigator. Go to the File Inspector on the right side of the Xcode window, and under **Target Membership**, select the **ExtensionsDemoTests** check box (Figure 21.1).

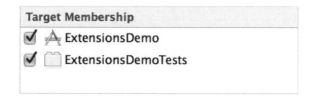

*Figure 21.1 Select the **ExtensionDemoTests** target membership.*

6. Select the **ExtensionDemoTests.swift** file in the Project Navigator. Enter the code **s.o** and the **occurrencesOfString** method appears in Code Completion (Figure 21.2).

```
func testExtension() {

    let s = "The quick brown fox jumped over the lazy gray dog"
    let count = s.occurrencesOfString( aString: String )
}
        M Int occurrencesOfString(aString: String)
```

Figure 21.2 The String extension appears in Code Completion!

7. Add the following code to the **testExtension** method:

```
func testExtension() {

let s = "The quick brown fox jumped over the
    lazy gray dog"

    let count = s.occurrencesOfString("the")
    XCTAssertEqual(count, 2)
}
```

This code checks the number of times "the" appears in the string. It should appear twice!

8. Set a breakpoint by clicking in the gutter to the left of the second line of code (Figure 21.3).

```
func testExtension() {

    let s = "The quick brown fox jumped over the lazy gray dog"
    let count = s.occurrencesOfString("the")

    XCTAssertEqual(count, 2)
}
```

Figure 21.3 Set a breakpoint on the second line of code.

9. To run this method, go to the Test Navigator by clicking the fifth button

from the left in the Navigator toolbar. Then click the arrow to the right of the **ExtensionDemoTests** node (Figure 21.4).

Figure 21.4 Run the unit test.

10. When you hit the breakpoint, click the **Step over** button in the Debug toolbar and the **count** variable is set to **2** in the Variables View (Figure 21.5).

```
func testExtension() {

    let s = "The quick brown fox jumped over the lazy gray dog"
    let count = s.occurrencesOfString("the")

    XCTAssertEqual(count, 2)                          Thread 1: step ov
    }

}
```

```
             0 ExtensionsDemoTest...sionsDemoTests)() -> (
▶  A  self = (ExtensionsDemoTests.ExtensionsDemoTests) 0x00007faac44dd8e0
▶  L  s = (String) "The quick brown fox jumped over the lazy gray dog"
▶  L  count = (Int) 2
```

Figure 21.5 Two occurrences have been found.

11. Click the Continue button in the Debug toolbar and Xcode indicates the **testExtension** method has passed.

Adding Computed Properties

Swift's extensions can add computed instance and type properties, but they can't add stored properties or property observers to existing properties.

Let's look at an extension that adds a computed instance property to the **UIImage** Cocoa Touch class.

1. In Xcode, select **File > Open** and navigate to the folder where you have stored this book's sample code. Drill down into the **ExtensionsDemo** project, select the **Extensions.playground** file and click **Open**.

2. The playground contains the following extension of the **UIImage** class:

```
extension UIImage {
    // Returns half-size version of current image
    var halfSizeImage: UIImage?
    {
        let halfWidth = self.size.width / 2
        let halfHeight = self.size.height / 2

        UIGraphicsBeginImageContext(CGSize(width:
            halfWidth, height: halfHeight))

        self.drawInRect(CGRectMake(0, 0,
            halfWidth, halfHeight))

        var image =
        UIGraphicsGetImageFromCurrentImageContext()

        UIGraphicsEndImageContext()
        return image
    }
}
```

This extension contains a single property named **halfSizeImage**. It takes the existing image (if any) and returns a half-size version of it. Let's give it a try.

3. Add the following code to the bottom of the playground:

```
var image = UIImage(named:"Book4iOS8.png")
```

This code creates a **UIImage** object from the **Book4iOS8.png** file, which I have added to this playground's resources.

When you enter this code, the image size is displayed in the playground's sidebar (Figure 21.6).

```
var image = UIImage(named:"Book4iOS8.png")        w 250 h 327
```

Figure 21.6 The image is 250x327.

4. Hover your mouse pointer to the right of the image size and click on the Quick Look icon (the eye) to see the image (Figure 21.7).

```
        UIGraphicsBeginImageContext
            (CGSize(width: halfWidth,
            height: halfHeigh
        self.drawInRect(CGReo
            halfWidth, halfHe
        var image =
            UIGraphicsGetImac
            ImageContext()
        UIGraphicsEndImageCor
        return image
    }
}

var image = UIImage(named:"Book4i
```

Figure 21.7 Hover over the Quick View icon to view the image.

5. Now add the following code that references the **halfSizeImage** extension property:

```
var imageHalf = image?.halfSizeImage
```

6. When you enter this line of code, the sidebar displays the size of the new image returned from this computed property, half the original size (Figure 21.8).

```
var imageHalf = image?.halfSizeImage        {Some w 125 h 164}
```

Figure 21.8 The half-size image is 125x164.

7. Hover your mouse pointer to the right of the new line of code and click the Quick View button to see the half-size image (Figure 21.9).

```
                    return nil
                }
                return charAtIndex
        }
    }

    var image = UIImage(named:"Book4iOS8.png")

    var imageHalf = image?.halfSizeImage
```

Figure 21.9 Quick view shows the half-size image.

The extension's computed property is working!

Adding Initializers

Swift's extensions also allow you to add initializers to an existing class. A few reasons why you may want to do this:

- To add more initialization options, making it more convenient to initialize the class.

- To create initializers that accept your own custom types as parameters.

Some basic rules governing adding initializers in an extension:

- You can add new convenience initializers, but not designated initializers or deinitializers.

- You are responsible for making sure instances are properly initialized after initialization is complete.

Let's check out an initializer extension to see how it works.

1. The **Extensions.playground** contains this extension:

```
extension UILabel {

    convenience init(text: String)
    {
        self.init()
        self.text = text
    }
}
```

This extension adds a convenience initializer to the **UILabel** class that accepts the label's text as a parameter.

2. Add the following code that uses the new initializer to the bottom of the playground:

```
var label = UILabel(text: "Swift Extension")
```

This code creates a new **UILabel** object with its **text** property set to **Swift Extension**.

3. Now add the following code that sets the text color to blue and sizes the label:

```
label.textColor = UIColor.blueColor()
label.frame = CGRectMake(0, 0, 150, 25)
```

4. Hover your mouse pointer in the sidebar to the right of the last line of code and click the Quick Look button to see a visualization of the label (Figure 21.10).

*Figure 21.10 The **UILabel** initializer extension at work*

The initializer extension successfully set the label's **text** property!

Adding Subscripts

Extensions.playground contains another extension that demonstrates how to add a subscript to an existing class:

```
extension String {

    // Returns the Character at the specified index
    subscript(index: Int) -> Character? {

        var charAtIndex: Character?

        if (index >= 0 && index < countElements(self))
        {
```

```
            var firstChar = self.startIndex
            charAtIndex = self[advance(startIndex,index)]
        }
        else
        {
            return nil
        }
        return charAtIndex
    }
}
```

This subscript accepts an integer index value and returns the character at that index.

1. Add the following code to the bottom of the playground to test this extension:

```
var s = "Brevity is the soul of wit"
s[0]
```

2. This code creates a **String** variable containing 26 characters, then requests the character at position 0.

    The results sidebar shows the values in Figure 21.11.

```
var s = "Brevity is the soul of wit"     "Brevity is the soul of wit"
s[0]                                      {Some "B"}
```

Figure 21.11 The subscript extension at work!

This is exactly right. The first character in the string is the letter **B**.

3. Try experimenting with other values, including negative numbers and numbers greater than 25. The subscript returns **nil** in both cases.

Adding Nested Types

Swift's extensions can add a nested type to a class, structure, or enumeration. Let's look at an example.

1. Select the **DateExtensions.swift** code file in the Project Navigator to see the following extension declaration:

```
extension NSDate {

    enum Month {
      case January, February, March, April, May,
        June, July, August, September, October,
          November, December, Unknown
    }

  class var currentMonth: Month {

      let cal = NSCalendar.currentCalendar()
      let flags: NSCalendarUnit = .MonthCalendarUnit
      let components = cal.components(flags,
            fromDate: NSDate.date())
      let monthNumber = components.month

      switch monthNumber {
         case 1:
         return .January
         case 2:
         return .February
         case 3:
         return .March
         case 4:
         return .April
         case 5:
         return .May
         case 6:
         return .June
         case 7:
         return .July
         case 8:
         return .August
         case 9:
         return .September
         case 10:
         return .October
         case 11:
         return .November
         case 12:
         return .December
         default:
         return .Unknown
         }
    }
}
```

This extension adds a nested **Month** enumeration to the **NSDate** class. It also adds a type property named **currentMonth** that returns the current month.

Let's give this extension a try.

2. Select **ExtensionsDemo.test** in the Project Navigator, and add the test method shown in Figure 21.12 to the file. Afterward, set a breakpoint on the code in the method.

```
func testDateExtension()
{
    var month = NSDate.currentMonth
}
}
```

Figure 21.12 Add the testDateExtension method to the unit test code file.

3. Go to the Test Navigator by selecting the fifth button from the left in the Navigation toolbar.

4. Hover your mouse pointer over the first **ExtensionDemoTests** node and click the **Run** button that appears.

5. When you hit the breakpoint, click the **Step over** button in the Debug toolbar (or if you're feeling curious, click the **Step into** button and step through the code).

When you step over the line of code in Figure 21.13, you see the current month displayed in the **month** variable. I ran this test in October, but if you are testing in a different month, that month will be in the Variables View.

```
func testDateExtension()
{
    var month = NSDate.currentMonth
}                                          Thread 1: step over
}
```

▽ ■ Ⅰ▷ ⌂ ↧ ↥ ⊲ ⊞ ⟩ 👕 ⟩ 🔟 0 Extensio...sts)0 -> 0

▶ Ⓐ **self** = (ExtensionsDemoTests.ExtensionsDemoTests) 0x00007fdf0b4ced50
Ⓛ **month** = (NSDate.Month) October

Figure 21.13 The nested class extension in action!

Extension Rules

A few more things to note about extensions:

- You can add more than one member to a class in a single extension.

- It's a best practice to add related methods to a single extension.

- There is no limit to the number of extensions you can add to a class.

- Members added to a class by an extension are inherited by subclasses. This makes extensions an extremely powerful feature!

Summary

- An extension allows you to extend a type without creating a subclass.

- You can extend types in the Cocoa Touch Framework.

- Here are the things you can add to a type using extensions:

  - Instance and type methods

  - Computed instance and computed type properties

  - Initializers

  - Subscripts

  - Nested types

  - Conformance to a protocol

- This is the basic syntax for declaring an extension:

```
extension TypeToExtend {

    // New extension members and/or behavior
}
```

- Swift's extensions can add computed instance and type properties, but they can't add stored properties or property observers to existing properties.

- Swift's extensions also allow you to add initializers to an existing class.

- You can add new convenience initializers, but not designated initializers or deinitializers.

- Make sure instances are properly initialized after initialization is complete.

- Swift's extensions can add a nested type to a class, structure, or enumeration.

Exercise 21.1

In this exercise, you will use what you have learned about extensions, subscripts, and strings to create an extension for the **String** class.

1. Open the **ExtensionsDemo** project in Xcode.

2. In the **StringExtensions.swift** code file, add the following subscript extension:

```
subscript (r: Range<Int>) -> String {
    let start = advance(self.startIndex,
    r.startIndex)
    let end = advance(self.startIndex,
    r.endIndex)
    return substringWithRange(Range(start: start,
    end: end))
}
```
This extension allows you to more easily get a range of characters from a string. For example:

```
myString[0...3]
```

3. Now add a second subscript extension that allows you to get the nth character in a string. (You can use the first subscript extension to accomplish this.)

Solution Movie 21.1

To see a video providing the solution for this exercise, you can enter the link below in your Web browser to see each step performed for you.

Movie 21.1

http://www.iOSAppsForNonProgrammers.com/B4M211.html

Chapter 22: Generics in the Real World

If you have read Apple's Generics documentation and are wondering how to use them in your own projects, this chapter is for you. You will learn how to take full advantage of generics in your everyday code as well as how to avoid constant type-casting that usually results from creating generalized code.

Sections in This Chapter

The Problem With Generalized Code

Every good app developer needs a base of generalized framework code they can use from the iOS projects they create. For example, in several of this book's projects, you have used the **mmBusinessObject** class. This class encapsulates Core Data, and using it in your projects helps you avoid repetitive code.

However, one of the downsides of generalized code is that many times in your project, you have to downcast from general to more specific types.

Let's look at a sample that demonstrates this problem.

1. Open the **GenericsDemo** project by selecting **File > Open...** from the Xcode menu. In the **Open** dialog, navigate to the folder where you have stored this book's sample code. Drill down into the **GenericsDemo** folder, select the **GenericsDemo. xcodeproj** file, and then click **Open**.

2. The Project Navigator contains most of the classes shown in the Figure 22.1 class diagram. On the left side of the diagram are the business classes. **Person** and **Company** are subclasses of **ABusinessObject**, which is in turn a subclass of **mmBusinessObject**.

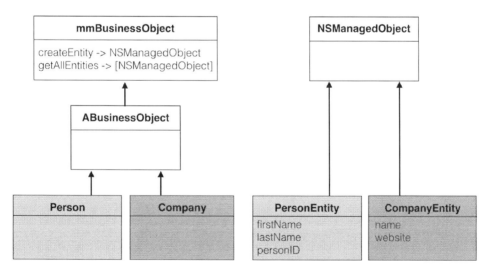

Figure 21.1 Business class relationships

On the right side of the diagram are the entity classes. **PersonEntity** and **CompanyEntity** are subclasses of **NSManagedObject**.

The **mmBusinessObject** class contains methods that create and manipulate entities. Since this is a custom framework-level class, its methods return instances of **NSManagedObject**. This allows you to use the **mmBusinessObject** class from any iOS project.

Your project-specific business classes, such as **Person** and **Company**, inherit these methods, which return **NSManagedObject** instances. However, they need to downcast the generalized **NSManagedObject** into **PersonEntity** and **CompanyEntity** objects to access entity-specific properties such as **firstName**, **lastName** and **personID** (Figure 22.1).

Let's take a closer look at this in code so you fully understand the relationship between these classes and the problem with generalized code.

3. Select the **mmBusinessObject.swift** file in the Project Navigator. Near the top of the file is the **createEntity** method, which returns an **NSManagedObject**:

```
func createEntity() -> NSManagedObject
```

Below this method is the **getAllEntities** method, which returns an array of **NSManagedObjects**:

```
func getAllEntities() -> Array<NSManagedObject>?
```

4. The **Person** and **Company** classes inherit these methods and therefore return the same types as **mmBusinessObject**. To verify this, select the **ViewController.swift** file in the Project Navigator. Check out the code in the **viewDidLoad** method:

```
var p = Person()
var personList = p.getAllEntities()
var personEntity = p.createEntity()

var c = Company()
var companyList = c.getAllEntities()
var companyEntity = c.createEntity()
```

This code creates a **Person** object, then calls its **getAllEntities** and **createEntity** methods. The second block of code creates a **Company** object and calls the same methods on that object.

5. Click on the **personList** variable and then go to the Quick Help Inspector on the right side of the Xcode window (Figure 22.2).

Figure 22.2 personList holds an array of NSManagedObjects.

It indicates the variable's type is an array of **NSManagedObjects**. This is determined by Swift's type inference, based on the **getAllEntities** method's return type.

6. Click on the **personEntity** variable. The Quick Help Inspector indicates it is of type **NSManagedObject**, based the **createEntity** method's return type (Figure 22.3).

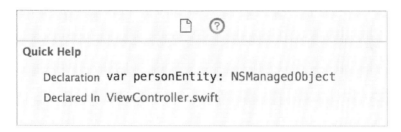

Figure 22.3 personEntity is of type NSManagedObject.

7. Clicking on the **companyList** variable, you'll see it holds an array of **NSManagedObjects**. Then clicking on the **companyEntity** variable, you'll see it is of type **NSManagedObject**. This is because the **getAllEntities** and **createEntity** methods are inherited by both the **Person** and **Company** classes, and both methods return objects of type **NSManagedObject**.

8. Let's try to access the properties of the **PersonEntity** object. Below the code that creates a **PersonEntity** object, add the last line of code in Figure 22.4, which tries to access the **firstName** property.

```
var p = Person()
var personList = p.getAllEntities()
var personEntity = p.createEntity()
personEntity.fir
```

*Figure 22.4 Try to access the **PersonEntity** object's **firstName** property.*

The **firstName** property doesn't appear in the Code Completion list, because the **personEntity** variable is of type **NSManagedObject**. You have to downcast the object to **PersonEntity** to see this property.

9. Delete the partial code you just entered, and let's add some code to perform the downcast.

A Non-Generic Solution

Let's look at one option for downcasting the return values of these inherited methods *without* generics.

In the **viewDidLoad** method, you *could* change the code as follows (but please don't):

```
var p = Person()
var personList = p.getAllEntities()
      as Array<PersonEntity>
var personEntity = p.createEntity()
      as PersonEntity

var c = Company()
var companyList = c.getAllEntities()
      as Array<CompanyEntity>
var companyEntity = c.createEntity()
      as CompanyEntity
```

This solution works. The return value of each method is downcast to the correct type of entity. However, this is a lot of work. Every time you call a business object method (and there are many more methods in the business object class than I am showing here), you have to write code that performs a downcast.

It's much less work to have each business object return the downcast type instead. To do this without generics, you can add methods to the **Person** and

Company classes that override existing methods or add completely new methods to return the desired types. For example (don't add this code yet):

```
class Person: ABusinessObject {
    override init() {
        super.init()
        self.entityClassName = "PersonEntity"
    }

    override func createEntity() -> PersonEntity {
        return super.createEntity() as PersonEntity
    }

    func getAllPersonEntities() ->
            Array<PersonEntity>? {
        return super.getAllEntities() as
            Array<PersonEntity>?
    }
}

class Company: ABusinessObject {
    override init() {
        super.init()
        self.entityClassName = "CompanyEntity"
    }

    override func createEntity() -> CompanyEntity {
        return super.createEntity() as CompanyEntity
    }

    func getAllCompanyEntities() ->
            Array<CompanyEntity>? {
        return super.getAllEntities() as
            Array<CompanyEntity>?
    }
}
```

This is a more acceptable solution. It accomplishes the goal of business objects returning **PersonEntity** and **CompanyEntity** objects. However, when you consider all the methods in the **mmBusinessObject** class (about 20 in the full version) and multiply that times the number of business objects in each project (20 to 30 in a large project), you quickly find yourself overriding several hundred methods. There's got to be a better way!

Enter generic methods.

The Generic Method Solution

You can incorporate generics in your projects in several ways. Let's start with a minimalist approach and create a generic method.

1. Since we are going to change the **mmBusinessObject** class to implement generics, let's leave the current class intact, and edit **mmBusinessObjectGeneric**, which is a copy of the class with a different name.

2. Select the **ABusinessObject.swift** file in the Project Navigator. Remember, this class is the superclass of both the **Person** and **Company** classes (Figure 22.1), so changing its superclass also changes the heritage of these other classes. Near the top of the class, change the superclass to **mmBusinessObjectGeneric**:

```
class ABusinessObject: mmBusinessObjectGeneric {
```

3. Select the **mmBusinessObjectGeneric.swift** file in the Project Navigator.

4. Near the top of the code file, locate the **createEntity** method (Figure 22.5).

```
// Create a new entity of the default type
func createEntity() -> NSManagedObject
{
    return NSEntityDescription.
        insertNewObjectForEntityForName(self.
        entityClassName, inManagedObjectContext:
        self.managedObjectContext!) as
        NSManagedObject
}
```

*Figure 22.5 The **createEntity** method in its "specific" form*

This method is not generic. It returns a *specific* value of type **NSManagedObject**. When we convert it to a generic method, any code that calls this method can specify the type of the return value.

5. Let's take the first step in making this method generic. Between the name of the method and the parentheses, add **<T>**:

```
func createEntity<T>() -> NSManagedObject
```

This is a ***type parameter***. It declares the letter **T** as a placeholder for a type within this method. In concept, this is similar to using *n* as a placeholder in an equation. The type parameter is replaced by an actual type when the method is called.

There is nothing magical about the letter **T**. You can specify a different letter or set of letters as the placeholder, but it's conventional to use **T** for "Type."

When you declare a type parameter for a method, it can specify:

- The method's parameter types

- The method's return type

- Types in the body of the method

Let's make use of this method's type parameter now.

6. Replace the **createEntity** method's **NSManagedObject** return type with the **T** placeholder:

```
func createEntity<T>() -> T
```

7. Next, change the **as NSManagedObject** operation at the bottom of the method to **as T**:

```
self.managedObjectContext!) as T
```

Figure 22.6 shows the three places you have used the type parameter. Now you're ready to call this generic method to see how it works at run time.

```
                        ①        ②
func createEntity<T>() -> T
{
    return NSEntityDescription.
        insertNewObjectForEntityForName(self.
        entityClassName, inManagedObjectContext:
        self.managedObjectContext!) as T
}
                                        ③
```

*Figure 22.6 **createEntity** as a generic method*

Testing the Generic Method

1. Select **ViewController.swift** in the Project Navigator.

2. Press **Command+B** to build the project. This displays a **Cannot convert the expression's type '()' to type 'T'** error for these lines of code:

```
var personEntity = p.createEntity()
var companyEntity = c.createEntity()
```

The compiler is complaining that you have not supplied enough information for it to determine the type it should substitute for the **T** placeholder in the **createEntity** method.

3. If you have used generics in other languages, your first instinct may be to pass the type to the method between angle brackets like this:

```
var personEntity = p.createEntity<PersonEntity>()
```

However, this produces the compiler error **Cannot explicitly specialize a generic function**.

4. Even though you can't explicitly specify the type in this way, specify the type of the **personEntity** variable where the method's return value is stored:

```
var personEntity: PersonEntity = p.createEntity()
```

This allows the compiler to infer that **PersonEntity** can replace the **T** placeholder as the **createEntity** method's return type. Go ahead and make this change.

5. Do the same for the **CompanyEntity** object:

```
var companyEntity: CompanyEntity =
    c.createEntity()
```

6. To see this code in action, set a breakpoint on the line of code shown in (Figure 22.7).

```
var p = Person()
var personList = p.getAllEntities()
var personEntity: PersonEntity = p.createEntity()
```

*Figure 22.7 Set a breakpoint on the call to **createEntity**.*

7. Click Xcode's **Run** button and execution stops on the breakpoint you just set.

8. Click the **Step into** button in the Debug toolbar. This moves execution to the **createEntity** method. The Variables View shows the **T** placeholder type is now **PersonEntity** (Figure 22.8). This is generics at work!

```
// Create a new entity of the default type
func createEntity<T>() -> T            Thread 1: step in
{
    return NSEntityDescription.
        insertNewObjectForEntityForName(self.
        entityClassName, inManagedObjectContext:
        self.managedObjectContext!) as T
}
```

self = (GenericsDemo.Person) 0x00007fe03b884cd0
$swift.type.T = (Builtin.RawPointer) GenericsDemo.PersonEntity

*Figure 22.8 The **T** placeholder type is **CompanyEntity**.*

9. Click the **Step out** button to run the **createEntity** method. This returns you to the **viewDidLoad** method, where you can see in the Variables View that the **personEntity** variable is of type **PersonEntity** (Figure 22.9). Click the **Stop** button.

```
var personEntity: PersonEntity = p.createEntity()
var c = Company()                      Thread 1: step out
```

self = (GenericsDemo.ViewController) 0x00007ffb6a723a00
p = (GenericsDemo.Person) 0x00007ffb6cb03a10
personList = ([NSManagedObject]?) 1 value
personEntity = (GenericsDemo.PersonEntity) 0x00007ffb6c870780

*Figure 22.9 **createEntity** returns a **PersonEntity** type.*

In this example, Swift was able to determine the correct type to substitute for **T** using type inference on the method's return value. This also works for methods with generic parameters as you will soon see.

Although generics are working properly in this example, you must still specify the type of the return variable. This doesn't completely solve the initial problem of having to explicitly declare types when accessing business object methods. There must be another way!

Enter generic classes.

Declaring Generic Classes

You used generic classes in *Chapter 10: Arrays & Other Collections.* Remember, when you declare a Swift Array or Dictionary, you specify the type of values contained in the collection. For example, the following code declares an array of type **String**:

```
var names: Array<String>
```

Swift lets you declare your own custom generic classes. Let's try it with **mmBusinessObjectGeneric**.

1. Select **mmBusinessObjectGeneric.swift** in the Project Navigator.

2. Add the following generic class declaration at the top of the code file:

    ```
    public class mmBusinessObjectGeneric<T:
        NSManagedObject>
    ```

    This type parameter declares that **T** is used as a placeholder for a type within the entire class.

    The **: NSManagedObject** in the declaration is a ***type constraint***. It specifies **mmBusinessObjectGeneric** only works with types of **NSManagedObject** or its subclasses. This allows the class to work with **PersonEntity** and **CompanyEntity** objects (subclasses of **NSManagedObject**), but not with objects of a completely different type such as **String** or **Integer**.

3. Since the generic class declaration encompasses the entire class, we can now remove the generic type declaration from the **createEntity** method.

Scroll down to the **createEntity** method and remove the **<T>** generic method declaration, but leave the other references to the **T** placeholder intact.

```
func createEntity() -> T
```

4. Press **Command+B** to build the project and you will get several compiler errors.

5. To examine one of these errors, in the Project Navigator, select the **ABusinessObject.swift** file. You can see the compiler error **Reference to generic type 'mmBusinessObjectGeneric' requires arguments in <...>** (Figure 22.10).

```
class ABusinessObject: mmBusinessObjectGeneric {
      ● Reference to generic type 'mmBusinessObjectGeneric' requires arguments in <...>
```

*Figure 22.10 The **ABusinessObject** compiler error.*

Now that **mmBusinessObjectGeneric** is declared as a generic class, we need to include a type argument in angle brackets whenever we reference it.

6. Since **mmBusinessObjectGeneric** only works with instances of **NSManagedObject** or its subclasses, change the **mmBusinessObjectGeneric** reference to:

```
class ABusinessObject:
        mmBusinessObjectGeneric<NSManagedObject>
```

This is similar to how you reference the Swift **Array** class, specifying the type of objects in the array.

7. Press **Command+B** to build the project. This generates a new compiler error, **Classes derived from generic classes must also be generic** (Figure 22.11).

```
class ABusinessObject: mmBusinessObjectGeneric<NSManagedObject> {
      ● Classes derived from generic classes must also be generic
```

Figure 22.11 Subclasses of generic classes must also be generic!

This is another requirement of generics in Swift. It means we must also declare **ABusinessObject** as a generic class.

8. Add the following generic declaration to make **ABusinessObject** a generic class:

```
class ABusinessObject<T: NSManagedObject>:
   mmBusinessObjectGeneric<NSManagedObject> {
```

Since **mmBusinessObjectGeneric** only works with instances of **NSManagedObject**, we should declare **ABusinessObject** to do the same.

9. Rather than repeating **NSManagedObject** twice in the class declaration, change the type of the **mmBusinessObjectGeneric** reference to **T**:

```
class ABusinessObject<T: NSManagedObject>:
      mmBusinessObjectGeneric<T> {
```

10. Press **Command+B** again and you can see the error has moved farther down the inheritance chain to the **Person** and **Company** classes.

11. Select **Person.swift** in the Project Navigator and add the following generic declarations:

```
class Person<T: PersonEntity>:
      ABusinessObject<T> {
```

This declares **Person** as a generic class with **T** as a placeholder that only works with instances of the **PersonEntity** class. The **T** placeholder is used as a type argument for the **ABusinessObject** superclass.

12. Select **Company.swift** in the Project Navigator and add the following generic declarations:

```
class Company<T: CompanyEntity>:
   ABusinessObject<T> {
```

This declares **Company** as a generic class that uses **T** as a placeholder, and only works with instances of the **CompanyEntity** class. The **T** placeholder is used as a type argument for the **ABusinessObject** superclass.

Figure 22.12 depicts the new generic class hierarchy.

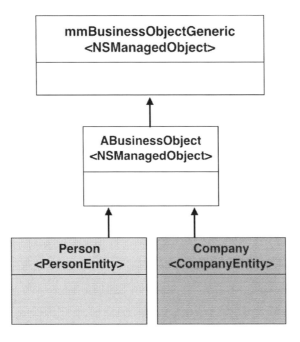

Figure 22.12 The new class hierarchy

13. Press **Command+B** and there are no more compiler errors!

Now you're ready to take these generic classes for a test drive!

Testing the Generic Class

1. Select **ViewController.swift** in the Project Navigator.

2. Remove the explicit variable types from the code that calls the **createEntity** method on the **Person** object:

   ```
   var personEntity = p.createEntity()
   ```
   This is no longer necessary, since the **Person** object effectively passes the **PersonEntity** type up through the inheritance chain where it is used in the **createEntity** method. Swift can now infer the return value type as **PersonEntity**.

3. Do the same for the code that calls **createEntity** on the **Company** object:

   ```
   var companyEntity = c.createEntity()
   ```

4. In the **viewDidLoad** method, click on the **personEntity** variable. The Quick Help Inspector shows it is of type **PersonEntity** (Figure 22.13).

*Figure 22.13 **personEntity** is of **PersonEntity** type.*

5. In the **viewDidLoad** method, click the **companyEntity** variable. The Quick Help Inspector shows the variable is of type **CompanyEntity** (Figure 22.14).

*Figure 22.14 The **companyEntity** variable is of type **CompanyEntity**.*

6. Add the following code to the **viewDidLoad** method to prove the **createEntity** method is returning entities of the correct type:

```
var p = Person()
var personList = p.getAllEntities()
var personEntity = p.createEntity()
personEntity.firstName = "Kevin"
personEntity.lastName = "McNeish"
println("Name: \(personEntity.firstName)
\(personEntity.lastName)")

var c = Company()
var companyList = c.getAllEntities()
var companyEntity = c.createEntity()
companyEntity.name = "Apple"
companyEntity.website = "www.apple.com"
println("Company: \(companyEntity.name) –
\(companyEntity.website)")
```

7. With the breakpoint still set on the line of code that creates a new
    PersonEntity (Figure 22.7), click Xcode's **Run** button. When the
    breakpoint is hit, click **Step into** in the Debug toolbar to step into the
    createEntity method on the **Person** object. The Variables View shows
    the **T** placeholder is of type **PersonEntity**, as it should be (Figure 22.15)!

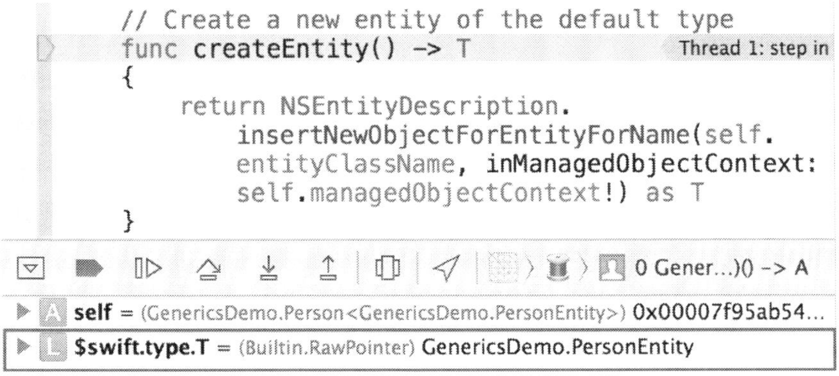

```
    // Create a new entity of the default type
    func createEntity() -> T                    Thread 1: step in
    {
        return NSEntityDescription.
            insertNewObjectForEntityForName(self.
            entityClassName, inManagedObjectContext:
            self.managedObjectContext!) as T
    }
```

self = (GenericsDemo.Person<GenericsDemo.PersonEntity>) 0x00007f95ab54...
$swift.type.T = (Builtin.RawPointer) GenericsDemo.PersonEntity

*Figure 22.15 The **T** placeholder is of type **PersonEntity**.*

8. Click **Step out** to return to the **viewDidLoad** method, and then click
    Step over four times to run the code that displays the property values in
    the Console:

```
Name: Kevin McNeish
```

9. Click **Step over** twice, then click Step In once to run the **createEntity**
    method on the **Company** object. The variables view shows the **T**
    placeholder is now of type **CompanyEntity** (Figure 22.16).

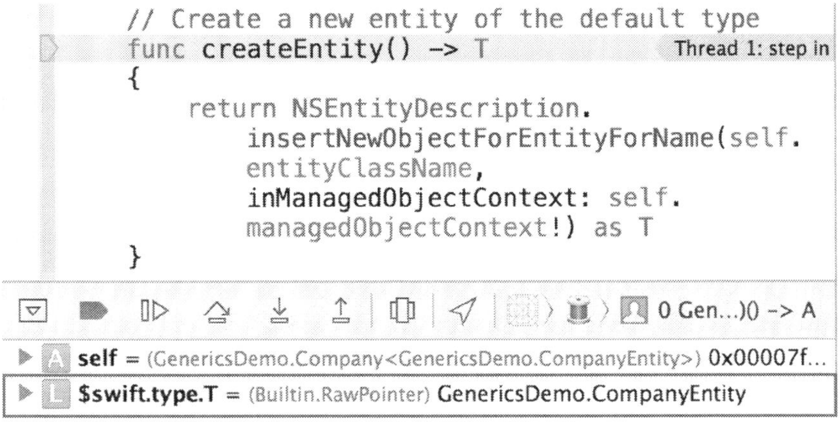

```
    // Create a new entity of the default type
    func createEntity() -> T                    Thread 1: step in
    {
        return NSEntityDescription.
            insertNewObjectForEntityForName(self.
            entityClassName,
            inManagedObjectContext: self.
            managedObjectContext!) as T
    }
```

self = (GenericsDemo.Company<GenericsDemo.CompanyEntity>) 0x00007f...
$swift.type.T = (Builtin.RawPointer) GenericsDemo.CompanyEntity

*Figure 22.16 The **T** placeholder is of type **CompanyEntity**.*

10. Click **Step out**, then click **Step over** four times to run the code that displays the property values in the Console:

```
Company: Apple - www.apple.com
```

11. Click Xcode's **Stop** button.

We have created a generic class whose methods can return the type that we specify!

Implementing Other Generic Methods

Once you have set up the generic class inheritance hierarchy, it's easy to implement other generic methods. Let's try this:

1. Select the **ViewController.swift** file in the Project Navigator.

2. Click on the **personList** and **companyList** variables and note the Quick Help Inspector indicates they are of the **Array<NSManagedObject>?** type. Let's change the **getAllEntities** method so it returns arrays of **PersonEntity** and **CompanyEntity** objects.

3. Select the **mmBusinessObjectGeneric.swift** file in the Project Navigator. Change the **getAllEntities** method's return type and **as** operation in the last line of code to **Array<T>?** as shown here:

```
func getAllEntities() -> Array<T>?
{
    var error: NSError?

    // Create the request object
    var request: NSFetchRequest = NSFetchRequest()

    // Set the entity type to be fetched
    var entityDescription : NSEntityDescription! =
    NSEntityDescription.entityForName(
      self.entityClassName,
      inManagedObjectContext:
      self.managedObjectContext!)

    request.entity = entityDescription
```

```
    // Execute the fetch
    var results = self.managedObjectContext?.
      executeFetchRequest(request, error: &error)

    return results as Array<T>?
}
```

4. Select the **ViewController.swift** file in the Project Navigator. Click on the **personList** and **companyList** variables and you can see their types are now **Array<PersonEntity>?** and **Array<CompanyEntity>?** just as they should be!

5. Feel free to run the project again, and check out the **personList** and **companyList** arrays first hand.

Overriding Generic Class Methods

Generics are the gift that keeps on giving, and that provides benefits for methods inherited from a generic class. Let's take a look at an example of this.

1. Select the **mmBusinessObjectGeneric.swift** file in the Project Navigator.

2. Change the **saveEntity**: method's parameter type from **NSManagedObject**, to **T**:

```
func saveEntity(entity: T) -> (state:
    SaveState, message: String?)
```

In the **mmBusinessObjectGeneric** class, the placeholder **T** is essentially **NSManagedObject**, so what does this buy us? Watch what happens when you override this method.

3. Select the **Person.swift** file in the Project Navigator. Below the initializer, type **saveEntity**, which displays the Code Completion option in Figure 22.17.

```
    saveEntity(entity: T) -> (state: SaveState, message: String?)
 M  saveEntity(entity: T) -> (state: SaveState, message: String?)
}
```

*Figure 22.17 **saveEntity** Code Completion*

4. Press **return** to fill in the method declaration, and then add the following code to the method:

```
class Person<T: PersonEntity> :
   ABusinessObject<T> {

   override init() {
    super.init()
    self.entityClassName = "PersonEntity"
   }

   override func saveEntity(entity: T) ->
     (state: SaveState, message: String?) {

      entity.personID = NSUUID().UUIDString
      return super.saveEntity(entity)
   }
}
```

5. Notice in the **saveEntity** method, the **entity** parameter is of type **PersonEntity** as indicated by the **personID** property on the **entity** object. That's because, at the **Person** class level, the **T** placeholder is declared as type **PersonEntity**.

6. If you override this same method in the **Company** class, the **entity** parameter in the **saveEntity** method is of type **CompanyEntity**:

```
class Company<T: CompanyEntity>: ABusinessObject<T> {

    override init() {
       super.init()
       self.entityClassName = "CompanyEntity"
    }

    override func saveEntity(entity: T) ->
      (state: SaveState, message: String?) {
         entity.website = "http://www.apple.com"
         return super.saveEntity(entity)
    }
}
```

This same magic is available for any method you subclass that has a generic parameter or return type. There is no type casting necessary!

More Rules of Generics

- You can specify more than one type parameter for a method or class by separating them with a comma. For example:

```
public class MyClass<T, P>
```

- Type constraints specify that a type parameter must inherit from a particular class or conform to a particular protocol. For example, the following type parameter specifies **T** must be a subclass of **MyType** and **P** must conform to **MyProtocol**:

```
public class MyClass<T: MyType, P: MyProtocol>
```

Generic Associated Types

You learned in *Chapter 20: Mastering Protocols and Delegates* that protocols allow you to define standard behavior for classes that are not necessarily related.

Just as Swift allows you to define generic types that are associated with a class, you can also define generic types associated with a protocol. Let's see how this works with our business object example.

Here is a protocol that implements the two business object methods used earlier in this chapter:

```
protocol BusinessObject {

    typealias T

    func createEntity() -> T

    func getAllEntities() -> Array<T>
}
```

The **typealias** keyword declares an associated generic type placeholder named **T**.

A class that adopts this protocol also uses the **typealias** keyword to specify **T**'s concrete type.

For example, in the following class declaration, the **MyPerson** class adopts the **BusinessObject** protocol. The **typealias = PersonEntity** statement declares **PersonEntity** as the concrete type of the generic **T** placeholder:

```
class MyPerson: BusinessObject {

    typealias EntityType = PersonEntity

    func createEntity() -> T {

        return EntityType()
    }

    func getAllEntities() -> Array<T> {
        return Array<T>()
    }
}
```

Alternately, you can manually replace each occurrence of the generic placeholder with the concrete type. This allows you to leave out the **typealias** statement because Swift can infer the type based on the concrete classes you specify:

```
class MyPerson: BusinessObject {

    func createEntity() -> PersonEntity {
        return PersonEntity()
    }

    func getAllEntities() -> Array<PersonEntity> {
        return Array<PersonEntity>()
    }
}
```

where Clauses for Associated Types

Just as you can specify constraints for types in a generic method or class, you can also specify constraints on associated types in protocols. You do this by means of the **where** clause.

For example:

```
func associateObjects<B1: BusinessObject,
    B2: BusinessObject
    where B1.T: PersonEntity, B2.T: CompanyEntity>
    (personObject: B1, companyObject: B2)
{
    // associate the objects
}
```

This method has two type parameters, **B1**and **B2.** The type constraint specifies that both of these types must implement the **BusinessObject** protocol:

The **where** clause goes further and specifies that the **B1** business object must have **PersonEntity** as its associated class, and the **B2** business object must have **CompanyEntity** as its associated class.

The **where** clause also allows you to specify that certain type parameters and associated types be the same. For example:

```
func associateObjects<B1: BusinessObject,
        B2: BusinessObject
        where B1.T == B2.T>
        (personObject1: B1, personObject2: B2)
{
        // associate the objects
}
```

The **where** clause for this method specifies that the associated types of the **B1** and **B2** objects must be the same.

Summary

- One of the downsides of using generalized code is that you often have to downcast from general types to more specific types many times in your project.

- You can declare individual generic methods in a class.

Generic Methods

- A **type parameter** declares a placeholder for a type within a method or class. For example:

```
func createEntity<T>() -> T
```

In concept, this is similar to using *n* as a placeholder in an equation. The type parameter is replaced by an actual type when the method is called.

- You can specify a different letter or set of letters as the placeholder, but it's conventional to use the letter **T**, which stands for "Type."

- When you declare a type parameter for a method, it can be used to specify:

  - The method's parameter types

  - The method's return type

  - Types in the body of the method.

- With generic methods, Swift can determine the concrete type to substitute for the generic placeholder using type inference. For example, you can specify the type of the **personEntity** variable where the method's return value is stored:

```
var personEntity: PersonEntity = p.createEntity()
```

This allows the compiler to infer that **PersonEntity** can replace the **T** placeholder as the **createEntity** method's return type.

Generic Classes

- You can declare an entire class as generic:

```
public class mmBusinessObjectGeneric<T:
    NSManagedObject>
```

- A **type constraint** specifies that a generic's type parameter must be a subclass of a particular type or conform to a particular protocol.

- Type constraints can specify that a type parameter inherit from a particular class or conform to a particular protocol. For example, the following type parameter specifies **T** must be a subclass of **MyType** and **P** must conform to **MyProtocol**:

```
public class MyClass<T: MyType, P: MyProtocol>
```

- You must include a type argument when referencing a generic class. For example:

```
mmBusinessObjectGeneric<NSManagedObject>
```

- Subclasses of generic classes must also be generic.

- You can specify more than one type parameter for a method or class by separating them with a comma. For example:

```
public class MyClass<T, P>
```

Associated Classes

- Just as Swift allows you to define generic types that are associated with a class, you can also define generic types associated with a protocol. For example:

```
protocol BusinessObject {

    typealias T

    func createEntity() -> T

    func getAllEntities() -> Array<T>
}
```

The **typealias** keyword declares an associated generic type placeholder named **T**.

- A class that adopts a protocol with an associated type also uses the **typealias** keyword to specify **T**'s concrete type. For example:

```
class MyPerson: BusinessObject {

    typealias EntityType = PersonEntity

    func createEntity() -> T {

        return EntityType()
    }

    func getAllEntities() -> Array<T> {
        return Array<T>()
    }
}
```

- Alternately, you can manually replace each occurrence of the generic placeholder with the concrete type. This allows you to leave out the **typealias** statement because Swift can infer the type based on the concrete classes you specify:

```
class MyPerson: BusinessObject {

    func createEntity() -> PersonEntity {

     return PersonEntity()
    }

    func getAllEntities() -> Array<PersonEntity> {
     return Array<PersonEntity>()
    }
}
```

Exercise 22.1

In this exercise, you will use what you have learned about generics to improve the **mmBusinessObjectGeneric** class.

1. Open the **GenericsDemo** project in Xcode.

2. Select the **mmBusinessObjectGeneric.swift** code file in the Project Navigator.

3. Delete the existing **entityClassName** property:

```
var entityClassName : String = ""
```

4. Replace it with the following **entityClassName** computed property:

```
// Gets the entity class name string from <T>
var entityClassName : String {
    var className = NSStringFromClass(T)
    if className.rangeOfString(".") != nil {
        className = className.pathExtension
    }
    return className
}
```

5. Fix the compiler errors in the **Person** and **Company** class files.

Solution Movie 22.1

To see a video providing the solution for this exercise, you can enter the link below in your Web browser to see each step performed for you.

Movie 22.1

http://www.iOSAppsForNonProgrammers.com/B4M221.html

Exercise 22.2

In this example, you will use what you have learned about generics to create a new business class.

1. Select the **GenericsDemo.xcdatamodeld** file in the Project Navigator.

2. Select **Editor > Add Model Version...** from the Xcode menu. Set the Version Name to **GenericsDemo2** and click **Finish**.

3. Select the **GenericsDemo.xcdatamodeld** parent node in the Project Navigator. Then, go to the File Inspector and under **Model Version**, change **Current** to **GenericsDemo2**.

4. Select **GenericsDemo2.xcdatamodel** in the Project Navigator.

5. In the Data Model editor, create a new **OfficeEntity** with two required string attributes named **building** and **officeNumber**.

6. Generate a new **OfficeEntity** class from the entity.

7. Create a new **Office** class subclassed from **ABusinessObject**, and use generics to associated it with the **OfficeEntity** class.

8. In the Data Model editor, select the **OfficeEntity** class, then go to the Data Model Inspector and set the **Class** to **GenericsDemo.OfficeEntity**.

9. Test the class in the view controller's **viewDidLoad**.

Solution Movie 22.2

To see a video providing the solution for this exercise, you can enter the link below in your Web browser to see each step performed for you.

Movie 22.2

http://www.iOSAppsForNonProgrammers.com/B4M222.html

Chapter 23: Understanding Closures

This chapter teaches you about passing references to functions and methods using the Target-Action design pattern. Then, it demonstrates the superiority of using closures to perform the same task, and helps you understand the best way of using closures in your own apps.

Sections in This Chapter

Closures is one of the more difficult Swift concepts to learn. To introduce the topic, we'll talk first about the ***target-action design pattern*** used throughout iOS apps, which allows you to store references to functions and methods. Then we'll work up to closures, which allow you to pass around blocks of code as objects.

Using the Target-Action Design Pattern

In all the code samples so far, you have worked with basic data types such as integers, Booleans, and strings, as well as references to more complex objects, storing these types in variables and passing them as arguments to functions and methods.

In Swift, you can also store and pass references to functions and methods. At first, this concept may seem a bit foreign, but it's used often in iOS app development. For example, Apple's iOS architecture implements a Target-Action design pattern. It is typically used to call a method in response to the user interacting with a user-interface control.

In this pattern, a user interface object holds two pieces of information for calling a method:

1. A ***target***, which is the object that possesses the method to be called.

2. An ***action***, which is the method to be called.

For example, Figure 23.1 shows a **Bar Button Item** (a button in a navigation bar or toolbar) that has **target** and **action** properties. In this example, the **target** property points to a view controller object and the **action** property points to a **flipBack** method. When the user taps the bar button item at run time, the **flipBack** method is called on the view controller.

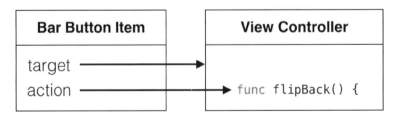

*Figure 23.1 A bar button item with **target** and **action** properties*

To see how this works, let's look at the **PickACard** sample project.

1. Open the **PickACard** project located in a subfolder where you have
    stored this book's sample code.

2. In the Project Navigator, expand the **PickACard** group and click on the
    Main.storyboard file. Scroll to the right of the storyboard to see the two
    main scenes—**Playing Card Back** and **Playing Card Front** scenes
    (Figure 23.2).

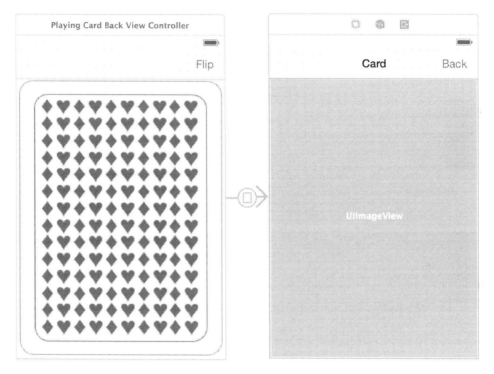

Figure 23.2 The playing card back and front scenes

The **Playing Card Back** scene shows the back of a playing card. When
you tap the **Flip** button on the right side of the navigation bar, the view
flips and displays the **Playing Card Front** scene. Code in the app gets a
random playing card from a deck of cards and displays it in the **Playing
Card Front** scene.

3. Let's run the app to see how it works. Click Xcode's **Run** button, and
    when the app appears in the Simulator, click the **Flip** button. This flips
    the view horizontally and displays a random card on the flip side of the
    view as in Figure 23.3 (since the card is random, yours will most likely be
    different!)

Figure 23.3 A random card on the flip side of the view

4. If you click the **Back** button, nothing happens. You are going to fix this so clicking the **Back** button flips the view to the back of the card.

5. Go back to Xcode and click **Stop**.

6. Next, click on the **PlayingCardFrontViewController.swift** file in the Project Navigator. This is the view controller code file associated with the **Playing Card Front** scene. Scroll to the bottom of the code file to see the **flipBack** method:

```
func flipBack() {

    self.dismissViewControllerAnimated(true,
        completion: nil)
}
```

This method calls the view controller's (**self**) **dismissViewControllerAnimated:completion:** method, which flips the view to the back of the card.

7. You need to tell the **Back** button to call this method when it's tapped. To do this, add the following code to the **viewDidLoad** method:

```
override func viewDidLoad() {
    super.viewDidLoad()

    self.imageView.image = UIImage(named:
        card.cardImageName)
    self.navItem.title = card.cardName

    self.btnBack.target = self
    self.btnBack.action = "flipBack"
}
```

This code sets the button's **target** property to **self** and its **action** property to "**flipBack**," as Figure 23.1 shows.

Notice you specify the name of the action method as a string literal. The button's **action** property is of type **Selector**. In Objective-C (the language the button was created in), a selector refers to the name of an Objective-C method. Apple has built an easy bridge between Swift and Objective-C by automatically converting Swift's string literals to selectors.

8. Let's run the app again and see what happens. Click the **Run** button, and when the app appears in the Simulator, click the **Flip** button to display a random card. At this point the **Back** button is "wired up" to a target object and action method. Click the **Back** button to flip the view to the back of the card.

Now flip back and forth between the views to display random playing cards.

Although here you set the target object and action method in code, you can set these in the Interface Builder editor simply by dragging from the Connections Inspector to the associated view controller code file. You learn much more about this in *Book 3: Navigating Xcode*.

Enhancing Your Code With Closures

A *closure* is a self-contained chunk of code, usually small, that can be passed around as an object (in fact, closures are Swift objects).

The term *closure* comes from the ability to capture and store references to (close over) constants and variables from the context they are defined in.

Closures are similar to blocks in Objective-C. In fact, blocks in the Cocoa Touch Framework are automatically imported into Swift as closures. Vice-versa, you can pass a Swift closure to Objective-C code that expects a block.

Closures can be executed:

1. As a callback when an operation has finished, or in response to an event

2. Simultaneously on multiple threads of execution

3. Over items in a collection

Apple has implemented the use of blocks/closures in a number of important places in the Cocoa Touch Framework (although not in enough places yet).

Now that you understand the Target-Action design pattern, let's compare this older methodology to the newer closures as we look at ***animations***.

An animation is a smooth transition from one user-interface state to another; for example, when one view slides out and another view slides in its place.

Animation Without Closures

Let's check out the **PickACard** project for a hands-on look at how animation works without closures.

1. Open the **PickACard** project.

2. Click Xcode's **Run** button. Notice a splash image (Figure 23.4) appears then slowly grows and fades.

Figure 23.4 The splash image grows and fades out.

3. To see how this animation works, go back to Xcode and press the **Stop** button.

4. Select **AppDelegate.swift** in the Project Navigator.

The **application:didFinishLaunchingWithOptions:** method at the top of the code file is called automatically when your app is first launched. Near the bottom of this method, a call is made to the **animateOldStyle** method.

The **animateOldStyle** method is called "old style" because it demonstrates performing animations without closures:

```
func animateOldStyle() {

    // Animate the splash view
    UIView.beginAnimations(nil, context: nil)
    UIView.setAnimationDuration(2.0)
    self.splashView.alpha = 0.0
    self.splashView.frame = CGRectMake(-60, -60,
    self.splashView.frame.size.width+120,
    self.splashView.frame.size.height+120)

    // Specify the delegate and selector
    UIView.setAnimationDelegate(self)
    UIView.setAnimationDidStopSelector("startupDone")
    UIView.commitAnimations()
}
```

The code in this method sets the animation duration to **2.0** seconds. It then specifies that during the two-second animation, the image view's **alpha** value decreases to zero (gradually making it invisible), and the **height** and **width** of the image view increases by 120 points. This produces the "grow and fade" animation effect.

Next, **self** (**AppDelegate**) is set as the delegate object and **startupDone** as the selector method to call when the animation completes. The call to **commitAnimations** kicks off the animation sequence.

Here is the **startupDone** selector method, which hides the splash view by removing it from its superview:

```
func startupDone() {

    self.splashView.removeFromSuperview()
}
```

The main point of this exercise is that a reference to the **startupDone** method is stored in the view's selector property and is called when the animation completes.

Figure 23.5 depicts the animation's order of events.

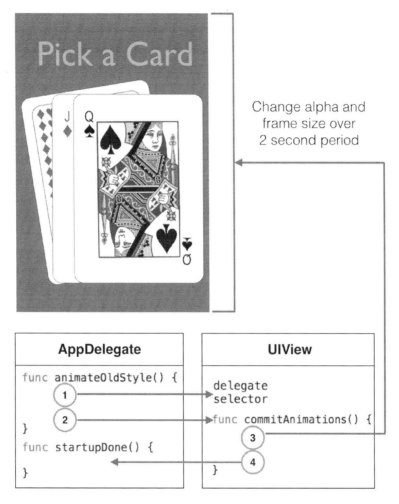

Figure 23.5 The animation sequence

1. The **AppDelegate** object stores a reference to itself in the view's **delegate** property and a reference to its **startupDone** method in the view's **selector** property.

2. **AppDelegate** calls the **UIView commitAnimations** method.

3. Over a two-second period, the splash view's **alpha** value is decreased and its **frame** size is increased.

4. After the two-second animation period, **UIView** calls the **startupDone** method, which removes the splash view from its parent view.

Now let's see how animations work when using closures.

Animation With Closures

The code that uses closures for animation is already included in the sample project. Let's take a look.

1. Open the **PickACard** project.

2. Select the **AppDelegate.swift** file in the Project Navigator, and scroll down until you see the **animateWithClosures** method (Figure 23.6).

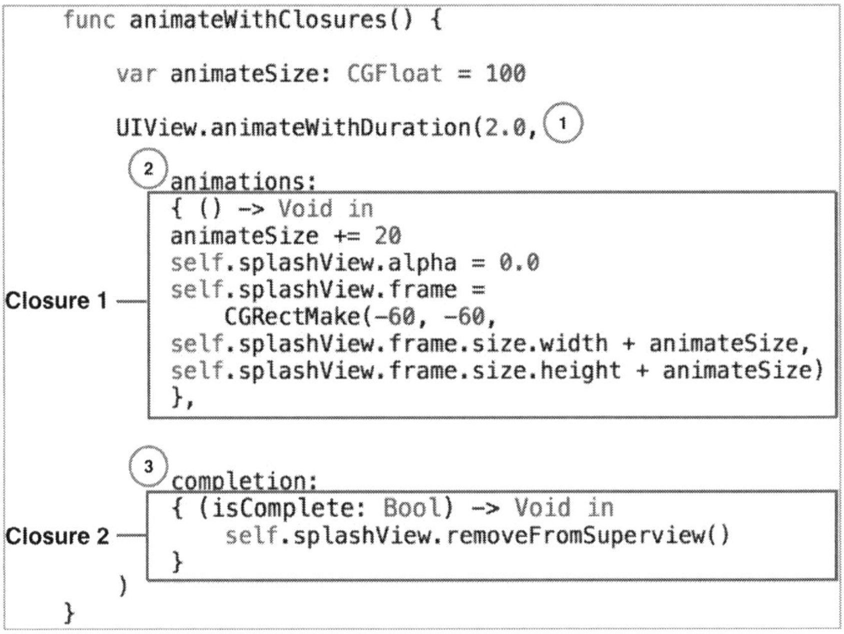

*Figure 23.6 Calling the **animateWithDuration:** method*

This code is more concise than the non-closure code. The **animateWithDuration:animations: completion:** method accepts three arguments as in Figure 23.6.

1. The duration of the animation, in seconds

2. An **animations** closure containing code that sets up the object properties to be animated

3. A **completion** closure that contains code that is executed when the animation completes.

By using closures, you can keep all the animation code in one place, instead of creating a separate method for the completion code.

Declaring an Inline Closure

In Figure 23.6, the closures can be declared inline and passed directly as arguments. Here is the basic syntax of a closure:

```
{ (arguments) -> ReturnType in
    // code statements
}
```

- Closures are contained within curly braces.

- Any arguments are listed after the opening curly brace within parentheses and separated by commas.

- The **in** keyword marks the beginning of the closure's code statements to be executed.

Closure 1 accepts no parameters (indicated by the empty parentheses) and it returns **Void** (nothing).

Closure 2 accepts a single boolean argument and also returns **Void**.

Here are several ways to simplify a closure expression:

- Unlike for regular methods, if a closure doesn't accept parameters, you can omit the empty parentheses.

- Leave out the **-> Void** declaration just as you would with regular methods.

- If a closure has neither parameters nor a return value, you can omit the **in** keyword.

- When passing a closure as an argument, Swift can infer the closure's parameter and return value types. This means you can omit the types when declaring a closure expression.

- Closures containing a single expression can omit the **return** keyword.

This means you can simplify the closure expression as in Figure 23.7.

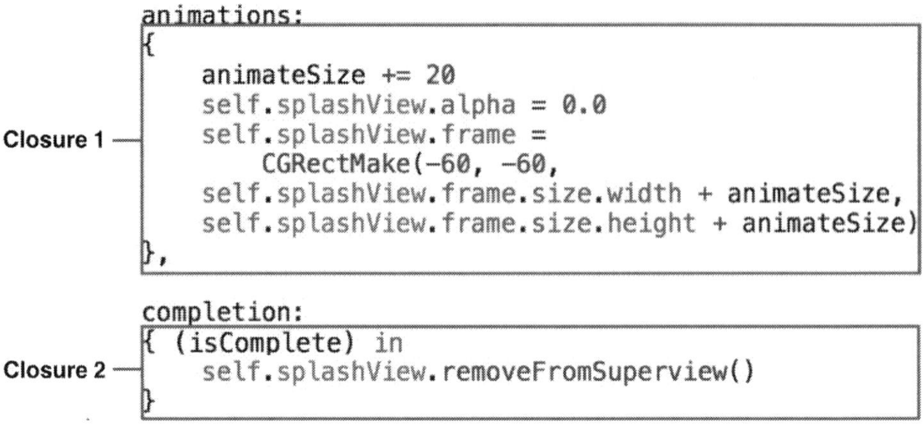

```
animations:
{
    animateSize += 20
    self.splashView.alpha = 0.0
    self.splashView.frame =
        CGRectMake(-60, -60,
        self.splashView.frame.size.width + animateSize,
        self.splashView.frame.size.height + animateSize)
},
```

Closure 1

```
completion:
{ (isComplete) in
    self.splashView.removeFromSuperview()
}
```

Closure 2

Figure 23.7 The simplified closure expression

Just because you *can* omit parameters and return value types doesn't mean you *should*. If the type declarations make your code more readable, then leave them in. Factoring code down to its barest essence can make it unreadable—a rookie-developer mistake. Always choose clarity over cleverness.

To further grasp closure syntax, let's see how **Closure 2**'s declaration differs from a regular method. At the top of Figure 23.8 is a *method* that is equivalent to **Closure 2**.

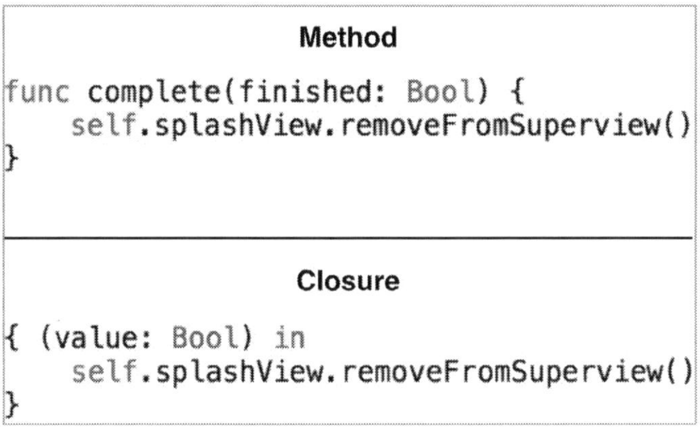

Method

```
func complete(finished: Bool) {
    self.splashView.removeFromSuperview()
}
```

Closure

```
{ (value: Bool) in
    self.splashView.removeFromSuperview()
}
```

Figure 23.8 Comparing a method and a closure

Some things to note:

- The name of the method is **complete**.

- Closures don't have names—they are *anonymous*.

- Method and closure parameters are declared using the same syntax, except the parameter declaration appears *before* the opening curly brace in a method, and *after* the opening curly brace in a closure.

Benefits of Closures

We'll learn more about closure syntax in just a bit, but let's talk about why closures are more desirable than selectors.

1. They allow you to locate the code to be executed near the code that is invoking it. As Figure 23.6 shows, you don't have to create a separate method that is called on completion of the animation. When you pass the code as a closure, your code is easier to read and understand.

2. Closures have access to any constants and variables that are in scope at the time the closure is declared. This means you don't have to pass arguments to give the closure the information it needs the way you do with a separate method. The closure can access the constants and variables directly.

This second point is discussed further in the next section.

Capturing Constants and Variables

The term *closure* describes the ability to close around constants and variables that are in scope at the time the closure is declared. If you declare a variable outside a closure, the closure can still access that variable.

For example, in Figure 23.6, the **animateSize** variable is declared in the same method as the closure, so this variable can be accessed from within the closure.

You can see by the first line of code in **Closure 1** (Figure 23.6) that the value of a captured variable can be changed within a closure.

Shorthand Argument Names

Swift automatically creates shorthand argument names for inline closure arguments, starting with **$0** for the first argument, then **$1**, **$2**, and so on. You can reference these arguments in the body of your closure.

Sometimes, shorthand argument names make your code more readable. For example, this code hasn't been simplified yet:

```
let alphabet =
        ["A","B","C","D","E","F","G","H","I","J","K",
        "L","M","N","O","P","Q","R", "S", "T", "U",
        "V", "W", "X", "Y", "Z"]

let vowels = "AEIOUY"

var consonants = filter(alphabet,
        { (str: String) -> Bool in
        return vowels.rangeOfString(str) == nil })
```

This code declares an **alphabet** array containing all letters in the English alphabet, and a **vowels** constant containing a string of English vowels. The next section of code uses Swift's **filter()** function to create a new array that only contains consonants.

As Figure 23.9 shows, Swift's **filter()** function accepts two arguments: an array to be filtered, and a closure that tests each item in the array. If the closure returns **true**, the item is added to the array. If it returns **false**, the item is not added to the array.

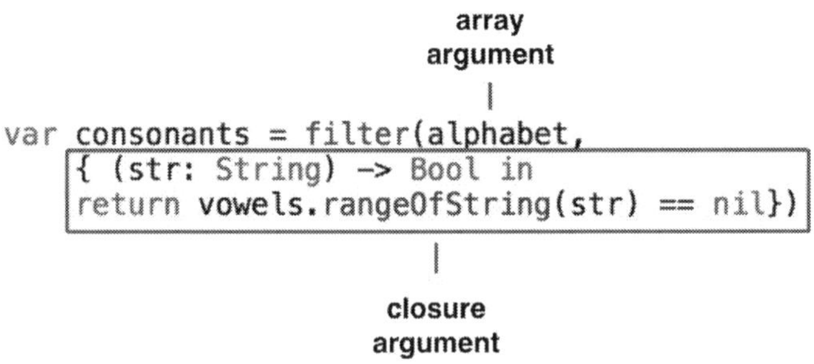

array
argument
|

```
var consonants = filter(alphabet,
{ (str: String) -> Bool in
return vowels.rangeOfString(str) == nil})
```

|
closure
argument

*Figure 23.9 Swift's **filter()** function*

As you have learned, you can remove the **return** statement because this is a single-statement closure:

```
var consonants = filter(alphabet,
        { (str: String) -> Bool in
        vowels.rangeOfString(str) != nil})
```

You can also remove the closure's return arrow and type, since Swift can infer the return type:

```
var consonants = filter(alphabet,
        { (str: String) in
        vowels.rangeOfString(str) == nil})
```

You can use Swift's shorthand argument names, which allow you to remove the explicit parameter declaration, as well as the **in** keyword:

```
var consonants = filter(alphabet,
        {vowels.rangeOfString($0) == nil})
```

This is as far as we can factor this closure down. The resulting code is far more readable than the original version. By including well-named variables, we can easily see that this line of code filters vowels from the alphabet and produces an array of consonants.

Ultimately, shorthand argument names work well in single-statement closures. Their overuse can create less readable code. For example:

```
if $0 {
        self.splashView.removeFromSuperview()
}
```

It's far better to use an argument name in this case:

```
if isComplete {
        self.splashView.removeFromSuperview()
}
```

Trailing Closures

When calling a function or method that accepts a closure as its final parameter, you have the option of using *trailing closure* syntax when passing the closure.

Trailing closure syntax moves the closure expression after the parentheses of the function or method call. Its purpose is to make your code more readable.

For example, here is the familiar **filter()** function call:

```
var consonants = filter(alphabet,
    {vowels.rangeOfString($0) == nil})
```

The **filter()** function accepts two arguments. The first is the **alphabet** array and the second is a closure. A comma separates the two, and the closing parenthesis indicates the end of the arguments list.

To change this to a trailing closure, delete the comma separating the arguments and move the trailing parentheses after the first argument:

```
var consonants = filter(alphabet)
        {vowels.rangeOfString($0) == nil}
```

When using trailing closure syntax, if the closure is the only argument being passed to the function or method, you can completely remove the parentheses.

When to Use Closures in Your Apps

As you saw in the animation example, it's common to use closures to execute code after a task of unknown duration completes.

A great example of this is retrieving data from the Web. Sometimes retrieval is nearly instantaneous, but usually it's not. You need to update the UI only after the data is retrieved. This is where closures can help.

Let's look at a sample app that doesn't use closures.

1. Open the **ClosureDemo** project located in a subfolder where you have stored this book's sample code.

2. Let's run the app to see what it does and then look behind the scene to see how it works.

3. At the top left of the Xcode window, set the **Scheme** to one of the iPhone options (such as **iPhone 6**).

4. Click Xcode's **Run** button. When the app appears in the Simulator, the first view contains a list of companies. By default, there is only one company, **Apple** (Figure 23.10).

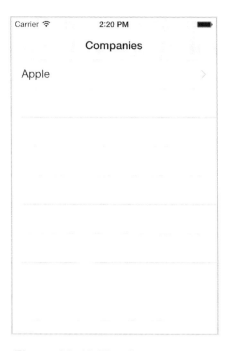

Figure 23.10 The Companies list

5. In the list of companies, click Apple to see a list of employees (Figure 23.11).

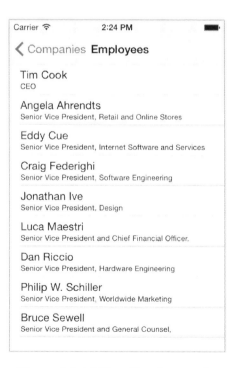

Figure 23.11 The Employees list

6. Go back to Xcode and click **Stop**.

Let's look at the code behind this app. In the Project Navigator, select the **CompanyViewController.swift** file.

At the top of the class file are two properties:

```
var company = Company()
var companyList = Array<CompanyEntity>()
```

The **company** property holds a reference to the **Company** business controller. The **companyList** property holds a reference to the list of companies, and is initialized to an empty **CompanyEntity** array.

The **viewDidLoad** method contains a code that calls the company object's **getAllEntities** method and stores the result in the **companyList** array:

```
self.companyList = self.company.getAllEntities()
```

The **tableView:numberOfRowsInSection** method returns the **count** property of the **companyList** array to indicate the number of companies in the list:

```
return companyList.count
```

The **tableView:cellForRowAtIndexPath:** method gets a **CompanyEntity** object from the **companyList** to configure each table view cell:

```
var companyEntity = companyList[indexPath.row]
cell.textLabel.text = companyEntity.companyName
```

Figure 23.12 depicts the order this code executes in.

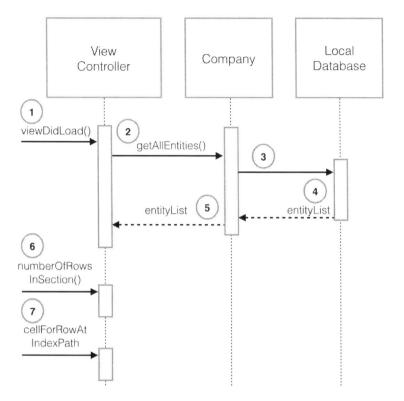

Figure 23.12 Sequence for displaying the Company list

1. The view controller's **viewDidLoad** method executes.

2. The **Company** object's **getAllEntities** method is called.

3. The **Company** object retrieves the **CompanyEntity** objects from the database on the local iOS device.

4. The list of entities is returned to the **Company** object.

5. The list of entities is stored in the view controller's **entityList** array.

6. The view controller's **numberOfRowsInSection:** method is called by the table view controller.

7. The **tableView:cellForRowAtIndexPath:** method is called by the table view once for each company in the list.

This sequence works well as long as you are retrieving entities from a local database.

However, when you retrieve entities from a Web database, you can't stall your app by waiting for the **Company** object to return the list of entities. Instead, you send a closure to the **Company** object containing code you want to be executed when the entities are available.

Let's create a method on the **mmBusinessObject** class that accepts a closure parameter.

Creating Methods That Accept Closures

Remember, a closure is a function you can pass around. So it can accept parameters and return a value. Figure 23.13 shows the basic syntax of a method that accepts a closure parameter:

Figure 23.13 Syntax of a closure parameter

- The parameters accepted by a closure are listed between parentheses and separated by commas.

- The return arrow (->) is followed by the type returned by the closure.

- If the closure doesn't return anything (**Void**), specify empty parentheses as the return type: -> **()**

In our example, the closure needs to accept an array of entities, and return **Void**. So let's create the method that accepts the closure parameter.

1. Expand the **Business Layer** node in the Project Navigator and select **mmBusinessObject.swift**.

2. Check out the existing **getAllEntities** method:

    ```
    func getAllEntities() -> Array<T>
    {
    ```

```
        return self.getEntities(sortedBy: nil,
        matchingPredicate: nil)
}
```

This is the method currently called from the view controller to return an array of entity objects.

3. Let's add a new version of this method that accepts a closure. Rather than returning an array of entities, our new method will pass the array of entities to the closure. Add the following method to the code file directly below the existing **getAllEntities** method:

```
func getAllEntities
    (closure: (entityList: Array<T>) -> ())
{
        var entities = self.getAllEntities()
        closure(entityList: entities)
}
```

Figure 23.14 breaks out the different parts of the closure parameter.

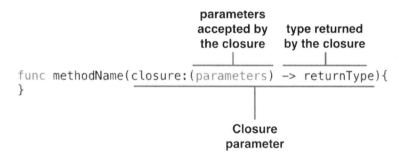

Figure 23.14 A breakdown of the closure parameter

This method accepts a single **closure** parameter. The closure passed to this method must accept an **entityList** parameter of type `Array<T>` and return nothing (`->` `()`).

4. The first line of code in the new **getAllEntities:** method makes a call to the existing **getAllEntities** method. The second line of code is important! It executes the closure, passing in an array of entities:

```
func getAllEntities
   (closure: (entityList: Array<T>) -> ())
{
    var entities = self.getAllEntities()
    closure(entityList: entities)
}
```

5. Now let's add code to the view controller that calls this new method. In the Project Navigator, select the **CompanyViewController.swift** file.

6. Comment out the following line of code that retrieves the list of entities and stores them in the **entityList**.

    ```
    //self.companyList = self.company.getAllEntities()
    ```

7. Now let's call the new method. Below the commented code, type self.company.get, and then select the second method in the Code Completion list (Figure 23.15).

```
//self.companyList = self.company.getAllEntities()
self.company.getAllEntities( closure: (entityList: Array<T>) -> () )
  M  Array<T> getAllEntities()
  M     Void getAllEntities(closure: (entityList: Array<T>) -> ()(entityList: Array<T>) -> ())
  M  Array<T>? getAllEntitiesSortedBy(sortDescriptor: NSSortDescriptor)
  M  Array<T> getEntities(sortedBy: NSSortDescriptor?, matchingPredicate: NSPredicate?)
  M  Array<T>? getEntitiesMatchingPredicate(predicate: NSPredicate)
  M  Array<T>? getEntitiesSortedBy(sortDescriptor: NSSortDescriptor, matchingPredicate: NSPredicate)
```

Figure 23.15 Select the second item in the list.

This adds the Code Completion template in Figure 23.16—the exact closure declaration we specified for this method (Figure 23.14).

```
self.company.getAllEntities( closure: (entityList: Array<T>) -> () )
```

Figure 23.16 The Code Completion template

8. Press **return**. This inserts the code in Figure 23.17.

```
self.company.getAllEntities { (entityList) -> () in
    code
}
```

Figure 23.17 The inserted code

9. Now let's replace the **code** placeholder with the code to be executed when

the list of entities is retrieved:

```
self.company.getAllEntities {(entityList) -> () in
        self.companyList = entityList
        self.tableView.reloadData()
}
```

This code stores the **entityList** array that is passed to the closure into the view controller's **companyList** array property. It then calls the table view's **reloadData()** method, which reloads the table view's rows.

In this example, we are not *really* retrieving data from the web. Doing so requires code beyond the scope of this book (although this will be covered later in the series). For now, it's important to understand how to pass a closure to a method executed at a later time.

Testing the Closure

Let's test the closure to see how it works at run time.

1. Select the **CompanyViewController.swift** code file in the Project Navigator.

2. Click in the gutter to the left of the first line of code you added to the **viewDidLoad** method (Figure 23.18).

```
override func viewDidLoad() {
    super.viewDidLoad()

    //self.companyList = self.company.getAllEntities()

    self.company.getAllEntities { (entityList) -> () in
        self.companyList = entityList
        self.tableView.reloadData()
    }
}
```

Figure 23.18 Set a breakpoint.

3. Click Xcode's **Run** button and when the app appears in the Simulator you will hit the breakpoint.

4. Click the Step Into button in the Debug Area toolbar three times to execute the code that passes the closure to the **getAllEntities** method. In

the Variables View in Figure 23.19 you can see the closure object has been successfully passed and its type is exactly what we specified in code.

```
func getAllEntities(closure: (entityList: Array<T>) -> ())
{                                                    Thread 1: step in
    var entities = self.getAllEntities()
    closure(entityList: entities)
}
```

```
☑  ●  I▷  ⬠  ↓  ↥  | ⎕ | ⊿ | ⊞ ⟩ 🗑 ⟩ ⎁ 0 ClosureDemo...A>) -> 0) -> ()
  A closure ((entityList: [T]) -> ())
▶ A self = (ClosureDemo.Company<ClosureDemo.CompanyEntity>) 0x7aa3c2a0
▶ L $swift.type.T = (Builtin.RawPointer) ClosureDemo.CompanyEntity
  L entities ([T])
```

Figure 23.19 The closure object has been passed.

5. Click Step Into once, and then click Step Over to move to the code that calls the closure (Figure 23.20).

```
func getAllEntities(closure: (entityList: Array<T>) -> ())
{
    var entities = self.getAllEntities()
    closure(entityList: entities)            Thread 1: step over
}
```

Figure 23.20 Getting ready to call the closure.

6. Click the Step Into button twice and you can see the closure is executed (Figure 23.21).

```
self.company.getAllEntities { (entityList) -> () in
    self.companyList = entityList            Thread 1: step in
    self.tableView.reloadData()
}
```

Figure 23.21 Executing the closure!

The array of entities is passed to the closure and the closure stores the array in the view controller's **companyList** property.

Figure 23.22 contains a sequence diagram that shows the sequence of events when retrieving and displaying a list of companies using a closure.

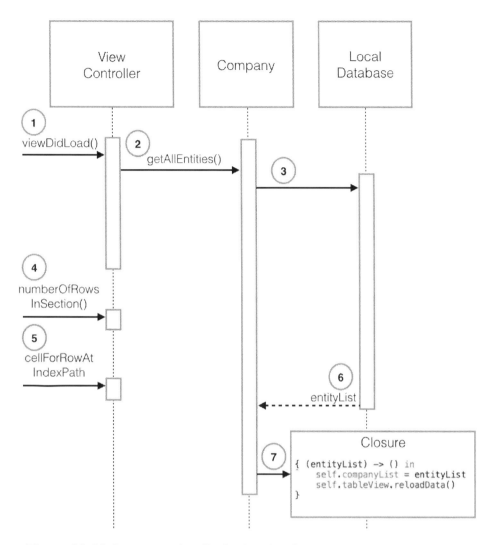

Figure 23.22 Sequence for displaying the Company list using a closure

Notice the table view calls the **numberOfRowsInSection** method (4) and the **cellForRowAtIndexPath** (5) before the array of entities is passed to the closure (7). At the point these methods are executed, the **companyList** array is empty and therefore produces an empty table view. That's why the closure must call the table view's **reloadData** method so the table view re-executes these methods after the **companyList** array contains a list of companies.

Passing Closure Algorithms

Now let's take a look at a more advanced example that demonstrates passing an algorithm as a closure:

1. Open the **PickACard** project.

2. In the Project Navigator, select the **Dealer.swift** file. Scroll towards the bottom of the code file to see the **shuffleDeckUsingClosure:** method:

```
func shuffleDeckUsingClosure(algorithm:
(inout deck: Array<CardEntity>, index:Int) -> ()){

    for i in 0..<self.deck.count {
        algorithm(deck: &self.deck, index: index)
    }
}
```

This method shuffles a deck of cards. You can pass in your own shuffling algorithm as a closure.

Based on this declaration, the **algorithm** closure you pass to this method must accept a **deck** of cards as an **inout** parameter and the **index** of the current card. The closure you pass to this method must return nothing as indicated by the empty parentheses:

```
(inout deck: Array<CardEntity>, index:Int) -> ())
```

The method contains a **for** loop that iterates through each card in the deck:

```
for i in 0..<self.deck.count {
        algorithm(deck: &self.deck, index: i)
}
```

The **algorithm** closure is called for each card. It is passed a reference to the deck of cards, and the index of the current card. It's up to the closure to shuffle the cards based on this information.

3. Farther down the code file is the **shuffleDeck** method:

```
func shuffleDeck() {

    self.shuffleDeckUsingClosure { (deck, index) in

    // Get a random number from 1-52
    let r =
        Int(arc4random_uniform(UInt32(deck.count)))
        swap(&deck[index], &deck[r])
    }
}
```

This method calls **shuffleDeckUsingClosure:,** passing a closure containing the Fisher-Yates shuffling algorithm. It generates a random number between 1 and 52, then swaps the card at the current position with the card at the random number position.

Figure 23.23 depicts the sequence of events:

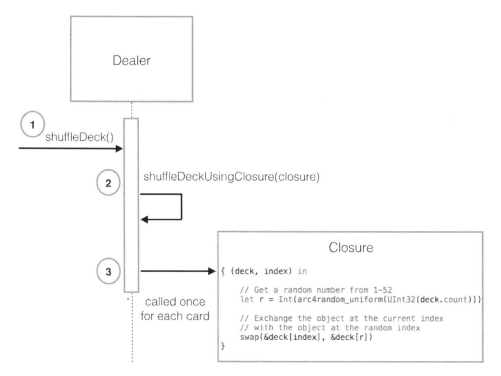

Figure 23.23 Calling the shuffling closure

1. **shuffleDeck** is called on the **Dealer** object.

2. **shuffleDeck** calls **shuffleDeckUsingClosure**, passing a reference to the closure object.

3. **shuffleDeckUsingClosure** calls the closure once for each card in the deck.

4. To see how the shuffling algorithm works at run time, click the fifth button from the left in the Navigation Toolbar to display the Test Navigator.

5. Expand the **PickACardTests** node and click on the **testShuffleDeck()** method. This method creates a **Dealer** object and displays the unshuffled deck in the Console. Next, it calls **shuffleDeck** on the object and displays the shuffled deck in the Console.

6. Set the breakpoint in the **testShuffleDeck** method shown in Figure 23.24.

```
func testShuffleDeck()
{
    var dealer = Dealer()

    println("Enumerating unshuffled deck:")
    for card in dealer.deck
    {
        println(card.cardName)
    }

    dealer.shuffleDeck()

    println("Enumerating shuffled deck:")
    for card in dealer.deck
    {
        println(card.cardName)
    }
}
```

Figure 23.24 Set a breakpoint in the test method.

7. Hover your mouse pointer over the **testShuffleDeck** method and click the **Run** button.

8. In the Console at the bottom of the Xcode window you can see the unshuffled card order (Figure 23.25).

```
Enumerating unshuffled deck:
Ace of Hearts
2 of Hearts
3 of Hearts
4 of Hearts
5 of Hearts
6 of Hearts
7 of Hearts
8 of Hearts
9 of Hearts
10 of Hearts
Jack of Hearts
Queen of Hearts
King of Hearts
Ace of Clubs
2 of Clubs
3 of Clubs
4 of Clubs
5 of Clubs
```

Figure 23.25 The un-shuffled card order

9. Click Continue in the Debug toolbar to see a shuffled card order. The list of cards you see will differ from that in Figure 23.26, because list is in random order.

```
Enumerating a shuffled deck:
2 of Diamonds
3 of Hearts
6 of Hearts
Ace of Clubs
7 of Diamonds
3 of Diamonds
4 of Hearts
Queen of Clubs
10 of Hearts
10 of Diamonds
Ace of Spades
Ace of Diamonds
8 of Hearts
9 of Hearts
4 of Spades
8 of Clubs
5 of Diamonds
9 of Diamonds
```

Figure 23.26 The shuffled card order

Summary

The key points of this chapter:

Target-Action Design Pattern

- In Swift, you can also store and pass references to functions and methods.

- Apple's iOS architecture implements a Target-Action design pattern that is typically used to call a method in response to the user interacting with a UI control.

- In the Target-Action pattern, a user interface object holds two pieces of information for calling a method:

    1. A target, which is the object that possesses the method to be called

    2. An action, which is the method to be called.

Closures

- A **closure** is a self-contained chunk of code, usually small that can be passed around as an object (in fact, closures are Swift objects).

- The term *closure* comes from the ability to capture and store references to (close over) constants and variables from the context they are defined in.

- Closures are similar to blocks in Objective-C.

- Blocks in the Cocoa Touch Framework are automatically imported into Swift as closures. Vice-versa, you can pass a Swift closure to Objective-C code that expects a block.

- Closures can be executed:

    1. As a callback when an operation has finished, or in response to the occurrence of an event

    2. Simultaneously on multiple threads of execution

    3. Over items in a collection

Closure Syntax

- Closures can be declared inline and passed directly as arguments.

- Here is the basic syntax of a closure:

```
{ (arguments) -> ReturnType in
      // code statements
}
```

- Closures are contained within curly braces.

- Any arguments are listed after the opening curly brace within parentheses and separated by commas.

- The **in** keyword marks the beginning of the closure's code statements to be executed.

- Here is an example of passing closures to a method:

```
func animateWithClosures() {

    var animateSize: CGFloat = 100

    UIView.animateWithDuration(2.0, ①

    ② animations:
Closure 1 ──  { () -> Void in
               animateSize += 20
               self.splashView.alpha = 0.0
               self.splashView.frame =
                   CGRectMake(-60, -60,
               self.splashView.frame.size.width + animateSize,
               self.splashView.frame.size.height + animateSize)
               },

    ③ completion:
Closure 2 ──  { (isComplete: Bool) -> Void in
                   self.splashView.removeFromSuperview()
               }
    )
}
```

Simplifying Closure Expressions

Here are several ways to simplify a closure expression:

- Unlike in regular methods, if a closure doesn't accept parameters, you can omit the empty parentheses.

- You can leave out the -> **Void** declaration just as you can with regular methods.

- If a closure has neither parameters nor a return value, you can omit the **in** keyword.

- When passing a closure as an argument, Swift can infer the closure's parameter and return value types. This means you can omit the types when declaring a closure expression.

- Closures containing a single expression can omit the **return** keyword.

Here is an example of simplified closure expressions:

```
animations:
{
    animateSize += 20
    self.splashView.alpha = 0.0
    self.splashView.frame =
        CGRectMake(-60, -60,
        self.splashView.frame.size.width + animateSize,
        self.splashView.frame.size.height + animateSize)
},
```
Closure 1

```
completion:
{ (isComplete) in
    self.splashView.removeFromSuperview()
}
```
Closure 2

Benefits of Closures

- They allow you to locate the code to be executed near the code that is invoking it.

- Closures have access to any constants and variables that are in scope at the time the closure is declared. This means you don't have to pass arguments to give the closure the information it needs the way you do with a separate method. The closure can access the constants and variables directly.

Capturing Constants and Variables

- The term *closure* describes the ability to close around constants and variables that are in scope at the time the closure is declared. If you declare a variable outside a closure, the closure can still access that variable.

Shorthand Argument Names

- Swift automatically creates shorthand argument names for inline closure arguments, starting with **$0** for the first argument, then **$1**, **$2**, and so on. You can reference these arguments in the body of your closure. For example:

```
var consonants = filter(alphabet,
    {vowels.rangeOfString($0) == nil})
```

Trailing Closures

- When calling a function or method that accepts a closure as its final parameter, you have the option of using *trailing closure* syntax when passing the closure.

- Trailing closure syntax moves the closure expression after the parentheses of the function or method call. Its purpose is to make your code more readable.

- Here is an example of a trailing closure:

```
var consonants = filter(alphabet)
    {vowels.rangeOfString($0) == nil}
```

- When using trailing closure syntax, if the closure is the only argument being passed to the function or method, you can remove the parentheses.

Creating Methods that Accept Closures

- It's common to use closures to execute code after a task of unknown duration completes.

- Here is the basic syntax of a method that accepts a closure argument:

- The parameters accepted by a closure are listed between parentheses and separated by commas.

- The return arrow (->) is followed by the type returned by the closure.

- If the closure doesn't return anything (**Void**), specify empty parentheses as the return type: `-> ()`.

- An example of a method that accepts a closure argument:

```
func getAllEntities
    (closure: (entityList: Array<T>) -> ())
{
        var entities = self.getAllEntities()
        closure(entityList: entities)
}
```

Here is a breakdown of this method's closure parameter:

- Blocks are a great way to pass different algorithms to a method.

Exercise 23.1

In this exercise, you will use what you have learned about closures to enhance the **ClosureDemo** project.

1. Open the **ClosureDemo** project in Xcode.

2. Change the **EmployeeViewController** to use the **getAllEntities** method that accepts a closure.

Solution Movie 23.1

To see a video providing the solution for this exercise, you can enter the link below in your Web browser to see each step performed for you.

Movie 23.1

http://www.iOSAppsForNonProgrammers.com/B4M231.html

Conclusion

Now that you have the basics of Swift under your belt, where do you go from here?

Where Do You Go From Here?

Now that you have climbed the Swift learning curve, what are your next steps in learning to create iOS Apps for the iPhone, iPad, and iPod touch?

One of your next steps is to learn more about Xcode. In this book, we have just scratched the surface of Xcode's capabilities. There is much to learn in laying out the user interface, writing code that responds to user interaction, testing your code, and making full use of the iPhone and iPad Simulators.

To get this knowledge quickly, and learn how to create some great sample Apps in the process, I recommend checking out the third book in this series, Navigating Xcode. Not only will you learn a lot about Xcode, but you will also learn much about app architecture and how to store and retrieve data on an iOS device.

When you create Apps for yourself or others, it's best to create a prototype first so you can get feedback from people representing your target audience. This saves a tremendous amount of time you would otherwise spend reworking your app when you put it in front of users for the first time. Xcode is a great prototyping tool and you should learn how to use it in this way before building your first app. If you haven't already read the first book in this series, Diving Into iOS, I highly recommend you check it out for great tips and practical information on creating app prototypes.

Ask Questions On Our Forum!

To get answers to your questions and engage with others like yourself, check out our forum:

http://iOSAppsForNonProgrammers.com/forum

Training Classes

I regularly teach hands-on training classes (with small class sizes) where you can learn more about iOS App development in a friendly, in-person environment. For more information, check out our web site:

www.iOSAppsForNonProgrammers.com/Training.html

Appendices

The appendices in this section of the book provide quick access to information on Swift functions, data types and operators.

Appendices:

Appendix A: Swift's Free Functions

abs()

```
Int32 abs(Int32)
```

Returns the absolute value of the specified integer.

```
T abs(x: T)
```

Returns the absolute value of **x**, where **x** conforms to protocol **SignedNumberType**.

Example:

```
abs(-10)  // Returns 10
```

advance()

```
T advance(start: T, n:T.Distance)
```

Returns the result of advancing **start** by **n** positions.

```
T advance(start: T, n: T.Distance, end: T)
```

Returns the result of advancing **start** by **n** positions, or until it equals **end**.

Example:

```
var s = "Waiting for Apple Watch"
let index = advance(s.startIndex, 12)
var sub = s.substringFromIndex(index)// Returns "Apple Watch"
```

assert()

```
Int32 abs(condition:Bool, message:String)
```

If the assertion evaluates to true, execution continues. If it evaluates to false, code execution ends and the app is terminated.

Example:

```
assert(a > 3, "a must be greater than 3")
```

contains()

```
Bool contains(seq: S, x: S.Generator.Element)
```

Checks a sequence (such as an array) for the specified element (the element must adopt the Equatable protocol).

Example:

```
var a = ["Apple","Orange","Banana"]
contains(a, "Apple")
```

count()

```
Int count(r: Range<I>)
```

Returns the number of items in a range.

Example:

```
count(0...100)
```

countElements()

```
Int count(x: T)
```

Returns the number of elements in a sequence, such as a String, Array, or Dictionary.

Example:

```
countElements("Imagination")
```

distance()

```
Int distance(start: T end: T))
```

Returns the distance between a start and end index.

Example:

```
var m = "Macintosh"
var charIndex1 = find(m, "i")
var charIndex2 = find(m, "o")
distance(charIndex1!, charIndex2!)
```

dropFirst()

```
T dropFirst(s: Seq)
```

Returns a sequence after dropping the first item

Example:

```
let s = "Apple"
dropFirst(s) // returns "pple"
```

dropLast()

```
T dropFirst(s: Seq)
```

Returns a sequence after dropping the first item

Example:

```
let s = "Apple"
dropLast(s) // returns "Appl"
```

dump()

```
T dump(x: T)
```

Dumps the contents of an object to the specified output stream (Console by default)

Example:

```
class Person {
    var firstName = "John"
    var lastName = "Doe"
}
var p = Person()
dump(p)
```

enumerate()

```
(index, value) enumerate(collection)
```

Returns a tuple containing the index number and value of the current collection item.

Example:

```
for (index, color) in enumerate(colors) {
    println("Color \(index) - \(color)")
}
```

equal()

```
Bool equal(a1: S1, a2: S2)
```

Compares two sequences and returns true if they have the same elements in the same order.

Example:

```
var a = ["Apple","Orange","Banana"]
var b = ["Apple","Orange","Banana"]
equal(a, b) // returns true
```

filter()

```
[S.Element] = filter(source: S, includeElement:
{ (s.Element) -> Bool in
        // code
})
```

Returns an array containing elements of type **S**, in order, that satisfy the test code in the **includeElement** closure.

Example:

```
var consonants = filter(alphabet,
      { (str: String) -> Bool in
      return vowels.rangeOfString(str) == nil })
```

find()

```
C.Index? find(domain: C, value:)
```

Returns the index of the element in the sequence, or **nil** if not found.

Example:

```
let a = ["A","B","C"]
find(a, "B")
```

insert()

```
insert(&x: newElement:, atIndex:)
```

Inserts a new element into x at the specified index.

Example:

```
var a = ["A","B","D"]
insert(&a, "C", atIndex: 2)
```

join()

```
join(separator: sequence:)
```

Inserts the specified separator between the elements of the sequence and returns the result.

Example:

```
var a = ["A","B","C"]
join("-", a)   // Returns A-B-C
```

lexicographicalCompare()

```
lexicographicalCompare(a1: a2:)
```

Returns true if a1 precedes a2 (is less than) in a lexicographical (dictionary) ordering.

Example:

```
lexicographicalCompare("Aardvark","Apple")
```

map()

```
map(source:C transform: (C.Element) -> T)
```

Returns an array containing the results of performing a transform closure over a source array.

Example:

```
let letters = ["A","B","C"]

// Outputs ["<A>","<B>","<C>"]
map(letters, { (var letter) -> String in
    "<"+letter+">"
})
```

max()

```
T max(x: T y: T))
```

Returns the greater of 'x' and 'y'.

Example:

```
max("A", "B") // Returns "B"
max(32, 54) // Returns 54
```

maxElement()

```
R.element maxElement(elements: R)
```

Returns the maximum element in a collection.

Example:

```
maxElement(["A", "B"]) // Returns "B"
maxElement([38, 99]) // Returns 99
```

min()

```
T min(x: T y: T))
```

Returns the lesser of 'x' and 'y'.

Example:

```
min("A", "B") // Returns "A"
min(32, 54) // Returns 32
```

minElement()

```
R.element maxElement(elements: R)
```

Returns the minimum element in the collection.

Example:

```
minElement(["A", "B"]) // Returns "A"
minElement([38, 99]) // Returns 38
```

print()

```
print(object:, target:)
```

Displays the textual representation of the value to standard output (Console by default).

Example:

```
print("Operation complete")
```

println()

```
println(object:, target:)
```

Displays the textual representation of the value followed by a new line to standard output (Console by default).

Example:

```
print("Operation complete") quickSort()
```

reduce()

```
U reduce(sequence:S initial:U combine:(U, element)
```

Reduces a sequence to a single value by repeatedly calling the **combine:** closure for each item.

Example 1:

```
var s = ["First name","Last name","Customer ID"]
// Joins all strings in array, separated by comma
reduce(s, "") { (value, character) -> String in
    value + ", " + character
}
```

Example 2:

```
var a = [1, 3, 5, 11]
// Adds all numbers in the array
reduce(a, 0) { (total, number) -> Int in

    total + number
}
```

reflect()

```
MirrorType reflect(x: T)
```

Returns a MirrorType which can be used to examine a type and its properties.

Example:

```
var person = Person()
let r = reflect(person)
r.count // Number of properties (3)
r.summary // Type (Person)
let p1 = r[0] // 1st property (name, MirrorType)
let p2 = r[0] // 2nd property (name, MirrorType)
```

reverse()

```
C reverse(source: C)
```

Returns an array containing elements of the source in reverse order.

Example:

```
var a = [1,2,3]
reverse(a) // returns [3, 2, 1]

var s = "abc"
reverse(s) // returns ["c","b","a"]
```

sizeof()

```
Int sizeof(T.Type)
```

Returns the memory footprint of the specified type.

Example:

```
sizeof(Int8)     // returns 1
sizeof(Int16)    // returns 2
sizeof(Int32)    // returns 4
```

sizeofValue()

```
Int sizeof(T)
```

Returns the memory footprint of the specified value.

Example:

```
var i: Int32 = 1
var d: Double = 1
sizeofValue(i)  // returns 4
sizeofValue(d)  // returns 8
```

sort()

```
sort(&a)
```

Sorts the items in the specified array.

Example:

```
var a = [3,2,1]
sort(&a)    // Changes array to [1,2,3]
```

sorted()

```
sorted(&a)
```

Returns a new array containing resorted items from the original array. Can pass an optional closure that performs the sorting algorithm.

Example:

```
var a = [3,2,1]
var b = sorted(a) // Creates new array [1,2,3]
```

split()

```
[S.Subslice] split(element:S, isSeparator:
(S.Generator.Element)) -> R(S.Generator.Element)  -> R
```

Splits the specified elements into an array based on the characters that the closure specifies as separators.

Example:

```
var splitArray = split("I am here") {$0 == " "}
// Returns ["I", "am", "here"]
```

startsWith()

```
Bool startsWith(s:S0, prefix:S1)
```

Returns true if the starting elements of the sequence are the same as the specified prefix.

Example:

```
startsWith("Apple, Inc", "Apple")    // true
startsWith(0...15, 0...5)            // true
var a = ["a","e","i","o","u"]        // true
startsWith(a, ["a"])                 // true
```

stride()

```
StrideThrough<T> stride(from:T, through:T by T.Stride)
```

Allows you to iterate through ranges with a step other than 1.

Example:

```
var array = ["blastoff","1","2","3","4","5"]
// stride:through outputs 5 4 3 2 1 blastoff
for i in stride(from:array.count-1, through:0, by: -1) {
    println(array[i])
}


var array = ["blastoff","1","2","3","4","5"]
// stride:to outputs 5 4 3 2 1
for i in stride(from:array.count-1, to:0, by: -1) {
    println(array[i])
}
```

swap()

```
Void swap(&a:T, &b:T)
```
Exchanges the values of **a** and **b**.

Example:

```
// Swap two cards in a deck of cards
swap(&deck[index], &deck[r])
```

toString()

```
String toString(inputEncoding: outputEncoding: input: output:
stopOnError:)
```

Returns the result of printing into a string.

Example:

```
toString(123) // Returns "123"
```

transcode()

```
Bool transcode(x:T)
```

Converts from one Unicode encoding to another.

Example:

```
let error = transcode(UTF32.self, UTF8.self,
    array.generate(), output, stopOnError: true)
```

underestimateCount()

```
Int underestimateCount(x:T)
```

Returns an estimate of the number of elements in the specified sequence without consuming the sequence. Returns **countElements()** for collections.

Example:

```
underestimateCount("abc") // returns 3
```

withExtendedLifetime()

```
Result withExtendedLifetime(x:T, f:() -> Result() -> Result)
```

Evaluates f() and returns its result, ensuring that x is not destroyed before f() returns.

Example:

```
withExtendedLifetime(myArray) { () -> () in
    // Closure code
}
```

Math Functions

sin()

```
Double sin(Double)
```

cos()

```
Double cos(Double)
```

tan()

```
Double tan(Double)
```

log()

```
Double log(Double)
```

sqrt()

```
Double sqrt(Double)
```

Working with C APIs

If you need to work with legacy C APIs or Objective-C APIs that take in-out parameters as pointers, check out these additional Swift functions:

withUnsafePointer()

```
Result withUnsafePointer(&arg:T body: (UnsafePointer<T>) ->
Result(UnsafePointer<T>) -> Result)
```

Invokes **body** with an **UnsafePointer** to **arg** and returns the result.

withUnsafePointers

```
Result withUnsafePointers(&arg0:A0, &arg1:A1, &arg2: A2, body:
(UnsafePointer<A0>, UnsafePointer<A1>, UnsafePointer<A2>) ->
Result)
```

Similar to **withUnsafePointer**, but passes pointers to **arg0**, **arg1**, and **arg2**.

Appendix B: Swift's Basic Data Types

Swift's basic data types are simple, *scalar* types that contain only a single value.

Data type	Description
Bool	Boolean value that can be true or false
char	A single character, such as the letter "x"
Int	An integer, or whole number (a number without a decimal point), On 32-bit platforms (iPhone 5 and earlier) it can hold a value between -2,147,483,648 to 2,147,483,647. On 64-bit platforms (iPhone 5s and newer) it can hold a value between -9,223,372,036,854,775,807 and 9,223,372,036,854,775,807. *Apple recommends that you use Int for most integers unless you need to work with a specific size of integer.*
Int8	An integer that holds a value between -128 and 127.
Int16	An integer that holds a value between -32,768 and 32,767.
Int32	An integer that holds a value between --2,147,483,648 and 2,147,483,647
Int64	An integer that holds a value between -9,223,372,036,854,775,807 and 9,223,372,036,854,775,807.
UInt	An unsigned integer, or whole number (a number without a decimal point), On 32-bit platforms (iPhone 5 and earlier) it can hold a value between 0 to 2,147,483,647. On 64-bit platforms (iPhone 5s and newer) it can hold a value between 0 and 9,223,372,036,854,775,807.
UInt8	An unsigned integer that holds a value between 0 and 127.
UInt16	An unsigned integer that holds a value between 0 and 32,767.
UInt32	An unsigned integer that holds a value between 0 and 2,147,483,647
UInt64	An unsigned integer that holds a value between 0 and 9,223,372,036,854,775,807.
Float	32-bit floating point number. Gets its name from the decimal point that can "float", or be placed anywhere in a number (for example, 1.234, 12.34, 123.4.
Double	64-bit floating-point number

Appendix C: Swift Operators

Operator	Description	Example
=	Assignment	a = b
+	Addition	a = b + c
-	Subtraction	a = b - c
*	Multiplication	a = b * c
/	Division	a = b / c
%	Remainder (that results from integer or floating point division)	a = b % c;

Operator	Description	Example
+=	Addition and assignment	a += b
-=	Subtraction and assignment	a -= b
*=	Multiplication and assignment	a *= b
/=	Division and assignment	a /= b
%=	Modulus and assignment	a = %= b
++	Return value then increment	a++
++	Increment then return value	a--
--	Decrement then return value	--a
--	Return value then decrement	--b
-	Unary minus; toggles sign	-a
+	Unary plus operator	+a
<=	Less than or equal to	a <= b;
>=	Greater than or equal to	a >= b;
==	Equal to	a == b
!=	Not equal to	a != b
===	Reference same object	a === b
!==	Not reference the same object	a !== b
!	Logical NOT	!a
&&	Logical AND	a && b
||	Logical OR	a || b
?:	Ternary conditional operator	a = b ? c : d
??	Nil coalescing; Unwraps optional if contains a value; otherwise returns default value	a ?? b
...	Closed range operator	a...b
..<	Half-Open range operator	a..<b
()	Cast	a = (b)c
&+	Overflow addition	a = b &+ c
&-	Overflow subtraction	a = b &- c
&*	Overflow multiplication	a = b &* c
&/	Overflow division	a = b &/ c
&%	Overflow remainder	a = b &% c

Bit Operators

Bit operations operate on integer values at the level of individual bits of information. You rarely use these in Swift programming, but they are listed for the sake of completeness.

Operator	Description	Example
~	Bitwise NOT (inverts all bits)	~a
&	Bitwise AND	a = b & c
|	Bitwise Inclusive OR	a = b | c

Operator	Description	Example
^	Bitwise Exclusive OR	a = b ^ c
~	Ones complement	a = ~b
<<	Left bit shift	a = a << 2
>>	Right bit shift	a = a >> 4
&=	Bitwise AND and assign	a &= b
|=	Bitwise Inclusive OR and assign	a |= b
^=	Bitwise Exclusive OR and assign	a ^= b
<<=	Left bit shift and assign	a <<= b
>>=	Right bit shift and assign	a >>= b

Glossary

Action　In the Target-Action design pattern, the action is the method to be invoked.

Animation　An animation is a smooth transition from one user-interface state to another. The user tapping a button that causes one view to slide out and another view to slide in is an example of an animation.

App　An app is a relatively small software application designed to perform one or more related tasks. In the context of this book, an app is specifically a software application that runs on an iPhone, iPod Touch or iPad.

ARC　See Automatic Reference Counting

Argument　An argument is an additional piece of data that is passed to an object in a message call.

You often see the words *argument* and *parameter* used interchangeably, but there is a subtle difference. An *argument* is a piece of data that you pass to a method. A *parameter* is a part of the method declaration that dictates the argument(s) to be passed to the method. In short, arguments appear in message calls, parameters appear in method declarations.

Assigment operator　To store a value into a property, variable or constant, you use the assignment operator, which is an equal (=) sign. It takes the value on its right and stores it into the property or variable on its left. For example:

```
var myString: String = "Swift"
```

Attribute　Attributes describe the characteristics of an object. Xcode's Attributes Inspector allows you to view and change the attributes of user-interface objects.

For every object *attribute* you see in Xcode's Attribute Inspector, there is a corresponding *property* in the class definition.

An object's attributes are defined as properties in the class blueprint from which the object was created. Each attribute has a default value, also specified in the class. After an object has been created, you can change the value of its attributes. You can change an attribute on one object without affecting any other objects.

In this context, attributes and properties are similar. In Xcode, an object has attributes; in Swift the class on which an object is based has properties.

Automatic Reference Counting   Starting in iOS 5, Apple introduced Automatic Reference Counting, or ARC, which deals specifically with memory management in your app. Before ARC was introduced, you had to manually insert **retain** messages in your code to increment your object's retain count, and **release** messages to decrement your object's retain count. When an object's retain count reaches zero, it is released from memory. Not sending the proper **retain** and **release** messages was a constant cause of *memory leaks* in iOS apps.

With Automatic Reference Counting, the compiler inserts **retain** and **release** messages in the compiled code for you based on the context of how your object is used.

Base class   A base class is a class that doesn't inherit from another class.

Bit operations   Bit operations operate at the level of individual bits of information. You rarely use these in Swift programming. Check out Appendix C: Swift Operators for a list of bitwise operations.

Breakpoint   A breakpoint is a debugging feature in Xcode that allows you to temporarily pause an App and examine the value of variables, properties, and so on.

Business Object   Business objects contain the core business logic of your App. They often represent real-world entities such as a customer, invoice, product, or payment.

Call stack   The call stack is a "breadcrumb trail" of how execution arrived at the current line of code (this line of code called that line of code which called this other line of code, and so on). Your App's call stack is displayed at run time in the Debug Navigator.

Camel case   Camel case is a term used to describe the capitalization style of symbols such as method and parameter names. A camel-cased name always begins with a lowercase letter, and then the first letter of each word in a compound word is uppercased (like a camel's head and its humps). For example, the method names **areYouOld** and **amIOld** are both camel cased.

Case sensitive   Swift is case sensitive, which means you must type the uppercase and lowercase letters exactly as the language expects, or you will encounter errors when you try to compile your code.

Cast   See **Explicit conversion**

Class   A class is like a blueprint for an object. You create objects from a class.

Class diagram   A class diagram is a formal representation of a class. It lists both the properties and methods of the class.

Closure   A closure is a self-contained chunk of code, usually small in size that can be passed around as an object. In fact, closure are full-fledged Swift objects.

Cocoa Touch Framework   The Cocoa Touch Framework is a set of many smaller frameworks (which contain sets of classes) each focusing on a set of core functionality that provides access to important features and services such as multi-touch gestures, user-interface controller, saving and retrieving data, maps, the camera, and the compass.

Code Completion   Code Completion is Xcode's way of helping you write code. Based on the characters you type, it provides its best guess as to what you need to complete a code statement.

Collection   A collection is a grouping of one or more related objects. Cocoa Touch Framework collection classes such as **NSArray**, **NSDictionary**, and **NSSet** allow you to group multiple items together into a single collection.

Comment   A comment is text that is added to a code file to provide an explanation of the functionality of a particular section of code. Comments are not code and are, therefore, not executed.

Compiler   A compiler is a software program that interprets, or converts the Swift code that you write into machine code, which an iOS device can actually execute.

Compound assignment operators   A compound assignment
operator is an operator that performs two operations. For example, the +=
operator adds the specified value and then stores the result back into a
variable or property. The -= operator performs subtraction, *= performs
multiplication, and /= performs division, each storing the resulting value back
into a variable or property.

Compound comparison   A compound comparison allows you to
perform multiple tests in a single *condition*. For example, in the following
code, one check is performed to determine if **iq** is less than **20**, and a second
check is performed to determine if **iq** is greater than **140**.

```
if iq < 20 || iq > 140 {

    // statements to be executed
}
```

Computed Property   Computed properties do not store a value but are
typically used to retrieve and manipulate values from other properties. For
example, a **fullName** property may join **firstName** and **lastName**
properties to compute its value.

Condition   A condition is an expression that is checked to determine if it
is true or false. For example, in the following **if** statement, the condition in
parentheses is checked, and if **age > 100** evaluates to **true**, the **println**
statement is executed.

```
if age > 100 {
    println("You are old!")
}
```

Constant   Constants are values that do not change after they are
declared. Sometimes constants are stand-alone, but they are often grouped
together with other related constants in an enumeration.

Convenience initializer   A convenience initializer is a secondary class
initializer that typically accepts fewer parameters than the designated
initializer, but then calls the designated initializer with defaults set for some
of the parameters.

Core logic   The core logic is the code in an App required to perform
actions when a user-interface object is touched or any other processing takes

place automatically. Whenever an App "does something," it requires code to execute a set of instructions.

Data   Data is the information and preferences maintained by an App. This can be as simple as storing the user's zip code or as complex as storing large amounts of data such as thousands of pictures and songs.

Delegate   A delegate is an object that performs a task for another object.

Designated initializer   A designated initializer is the main initializer for a class. It initializes all properties declared in the class, and is responsible for calling an initializer in its superclass (if it has is a superclass.)

Dictionary literal   You can initialize a Dictionary with a dictionary literal, which is a list of **key: value** pairs separated by commas, between square brackets. For example:

```
var countries: Dictionary<String, String> =
        ["AT": "Austria",
        "BG": "Bulgaria",
        "CH": "Switzerland",
        "DE": "Germany"]
```

Discoverability   Discoverability is a measure of how easy is it to discover, or find the code that you need to perform a particular task.

Downcasting   When you treat an instance as if it were a class lower in the inheritance chain (for example, its subclass), it's called downcasting.

Enumeration   An **enumeration** is a group of related constants. Enumerations and their member names are Pascal cased and typically begin with a suffix that describes what type that they are. For example, in the **UITextBorderStyle** enumeration, each member of the enumeration begins with the prefix "UITextBorderStyle":

* **UITextBorderStyle.Bezel**

* **UITextBorderStyle.Line**

* **UITextBorderStyle.None**

- **UITextBorderStyle.RoundedRect**

Explicit conversion   An explicit conversion, also known as a *cast*, is a conversion from one data type to another that you perform manually in code.

For example, the following code explicitly converts an integer to a Float:

```
var f = Float(i)
```

Extension   In Swift an extension allows you to add functionality to an existing class, structure, or enumeration. This is the basic syntax for declaring an extension:

```
extension TypeToExtend {

    // New extension members and/or behavior
}
```

Factory method   A factory method is a method that creates an object.

Failable Initializer   A failable initializer returns an object if the initialization succeeds, or a **nil** if it doesn't. For example, the following initializer returns an object if you specify a valid enumeration raw value and **nil** if you don't:

```
let op: Operation? = Operation(rawValue: "+")
```

Forced unwrapping   One way to unwrap an optional value is to use **forced unwrapping**—add an exclamation mark (!) after the optional to explicitly unwrap it. For example:

```
firstAndMiddleNames = firstName + " "  + middleName!
```

Note: Only used forced unwrapping if you are absolutely sure the optional does not contain a **nil**, or you will get a run time error!

Frame   A frame is a rectangle that specifies a user-interface object's position on the user interface (in x and y coordinates) as well as its width and height.

Function   A function is a lot like a method; it groups together one or more lines of code that perform a specific task. However, unlike a method, a function is not attached to an object or a class; it's stand-alone or "free floating."

Getter   A getter is one of the two methods associated with a property. It gets the value of the property, usually from an associated instance variable.

High-level language   Swift is a high-level language, meaning it is closer to human language than the actual code an iOS device executes when it is running your app.

Immutable   Swift is a high-level language, meaning it is closer to human language than the actual code an iOS device executes when it is running your app.

Implicit conversion   Swift performs an implicit conversion when upcasting to a class higher up in the inheritance chain.

Implicitly Unwrapped Optionals   Implicitly unwrapped optionals do not need to be unwrapped using either forced unwrapping (!) or optional binding because they are unwrapped implicitly (automatically.) They are declared using an exclamation mark (!) rather than a question mark (?).

Index   When used in the context of an Swift collection, an index is a number that references an item by its position in the collection.

Inheritance   Inheritance is a basic principle of object-oriented programming. It refers to the concept that a class can be based on, or inherit its attributes (properties) and behavior (methods) from, another class.

Initializer   An initializer method returns a fully initialized object that has all of its properties set to default values, and performs any other setup the object needs.

Instance   An object created from a class is referred to as an instance of the class.

Instance method   Instance methods are methods called on instances of an object—meaning you create an object from a class, and then call a method on the object.

Instantiate   The term instantiate refers to the act of creating an instance of a class. The process of instantiation creates an object from a class definition.

Lazy Stored Property   A **lazy stored property**'s in-line initialization code is not executed until the property is first accessed by another line of code. This is particularly useful in situations where the initialization code is creating an object that takes a while to create.

Just add the lazy modifier to declare a lazy stored property:

```
lazy var webCalculator = WebCalculator()
```

Local variable   Variables declared within a method are known as local variables because they can only be accessed locally from within the method in which they are declared.

Localize   The term localize is used in iOS and other software platforms to describe the process of translating and adapting your app to different cultures, countries, regions, or groups of people.

Machine code   Machine code is an instruction set consisting of bits of data (ones and zeroes) specific to a particular processor. The compiler generates machine code from the Swift code that you write.

Memory leak   A memory leak is a situation whereby an app continually eats up memory until all memory allocated to the app is eventually consumed.

Method   The behavior of an object, or the actions that it can perform, are defined in the class blueprint as methods. A method is comprised of one or more (usually more) lines of code grouped together to perform a specific task.

Method Call   A method call is the act of calling a method on an object.

Method signature   A method signature is the name of the method and the number of and type of its parameters, not including the return type.

Mutable   A mutable object is one that can be changed after it is created. For example, Swift's **Array** and **Dictionary** classes are collections that can be changed (items can be added, removed, and edited) after the collection is created, if you store the collection in a variable. These collections are immutable if you store them in a constant.

Object   Software objects are similar to real-world objects. They have both attributes and behaviors. apps have user-interface objects such as text fields, sliders, web views, and labels, as well as *business objects* that contain the app's core logic and represent real-world entities such as a Customer, Address, Album, Song, and Calculator.

In Swift, you create objects at run time from classes, which act like blueprints.

Operating System   On an iOS device, iOS is the operating system. It is the software provided by Apple that manages the device hardware and provides the core functionality for all apps running on the device.

Optional Binding   Optional binding allows you to test if an optional contains a value, and if so, store that value in a temporary variable or constant. This is shown in the **if** condition in the following code:

```
var firstName: String = "Ryan"
var middleName: String? = "Michael"
var firstAndMiddleNames: String

if let middle = middleName
{
        firstAndMiddleNames = firstName + " " + middle
}
else
{
        firstAndMiddleNames = firstName
}
```

Optionals   Optionals are a key feature of the Swift programming language. They allow you to specify that a variable or constant may potentially contain a **nil** (nothing). You add a question mark after the the type of a value to indicate the value is optional. For example:

```
var middleName: String?
```

Override   You can override a method inherited from a superclass by creating a method with the same signature in the subclass. Overriding allows you to extend an inherited method or completely change its implementation.

Parameter   A **parameter** is a part of the method declaration that dictates the argument(s) to be passed to the method. For example, the following method has a parameter named **value** of type **Double.**

```
func addToTotal(value: Double)
{

}
```

You often see the words argument and parameter used interchangeably, but there is a subtle difference. An argument is a piece of data that you pass to a method. A parameter is a part of the method declaration that dictates the argument(s) to be passed to the method. In short, arguments appear in message calls, parameters appear in method declarations.

Pascal case   Pascal case is a term used to describe the capitalization style of symbols such as class names. A Pascal cased symbol always begins with an uppercase letter, and then the first letter of each word in a compound word is capitalized—for example, **InvoiceDetail** and **PatientHistory**.

Polymorphism   Polymorphism is one of the core principles of object-oriented programming. This term refers to the ability of a class to take many different forms. Polymorphism allows you to declare a variable of a particular type, and then store a reference to an object of that type or *any of its subclasses* in that variable.

For example, you can declare a variable of type **UIControl**, and then store a reference to any class that is a subclass of **UIControl**:

```
var control: UIControl
control = UITextField()
control = UIButton()
control = UISwitch()
```

Polymorphism allows you to write more generic code that works with families of objects rather than writing code for a specific class.

Processor   A processor is a central processing unit, or CPU. It is the hardware within a device that carries out programming instructions. For example, the iPhone 6 and 6 Plus use the Apple A8 processor, and the iPad Air 2 uses the A8x processor.

Programmatically   When you perform an action in code, it is considered to be done **programmatically** or in the program's code.

For example, if you add a user-interface control to a view by writing code (rather than dragging an dropping it on a view at design time), you are doing it programmatically.

Property   A property is the part of a class definition that describes a class's attributes or characteristics. A property defined in a class corresponds to an object attribute in Xcode, which can be viewed using the Attributes Inspector.

Property observer   Property observers allow you to perform an action when the value of a property is changed.

You can create property observers on stored properties that you declare in your custom classes, or on stored or computed properties that you inherit from a superclass.

Protocol   A **protocol** is an advanced feature of Swift that allows you to define a standard set of behavior that other classes can implement.

For example, the **UIPickerViewDataSource** protocol declares methods required by an object that wants to act as a data source for the picker view, and the **UIPickerViewDelegate** protocol declares methods required by an object that wants to act as a delegate for the picker view.

Protocols are equivalent to *interfaces* in languages such as Java and C#.

Required Initializer   A required initializer is an initializer that must be implemented in subclasses. You add the **required** modifier to an initializer to indicate that is required:

```
class Translator {

    required init()
    {
    }
}
```

Return arrow   The **return arrow** symbol, ->, is used to separate a method or function's parameter list from its return value and is followed by the type of the return value. For example:

```
func getTotal() -> Double {

    // Return a double value
}
```

This method returns a value of type Double.

Run time   Run time is when an app is running in the Simulator or on an iOS device.

Scalar values   Scalar refers to primitive data types that contain only a single value such as Booleans, integers, and doubles.

Setter   A setter is one of the two methods associated with a property. It sets the value of the property, usually by storing it to an associated instance variable.

Signature   See **Method signature**

Statement   In Swift, a statement is a line of code that ends in a semicolon. Note that a statement can span multiple physical lines in a source code file, but is still considered a single statement.

Stored Property   Stored properties are the most common type of property. They store a value associated with an instance of a class or a class itself. They can be either variable stored properties where the value can change or constant stored properties where the value does not change.

String interpolation   String interpolation allows you to build a string from a mix of string literals, variables, constants, and expressions. All you have to do is place the values you want to convert inside parentheses and prefixed by a backslash. For example:

```
var count = 10
let message = "There are \(count) students."
```

String Literal   A string literal is a sequence of characters surrounded by double quotes. Here is an example of a string literal:

```
let myString = "Swift"
```

Strong reference cycle   A strong reference cycle occurs when two objects have a strong reference to each other, and therefore neither object can be released.

Structure   Although not really a collection, Swift's **structures** allow you to group values together as a single unit.

For example, the following code declares a structure named **SATScores** that has three members of type integer named **writing**, **math**, and **reading**:

```
struct SATScores {

    var writing: Int = 0
    var math: Int = 0
    var reading: Int = 0
}
```

Subclass   In an inheritance relationship, a subclass is a class that is derived from another class (its superclass). It is sometimes referred to as a "child class." In Swift, a class can have zero, one, or many subclasses.

Subscript syntax   Subscript syntax is used to reference an item in a collection. You specify the name of the array followed by square brackets that contain the index of the item. For example:

```
names[0] = "Mia"
```

Superclass   In an inheritance relationship, the superclass is a class from which other classes are derived, and is sometimes referred to as a "parent class." In Swift, a class can only have one superclass.

Target   In the Target-Action design pattern, the target is the receiver of the message.

Target-Action design pattern   In the Target-Action design pattern, an object holds two pieces of information for sending a message:

1. A **target**, which is the receiver of the message and

2. An **action**, which is the method to be invoked.

Tuple   **Tuples** provide a way to create a group of related values that can be of different types. They are particularly useful in returning multiple values from a method.

Type Alias   A **type alias** allows you to assign a different name to an existing class. For example:

```
typealias CoreDataWrapper = mmBusinessObject
```

Type constraint   A type constraint specifies that a generic's type parameter must be a subclass of a particular type or conform to a particular protocol.

For example, the following type constraint specifies that **mmBusinessObjectGeneric** only works with types of **NSManagedObject** or its subclasses.

```
public class mmBusinessObjectGeneric<T: NSManagedObject>
```

Type inference   Type inference refers to a compiler's ability to examine a value in the context in which it is used and infer, or figure out, the type of the value.

Type method   Type methods are methods that belong to the class itself, meaning that you pass the message to the class directly without creating an instance of the class.

Type parameter   A **type parameter** is a feature of Swift's generics. It declares a placeholder for a type within this method. This is similar in concept as using *n* as a placeholder in an equation. The type parameter is replaced by an actual type when the method is called. For example:

```
func createEntity<T>() -> NSManagedObject
```

Type properties   Type properties belong to the class itself rather than to any instance of that class. No matter how many instances you have, there is only ever one copy of a type property.

UI   UI is an acronym for User Interface.

Unit testing   Unit testing is a testing method by which individual units of your app (usually a single method is considered to be one unit) are tested to make sure your app as a whole is ready to be released.

Unordered collection   An unordered collection, such as the **Dictionary** class, contains items that are in no particular order.

Upcasting   When you treat an instance as if it were a class higher in the inheritance chain (for example, its superclass), it's called **upcasting**.

User interface   The user interface is the part of the app that the user sees and interacts with by touch. It includes buttons, text fields, lists, and, as is the case with many games, the entire touch-screen surface.

Value binding   In a **switch** statement, when you store the value being examined by a **case** in a constant or variable, this is known as value binding.

Variable   A variable is a place in memory where you can store and retrieve information. It's called a variable because you can change the information that you store in it. You can store one piece of information in a variable but then, later on, store another piece of information in the same variable.

View   A view contains one screen of information on an iOS device.

View Controller   Every view in an iOS App has a view controller that works behind the scenes in conjunction with the view.

It has properties that (among other things):

• Indicate if the user can edit items in the view,

• Report the orientation of the user interface (portrait or landscape), and

• Allow you to access user-interface elements.

It has methods that:

• Allow you to navigate to other views,

• Specify the interface orientations that the view supports, and

- Indicate when the associated view is loaded and unloaded from the screen.

View-controller objects are based on the Cocoa Touch Framework's **UIViewController** class or one of its subclasses.

About the Author

So, I was supposed to be a hardware guy.

While I was in college majoring in electronic engineering, I worked at a small company as I paid my way through school. Brian, the head of the software department, would tell me on a regular basis "You know, I think you're a software guy!"

Hardware guys typically do *not* want to be software guys, so I just ignored it as good-natured harassment. Then one day I decided to get him off my back by giving it a try.

As they say, the rest is history. I fell in love with writing software, and the honeymoon is definitely not over!

I learned that writing software is a *very* creative process. In just a matter of hours, I could conceive an idea, create a software design and have it up and running on a computer.

The first software I wrote was a tutorial program that helped new computer users understand how a computer works (this was not long after the birth of the PC). I came up with the idea after watching new computer users give up on themselves before they started.

Since then, I've devoted my teaching career to making difficult concepts easy to understand. So, when Apple released the iPhone and a platform for building Apps, I immediately started teaching classes to empower others to join this software revolution and share in the fun. Maybe you'll find you're a software "guy" too. — Kevin

Books in This Series by Kevin McNeish

1. *Book 1: Diving In*

2. *Book 2: Flying with Objective-C*

3. *Book 3: Navigating Xcode*

4. *Book 4: Learn to Code in Swift*

Questions and Comments for the Author

Email me at:

kevin@iOSAppsForNonProgrammers.com.

Rate and Recommend This Book

If you have enjoyed this book and think it's worth telling others about, please leave your comments and rating for this book on our Amazon book page and tell your friends. Thanks!

Made in the USA
Lexington, KY
20 December 2014